Joseph the Carpenter

History of Biblical Interpretation Series
5

ISSN 1382-4465

Deo Publishing

JOSEPH *the* CARPENTER

*His Reception in Literature and Art
from the Second to the Ninth Century*

Philip W. Jacobs

BLANDFORD FORUM

History of Biblical Interpretation Series, 5

ISSN 1382-4465

Copyright © 2016 Deo Publishing
P.O. Box 6284, Blandford Forum, Dorset DT11 1AQ, UK

All rights reserved. No part of this publication may be reproduced, translated, stored in a retrieval system, or transmitted in any form or by any means, electronic, mechanical, photocopying, recording or otherwise, without prior written permission from the publisher.

Printed by Henry Ling Ltd, at the Dorset Press, Dorchester, DT1 1HD, UK

British Library Cataloguing-in-Publication data
A catalogue record for this book is available from the British Library

ISBN 978-1-905679-34-8

Contents

Acknowledgments vii
Abbreviations... ix
Illustrations x

Part I
Introduction – Problem, History of Research, and Methodology 1

Part II
The Canonic Portrayals of Joseph 25

Chapter 1
The Portrayal of Joseph the Carpenter in the Gospel of Matthew 27

Chapter 2
The Portrayal of Joseph the Carpenter in the Gospel of Luke 46

Chapter 3
The Portrayal of Joseph the Carpenter in the Gospel of John 69

Conclusion
The Canonic Portrayals of Joseph the Carpenter... 77

Part III
**The Response of Later Christian Narrators and Their Communities
to the Canonic Portrayals of Joseph** 81

Chapter 4
The Portrayal of Joseph the Carpenter in the Infancy Gospel of James 83

Chapter 5
The Portrayal of Joseph the Carpenter in the Infancy Gospel of Thomas 96

Chapter 6
The Portrayal of Joseph the Carpenter in the History of Joseph the Carpenter 111

Chapter 7
The Portrayal of Joseph the Carpenter in the Gospel of Pseudo-Matthew 128

Conclusion
The Non-Canonic Portrayals of Joseph 143

Part IV
The Response of Later Christian Artists and Their Communities to the Canonic Portrayals of Joseph 147

The Beginnings of Christian Art and the Reception and Assimilation of Canonic and Non-Canonic Texts by Artists in the Early Christian and Early Medieval Periods 149

Chapter 8
Portraits of Joseph in Compositions of the First Dream of Joseph and the Annunciation to Joseph 162

Chapter 9
Portraits of Joseph in Compositions of the Water Test 186

Chapter 10
Portraits of Joseph in Compositions of the Journey to Bethlehem 194

Chapter 11
Portraits of Joseph in Compositions of the Nativity 206

Chapter 12
Portraits of Joseph in Compositions of the Adoration of the Magi 218

Conclusion
The Artistic Portrayals of Joseph 234

Part V
Conclusions and Implications 241

Appendix:
Artistic Portrayals of Joseph c. 300 – 800 CE According to Theme 246

Bibliography 248
Index of Names 263
Index of Biblical and Other Source References 267

Acknowledgments

The idea to explore the subject of the reception history, interpretation, and portrayal of Joseph the Carpenter in the history of western literature and art first emerged some years ago and was inspired by my initial reading of Dr. Dan Via's article on 'Narrative World and Ethical Response: The Marvelous and Righteousness in Matthew 1-2' which highlighted the significance of Joseph.[1] It reemerged some years later as I sat reflecting upon prospective topics for homilies one Advent season and realized that in all my years in the Protestant Christian church I had never heard a sermon on the subject of Joseph and his role in the birth and life of Jesus of Nazareth. Since then I have engaged in substantial reflection on this subject from several perspectives and been encouraged in my exploration of this topic by an amazing amalgam of friends and advisors, including Dr. Paul Barolsky, Commonwealth Professor of Art History at the University of Virginia; Dr. Harry Gamble, Department of Religion, University of Virginia; Dr. Timothy Lyons, Chair, Department of Endocrinology, University of Oklahoma; my thesis supervisor, Dr. John Christopher Thomas, Clarence J. Abbott Professor of Biblical Studies, Pentecostal Theological Seminary, USA and Director of the Centre for Pentecostal and Charismatic Studies, Bangor University, Wales; and my closest colleague and friend, Rev. Dwain DePew. Additional support and reflection has also been provided by Dr. Lee Roy Martin, Professor of Old Testament, Pentecostal Theological Seminary, Tennessee, my fellow Bangor University PhD students, notably, Dr. Larry McQueen, Melissa Archer, Odell Bryant, Michelle Marshall, Jeff and Karen Holly, Steffen Schumacher, Dr. Chris Green, and Randall Auckland.

Further, I am especially grateful for the efforts of Mr. Frank Carter, former Chair, Department of Humanities and Fine Arts, Cape Fear Community College, Wilmington, North Carolina who encouraged me to apply for a sabbatical and supported me in the process. Just as well, I

---

[1] Dan O. Via, 'Narrative World and Ethical Response: The Marvelous and Righteousness in Matthew 1–2', *Semeia* 12 (1978), pp. 123-50. This reading took place in a graduate seminar on New Testament Ethics taught by Dr. Via at the University of Virginia.

am most thankful for the support of the former President of our college, Dr. Eric McKeithan, and Cape Fear Community College's Board of Trustees who gave final approval for this sabbatical. It permitted me to engage in further research and study at Duke University and Cambridge University at a critical juncture in this project. Additionally, thanks must also be offered to Susan Mock, librarian extraordinare at Cape Fear, who handled numerous requests for inter-library loans and did so with diligence and kindness.

In addition, I am most grateful for the support I received through the graciousness and love of my mother, Helen Saturday Jacobs, who helped make this study feasible. Though she died shortly before this work was finished I have no doubt that she would have celebrated its appearance.

With respect to the guidance and supervision I have received from Dr. John Christopher Thomas, I cannot say enough. His scholarly acumen, support, and encouragement throughout this project have been immense and there is little question that it would not have reached fruition without his enduring patience and wisdom and compassion.

Finally, I am immensely grateful to my beloved wife, Mimi Langlois. Without her encouragement and constant support this research would never have come to fruition. She has tolerated my absence on numerous occasions and always offered prayerful and loving support. At the same time, I am very thankful to my two children, Thomas Jacobs and Anna Jacobs, as well as numerous other friends and colleagues.

In the process of my study, I have been aided by the services of the staff at several libraries, including the librarians at Cape Fear Community College, Duke University, Tyndale House, the Fitzwilliam Museum Library, Cambridge University, the National Gallery of Art in Washington, DC, Catholic University of America, the University of Virginia, and the library of the British Museum.

Abbreviations

ACCS	Ancient Commentary of Christian Scripture
ACW	Ancient Christian Writers
ANF-II	*Ante-Nicene Fathers: Second Series*
ArtB	*Art Bulletin*
BAGD	Walter Bauer, William F. Arndt, F. William Gingrich, and Frederick W. Danker, *A Greek–English Lexicon of the New Testament and Other Early Christian Literature* (Chicago: University of Chicago Press, 2nd edition, 1958).
BSJSF	*Bibliographie sur saint Joseph et la sainte Famille*
CBQ	*Catholic Biblical Quarterly*
CCA	Corpus Christianorum. Series Apocryphorum
CJ	*Cahiers de Josephologie*
CoptE	Coptic Encyclopedia
EDNT	Horst Balz and Gerhard Schneider (eds.), *Exegetical Dictionary of the New Testament* (3 vols.; Grand Rapids: Eerdmans, 1990-1993).
GPM	*Gospel of Pseudo-Matthew*
GRBS	*Greek, Roman, and Byzantine Studies*
HJC	*History of Joseph the Carpenter*
HTR	*Harvard Theological Review*
IGJames	*Infancy Gospel of James*
IGThomas	*Infancy Gospel of Thomas*
JBL	*Journal of Biblical Literature*
JECS	*Journal of Early Christian Studies*
JSNT	*Journal for the Study of the New Testament*
JSNTS	Journal for the Study of the New Testament Supplement Series
LCC	*Library of Christian Classics*
LCI	*Lexikon der christlichen Ikonographie*
LNTS	*Library of New Testament Studies*
NIDNTT	Colin Brown (ed.), *New International Dictionary of New Testament Theology* (3 vols.; Grand Rapids: Zondervan, 1975-78)
NPNF-I	*Nicene and Post-Nicene Fathers: First Series*
NPNF-II	*Nicene and Post-Nicene Fathers: Second Series*
NTS	*New Testament Studies*
TDNT	Gerhard Kittel and Gerhard Friedrich (eds.), *Theological Dictionary of the New Testament* (trans. Geoffrey W. Bromiley; 10 vols.; Grand Rapids: Eerdmans, 1964-1976).
ZAC	*Zeitschrift für antikes Christentum*
ZNW	*Zeitschrift für die neutestamentliche Wissenschaft*

Illustrations

Figure 1. Sarcophagus, Arles, *First Dream of Joseph and Annunciation to Joseph*, Gallic, Fourth Century, Musée de l'Arles Antique, Arles, France

Figure 2. Mosaic, *Annunciation to Mary and First Dream of Joseph and Annunciation to Joseph*, Roman, Fifth Century, Santa Maria Maggiore, Rome, Italy

Figure 3. Mosaic, *First Dream of Joseph and Annunciation to Joseph*, Roman, Fifth Century, Santa Maria Maggiore, Rome, Italy

Figure 4. Ivory Plaque, *First Dream of Joseph and Annunciation to Joseph and the Journey to Bethlehem*, Cathedra for Archbishop Maximianus of Ravenna, Byzantine, 546-556, Archiepiscopal Museum, Ravenna, Italy

Figure 5. Ivory Plaque, *First Dream of Joseph and Annunciation to Joseph*, Cathedra for Archbishop Maximianus of Ravenna, Byzantine, 546-556, Archiepiscopal Museum, Ravenna, Italy

Figure 6. Sarcophagus, Le Puy, *First Dream of Joseph and Annunciation to Joseph and Marriage of Joseph and Mary*, Gallic, Fourth Century, Musée Crozatier, Le Puy-en-Velay, France

Figure 7. Sarcophagus, Le Puy, *First Dream of Joseph and Annunciation to Joseph*, Gallic, Fourth Century, Musée Crozatier, Le Puy-en-Velay, France

Figure 8. Ivory Plaque, *Water Test*, Cathedra for Archbishop Maximianus of Ravenna, Byzantine, 546-556, Archiepiscopal Museum, Ravenna, Italy

Figure 9. Ivory Book Cover, St. Lupicin Gospels, *Water Test*, Byzantine, Sixth Century, Bibliotheque Nationale, Paris, France

Figure 10. Ivory Plaque, *First Dream of Joseph and Annunciation to Joseph and Journey to Bethlehem*, Cathedra for Archbishop Maximianus of Ravenna, Byzantine, 546-556, Archiepiscopal Museum, Ravenna, Italy

Figure 11. Ivory Plaque, *Journey to Bethlehem*, Cathedra for Archbishop Maximianus of Ravenna, Byzantine, 546-556, Archiepiscopal Museum, Ravenna, Italy

Figure 12. Ivory Book Cover, St. Lupicin Gospels, *Journey to Bethlehem*, Byzantine, Sixth Century, Bibliothèque Nationale, Paris, France

Figure 13. Ivory Pyx, *Journey to Bethlehem*, Syrian-Palestinian, Sixth Century, Staatliche Museen Preußischer Kulturbesitz, Berlin, Germany

Figure 14. Ivory Book Cover, Murano Ivories, *Journey to Bethlehem*, Syrian, Sixth-Eighth Century, Louvre, Paris, France

Figure 15. Ivory Book Cover, *Nativity*, Italian, Fifth Century, Cathedral Treasury of Milan, Italy

Illustrations   xi

Figure 16. Illuminated Manuscript Parchment, Rabbula Codex, *Nativity*, Syrian, Monastery of St. John Zagba, 586 CE, Biblioteca Laurenziana, Florence, Italy

Figure 17. Ivory Book Cover, Dagulf Plaque, *Nativity*, Court of Charlemagne (?), Eighth-Ninth Century, Bodleian Library, Oxford, England

Figure 18. Ivory Plaque, *Nativity*, Syrian-Palestinian, Seventh-Eighth Century, Dumbarton Oaks, Washington, DC

Figure 19. Sarcophagus, 'Sarcophagus of the Two Testaments' or 'The Dogmatic Sarcophagus,'*Adoration of the Magi*, Roman, Fourth Century, Museo Pio Cristiano (the Vatican Museum), Rome, Italy

Figure 20. Sarcophagus, *Adoration of the Magi*, Cherchell, Algeria, Fourth Century, Louvre, Paris, France

Figure 21. Mosaic, *Adoration of the Magi*, Roman, Fifth Century, Santa Maria Maggiore, Rome, Italy

Figure 22. Mosaic, St. Peter's Basilica, *Adoration of the Magi*, Roman, Eighth Century, Basilica of Santa Maria in Cosmedin, Rome, Italy

Part I

Introduction

The Problem

In the history of Western art and literature much attention and many studies have been directed to the subjects of the nature and character of the portrayal of two figures in the Holy Family, Jesus and Mary. However, only a few scholars have shown serious interest in the subject of the portrayal of *the other person* in the Holy Family, Joseph the Carpenter. Further, none have formally focused on the reception history and interpretation of the canonic portrayals of Joseph, in Matthew, Luke, and John, in the first several centuries of Christian literature and art (the *Wirkungsgeschichte* of these New Testament representations). This is the case despite the fact that most of these literary portrayals are found within two of the most popular and studied narrative sections of the New Testament (birth and early childhood sections of Matthew and Luke) and despite the fact that numerous and significant literary and artistic records of their later reception and development are extant from the early Christian and early medieval periods.

The purpose of this study is to offer an examination of these initial narrative portrayals and further examinations of four later texts and eighteen later images that document their reception; to review the earliest literary portrayals and to trace and record the development of the *Wirkungsgeschichte*, the history of the reception, of the canonic representations of Joseph in Christian literature and art, from approximately 150 CE to 800 CE. Thus, the objective of this thesis is to fill a significant lacuna in contemporary scholarship.

The History of Research

In order to fill this lacuna it is necessary initially to review the work of those scholars who have shown an implicit interest in the *Wirkungsgeschichte* (which this study assumes includes and encompasses the 'history of interpretation,' *Auslegungsgeschichte*, as defined by the biblical scholar,

Ulrich Luz) of the New Testament nativity narratives and accounts pertaining to Joseph the Carpenter.[1] Therefore, their work will be noted in this history of research.

Research in Biblical Studies

While several biblical scholars have provided very brief insight into the character, role, and portrayal of Joseph in the gospels of Matthew, Luke, and John through the means of textual, historical, form, and redaction critical studies found in commentaries, only four have focused upon the character of Joseph in a significant way, namely Raymond Brown, Dan Via, Ulrich Luz, and Joseph Fitzmyer. Thus, the attention of this initial review of related scholarship in biblical studies will focus upon the research of these four individuals.

Raymond Brown

In his groundbreaking work, *The Birth of the Messiah*, Raymond Brown pays particular attention to the role and portrayal of Joseph, especially in the Gospel of Matthew.[2] Using the methods of form and redaction criticism, Brown highlights the importance of Joseph within this narrative. Consequently, he acknowledges that 'the Matthean infancy narrative ... centers upon Joseph' and that Mary 'figures only on a secondary level'.[3] In addition, Brown goes so far as to suggest that 'the figure of Joseph holds the narrative together'.[4] He believes this because he sees Joseph as the character in the narrative that maintains 'the continuity' between Israel and the new movement of Jews and Gentiles.[5] It is he who, as the central subject of the infancy narrative, brings together the salvation history of the Hebrew people and the salvation history of the rest of the

---

[1] This study accepts the definition of *Wirkungsgeschichte* articulated by Ulrich Luz in his commentary *Matthew 1–7* (trans. James E. Crouch; Minneapolis, MN: Fortress Press, 2007), p. 61. Luz writes: 'Under "history of interpretation" (*Auslegungsgeschichte*) I understand the interpretations of a text particularly in commentaries. Under the "history of influence of the text" (*Wirkungsgeschichte*) in the narrower sense I want to understand how the text is received and actualized in media other than commentaries-in verbal media such as sermons, canonic documents, and "literature," as well as in nonverbal media such as art and music, and in the church's activity and suffering, that is, in church history ... At the same time, I understand the "history of the influence of the text" (*Wirkungsgeschichte*) to be a more inclusive concept that includes "history of interpretation" (*Auslegungsgeschichte*) and "history of the influence of the text" (*Wirkungsgeschichte*) in the narrower sense.' It is believed that Luz's broader definition of this interpretive method and process permits the acknowledgment of the work of other scholars who have worked in the fields of non-canonic studies, church history, and art history.

[2] Raymond Brown, *The Birth of the Messiah* (Garden City, NY: Doubleday, 1977).

[3] Brown, *The Birth of the Messiah* (1977), p. 33.

[4] Brown, *The Birth of the Messiah* (1977), pp. 231-32.

[5] Brown, *The Birth of the Messiah* (1977), p. 231.

world. It is Joseph who, as Brown says, 'protects Jesus from the hostile authorities of his own people and brings him to safety to Galilee of the Gentiles'.[6] It is he who, according to Brown, in his righteous, obedient, and faithful acts, offers us, by his example in the Matthean account of the nativity and infancy, 'the Gospel and its destiny in miniature'.[7] For this reason, by his emphasis upon the significance of Joseph in Matthew, Brown provides an important foundation for further reflection and analysis on the portrayal of Joseph within the New Testament.

Nevertheless, significant as his analysis is with respect to the portrayal of Joseph in Matthew, he seems reluctant to see the importance of Joseph in Luke. This is obvious in both his earlier reflections about Joseph in the first edition of *The Birth of the Messiah* as well as in his later observations found in the second and final edition of this text. He acknowledges Joseph's presence in the first two chapters of Luke, noting he is 'betrothed' to Mary who is 'pregnant', whom God has chosen to bear 'a Savior who is Messiah and Lord'.[8] Brown also recognizes that Luke identifies Joseph as 'the father of Jesus' (2.48) and has twice stressed that Joseph was of the house of David (1.27 and 2.4)', remarks that affirmed that 'in a Jewish mindset, through Joseph's acknowledgment, Jesus could be legally, even if not biologically, Joseph's son and thus share Joseph's Davidic descent'.[9] Further, Brown confirms that 'Jesus' parents' were spiritually obedient Jews who followed the 'laws involving the Temple and sacrifices (2.22-24,39,41)'.[10] And, yet, he is unable to say little more about the role and place of Joseph in Luke and concludes that 'Joseph will never be more than a shadow figure or speak in the Jesus story'.[11]

Dan Via

In his article, 'Narrative World and Ethical Response: The Marvelous and Righteousness in Matthew 1-2', Via engages in 'a more or less internal literary analysis of the surface structure of this narrative in relation to its deeper structures and the implications of the narrative world for ethical responsibility'.[12] In the process, he primarily attempts to integrate this 'aesthetic' literary analysis with a 'structural' analysis.[13] This particular structural analysis is based upon A.J. Greimas' 'test sequence' which consists of five functions: '(1) Mandating, (2) Acceptance (or Rejection),

---

[6] Brown, *The Birth of the Messiah* (1977), p. 232.
[7] Brown, *The Birth of the Messiah* (1977), p. 232.
[8] Brown, *The Birth of the Messiah* (1977), pp. 287, 393.
[9] Raymond Brown, *The Birth of the Messiah* (New Haven and London: Yale University Press, 1993), p. 589.
[10] Brown, *The Birth of the Messiah* (1993), p. 625.
[11] Brown, *The Birth of the Messiah* (1993), p. 642.
[12] Via, 'Narrative World and Ethical Response', pp. 123-50.
[13] Via, 'Narrative World and Ethical Response', p. 129

(3) Confrontation, (4) Success or Domination, (5) Consequence, Attribution, or Communication'.[14] Each of these functions is contained within the three different types of 'tests' Greimas believes should be applied in an analysis of a narrative. These three 'tests' are identified by him as 'qualifying, main, and glorifying'.[15] Still, Via goes on to qualify his use of Greimas' method by stating that his 'analysis ... will to a large extent be limited to the functions ... and their surface manifestations' and this is especially evident in his reflections on the portrait of Joseph in the Matthean narrative.[16]

Having enunciated his methodology, Via relates that he believes Joseph is the protagonist ('the subject mandated to pursue a task') of Matthew 1-2 and believes Joseph (who is acknowledged as 'righteous') and 'his story' represent a 'semantically packed miniature' of the Matthean portrayal of Jesus, 'his story', and 'the righteousness demanded of his disciples'.[17] In the process, Via acknowledges that Joseph's identity as 'a righteous man' is largely portrayed in this biblical account 'by his actions, by his decisions to render a difficult obedience'.[18]

In his recounting of Joseph's 'decisions' Via addresses Joseph's initial 'decision' in response to his realization that Mary has become pregnant. In this case, Via recognizes that while Joseph's 'righteousness disposes him to obey the law', the quality of it also leads him to decide to do this 'quietly' so as to protect Mary (and the child she bears) from possible punishment and even death.[19] Further, Via argues, it is this very ethical dilemma of Joseph, highlighted in his 'embarrassment' over his discovery about Mary that leads to a 'dramatic encounter of self with self, God, and the world' that leads him to make new decisions.[20] It is this 'dramatic encounter', facilitated by the annunciation of the angelic messenger during Joseph's first dream that changes everything and ultimately reshapes his understanding of righteousness, the law, his relationship with Mary

---

[14] Via, 'Narrative World and Ethical Response', p. 129.
[15] Via, 'Narrative World and Ethical Response', p. 129, adds: 'All three have the same five functions, but they are differentiated in that the Consequence or Attribution function differs in each of them in content with regard to the object communicated. In the qualifying test power or a helper is attributed to the hero; in the main test a good or value, liquidation of lack, is communicated to him; and in the glorifying test recognition, or a message, is attributed to him (Greimas: 197, 202-203, 206; Calloud: 28). Obviously, in order to distinguish the three tests, it was necessary to give the fifth function a more specific semantic content than it has in the test sequence per se. Therefore, the three-test pattern is less abstract (less "deep") than the simple test sequence and should be called, in our frame of reference, an "intermediate" structure.'
[16] Via, 'Narrative World and Ethical Response', p. 129.
[17] Via, 'Narrative World and Ethical Response', pp. 123, 133.
[18] Via, 'Narrative World and Ethical Response', p. 127.
[19] Via, 'Narrative World and Ethical Response', pp. 127, 133.
[20] Via, 'Narrative World and Ethical Response', p. 133.

(and the child she bears), and his identity and purpose in life. For in this 'encounter' Joseph is commanded to reverse his present course, and to 'take Mary as his wife', and make Jesus 'his legal, adopted son and thereby also son of David'.[21] Therefore, in his analysis of the portrayal of Joseph in Matthew 1-2, Via suggests that it is Joseph's acceptance of the angelic message and command that reveals both the consistency in his character ('he persistently has the disposition to do the will of God') and his moral and spiritual 'flexibility and openness' ('displayed in his capacity – seen especially in his first decision – to change his view of what the will of God requires and of how one knows it').[22]

Ulrich Luz

A pioneer in the use and application of *Wirkungsgeschichte* in the interpretation of the New Testament, Ulrich Luz, has contributed three significant studies on the Gospel of Matthew, namely, *Matthew in History: Interpretation, Influence and Effects* (1994), *The Theology of the Gospel of Matthew* (1995), and *Matthew 1-7*, initially published in English in 1989, and later adapted and reissued in 2007.[23] This in turn has been followed by the publications of two other volumes in his Matthean commentary series: *Matthew 8-20* and *Matthew 21-28*.[24] It is his volume on Matthew 1-7 that is most relevant for the present study. In his examination of the first two chapters of Matthew, Luz acknowledges Joseph's importance and centrality, particularly in his comments on 1.18-25 and 2.13-23.[25] Even so, significant as Luz's comments are with regard to Joseph's character and role in the narrative, he makes only brief references and allusions to Joseph in his discussion of the *Wirkungsgeschichte* of the first two chapters of Matthew.

With respect to 1.1-17, Luz recognizes that most interpreters in the ancient church did not concur with the idea that Joseph's genealogy 'demonstrated the Davidic descent because ... he was Jesus' legal father ...', and notes that most acknowledged Matthew's genealogy as "Joseph's"'.[26] In his comments on the second pericope (1.18-25), Luz focuses upon the reception history of 1.25. With regard to this verse, he

---

[21] Via, 'Narrative World and Ethical Response', p. 134.
[22] Via, 'Narrative World and Ethical Response', p. 137.
[23] His publications include: Ulrich Luz, *Matthew in History: Interpretation, Influence, and Effects* (Minneapolis, MN: Fortress Press, 1994); *The Theology of the Gospel of Matthew* (trans. J.B. Robinson; Cambridge: Cambridge University Press, 1995); *Matthew 1–7* (trans. Wilhelm C. Linss; Minneapolis, MN: Fortress Press, 1989) and *Matthew 1–7* (trans. James E. Crouch; Minneapolis: Fortress Press, 2007).
[24] Ulrich Luz, *Matthew 8-20* (trans. James E. Crouch; Minneapolis, MN: Fortress Press, 2001) and Ulrich Luz, *Matthew 21-28* (trans. James E. Crouch; Minneapolis, MN: Fortress Press, 2005).
[25] Luz, *Matthew 1–7*, 1989, p. 115 and *Matthew 1–7*, 2007, p. 94.
[26] Luz, *Matthew 1–7*, 2007, pp. 86-87.

notes that Joseph's presence raises questions about the nature of his relationship with Mary following the birth of Jesus and this, in turn, leads Luz into an extensive discussion about Mary and the role of this verse with regard to later discourse about the theological doctrine of Mary's perpetual virginity.[27] Curiously, Luz does not explore these matters with respect to Joseph in any depth or reflect upon later theological or artistic portrayals of Joseph based upon this pericope.

This lack of attention to Joseph is also evident in his discussion of the *Wirkungsgeschichte* of the pericopes in the second chapter of Matthew. In his analysis of the *Adoration of the Magi* in 2.1-12, Luz gives serious consideration to the representations of Mary, the Christ child, and the Magi in the later interpretations of numerous church fathers and theologians. Further, he also gives serious consideration to their representations in the later images of some artists (including two notable images, the composition of *The Epiphany* in the large anonymous mosaic in S. Maria Maggiore in Rome and the composition of the central panel of the triptych of the *Adoration of the Magi* by Rogier van der Weyden in the Alte Pinakothek in Munich in which Joseph is present). Yet, Luz ignores the reflections and portrayals of these interpreters and artists with respect to Joseph.[28] Neither does Luz include any later interpretations and portrayals of Joseph in his discussion of the 'Flight to Egypt and Move to Nazareth' in 2.13-23. This is especially surprising since this particular pericope has evoked much response from later narrators, church fathers, theologians, and artists and invited fascinating representations and compositions of the Carpenter.[29]

Joseph A. Fitzmyer

In a lecture given at St. Joseph's University in 1997 in Philadelphia and later published by that institution under the title, *Saint Joseph in Matthew's Gospel*, the Jesuit scholar, Joseph A. Fitzmyer, reflects upon the topics of 'Joseph's Name', 'The Ancient Sources that Tell Us about Joseph, the Husband of Mary', and 'The Picture of Joseph in Matthew's Gospel'.[30] In the process, Fitzmyer provides much information about the portrayal of Joseph in both Matthew and Luke, noting 'the important role that Joseph plays in the infancy narrative (Matthew)' and draws a substantial analogy between the Joseph of the New Testament and the Joseph of

---

[27] Luz, *Matthew 1–7*, 2007, p. 98.
[28] Luz, *Matthew 1–7*, 2007, pp. 106-11.
[29] Luz, *Matthew 1–7*, p. 124.
[30] Joseph A. Fitzmyer, *Saint Joseph in Matthew's Gospel* (Philadelphia: Saint Joseph's University Press, 1997).

Genesis, whom Fitzmyer identifies as the 'famous guardian of a patriarchal family in Israelite history'.³¹ However, it is striking that though Fitzmyer acknowledges Joseph is identified by the writer of Matthew as the 'husband' of Mary and the 'father' or 'foster-father' of Jesus and as a 'righteous' and 'obedient' Jew, he most often speaks of him as 'Joseph the guardian' and summarizes Joseph's activity in Matthew as 'providing safety and guardianship for Mary and Jesus'.³² Thus, while Fitzmyer goes into some detail about the character of Joseph within Matthew and the rest of the New Testament, his theological assumptions about Joseph's virginity and his primary role (that he is 'Joseph the guardian'), seriously inhibit his analysis and his conclusions about Joseph's role and portrayal within the gospels narratives of the birth and infancy of Jesus.³³ As a result many aspects of Joseph's portrayal in Matthew are left unexplored.

Research in Non-canonic Studies

Although Joseph the Carpenter is a prominent figure in the Infancy Gospel of James, the Infancy Gospel of Thomas, the History of Joseph the Carpenter, and the Gospel of Pseudo-Matthew, only one scholar has taken formal interest in his character, role, and portrayal in this material, namely, Ronald Hock. Specifically, Hock reflects on the reception history of the New Testament portrayals of Joseph in Christian non-canonic literature.³⁴

Ronald Hock

While Ronald F. Hock's main goals in *The Infancy Gospels of James and Thomas* are to provide new English translations, updated Greek texts, along with introductions and commentaries for both of these early Christian apocrypha, he, nonetheless, offers important insights into the

---

[31] Fitzmyer, *Saint Joseph in Matthew's Gospel*, pp. 2-4, 12, 17-20.

[32] Fitzmyer, *Saint Joseph in Matthew's Gospel*, pp. 2, 3, 4, 7, 12-13, 17, 19-20. Fitzmyer further highlights his conviction that Joseph's primary function is that of 'guardian' by drawing a direct parallel between the Joseph of Genesis (who he also identifies as 'the guardian of his family') and the Joseph of Matthew.

[33] Fitzmyer, *Saint Joseph in Matthew's Gospel*, pp. 4, 16, 17, 20.

[34] Ronald F. Hock. *The Infancy Gospels of James and Thomas* (Santa Rosa, CA: Polebridge Press, 1995). While Wolfgang A. Bienert, 'The Relatives of Jesus', in Wilhelm Schneemelcher (ed.), *The New Testament Apocrypha: Gospels and Related Writings* I (trans. Robert McL.Wilson; Louisville, KY: Westminster/John Knox Press, 1991), pp. 470-85 and J.K. Elliott, *The Apocryphal New Testament* (Oxford: Clarendon Press, 2004), pp. 48-51, 68-69, 84-86, 111, and *A Synopsis of the Apocryphal Nativity and Infancy Narratives* (Leiden and Boston: Brill, 2006), pp. ix–x, xvi, make mention of Joseph, they do not formally reflect on the reception history of the New Testament portrayals of Joseph in Christian non-canonic literature. The same may be said with regard to the work of Reidar Aasgaard, *The Childhood of Jesus: Decoding the Apocryphal Infancy Gospel of Thomas* (Eugene, OR: Cascade Books, 2009).

Wirkungsgeschichte of the New Testament portrayals of Joseph in certain circles within early Christianity.[35] Although he acknowledges with Elliott that much of the focus of these two narratives is on stories about Mary and evolving Mariology, Hock's approach to them permits him to reflect seriously upon their authors' representations of Jesus and Joseph. In the process, Hock identifies several perceptions the authors (and likely their communities) held about Joseph, which constitutes an important contribution to the reception history of the New Testament portrayals of Joseph.

Hock finds the image of Joseph in the Infancy Gospel of James to be quite different from his portrait in the canonic Gospels. While he admits the author of this second century non-canonic narrative makes use of the material relevant to the canonic portrayal of Joseph in Matthew 1-2 and Luke 1-2 and keeps significant portions of the outline of the canonic narrative in place, Hock recognizes that the author introduces important innovations into his characterizations and narrative, including specific innovations that profoundly alter the canonic portrait of Joseph.[36] Among other places, these innovations appear with regard to Joseph's concern about Mary's pregnancy and include, as Hock notes, 'a soliloquy by Joseph about Mary's condition (13:1-5)' and 'a confrontation between Joseph and Mary (13:6-10)'.[37]

Hock believes the most significant innovations occur in 'Joseph's characterization', changes that he argues 'are necessitated by the author's emphasis on Mary's purity...'[38] In addition, this author makes every effort in the tone, demeanor, and substance of the words he places in Joseph's mouth, to build a spiritual and psychological wall between Joseph and Mary, to remove any suggestion of a close personal relationship or intimacy between the couple during the period of the birth of Jesus (19.1-13) or later (9.8).[39]

At the same time, Hock finds even more innovation in the image of Joseph in The Infancy Gospel of Thomas, a collection of several stories about the childhood of Jesus.[40] Here, as he notes, Joseph is placed into a largely new role where he must father, as it were, a 'new' Jesus who is 'a vindictive, arrogant, unruly child' who, as J.K. Elliott puts it, 'seldom acts in a Christian way'.[41] Thus, the author of this infancy gospel offers

---

[35] Hock, *The Infancy Gospels of James and Thomas*, pp. 22-25, 85-86.
[36] Hock, *The Infancy Gospels*, pp. 22-25.
[37] Hock, *The Infancy Gospels*, p. 23.
[38] Hock, *The Infancy Gospels*, p. 25.
[39] Hock, *The Infancy Gospels*, pp. 24-25.
[40] Hock, *The Infancy Gospels*, pp. 85-86.
[41] Hock, *The Infancy Gospels*, p. 86, quoting Elliott from p. 68 of the *Apocryphal New Testament*.

a further portrait of Joseph that not only stands in tension with the earliest canonic image and the portrayal offered by the author of the Infancy Gospel of James, but contributes extra elements to the narrative portrayal of Joseph that further stretch the parameters of the conception and image of the Carpenter in early Christianity. Among these elements is the fact that in this gospel Joseph is a very active father who is substantially engaged with Jesus.

In placing his analyses of these non-canonic gospels side by side, Hock permits his readers to perceive the differences and similarities between these respective portraits of Joseph; differences and similarities that highlight both the apologetic concerns of the early church and the fluidity in the perception of the role of the Carpenter.

Research in Church History

While several scholars in the field of church history have made contributions to an understanding of the portrayal of Joseph, four in particular, Joseph Seitz, Francis Filas, Geoffrey Parrinder, and Joseph Lienhard engage in implicit attempts to attend to the *Wirkungsgeschichte* of the New Testament portrayals of Joseph.[42] Thus, the attention of this initial review will be upon their work.

Joseph Seitz

In a text published in 1908, the Jesuit scholar, Joseph Seitz, made a substantial effort to document and survey the history of devotion to Joseph.[43] In order to accomplish this task, he sought to document and examine evidence about Joseph found in relevant literary and theological sources (including the narratives of the New Testament and Christian non-canonic writers, the theological writings of the church fathers, and the later writings of medieval and renaissance theologians and spiritual writers) and in related works of art (covering the period of the earliest Christian art to that of renaissance artists and artisans). In so doing, Seitz, brought new attention to Joseph and, by means of the quantity of evidence he presented, challenged scholars to reconsider Joseph's role and importance in Christian salvation history. Accordingly, Seitz offers a wide array of literary, theological, and artistic evidence to support his conviction that devotion to Joseph grew over time, became substantial within the medieval period, and reached an appropriate height by the

---

[42] While Joseph has been the subject of several other texts and articles within Catholic literature, this work is primarily devotional. Therefore, it is not included in this survey.

[43] Joseph Seitz, *Die Verehrung des hl. Joseph in ihrer geschichtlichen Entwicklung bis zum Konzil von Trient dargestellt* (Freiburg im Breisgau: Herder, 1908).

time of the Council of Trent. In the process, he provides evidence to aid in the analysis of the *Wirkungsgeschichte* of the New Testament images of Joseph.

While the strength of his text is found largely in its breadth, this breadth also reveals its limitation. This limitation is demonstrated, among other places, in his work in chapter three which covers the early Christian and early medieval periods that are the focus of this study. Although he provides some critical documentation in these chapters, Seitz inevitably misses much evidence that explains the development of the *Wirkungsgeschichte* of the New Testament images of Joseph. Further, Seitz's work is limited by certain theological assumptions that underlie his study (namely, the assumption that Joseph was a virgin throughout his life and the assumption that he and Mary never consummated their relationship and had a family, as the early gospel texts may suggest). Among other things, these underlying assumptions lead him to negate part of the portrayal of Joseph in the New Testament and dismiss the significance of Joseph's role in the Christian non-canonic literature. Thus, ultimately, both the breadth of Seitz's work and these two particular assumptions inhibit its value with respect to the narratives and art addressed in this analysis.

Francis Filas

Much the same can be said in regard to the research of the Jesuit scholar, Francis Filas, who spent a large portion of his academic career engaged in analysis of the portrayal of Joseph as his publications indicate.[44] While all of his volumes reveal an implicit interest in the *Wirkungsgeschichte* of the New Testament images of Joseph, this interest seems most notable in his last.[45]

Heavily dependent upon Seitz's earlier work, in *Joseph, the Man Closest to Jesus*, Filas examines the evolution of devotion to Joseph from the earliest years of Christianity to the modern period.[46] In the process, Filas focuses upon some subjects that are relevant to this analysis, notably, the

---

[44] His publications include the following: Francis Filas, *The Man Nearest to Christ: Nature and Historic Development of the Devotion to St. Joseph* (Milwaukee, WI: Bruce, 1944); *Joseph and Jesus: A Theological Study of Their Relationship* (Milwaukee, WI: Bruce, 1952); *Joseph Most Just: Theological Questions about St. Joseph* (Milwaukee, WI: Bruce, 1956); and *Joseph, the Man Closest to Jesus: The Complete Life, Theology, and Devotional History of St. Joseph* (Boston: Daughters of St. Paul, 1962).

[45] Francis Filas, *Joseph, the Man Closest to Jesus: The Complete Life, Theology, and Devotional History of St. Joseph*.

[46] Filas, *Joseph, the Man Closest to Jesus: The Complete Life, Theology, and Devotional History of St. Joseph*, p. 15, acknowledges his heavy dependence upon the work of Seitz.

portrayal of Joseph in the canonic and non-canonic gospels and the history of devotion to Joseph in the early centuries and in the Byzantine Church.

However, as in the case of the work of Seitz, much of Filas' writing is shaped by the two underlying assumptions that informed Seitz as well, and by an even more heightened desire to defend additional Catholic doctrine. It is also influenced by Filas' desire to cover even a larger time period than Seitz; a goal that inevitably diminishes the strength of this text as well as the quality of his scholarship.[47] Therefore, while there is much to commend this large work, it has limited value for this thesis.

Geoffrey Parrinder
Rebutting the 'traditional belief in a virginal conception of Jesus', Parrinder asserts in, *Son of Joseph: The Parentage of Jesus*, his own belief that Joseph was the biological father of Jesus.[48] Using the historical critical method, he engages in considerable reflection upon the heritage of the historical Jesus, as it can be discerned, in both the New Testament and early Christian non-canonic gospels. This leads Parrinder to conclude, among other things, that some early Christian narratives, theology, and art (based upon this 'traditional belief') distorted the identity of Jesus and diminished the role and significance of Joseph in Jesus' life. Consequently, summarizing his thoughts in a chapter entitled, 'Joseph', Parrinder argues that Joseph played a substantial role in the life of Jesus. In his role as a Jewish father, he believes Joseph helped determine Jesus' earthly vocation as a carpenter, had a significant influence on Jesus' spiritual beliefs and ideas, very possibly shaped Jesus' conception of God as 'father' and, naturally, led people who knew both to identify Jesus as 'son of Joseph'.[49]

The priority he gives the canonic narratives is a reminder that their portrayals of Joseph must first be sufficiently reviewed and analyzed before a study of the development of the *Wirkungsgeschichte* of the New Testament images of Joseph can truly begin.

---

[47] Thus, Filas spends a lot of time focused upon certain subjects that are not directly relevant to the concerns of the present study. These include the subjects of Joseph's ancestry, 'Joseph's miraculous selection', his relationship to the 'brethren of the Lord', the prospect of his 'earlier marriage', the authenticity of his marriage to Mary, the issue of 'Joseph's fatherhood', and other matters that are particularly relevant to the Catholic tradition.

[48] Geoffrey Parrinder, *Son of Joseph: The Parentage of Jesus* (Edinburgh: T. & T. Clark, 1992).

[49] Parrinder, *Son of Joseph: The Parentage of Jesus*, pp. 110-15.

Joseph Lienhard

In his brief study, *St. Joseph in Early Christianity*, Lienhard, also a member of the Society of Jesus, reflects on the *Wirkungsgeschichte* of the New Testament portrayals of Joseph in early Christian non-canonic and patristic writings.[50] Although he considers the representations of Joseph in several of the early non-canonic writings (the Infancy Gospel of Thomas, the Gospel of Pseudo-Matthew, the Arabic Gospel of the Infancy, and the History of Joseph the Carpenter) in relationship to the canonic gospel images, he focuses most of his attention on the narrative of the Infancy Gospel of James, the narrative he considers the most important and influential theological text within Christian apocrypha. Among other things, Lienhard identifies 'several important, but problematic, assertions [within it] ... not accounted for in the gospels', including assertions about Joseph that later authors further developed or embellished; assertions that dramatically shaped patristic interpretations of Joseph.[51]

Research in Art History

Although much research in art history has focused on representations of the holy family, a significant amount of this work has centered on the two figures of the Christ-child and Mary or upon the figure of Mary alone; with little reflection on the figure of Joseph. Numerous examples of this concentration can be found within the standard catalogue raisonnes of both major and minor artists as well as in numerous special studies. Of the various scholars who consider the portrayal of Joseph the

---

[50] Joseph Lienhard, *St. Joseph in Early Christianity* (Philadelphia: St. Joseph's University Press, 1999).

[51] Lienhard, *St. Joseph in Early Christianity*, pp. 9 and 11. Lienhard believes the church fathers' interests were primarily centered on providing answers to certain questions that addressed, among other issues, the apparent conflict between Matthew's account of the genealogy of Joseph and Luke's, the interpretation of the gospel references to the brothers and sisters of Jesus, and the marital status and position of Joseph. The patristic fathers believed these were very serious issues; issues that raised questions with respect to Jesus' divinity, Mary's virginity, the nature of Joseph's fatherhood of Jesus, Joseph's marital and sexual status, and the nature and character of the relationship between Joseph and Mary. Therefore, they devoted a lot of time and effort to these questions. Having posed these issues, Lienhard, *St Joseph in Early Christianity*, pp. 11-56, then goes on to provide an interpretation of the patristic responses to them and to offer an extensive anthology entitled, 'Principal Passages from the Fathers of the Church on St. Joseph' that details the perceptions and thoughts of Justin Martyr, Irenaeus, Julius Africanus, Origen, Ambrose, Hilary, Augustine, and Chrysostom, Pseudo-Augustine, and Pseudo-Origen, among others.

Carpenter, the work of Gertrud Schiller, Tom Pitts, and Brigitte Heublein, disclose implicit attempts to attend to the development of the *Wirkungsgeschichte* of the earliest gospel portrayals of Joseph.[52]

Gertrud Schiller

In her two-volume text, *The Iconography of Christian Art*, Gertrud Schiller reveals an interest in some of the portrayals of Joseph the Carpenter in the history of Western art.[53] Indeed, in contrast to many other art historians, she makes brief but important efforts to detail the history of Joseph's role and portrayal in early Christian and early medieval art, the periods of interest for this study as well as in later periods. Within the context of her discussion of the broader subject of 'The Birth and Childhood of Christ', Schiller documents the fluidity and variety in the artistic representations of Joseph in the evolution of the *Wirkungsgeschichte* of the earliest gospel portrayals of Joseph through the means of several images that recount the Matthean and Lukan nativity scenes. In the process, she creates one of the most important analyses of the development of the reception history of the Matthean and Lukan accounts of Joseph in art history, research that will be given serious consideration.

Among other images, Schiller draws attention to several significant portrayals and interpretations of Joseph in the mosaic pictorial cycle of the birth and childhood of Jesus in the triumphal arch of the Santa Maria Maggiore, the earliest and only extant Roman cathedral from the first half of the fifth century. Created, under the direction of Pope Sixtus III, following the important Council of Ephesus in 431, in which the larger church declared Mary, the mother of Jesus, to be *theotokos*, 'the bearer of God', this cathedral was the first to be dedicated to the virgin Mary.[54] As Schiller notes, it is these images of Joseph, inspired from the Matthean and Lucan narrative events of the *Annunciation to Mary and the Annunciation to Joseph*, the *Adoration of the Magi*, the *Presentation in the Temple and Joseph's Second Dream*, and the *Three Magi before Herod* as well as a scene from an early unknown non-canonic gospel, the *Greeting of the Holy Family by Afrodisius at Sotinen in Egypt during the Flight into Egypt*, that provide some of the most memorable and fascinating representations of the canonic and non-canonic accounts of the Carpenter.

---

[52] While the great scholar of early Christian images, Wilpert, Giuseppe, *I Sarcofagi Cristiani Antichi*, vols. I-V (Roma: Pontificio Istituto di Archeologia Cristiana, 1929-1936), periodically reflects upon the presence and portrayal of Joseph, he does not engage in the kind of concentrated reflection found in the work of these other authors.

[53] Gertrud Schiller, *The Iconography of Christian Art*, 2 vols. (trans. Janet Seligman; Greenwich, CT: New York Graphic Society, 1971).

[54] Schiller, *The Iconography of Christian Art*, I, pp. 26-27.

Tom Pitts

In his 1988 PhD dissertation, 'The Origin and Meaning of Some Saint Joseph Figures in Early Christian Art,' completed at the University of Georgia, Pitts asserts that the 'image of St. Joseph ... in the art of the early Catholic church was, in certain examples, based on classical figures that were chosen as models for their ability to communicate Joseph's appearance and emotional state as related by the Bible and earliest non-canonic narrative.'[55] He explores this thesis by surveying classical pagan images and determining which of these prototypes bear the closest resemblance to images of Joseph created within the first several centuries of Christianity.

Before Pitts begins this substantial survey and comparison, he documents and evaluates three early Christian literary sources in chapter 1, notably, the two nativity accounts in the Gospels of Matthew and Luke and the account of the non-canonic *Infancy Gospel of James*, that he is convinced informed early representations of Joseph with regard to his appearance and emotional state. He does this in order to determine 'the variety of emotions to which the artisans needed to refer' in their compositions of Joseph.[56] In the end, it is his belief that the authors of Matthew, Luke, and the *Infancy Gospel of James*, leave their readers with the impression that the most dominant emotions 'experienced by Joseph' were 'sadness and anxiety ...'[57]

Once he completes his discussion of the literary and theological background of early portrayals of Joseph, Pitts then seeks to substantiate his thesis by means of a survey and comparison of antique classical images and early images of Joseph. In order to establish that specific resemblances do exist, Pitts compares the classical images with the portrayals of Joseph. Using the diverse categories of body type, age, beard, hair length, costume, gesture, placement in the composition, similar situations, character traits, and emotions, he precedes to make the case, in the rest of his text that substantial parallels exist between several different classical pagan figures and early figures of Joseph.

In ch. 2, Pitts asserts that one of the basic types of Joseph, often described as the 'depressed-appearing' or 'mourning Joseph', bears a close relationship to antique images of anonymous mourners. As he notes, the 'type of Joseph who sits with his head on the palm of his hand', in fact, has antecedents in classical philosopher figures as well as Roman capta figures and, thus, should be interpreted more broadly.[58] Referring to

---

[55] Tom Richardson Pitts, 'The Origin and Meaning of Some Saint Joseph Figures in Early Christian Art', PhD dissertation (Athens, GA: University of Georgia, 1988), p. iii.

[56] Pitts, 'The Origin and Meaning of Some Saint Joseph Figures', p. 85.

[57] Pitts, 'The Origin and Meaning of Some Saint Joseph Figures', p. 85.

[58] Pitts, 'The Origin and Meaning of Some Saint Joseph Figures', p. 22.

several examples of early Christian portrayals of this type of Joseph, he asserts that this pose and gesture, in some compositions, also represents other emotions or mental states, aside from that of mourning, including, 'attention to the will of God', 'watchfulness over the safety of the mother and child', and 'worry, thought, sleep, and submission'.[59]

In his concluding remarks, Pitts offers an excellent summary of the challenges that confronted early Christian artists with respect to their construction of Joseph's portrayal, challenges that even remained for later Christian artists. He writes:

> The creators of early Christian art confronted a difficult problem in the task of creating the first Joseph images. In their cast of classical figures no one figure could best be adapted as the basis for the saint in all his various roles. In addition, there was scant literary description of the man. This situation was complicated by the artisan's goal of creating a Joseph figure that expressed a vast range of human emotion. Also, to complicate the matter was the early Church's two attitudes toward the Saint. On the one hand, he was an important witness to the birth and protector to the child and mother, and on the other hand he was a threat to the belief that Christ was of virgin birth and that Mary was forever pure. The artisans responded to this complex situation and produced the first images of the husband of Mary by utilizing a multiplicity of sources for body types, dress, and character features, and they adopted the time-tested language of gestures from the classical realm.[60]

Brigitte Heublein

In a text published in 1998, Brigitte Heublein addresses the subject of the iconography of Joseph in German and Dutch contexts from the medieval to the renaissance periods.[61] Thus, the focus of her attention is only upon a limited scope of the artistic representation of Joseph. She also shows minimal interest in a formal analysis of the *Wirkungsgeschichte* of the earliest gospel portrayals of Joseph although her own analyses inevitably lead to the documentation of later examples that reveal specific responses to this narrative record.

In ch. 2 of her discussion of the portrayal of Joseph (in scenes of the birth of Jesus) in the early Christian and early medieval periods, she provides both evidence and commentary on several works of art that constitute important examples of this development.[62] These include, among others, portrayals of Joseph in artistic scenes related to the birth of Jesus in carved sarcophagi from Arles and Le Puy, in ivory-carved images in the cathedra of Maximian in Ravenna, in an illuminated manuscript

---

[59] Pitts, 'The Origin and Meaning of Some Saint Joseph Figures', p. 85.
[60] Pitts, 'The Origin and Meaning of Some Saint Joseph Figures', p. 85.
[61] Brigitte Heublein, *Der 'verkannte' Joseph: Zur mittelalterlichen Ikonographie des Heiligen im deutschen und niederländischen Kulturraum* (Weimar: VDG, 1998).
[62] Heublein, *Der 'verkannte' Joseph*, pp. 19-62.

composition in the Syrian Rabula Codex in Florence, and in ivory-carved book covers from Milan, examples which will be both acknowledged and evaluated in this study.[63]

A review of the history of research of both explicit and implicit scholarly studies of the development of the *Wirkungsgeschichte* of the Matthean, Lukan, and Johannine portrayals of Joseph the Carpenter in the fields of biblical studies, non-canonic studies, church history, and art history suggests that a scholarly examination to trace and document these representations of Joseph the Carpenter in Christian literature and art is necessary and appropriate to fill this scholarly lacuna.

The Methodology

The methodology of this study is based upon the work of Hans-Georg Gadamer who introduced the idea of *Wirkungsgeschichte*, the history of influence, in his 1960 work, *Wahrheit und Methode*.[64] It is founded on Gadamer's assertion that a 'true historical object is not an object at all, but the unity of the one and the other, a relationship that constitutes both the reality of history, *die Wirklichkeit der Geschichte*, and the reality of historical understanding, *die Wirklichkeit des geschichtlichen Verstehens*'.[65] To acknowledge this is to accept the marriage between the reality of history and the reality of historical understanding and to recognize the potentialities for interpretation and scholarship despite our own historicity and limitations.

These potentialities for interpretation have been recognized by many scholars including Hans Robert Jauss and Ulrich Luz. Some twenty years after the publication of Gadamer's *Wahrheit und Methode*, Hans Robert Jauss, a student of Gadamer's at Heidelberg, created what he described as an aesthetic of reception, *Rezeptionsästhetik*, his own hermeneutical theory, in his text, *Towards an Aesthetic of Reception*.[66] In it he argued that 'A literary work is not an object that stands by itself and that offers the same view to each reader in each period. It is not a monument that monologically reveals its timeless essence.'[67] Rather, it is an object whose meaning can only be actualized as different generations and groups of readers engage the text and interpret it. This is certainly true for the

---

[63] Heublein, *Der 'verkannte' Joseph*, pp. 21-22, 23, 31, 34.

[64] Hans-Georg Gadamer, *Wahrheit und Methode: Grundzüge einer philosophischen Hermeneutik* (Tübingen: J.C.B. Mohr, 1960).

[65] Hans-Georg Gadamer, *Truth and Method* (trans. J. Weinsheimer and D. Marshall; London: Sheed & Ward, 1975 and 1989), pp. 283 and 299.

[66] Hans Robert Jauss, *Toward an Aesthetic of Reception* (trans. Timothy Bahti; Minneapolis, MN: University of Minnesota Press, 1982).

[67] Jauss, *Toward an Aesthetic of Reception*, p. 21.

biblical narrative which, in one way or another, has always been an 'interpreted' text.[68]

At the same time Jauss asserted that modern interpreters can only really understand texts if they take into account their readers, those who have engaged the texts and interpreted them.[69] For this reason, it is essential that the modern scholar attempt to recognize the different presuppositions readers have brought to their interpretations of particular texts, the 'horizons of expectation' (*Horizonte der Erwartung*) the readers hold that have informed and shaped their interpretations.[70]

Likewise, building upon the work of Gadamer, New Testament scholar Ulrich Luz has further developed his own ideas with respect to *Wirkungsgeschichte*. As a result, he has become convinced that

> In a special sense the history of the text's influence that goes beyond the history of interpretation reminds us that understanding a biblical text takes place not only through determining what it says, but also through doing and suffering; through singing, painting, and composing poetry ...[71]

Subsequently, this has encouraged other scholars to consider the evidence of other factors, such as other types of literature and art, in their own interpretations of New Testament texts and literature. Certainly this can be seen in the early work on the history of effects of A.C. Thiselton,[72] R.C. Trexler,[73] and M.M. Mitchell.[74] Such considerations are also visible, among other places, in the essay, 'The Annunciation: A Study in Reception History,' by Tord Fornberg, and the study, *Walking on Water: Reading Mt. 14:22-33 in the Light of its Wirkungsgeschichte* by

---

[68] Mary Chilton Callaway, 'What's the Use of Reception History?', p. 5. Paper presented at the Annual Meeting of the Society of Biblical Literature, 2004.

[69] Jauss, *Toward an Aesthetic of Reception*, pp. 18-36, goes into this in some detail in this text.

[70] J.F.A. Sawyer, 'The Role of Reception Theory, Reader-Response Criticism and/or Impact History in the Study of the Bible: Definition and Evaluation', p. 5. This article is found at http://www.bbibcomm.net/downloads/sawyer2004.pdf. In speaking about this concept in the singular, Sawyer translates the German term as *Erwartungshorizont*. However, in the plural, as Sawyer uses it above, it would read, *Horizonte der Erwartung*.

[71] Luz, *Matthew 1–7*, p. 64.

[72] A.C. Thiselton, *The First Epistle to the Corinthians: A Commentary on the Greek Text* (Cambridge and Grand Rapids: Eerdmans, 2000).

[73] R.C. Trexler, *The Journey of the Magi: Meanings in History of a Christian Story* (Princeton: Princeton University Press, 1997).

[74] M.M. Mitchell, *The Heavenly Trumpet: John Chrysostom and the Art of Pauline Interpretation* (Tübingen: Mohr Siebeck, 2000).

Rachel Nicholls, both of which exemplify the different ways the *Wirkungsgeschichte* of a New Testament document can be explored and offer suggestions for how the present study might be conducted.[75]

In Fornberg's attempt to address the subject of 'The Reception of the New Testament as a Continuing Process', he engages in an examination of the text of the *Annunciation to Mary*, found in Lk. 1.26-38.[76] In the process, he traces and documents several literary, liturgical, and artistic responses to this pericope. Thus, he presents a broad and extensive collection of 'effects' from the early Christian period to the modern age.[77] Detailing these, Fornberg records responses to the *Annunciation of Mary* in the writings of theologians (from Ignatius to Thomas à Kempis to modern Protestant and Catholic theologians), in other Christian narratives (from the *Protevangelium of James* to the *Biblia Pauperum* to later Marian narratives), in the establishment of certain liturgical events and practices (from the development of Apostolic and Niceno-Constantinopolitan Creeds to the emergence of the feast of the Annunciation and the practice of the Rosary), and in a variety of art (from the earliest image in the Christian catacombs to the innumerable portrayals of this scene in later Christian art).[78]

In her monograph, *Walking on Water: Reading Mt. 14:22-33 in the Light of its Wirkungsgeschichte*, Nicholls, approaches her exploration of the history of reception of this text by first engaging in 'historical critical' and 'literary critical' examinations of it.[79] Following this, she compares two different 'clusters' or types of 'effects' (one, literary, and one, artistic).[80] In the process, she first analyzes 'how the story is understood in some mid-late nineteenth-century theological texts' (notably, in the early nineteenth century writings of H.E. Paulus, and the mid-late nineteenth century writings of, R.C. Trench, B.F. Westcott, D.F. Strauss, W. Hanna, F. Schleiermacher, J.B. Mozley, and F.W. Farrar).[81] In order to comprehend these later theological 'effects', Nicholls takes into account the different authors' perceptions about miracles and their views of the credibility of 'the accounts of the miracles in the Gospels'.[82] By

---

[75] Tord Fornberg, 'The Annunciation: A Study in Reception History', in Mogens Muller and Henrik Tronier (eds.), *The New Testament as Reception History* (Library of New Testament Studies 230; London: T. & T. Clark, 2002), pp. 157-80 and Rachel Nicholls, *Walking on Water: Reading Mt. 14:22-33 in the Light of its Wirkungsgeschichte* (Leiden and Boston: Brill, 2008).

[76] Tord Fornberg, 'The Annunciation: A Study in Reception History', p. 157.

[77] Despite his analysis of this passage, Fornberg makes no reference to the figure and presence of Joseph.

[78] Tord Fornberg, 'The Annunciation: A Study in Reception History', pp. 158-80.

[79] Rachel Nicholls, *Walking on Water*, p. 26.

[80] Rachel Nicholls, *Walking on Water*, pp. 26, 127-86.

[81] Nicholls, *Walking on Water*, pp. 26, 127-86.

[82] Nicholls, *Walking on Water*, p. 99.

doing so, Nicholls believes she is able to 'bring into focus the thought of their period about walking on the water.'[83]

She next considers how this New Testament account is understood in six artistic works.[84] The first composition comes from the earliest period of Christian history and is a mid-third century fresco fragment from the Dura Europus [Syria] Collection at Yale University Art Gallery, in New Haven, Connecticut.[85] The next four works come from the medieval and early renaissance period and include a mid-late twelfth century marble bas-relief of 'Jesus Walking on the Water' by the Master of Cabestany in the Museu Frederic Mares, in Barcelona, Spain; an early fourteenth century tempera on panel of the 'Appearance on Lake Tiberias' [from the Maesta] by Duccio, in Saint Peter's Basilica, in Rome, Italy; an early fourteenth century mosaic of the 'Navicella' by Giotto, also in Saint Peter's Basilica, in Rome, Italy; and an early fifteenth-century tempera on panel of 'St. Peter Walking on the Water' by Luis Borrassa, also in the Church of Santa Maria in Terrassa, Spain.[86] Lastly, Nicholls considers a modern Christian painting, a twentieth century oil on wood of 'Walking on Water' by Christina Saj, located in the collection of the artist, in America.[87] In Nicholl's examination of these later artistic effects, she considers each 'in isolation from the other' and takes into account a variety of 'factors', including, the materials used, the size and condition of the work, the use of colour, light, line, texture, depth, symmetry, space and so on; according to what is appropriate to the particular image.[88] She thinks it is also essential 'to consider ... any indications of the context and purpose for which it [the artifact] was intended.'[89]

Thus, both Fornberg's and Nicholls' analyses offer a variety of criteria to consider in the evaluation of the various 'effects' related to New Testament texts.

Finally, the growing interest in *Wirkungsgeschichte* can also be seen in the series of Blackwell Bible Commentaries, edited by John Sawyer, Christopher Rowland, and Judith Kovacs. Writing about this series, Kovacs and Rowland note in their *Revelation* volume that its purpose is to reveal the 'richly varied appropriations of each biblical book', including historical interpretations from the arts as well as theology.[90] Engaging in

---

[83] Nicholls, *Walking on Water*, p. 100.
[84] Nicholls, *Walking on Water*, pp. 26, 99-126, 127-86.
[85] Nicholls, *Walking on Water*, pp. 135-44.
[86] Nicholls, *Walking on Water*, pp. 145-74.
[87] Nicholls, *Walking on Water*, pp. 175-83.
[88] Nicholls, *Walking on Water*, pp. 100 and 133.
[89] Nicholls, *Walking on Water*, p. 134.
[90] Judith Kovacs and Christopher Rowland, *Revelation* (Oxford: Blackwell Publishing, 2004), p. xii.

an analysis with similarities to Fornberg's, Kovacs and Rowland record responses from the early age of Christianity to the contemporary age. Thus, they also offer a wide and diverse selection of 'effects' with respect to different parts of the narrative that include the Apocalypse's 'textual history', 'the Tyconian-Augustinian approach to the Apocalypse'(with its belief that it is a source of insight into the 'present life of the Christian' rather than 'a blueprint for church history or world history or as a means of calculating the time of the end'), the interpretations of the medieval monk, Joachim of Fiore (who 'saw the Apocalypse as a hermeneutical key to both the entire scriptures and the whole of history'), Lutheran and Calvinist reformers (who saw it as a foil against Catholics), radical Anabaptist reformers (who, likewise, saw it as a foil against both their fellow Protestants and the Catholic Church), and the Romantic poets of the late eighteenth and nineteenth centuries (who saw the text 'in existential terms with its conflicts related to the spiritual life of the individual').[91] At the same time, Kovacs and Rowland also consider more modern theological perspectives, including those that believe the Apocalypse should be interpreted 'as a repository of prophecies concerning the future' (such as John Mede, John Nelson Darby, and Hal Lindsey), those that think it should be interpreted in terms of 'the circumstances of John's own day' (such as the historical critics who follow Hugo Grotius, in particular, R.H. Charles), and those who are convinced it is an ongoing prophetic judgment upon humanity's hubris, pessimism and need for salvation beyond itself (such as Karl Barth and Ernst Bloch).[92] Then, they take into account the different ways the Apocalypse has been appropriated in music, art, architecture, and in the liturgy and worship of the Christian church.[93] Thus, when they turn to a close examination of the narrative, they pull from these various resources.[94]

Inspired by the groundbreaking work of Gadamer, Jauss, Luz, and later efforts of other scholars, this analysis of the development of the *Wirkungsgeschichte* of the Matthean, Lukan, and Johannine portrayals of Joseph will employ a method designed to address appropriately the subject of this thesis, as well as contribute methodologically to this emerging discipline. Treating the narratives (both canonic and non-canonic) as portraits in and of themselves, like the artistic images that will be examined, this study will consist of three basic parts (Parts II, III, and IV).

Part II will focus on the canonic portrayals of Joseph. Chapters 2, 3, and 4 will concentrate on the representation(s) of Joseph in the canonic

---

[91] Kovacs and Rowland, *Revelation*, pp. 14-24.
[92] Kovacs and Rowland, *Revelation*, pp. 24-29.
[93] Kovacs and Rowland, *Revelation*, pp. 29-38.
[94] Kovacs and Rowland, *Revelation*, pp. 39-246.

literature (in the Gospels of Matthew, Luke and John) by means of literary and narrative analysis, seeking to identify image(s) of Joseph in order that the response to and reception of those canonic portrayals in the work of later interpreters in theological literature and art can be traced.

In Part III the focus will be upon the responses of certain later Christian writers and their communities to the canonic portrayals of Joseph. In Chapters 5, 6, 7 and 8, attention will be centered upon the development of the canonic portrayals of Joseph in the non-canonic narratives of the *Infancy Gospel of James*, the *Infancy Gospel of Thomas*, the *History of Joseph the Carpenter*, and the *Gospel of Pseudo-Matthew*.

Initially, in order to understand the response of these later Christian writers and their communities to the canonic portrayals of Joseph, consideration will first be given to the issues of the date, provenance, language, stability of the text, history of translation and dissemination, availability and accessibility, purpose, and content of each non-canonic narrative, to the extent to which they can be ascertained.

Second, attention will be directed to the characterization of Joseph; to the particular way(s) he is portrayed within the text. This will include consideration of the varied details each narrative reveals about Joseph's age, his physical features and characteristics, demeanor, and posture; his proximity to Mary and the Christ-child; his physical position and location within the particular event or scene in which he is portrayed (i.e. within the narrative background or foreground of the image); the roles and actions in which it appears he engaged; and the different ways he and Mary are juxtaposed as complementary or contrasting figures.

Third, the focus will then turn to the independence the narrator's work reveals between itself and canonic and earlier non-canonic literary referents, as appropriate; its substantial or minimal difference from possible narrative referents; to the role earlier canonic and non-canonic portrayals of Joseph (narrative and artistic) may or may not have had in the portrayal of Joseph in each non-canonic narrative; i.e. to the distinctiveness of the portrayal of Joseph in each of these texts.

Fourth, an effort will be made to determine if and how a specific narrator received or assimilated canonic as well as earlier non-canonic narratives; if he/she may have created their own non-canonic portrayals of Joseph independent of received (and certainly later) non-canonic texts; and if and how a specific narrator may have been influenced by prior visual iconographies of Joseph.

Fifth, in light of the information discovered from the analysis of these initial four concerns, attention will then turn to the perceptions and beliefs these specific narratives suggest their narrators and their respective ecclesiastical communities appear to have held with regard to Joseph.

Sixth, and finally, conclusions will be drawn with respect to portrayal of Joseph that is found in each non-canonic narrative and the nature and significance of its response to the canonic portraits of Joseph in Matthew, Luke, and John. At the same time, it will be determined if the representation of Joseph in each non-canonic narrative reveals evidence of a pattern or trajectory that largely affirms and enhances his portrayal and role found in the canonic accounts or evidence of a pattern or trajectory that largely dismisses and diminishes this portrayal.

In Part IV the focus will be upon the responses of certain later Christian artists and their communities to the canonic portrayals of Joseph. Chapters 9, 10, 11, and 12 will focus on the development of the Matthean, Lukan, and Johannine portrayals of Joseph and the responses to them found in eighteen different portraits of Joseph in Christian sarcophagi, mosaics, ivories, and other artistic images within the period between c. 300 and c. 800 CE.

In contrast to the prior analyses in Parts II and III that were organized according to the approximate respective chronology of each narrative, in this case, in Part IV, this review will begin with some initial remarks about the beginnings of Christian art and the ways Christian artists/artisans may have received and assimilated canonic as well as non-canonic texts related to narrative portrayals of Joseph (a matter that will be addressed in more detail later in the essay).

The formal examination of eighteen art portrayals (that include portraits of Joseph) will follow and will be organized according to five specific iconographic themes/subjects found in canonic or non-canonic literature. The first images to be examined will be representations of the *First Dream of Joseph and the Annunciation to Joseph* that will be reviewed in Chapter 8. These will be followed by compositions of the four other themes, notably, the *Water Test* (in Chapter 9), the *Journey to Bethlehem* (in Chapter 10), the *Nativity* (in Chapter 11), and the *Adoration of the Magi* (in Chapter 12).

Next, consideration will first be given to the theme/subject, date, provenance, as well as these matters can be determined.[95]

---

[95] Although the provenance of certain objects can be determined with relative certainty, that is not the case with others, as O.M. Dalton, *Catalogue of the Ivory Carvings of the Christian Era* (London: Trustees of the British Museum, 1909), pp. xliii-xliv, notes in his remarks on ivory compositions. He acknowledges it is 'often very difficult to date (ivories) with precision or assign (them) to any particular locality'. Few ivories provide inscriptions that would help in this regard. As Dalton (p. xliv) so succinctly states: 'The fact that a given ivory has been preserved for centuries in one place is no proof that it was made in the same part of the world for ... such objects traveled in every direction as gifts or merchandise from a very early period. The migratory habits of the makers tend to increase the difficulty. In the earlier centuries of the Middle Ages ivories were chiefly made in the great monasteries; and monks who were distinguished for any particular craft, whether carving, enamelling, or goldsmith's work, might be summoned to distant houses of their order, or their services might be requisitioned by high ecclesiastics or secular rulers with whom their own superiors entertained friendly relations: in this way

Second, attention will be directed to the way and manner in which Joseph is portrayed and characterized in each composition. In this regard, as with the narratives, the focus will be directed to: the age of Joseph; his physical features, characteristics, demeanor, and posture; his proximity to Mary and the Christ-child; his physical position and location within the particular composition (i.e. within the background or foreground of the image); the roles and actions in which he appears to be engaged; and, finally, to the different ways Joseph and Mary are juxtaposed as complementary or contrasting figures.

Third, an attempt will be made, with regard to each work of art, to determine if and how a specific artist/artisan may have received or assimilated canonic as well as non-canonic texts; if he/she exercised independence from possible canonic and non-canonic literary referents and from prior visual portrayals of Joseph; and , thus, if the work reveals a distinctiveness.

Fourth, in light of the information gleaned from the analysis of these initial three concerns, consideration will be directed to the perceptions and beliefs these specific art works suggest their artists/artisans and their respective ecclesiastical communities, patrons, commissioners or guilds, appear to have held with respect to Joseph.

Fifth, and finally, consideration will be given as to whether or not an artistic portrayal of Joseph reveals evidence of a trajectory that largely affirms and enhances the portrayal and role of Joseph found in the canonic accounts or evidence of a trajectory that largely dismisses and diminishes this portrayal and role.

Part V of this study will be devoted to the conclusions and implications of these prior analyses. Subsequently, the results of the study will be summarized, their contribution to scholarship noted, and their implications for further academic research considered.

---

the style of the same man might affect the art of places situated at considerable distances from each other.'

Part II

The Canonic Portrayals of Joseph (70-100 CE)

The Gospels of Matthew, Luke, and John

The earliest literary representations of Joseph the Carpenter are found in the first-century narratives of Matthew, Luke, and John, likely written in the last quarter of the first century of the common era.[1] Joseph figures most prominently in the Matthean representation, a position highlighted not only by his acknowledged roles as the betrothed and husband of Mary and the legal father of Jesus, but also by his repeated responses and obedience to the direction of God mediated through an angelic messenger through dreams.[2]

---

[1] Although there are differences with respect to the dates of these gospel narratives, most scholars concur with this assessment. See Luke T. Johnson, *The Writings of the New Testament* (Minneapolis, MN: Fortress Press, 1999), pp. 187-88, 214, 526; Delbert Burkett, *An Introduction to the New Testament and the Origins of Christianity* (Cambridge: Cambridge University Press, 2002), pp. 181, 196, 216; Paul J. Achtemeier, Joel B. Green and Marianne Meyer Thompson, *Introducing the New Testament: Its Literature and Theology* (Grand Rapids and Cambridge: Eerdmans, 2001), p. 4.

[2] In the Matthean narrative 'Joseph' is mentioned by name seven times (1.16, 18, 19, 20, 24; 2.13, 19). He is also identified as the 'husband' of Mary two times (1.16, 19). In turn, Mary is identified as his 'betrothed' or 'wife' three times (1.18, 20, 24). With respect to this and other ways Joseph is conjoined to Mary and the child, it should be noted that Joseph is either united with Mary or with Mary and the child on fourteen occasions (1.16, 18, 19, 20, 21, 24, 25; 2.13, 14, 15, 20, 21, 22, 23). However, Joseph is never formally designated the 'father' of Jesus. Nonetheless, Jesus is identified as the 'son' of Joseph in Matthew 13.55 where he is recognized by residents of Nazareth as 'the carpenter's son'. Most importantly with respect to Joseph's prominence in the narrative, Joseph is the primary subject of the dramatic action in most of the Matthean nativity account.

With respect to Joseph's prominence in Matthew see Brown, *The Birth of the Messiah*, p. 33, who acknowledges 'the Matthean infancy narrative ... centers upon Joseph' and that Mary 'figures only on a secondary level'. As has been previously acknowledged, other biblical scholars also infer the primacy of Joseph. They include Pierre Bonnard, *L'évangile selon Saint Matthieu* (Neuchâtel, Paris: Delachaux et Niestlé, 1963), pp. 14-19; Eduard Schweizer, *The Good News According to Matthew* (trans. David E. Green; London: SPCK, 1976), pp. 30-43; Tarcisio Stramare, 'Son of Joseph from Nazareth', *Cahiers de Joséphologie*, 26.1 (trans. Larry M. Toschi, Montreal: Centre de recherche et de documentation Oratoire Saint-Joseph du Mont-Royal, 1978), pp. 31-32; Via, 'Narrative World and Ethical Response: The Marvelous and Righteousness in Matthew 1-2', pp.

Joseph is also important in Luke. However, here, Joseph plays a subsidiary role, particularly to the character of Mary, a role overshadowed by the extensive narration about Mary's encounter with Gabriel, her selection as the mother of Jesus, and her purity and obedience.[3] Nonetheless, Joseph's interaction and action, particularly in conjunction with Mary, expand his image and reveal a portrait worthy of extensive study.

In turn, Joseph is also mentioned twice in John. These references, though often forgotten or ignored, also warrant consideration.[4]

Thus, the main concern of this chapter will be to focus on these three respective portraits of Joseph in order to identify properly the New Testament images of Joseph.

126-27, 132-39; Daniel J. Harrington, *The Gospel of Matthew* (Collegeville, MN: The Liturgical Press, 1985), p. 30; Frederick Dale Bruner, *The Christbook: Matthew 1-12* (Waco, TX: Word Books, 1987), pp. 35-36; W.D. Davies and D.C. Allison, *The Gospel According to Saint Matthew* (Edinburgh: T & T Clark, 1988) I, pp. 183–85; Robert H. Smith, *Matthew* (Minneapolis, MN: Augsburg Publishing House, 1989), p. 35; Leon Morris, *The Gospel According to Matthew* (Grand Rapids: Eerdmans, 1992), pp. 26-27, 32; Donald Senior, *The Gospel of Matthew* (Nashville,TN: Abingdon Press, 1997), p. 89; Craig S. Keener, *A Commentary on the Gospel of Matthew* (Grand Rapids and Cambridge: Eerdmans, 1999), pp. 86-96; Edwin D. Freed, *The Stories of Jesus' Birth* (Sheffield: Sheffield Academic Press, 2004), pp. 33-34; John Nolland, *The Gospel of Matthew* (Grand Rapids and Cambridge: Eerdmans, 2005), pp. 94-98, 103, 116; Stanley Hauerwas, *Matthew* (Grand Rapids: Brazos, 2007), pp. 35-36; R.T. France, *The Gospel of Matthew* (Grand Rapids and Cambridge: Eerdmans, 2007), pp. 39-40; Luz, *Matthew 1–7*, pp. 93-97.

[3] In addition to Mary, the Christ-child also has a prominent position with respect to Joseph that is especially highlighted in the final pericope of chapter two of the gospel where he becomes the central character. Mary's prominence and critical role is evident in several places within his nativity narrative (see especially Lk. 1.26-38, 39-45, 46-56; 2.1-7, 16-19, 34-35, 48-51).

[4] John 1.45; 6.42.

1

The Portrayal of Joseph the Carpenter in the Gospel of Matthew

The account of the nativity of Jesus in the Matthew is relatively short and may be briefly summarized. In ch. 1, the readers are presented a genealogy of Jesus as well as accounts of the marital relationship of Joseph and Mary, Joseph's fear and concern at the discovery of Mary's pregnancy, his struggle with this discovery, Joseph's first dream (directing him to accept the child of Mary as of the Holy Spirit and to name the child, 'Jesus'), his acceptance of Mary and her pregnancy, his abstention from sexual intimacy with Mary, the birth of Jesus, and Joseph's naming of the child. In ch. 2, in turn, readers are presented the accounts of the adoration of the Magi, Joseph's second dream (directing him to take Mary and the child and flee to Egypt), the flight into Egypt, the residence in Egypt, Joseph's third dream (directing him to return to the land of Israel), and the return of the family from Egypt to Galilee. Finally, there is also reference to Joseph later in the Gospel (Mt. 13.55), within the pericope concerning the rejection of Jesus in the synagogue in Nazareth (13.54-58). Although this reference is brief, it is important, and also warrants further examination.

Thus, readers are introduced to a fascinating portrait of the Joseph in the Matthean nativity that invites acknowledging and analyzing three main issues, through the means of literary and narrative analyses: (1) the ways Joseph is presented and represented, (2) the respective characteristics and roles that are attributed to and associated with him and, in turn, (3) when and how he is juxtaposed with Mary, and the child, as well as other narrative figures.

The first formal mention of 'Joseph' (Ἰωσήφ) is found in the last part of the first section of the nativity account, in the pericope concerning the genealogy of Jesus (1.1-1.17), in 1.16b. Here, readers are told that through his father, Jacob (Ἰακώβ, 1.16), Joseph has descended from very important spiritual Hebrew males, including Abraham, Issac, and [the earlier] Jacob, the father of [the earlier] Joseph (1.2), and King David and Solomon (1.6); as well as four important foreign female figures, Tamar

(1.3), Rahab (1.5), Ruth (1.5), and the wife of Uriah [Bathsheba] (1.6).[1] This long list of Hebrew males would certainly have impressed the readers, and likely evoked contemplation on the longstanding fidelity and faithfulness of God. Nevertheless, the presence of the specific women in this list of descendants, unexpected and provocative characters and outsiders as they were, may well have evoked the most surprise and reflection and served as a literary precursor to the forthcoming surprises of the special roles of the previously unheralded Joseph and Mary in the salvation drama and the miraculous birth of the Messiah (1.16b, 18-25).[2] Still, the primary purpose of this extensive genealogy of the past, indicated in the long list of expected and unexpected heirs of Abraham and David (1.2-16), appears to be to connect Joseph with the past, present, and future of the Hebrew people.[3]

Following this important narration (1.1-16a) of the biological and spiritual children of Abraham and David, which provides an historic, spiritual, and familial context for Joseph, he is formally introduced to the

---

[1] With respect to the different ways the women in this genealogy have been understood, see especially Bonnard, *L'Évangile selon Saint Matthieu*, p. 16; H. Benedict Green, *The Gospel According to Matthew* (Oxford and London: Oxford University Press, 1975), pp. 52-53; Schweizer, *The Good News According to Matthew*, pp. 24-25; Brown, *The Birth of the Messiah* (1977), pp. 71-74; Brown, *The Birth of the Messiah* (rev. ed., 1993), pp. 590-96; Harrington, *The Gospel of Matthew*, pp. 28, 30-32; Bruner, *The Christbook*, pp. 5-8; Davies and Allison, *The Gospel According to St. Matthew* I, pp. 170-74, 187-88; Smith, *Matthew*, pp. 32-33; Craig L. Blomberg, *The New American Commentary: Matthew*, vol. 22 (Nashville, TN: Broadman Press, 1992), pp. 55-56; Margaret Davies, *Matthew: Readings* (Sheffield: Sheffield Academic Press, 1993), p. 31; Donald A. Hagner, *Matthew 1-13* (Dallas, TX: Word Books, 1993), pp. 10-12; David E. Garland, *Reading Matthew* (New York: Crossroad, 1999), pp. 17-19; Keener, *A Commentary on the Gospel of Matthew*, pp. 78-81; France, *The Gospel of Matthew*, pp. 35-38; Warren Carter, *Matthew and the Margins* (JSNTS 204; Sheffield: Sheffield Academic Press, 2001), pp. 58-61; Robert H. Mounce, *Matthew* [NIBC] (Peabody, MA: Hendrickson, 2002), pp. 8-9; Rudolf Schnackenburg, *The Gospel of Matthew* (trans. Robert R. Barr, Grand Rapids and Cambridge: Eerdmans, 2002), p. 17; Freed, *The Stories of Jesus' Birth*, p. 32; Hauerwas, *Matthew*, pp. 31-32; Luz, *Matthew 1-7*, pp. 83-85.

[2] Reflecting on what readers must have thought, Daniel Patte, *The Gospel According to Matthew* (Philadelphia: Fortress Press, 1987), p. 19, writes that they 'can only marvel at God's interventions which raised up children of Abraham with the help of these progenitors but also in spite of them.' Therefore, 'The generation of the ... children of Abraham and of David is not merely the result of natural, human procreation but is also the result of supernatural interventions, as is the case of Jesus' birth.' Thus, from his perspective, Patte argues that 'Jesus belongs to this genealogy ... because he fully belongs to this genealogy of people who are children of David and Abraham thanks to God's interventions'.

[3] Alfred Plummer, *An Exegetical Commentary on the Gospel According to St. Matthew* (London: Robert Scott, 1928), p. 2, notes that 'Neither Jew nor Gentile would derive the birthright of Jesus from his mother'. Thus, it is natural that the genealogy of Jesus is based upon his relationship with Joseph; his being seen or believed to be the true heir of Joseph.

readers by name (1.16). Bringing the long genealogy of Jesus to a conclusion, Matthew writes: 'and Jacob the father of Joseph the husband of Mary, of whom Jesus was born, who is called the Messiah' (Ἰακὼβ δὲ ἐγέννησεν τὸν Ἰωσὴφ τὸν ἄνδρα Μαρίας ἐξ ἧς ἐγεννήθη Ἰησοῦς ὁ λεγόμενος Χριστός, 1.16).[4] Several things are revealed in these words. First, readers are told that 'Jacob' is 'the father' of Joseph. However, the same is not said with respect to Joseph and Jesus as Daniel Patte notes. He writes that

> The hand of Matthew can again be seen in the last entry (1.16b), which disrupts the pattern set in the rest of the genealogy. In 1.2-16a, the active form of the verb 'to beget' is used ... while the passive form is used in 1.16b. This last statement announces the story of Jesus' birth (1.18-25). It leads the readers to contrast the ordinary conceptions of David and Joseph with the extraordinary conception of Jesus. They could now wonder whether the genealogy should be viewed as that of Joseph, who is called 'son of David' by no less an authority than 'an angel of the Lord' (1.20), rather than that of Jesus. In other words, the text creates a tension between the adoption and the miraculous conception. Is Jesus 'son of David' merely because of his adoption by Joseph, who belongs to the biological lineage of David while Jesus does not? But Matthew clearly wants to say that Jesus is son of David both because of the adoption of Joseph and because of the miraculous conception, since he relates the miraculous conception, to the genealogy (1.16). Even though Jesus' conception is extraordinary, it is not out of place.[5]

Thus, early in the narrative, readers suspect that Joseph is not the biological father of Jesus. Nonetheless, with the acknowledgment that Joseph is 'the husband of Mary' (τὸν ἄνδρα Μαρίας, 1.16), Joseph's authority over the child, as well as his responsibility toward him (that will be fully revealed in Joseph's formal acceptance of Mary and his naming of the child, 1.24-25) is recognized.[6] At the same time, Joseph's marital relationship with Mary, as well as his familial relationship with both

---

[4] This translation of the Greek text and the accompanying translations from the New Testament (in this study) are taken from the National Council of Churches of Christ in the United States of America, *The HarperCollins Study Bible* (New Revised Standard Version Bible 1989; New York: HarperOne, 2006).

[5] See Patte, *Gospel According to Matthew*, pp. 18-19.

[6] In this regard, see R.V.G. Tasker, *The Gospel According to St. Matthew* (Grand Rapids: Eerdmans, 1976), pp. 32-33; Via, 'Narrative World and Ethical Response: The Marvelous and Righteousness in Matthew 1-2', pp. 131-34; Robert H. Gundry, *Matthew* (Grand Rapids: Eerdmans, 1982), pp.18-26; John P. Meier, *Matthew* (Wilmington, DE: Michael Glazier, 1985), pp. 7, 9; and Francis W. Beare, *The Gospel According to Matthew* (Peabody, MA: Hendrickson, 1987), p. 61. Especially note the remarks of Davies and Allison, *The Gospel According to Saint Matthew* I, p. 185. They write: '... Matthew has in mind legal, not necessarily physical, descent, that is, the transmission of legal heirship; and the idea of paternity on two levels – divine and human, with position in society being determined by the mother's husband – was familiar in the ancient near east. In addition, the Mishnah relates, "If a man said, 'This is my son', he may be believed"; and

Mary and Jesus is established. In addition, the words 'Mary, of whom Jesus was born' (Μαρίας ἐξ ἧς ἐγεννήθη 'Ιησοῦς, 1.16) specify the limits of Joseph's engagement in the generation of Jesus. In turn, these words also identify Mary as the biological mother of Jesus and a unique figure in the narrative account. Finally, it should also be noted that the last two verses of the genealogy clarify the identity of Joseph, specifically with respect to his relationship with Jesus (1.16b) and Mary (1.16). In particular, they acknowledge, (ahead of the next pericope, 1.18-25) that Joseph is the legal father of Jesus. As such, they directly connect him to the rest of the story of the birth and earliest childhood of the Christ (1.18–2.23).

Therefore, although Joseph's genealogical background provides authority and credibility to this character, his selection and call to be the husband of Mary and the earthly father of Jesus is still, in many respects (as was the selection and call of the foreign and provocative women in the genealogy), unexpected, a surprise. Although he is identified as a 'son of David' (υἱὸς Δαυίδ, 1.20), there is no indication that he is either a person of present spiritual power or influence within the Hebrew spiritual community or a person of present political power or influence as some within his genealogy were. Nonetheless, the readers discover God sometimes chooses individuals as Joseph and the 'foreign' women to enact and fulfill his will. Joseph and these women, stand as spiritual precursors and models for the readers of the mysterious and marvelous ways God may use Jews as well as Gentiles who are faithful and obedient to enact and fulfill his will. So it is not surprising that as the readers reflect upon what they have read in the genealogy that they find themselves challenged both to contemplate the mysterious and unexpected ways God acts and the faith and obedience to which all the followers of God seem called.

---

according to Matthew (and presumably his tradition) Joseph gave Jesus his name and thereby accepted the role of father. With respect to this see also Heinrich August Wilhelm Meyer, *Critical and Exegetical Handbook to the Gospel of Matthew* (Edinburgh: T. & T. Clark, 1877), p. 59; Bonnard, *L'Évangile selon Saint Matthieu*, p. 17; William Hendriksen, *The Gospel of Matthew* (Edinburgh: The Banner of Truth Trust, 1974), pp. 128-29; Schweizer, *The Good News According to Matthew*, pp. 25-26; Stramare, 'Son of Joseph from Nazareth,' p. 37; Harrington, *The Gospel of Matthew*, pp. 38-39; Bruner, *The Christbook*, pp. 12-13; Garland, *Reading Matthew*, pp. 19-20; Keener, *A Commentary on the Gospel of Matthew*, pp. 94-95; Nolland, *The Gospel of Matthew*, pp. 103; and France, *The Gospel of Matthew*, pp. 46-59, as well as others. It is intriguing and quite appropriate that France, in his commentary on the Gospel of Matthew, entitles the early section of the narrative, 1.18-25 on p. 46, 'Joseph, Son of David, accepts Jesus as His Son'.

1. *The Portrayal of Joseph in the Gospel of Matthew*

As the readers encounter the next section of the narrative (1.18-25), they already know of Joseph's distinguished biological and spiritual heritage and his place within the history of the Hebrew people. While aspects of this heritage may be alluded to in this new pericope in order to emphasize further Joseph's importance and spiritual authority, the readers also discover new elements in the portrait of Joseph that expand and further illuminate Joseph's image as well as his relationship with Mary and the child.[7]

> Now the birth of Jesus the Messiah took place in this way. When his mother Mary had been engaged to Joseph, but before they lived together, she was found to be with child from the Holy Spirit. Her husband, Joseph, being a righteous man and unwilling to expose her to public disgrace, planned to dismiss her quietly. But, just when he had resolved to do this, an angel of the Lord appeared to him in a dream, and said, 'Joseph, son of David, do not be afraid to take Mary as your wife, for the child conceived in her is from the Holy Spirit. She will bear a son, and you are to name him Jesus, for he will save his people from their sins.' All this took place to fulfill what had been spoken by the Lord through the prophet: 'Look, the virgin shall conceive and bear a son, and they shall name him Emmanuel,' which means, 'God with us.' When Joseph awoke from sleep, he did as the angel of the Lord commanded him; he took her as his wife, but had no marital relations with her until she had borne a son; and he named him Jesus (Mt. 1.18-25).

One of the first things readers learn about Joseph's relationship with Mary is that he discovered she was 'with child' ('pregnant', ἐν γαστρὶ ἔχουσα, 1.18) before they formally lived together and engaged in sexual relations. Further, they are informed that Joseph was not initially aware, as they have been informed, that Mary's pregnancy was 'from the Holy Spirit' (ἐκ πνεύματος ἁγίου, 1.18). Thus, they understand that Joseph faces a personal crisis.

Even so, following this revelation, the readers are also quickly informed that Joseph is 'righteous' (δίκαιος ὤν, 1.19), an attribution that suggests the way in which readers are to perceive him as well as what they may expect of him.[8] At the same time, they also discover that this

---

[7] Beare entitles this section of the nativity narrative, Mt. 1.18-25, 'The Annunciation to Joseph' which is in many respects a more appropriate title than that of 'The Birth of Jesus' or parallel titles. See Beare, *The Gospel According to Matthew*, p. 61.

[8] Via, 'Narrative World and Ethical Response: The Marvelous and Righteousness in Matthew 1–2', p. 136, believes Matthew represents Joseph as a 'consistent' figure within the narrative. He writes that 'the character of Joseph is consistent in that he persistently has the disposition to do the will of God.'

With respect to the attribution of *dikaios* to Joseph, see the work of the following scholars, including Meyer, *A Critical and Exegetical Handbook to the Gospel of Matthew*, pp. 68-69; Alan Hugh McNeile, *The Gospel According to St. Matthew* (London: Macmillan, 1915), p. 7; Bonnard, *L'évangile selon Saint Matthieu*, pp. 19-20; Albright and Mann,

'qualification and attribution' of 'righteousness', as Via notes, will be exemplified 'primarily by his actions, by his decisions to render a difficult obedience' in the face of the present dilemma (1.19), as well as later challenges and dilemmas in later passages.[9]

Thus, in the face of the present dilemma, Joseph must decide how he will respond. On the one hand, the narrative reveals that he could act in

---

Matthew, p. 8; Hendirksen, *The Gospel of Matthew*, pp. 130-31, 145-46; Green, *The Gospel According to Matthew*, p. 55; Schweizer, *The Good News According to Matthew*, pp. 30-31; Stramare, 'Son of Joseph', pp. 56-59; Via, 'Narrative World and Ethical Response: The Marvelous and Righteousness in Matthew 1-2', pp. 126-27, 133-43; A. Tosato, 'Joseph Being a Just Man (Matt 1:19)', *Catholic Biblical Quarterly* 41 (1979), pp. 542-51; Gundry, *Matthew*, p. 21-22; Harrington, *The Gospel of Matthew*, pp. 34-40; Beare, *The Gospel According to Matthew*, p. 68; Bruner, *The Christbook: Matthew 1-12*, p. 22; Senior, *The Gospel of Matthew*, p. 89; Davies and Allison, *The Gospel According to Saint Matthew* I, pp. 202-205; Smith, *Matthew*, pp. 35-36; Blomberg, *Matthew*, p. 58; Morris, *The Gospel According to Matthew*, pp. 27-28; Hagner, *Matthew 1-13*, p. 18; Garland, *Reading Matthew*, p. 22; Keener, *A Commentary on the Gospel of Matthew*, pp. 87-95; Carter, *Matthew and the Margins*, pp. 67-68; Mounce, *Matthew*, p. 10; Schnackenburg, *The Gospel of Matthew*, pp. 18-20; Nolland, *Gospel of Matthew*, pp. 94-96; France, *Gospel of Matthew*, pp. 51-52; Hauerwas, *Matthew*, pp. 35-36; Luz, *Matthew 1 - 7* (2007), pp. 94-95, and H.W. Basser, *The Mind Behind the Gospels: A Commentary to Matthew 1-14* (Brighton, MA: Academic Studies Press, 2009), pp. 31-33.

Brown's discussion in *Birth of the Messiah* (1977), pp. 125-27, is particularly noteworthy. He remarks that Matthew makes every effort to portray Joseph as an 'upright' person (1.19), who is a faithful Jew and 'observant of the Law,' whose piety is above reproach. From Brown's perspective Joseph's *dikaios*, his 'righteousness' or 'uprightness' is informed by mercy (Mt. 1.19). It is for this reason that Joseph acts as he does. According to Brown, *Birth of the Messiah* (1977), pp. 125, 138-39, Joseph's *dikaios* is also exemplified through his obedience (as a 'son of David', himself) to the angel. The angel commands Joseph to take the pregnant Mary (and thus her child) into his home (1.20) and to name the forthcoming child (1.21). Joseph, in turn, fulfills both commands. Thus, through his obedience, the first 'son of David', Joseph, affirms that Jesus is also truly the 'son of David' (1.1). Brown substantiates the implications of Joseph's responses to the angel's commands by attesting to the fact that according to Jewish teaching 'the law prefers to base paternity on the man's acknowledgment. The Mishna *Baba Bathra* 8.6 states the principle: "If a man says, 'This is my son,' he is to be believed." Joseph, by exercising the father's right to name the child (cf. Lk. 1:60-63), acknowledges Jesus and thus becomes the legal father of 'the child'. Brown (*Birth of the Messiah*, p. 139 n. 18) writes: 'Legal father is a better designation than foster father or adoptive father. Joseph does not adopt someone else's son as his own; he acknowledges his wife's child as his legitimate son, using the same formula by which other Jewish fathers acknowledged their legitimate children.' The references to Isaiah in 1.23 are taken from two Septuagint sources: Isa. 7.14; 8.8, 10. In this regard see also Brown, *Birth of the Messiah* (rev. ed., 1993), pp. 605, 625.

[9] Via, 'Narrative World and Ethical Response: The Marvelous and Righteousness in Matthew 1-2', pp. 126-27. With respect to Joseph's dilemma, also note the further comments of Via (p. 133): '... Joseph, knowing less than the readers, believes that the pregnant Mary has been unfaithful. Since his righteousness disposes him to obey the law, he knows that he must divorce her because an engaged woman who consorts with another man is legally guilty of adultery, and the law demands the trial and punishment of an adulteress (Deut 22. 22-27).'

reaction to his discovery of the pregnancy of Mary in such a way that she would face 'public disgrace' (αὐτὴν δειγματίσαι, 1.19). However, he negates this prospect as a real option and decides to resolve the humiliating dilemma 'quietly' (λάθρᾳ, 1.19), in a way that will protect Mary and the child. Still, his reluctance to expose Mary in their community and society, important and virtuous as these qualities seem, do not necessarily lead him in the direction God wants him to go (1.19-20).[10] As such, his desire to live his life in righteous obedience to God (1.20-25), permits Joseph to receive and accept direction and revelation from God, in the present and the future, through the means of an 'angel of the Lord in a dream' (ἄγγελος κυρίου κατ' ὄναρ, 1.20); direction and revelation that lead him eventually to fulfill the immediate will of God (1.21-23).[11] This, in turn, enables him, paradoxically, to expand his understanding of what it means to be righteous and obedient to God and to perceive Mary's pregnancy and the forthcoming child, 'the child conceived in her' (τὸ γὰρ ἐν αὐτῇ γεννηθὲν, 1.20) in a completely new light.[12] Thus, readers come to understand Joseph's character through what he does, through the specific actions he takes in response to unfolding personal events and the direction of God mediated through an angelic messenger.

Further, this 'qualification' and 'description' of Joseph as 'righteous' connects him directly with the purpose of the life of 'the child' who he is to declare to be his son and raise and nurture (1.24-25); the one who, as the text later reveals, has come 'to fulfill all righteousness' (πληρῶσαι πᾶσαν δικαιοσύνην, 3.15). As such, this text and these series of events

---

[10] Patte (*Matthew*, p. 26) notes that 'Joseph's righteousness was of no help to him to gain the proper perspective of the situation. In fact ... it is as "righteous" that Joseph makes an incorrect evaluation of the situation, and this even though his righteousness is the better righteousness (5.20) of a person who has mercy and compassion (5.38-48; 7.12) for someone else. This is indicated by his wanting to divorce Mary quietly so as not to expose her to shame (1.19). Yet such a righteousness is not enough.'

[11] Meier (*Matthew*, p. 7) comments that Joseph 'is "just" in a double sense: he wishes to show loyalty and kindness to Mary, yet he must satisfy the requirement of the Law not to countenance adultery.' However, with regard to this, Via ('Narrative World and Ethical Response: The Marvelous and Righteousness in Matthew 1-2', p. 133) concludes that it is the very circumstance of this dilemma and crisis that leads Joseph and, in turn, the readers of the text, to reevaluate and change their 'understanding of righteousness'.

[12] As Via ('Narrative World and Ethical Response', p. 137) acknowledges, Joseph's belief that God has revealed his presence and word in the dream mediated by the angel, leads Joseph to 'allow the law to be complemented, if not temporarily suspended ...' and permits Joseph to perform 'a specific act grounded in a reorientation of his existential and moral self-understanding.' Additionally, it is also the case, as Patte (*Matthew*, p. 27) suggests, that it is God's intervention that establishes 'Joseph's vocation – of taking Mary as his wife and of adopting Jesus.' This is accomplished, Patte argues 'by providing Joseph with ... the correct evaluation of the situation'.

(1.18-25) provide an important lesson for readers about the interconnectedness of spirituality and morality. In addition, as the text reveals these insights, it also invites and permits the readers, in their reading and contemplation, to recognize and acknowledge Joseph as a spiritual exemplar, whose close relationship with God is exemplified here (1.18-25) as well as at other key places within this nativity narrative (2.13-15, 19-21, 22) and to imitate him. Further, along with these representations and portrayals, the image of Joseph as a guardian or caretaker of Mary and the child, is also suggested (1.23-25) as well as highlighted and illuminated in the narrative (2.14-15, 2.21-22, 23).

Thus, it is not surprising that the readers find themselves both comforted and challenged by the example of Joseph; comforted by the fact that God has chosen one who is not unlike them and used him in such special and holy ways; challenged by the realization that his character and life is defined, in large part, by his faith and obedience, by his positive and specific actions in response to the special, surprising, and gracious actions of God (1.18-25; 2.13-15, 19-23); a faith and obedience that they are also called to exhibit. As such, as they read further the readers are challenged to contemplate the meaning of their own lives and the significance of their own actions within the drama of salvation history.[13]

In turn, along with his new spiritual understanding, Joseph's genealogical and spiritual heritage is also underscored, especially when the readers are reminded that this Joseph, the husband of Mary, is also a 'son of David' (υἱὸς Δαυίδ, 1.20), an identification that he bestows upon Jesus in his decision to obey the revelation of God and name the child (1.25), the name the readers have already read (1.1) and already know.[14] Joseph's genealogical and spiritual heritage is reemphasized when it is observed that Joseph is also, as his spiritual forefather Joseph, a person of such extraordinary spiritual depth that he is the only person in the narrative that God addresses through the means of an angelic messenger and directs through dreams (1.20).[15]

---

[13] See Patte, *Matthew*, p. 22.

[14] In this regard, note the words of Patte (*Matthew*, pp. 27-28), 'The miraculous conception is complemented by the adoption of Jesus by Joseph. Even though the role of divine interventions in human affairs is now unambiguous in the miraculous conception, it does not abolish or bypass the role of human beings. The purpose of God's action – that Jesus be the son of David, the Christ, who will save his people and be the manifestation of the Holy among us – is realized only because Joseph received a vocation and accepted carrying it out. Note that it is Joseph who has the essential role of naming the child "Jesus" (1.21 and 25).' It seems this insight is informed by an earlier reflection of Patte's. See Patte, *Matthew*, p. 20.

[15] This genealogy appears to associate Joseph with a particular figure in Hebrew history and literature, [the earlier] Joseph, the great dreamer of the Hebrew people whose dreams brought hope to his people and led him ultimately to guide and protect his people

At the same time, the angel's direction to Joseph to take Mary as his wife and become her husband also reveals God's choice, 'taking', and selection of Mary; a choice and selection confirmed by the angel's revelation that the child within her is from God's Holy Spirit (1.20).[16] Once Joseph clearly comprehends the significance of this first angelic visit and the revelation that the child is a creation of the Holy Spirit of God, his understanding of his responsibility to Mary and the child are heightened, as seen in his immediate responses to both unfolding events in the story and further angelic visits and messages (2.13-15, 19-23). Further, both Joseph's actions and the angelic revelations disclose God's choice and selection of Joseph, God's 'taking' of him to be the husband of Mary and the father of her child; a choice and selection confirmed by the angel's further revelation and direction to Joseph that he is to name the child and specifically name him, 'Jesus' ('Ἰησοῦν, 1.21).[17] In addition, they highlight Joseph's significance in the story.

Next, the readers are clearly told that everything that has been said up to this point in the narrative (1.1–1.21) has occurred in order to fulfill

---

for many generations (Genesis 37–50). Although not directly mentioned, this Joseph would certainly be remembered and come to the mind of many who read and heard the words of this text. In turn, both the recollection of this earlier Joseph and his deeds, as well as the patriarch's role and importance in Hebrew history, would give Joseph a special authority and credibility within this narrative.

Meier, *Matthew*, p. 7, believes this dream motif involving Joseph is 'reminiscent of the dreams granted to the patriarchs in Genesis', particularly that of the 'patriarch Joseph'. Likewise, see Bonnard, *L'évangile selon Saint Matthieu*, pp. 20-21; Green, *The Gospel According to Matthew*, p. 55; Davies, *Matthew*, p. 32; Carter, *Matthew and the Margins*, p. 68; Mounce, *Matthew*, p. 10. In contrast, Derek S. Dodson, *Reading Dreams* (Library of New Testament Studies 397, London: T. & T. Clark, 2009), pp. 139-47, sees the strongest parallels between Greco-Roman dream narratives.

In turn, Senior, *Matthew*, p. 90, believes 'Matthew's portrayal of Joseph' recalls the 'Joseph of the Hebrew scriptures (Genesis 37–50)'. In addition, adapting the thoughts of Patte, *Matthew*, p. 22, to the figure of Joseph', instead of Jesus', it also seems appropriate to note that Joseph 'is not the puppet of a God who would have predetermined his existence; he is a person called by God for a specific and extraordinary vocation and given the means or qualifications to do it. He is a person free to respond to this call.' With respect to this special revelation that Joseph receives here and later in the nativity account, Luz, *Matthew 1–7* (1989), p. 138, does note 'as a fine nuance that only Joseph is held worthy of the [actual] appearance of an angel' [within Matthew's account] (1.20; 2.13, 19). See also, in this regard, Patte, *Matthew*, p. 23. He believes 'Matthew presupposes that his readers are familiar with Scripture and view it as containing promises that are fulfilled in Jesus' time'.

[16] It should be noted that this is the second and last place in the Matthean nativity where direct reference is made to the intervention of the Holy Spirit. See also Mt. 1.18. This manifestation of the angelic messenger in Joseph's first dream, as well as in the dreams that follow, appears closely connected with, if not part and parcel of, the earlier manifestation of the Spirit in the generation of the child in Mary.

[17] This name reflects the fact that the purpose of the child's life will be the salvation of humanity from sin (1.21).

the prophecies of Isaiah (Isa. 7.14; 8.8). This is followed by Joseph's immediate and obedient response (1.24) to the revelation of the angelic messenger, which additionally reveals Joseph's faith and is a sign of God's presence within the story for the readers.[18]

Therefore, in the second pericope in the Matthean account, 1.18-25, concerning the birth of Jesus, Joseph is in the center of the dramatic action (1.19-21), a position he reassumes in the fourth pericope (2.13-23). In contrast, Mary is in a largely subsidiary and passive role.[19] And, yet, Mary does not play an insignificant role for she is clearly identified as the biological mother of Jesus (1.16), a figure central in the narrative of this Gospel (1.18), and a virgin (1.16 and 1.25).[20] Indeed, Mary's role as 'his mother' (τῆς μητρὸς αὐτοῦ) is emphasized by the repetition of this designation on six occasions (1.18; 2.11, 13, 14, 20, 21).[21] Further, Joseph is twice described as the 'husband' of Mary (τὸν ἄνδρα Μαρίας, 1.16 and ὁ ἀνὴρ αὐτῆς, 1.19). In turn, she is identified as 'his wife' (τὴν γυναῖκα αὐτοῦ, 1.24).[22] At the same time, it seems equally important to

---

[18] Meier (*Matthew*, p. 9) is convinced the pattern of 'command-and-execution-of-command', represented in this verse (1.24), and repeated elsewhere in the nativity account, 'appears a number of times in the gospel to stress that a true disciple obeys immediately and perfectly'. He adds that this obedience is also evident in Joseph's willingness to forego 'marital intercourse' with Mary for the time being (1.25).

[19] As previously recognized, Brown (*Birth of the Messiah*, p. 33) notes this early in his commentary on the Gospel. Keener, *Gospel of Matthew*, p. 88; Nolland, *Gospel of Matthew*, p. 116; France, *Gospel of Matthew*, pp. 39-40 and Luz, *Matthew 1–7* (2007), pp. 90-91, 94, also acknowledge the subsidiary and passive role of Mary.

[20] Brown (*Birth of the Messiah*, p. 132) believes that Matthew's primary concern in the references to Mary's virginity in vv. 16, 25 is to emphasize that Mary is a virgin at the time of Jesus' birth 'so that the Isaian prophecy will be fulfilled ...' Several other scholars concur with Brown's conclusion. See also Meyer, *Critical and Exegetical Handbook to the Gospel of Matthew*, pp. 65-75; Bonnard, *L'Évangile selon Saint Matthieu*, pp. 17-22; W.F. Albright and C.S. Mann, *Matthew* (Garden City, NY: Doubleday, 1971), pp. 7-8; Hendriksen, *The Gospel of Matthew*, pp. 130-45; Green, *Matthew*, pp. 54-56; Schweizer, *The Good News According to Matthew*, pp. 25-35; Via, 'Narrative World and Ethical Response: The Marvelous and Righteousness in Matthew 1-2', pp. 132-33; Allen, *A Critical and Exegetical Commentary on Matthew*; H.P. Hamann, *Chi Rho Commentary on the Gospel According to Matthew* (Adelaide, AU: Lutheran Publishing House, 1984), pp. 14-16; Harrington, *The Gospel of Matthew*, pp. 34-40; Bruner, *The Christbook: Matthew 1-12*, pp. 66-72; Smith, *Matthew*, pp. 35-39; Blomberg, *Matthew*, p. 61; Davies, *Matthew*, pp. 31-34; Hagner, *Matthew* , pp. 47-59; Carter, *Matthew and the Margins*, pp. 66-72; Jack Dean Kingsbury, 'The Birth Narrative of Matthew', in David E. Aune (ed.), *The Gospel of Matthew in Current Study* (Grand Rapids and Cambridge: Eerdmans, 2001), pp. 154-65; Mounce, *Matthew*, pp. 9-11; Freed, *The Stories of Jesus' Birth*, pp. 56-69; Hauerwas, *Matthew*, p. 36; Luz, *Matthew 1–7* (2007), pp. 93-97, 183-84; Basser, *The Mind Behind the Gospels*, pp. 28-38.

[21] Further, Matthew indirectly identifies Mary as the child's mother on six other occasions (1.16, 20, 21, 23, 25, and 2.1).

[22] Brown (*Birth of the Messiah*, p. 125) notes that Matthew goes to some length to establish a portrait of Joseph as the real husband of Mary, as Matthew admits in verses

note that Mary's child, the child Joseph is commanded by the angel to name, 'Jesus' (Ἰησοῦν, 1.21), is not Joseph's biological heir (1.16), as the reader can see by the designation (proffered by the angel to Joseph) of the child as 'a son' (υἱὸν, 1.21, 23, 25). In addition, it is evident that Mary has been chosen, in part, because she has not had a sexual relationship with a man (1.18, 20, 23, 25). Further, at this point, a clear demarcation is also drawn between Joseph and the child by the identification of the child, just noted, as 'a son' (1.21, 23, 25) and the reference to Mary as 'his mother' (1.18), and the absence of any reference to Joseph as his father; a demarcation that appears to be reflective of a certain ambiguity with respect to Joseph's relationship to both the 'son' and 'his mother'. Thus, this division is highlighted for the reader.

In contrast to the second pericope, the third pericope, 2.1-12, concerning the adoration of the Magi, serves as a transitional section between the second (1.18-25) and the fourth pericope (2.13-23) that marks an intermission in the direct activity and centrality of Joseph.[23] Nonetheless, the dramatic action in this pericope moves the story forward, and in so doing, makes the fourth and final pericope of the narrative more comprehensible.[24]

---

sixteen, nineteen, twenty, and twenty-four. He claims that 'since Joseph and Mary have taken the first step in the matrimonial procedure by exchanging consent (betrothal), they are truly "husband" and "wife".' With respect to this, see also Alan Hugh McNeile, *The Gospel According to St. Matthew*, pp. 6-7; David Hill, *The Gospel of Matthew* (London: Marshall, Morgan, and Scott, 1972), pp. 77-78; Tasker, *The Gospel According to St. Matthew*, pp. 34-35; Gundry, *Matthew*, p. 21; Beare, *The Gospel According to Matthew*, pp. 66-67; Davies and Allison, *The Gospel According to Saint Matthew* I, pp. 182-84, 202-205, 218; Keener, *Gospel of Matthew*, pp. 85-95; Luz, *Matthew 1–7* (2007), pp. 93-94.

[23] Hill sees evidence of dependence on the Moses stories in chapter two of the Matthean nativity. See Hill, *The Gospel of Matthew*, pp. 81-85 and 86. Allen, also believes 'Moses is in mind in 2.1-13.' See Allen, *Commentary on the Gospel According to St. Matthew*, pp. 16 and 18. Beare is also convinced that this pericope and the rest within the Matthean nativity are modeled after 'the story of Moses'. See Beare, *The Gospel According to Matthew*, pp. 72, 75. Further, see Schweizer, *The Good News According to Matthew*, pp. 39-43. In turn, Senior (*Matthew*, p. 91) believes much of 2.1-18 'recalls the events concerning Moses' birth'.

In contrast to these scholars, Albright and Mann, *Matthew*, p. 18, do not see the clear connections others note. In concordance with them, Morris, *The Gospel According to Matthew*, p. 34, argues there is 'no evidence that the writer of this Gospel used them [stories about Moses] as a basis for composing stories about Jesus'.

[24] Ulrich Luz, *Matthew 1–7* (2007), p. 109. See also Via, 'Narrative World and Ethical Response', pp. 134-35; Davies and Allison, *The Gospel According to St. Matthew*, I, pp. 252-54; France, *Gospel of Matthew*, p. 75 with respect to the unity of this narrative content.

Here, in contrast to the previous pericope, the lack of a specific reference to Joseph suggests he is either disengaged or absent from the encounter between the Magi and Mary and the Child.[25] However, the righteous, obedient, and pious Joseph would likely be in the mind of the readers as they first read of King Herod, as would the substantial contrast between these two characters, which would become more evident in later parts of the narrative (2.13-15, 16-18, 19-22).[26]

> In the time of King Herod, after Jesus was born in Bethlehem of Judea, wise men from the East came to Jerusalem, asking, 'Where is the child who has been born king of the Jews? For we observed his star at its rising, and have come to pay him homage.' When King Herod heard this, he was frightened, and all Jerusalem with him; and calling together all the chief priests and scribes of the people, he inquired of them where the Messiah was to be born. They told him, 'In Bethlehem of Judea; for so it has been written by the prophet: "And you, Bethlehem, in the land of Judah, are by no means least among the rulers of Judah; for from you shall come a ruler who is to shepherd my people Israel."' Then Herod secretly called for the wise men and learned from them the exact time the star had appeared. Then he sent them to Bethlehem, saying, 'Go and search diligently for the child; and when you have found him, bring me word, so that I may also go and pay him homage.' When they had heard the king they set out; and there, ahead

---

[25] Meyer (*Critical and Exegetical Handbook of the Gospel of Matthew*, p. 89) does not believe Joseph's absence is 'important' or particularly telling. However, Bonnard (*L'Évangile selon Saint Matthieu*, p. 27) disagrees, noting that the lack of mention of Joseph is 'contrary to its Davidic concern ...' Schnackenburg (*The Gospel of Matthew*, pp. 23-24) concurs and states that Joseph's absence 'is striking'. See also Davies and Allison, *The Gospel According to Saint Matthew*, p. 36 and Carter, *Matthew and the Margins*, p. 81, in this regard. Meier (*Matthew*, p. 12) notes that the 'center of attention' is now upon 'the child and his mother'. He cites 2.11, 13, 14, 20, 21 in this regard and appears to conclude, with respect to the rest of the narrative, that 'Joseph ... appears only when needed.' In turn, Luz (*Matthew 1–7* [1989], p. 137) notes that the 'formulation' of 2.11 and the 'omission of Joseph indicate the special position of Mary in the sense of 1.18-25'. Hagner (*Matthew 1-13*, pp. 30-31) agrees. In a similar spirit, Brown (*Birth of the Messiah*, pp. 166-200) does not comment on the absence or omission of Joseph or explore the possibility that Joseph's presence is implied, in light of the mention of the 'house' presumably shared by Joseph and Mary (2.11) and, in light of the immediate introduction of Joseph in the second half of the chapter (2.13). In Brown, *Birth of the Messiah* (rev. ed., 1993), pp. 614-15, he revisits the subject of 'the house' and argues that 'Matt has never mentioned Joseph and Mary being anywhere but Bethlehem; he has told us that Joseph took Mary (home) in 1:24; he tells in 2:11 that the magi came into the house where they found the child with Mary his mother; and in 2:22-23 he explains that the reason that the family did not return to Bethlehem and went instead to Nazareth was apprehension about Archelaus.' See also Gundry, *Matthew*, p. 31 and Blomberg, *Matthew*, pp. 65-66.

In contrast to many other scholars, Hendriksen (*The Gospel of Matthew*, pp. 170-71) and Schweizer (*The Good News According to Matthew*, pp. 37-43) assume Joseph is present with 'his family' and the event occurs at the 'house of Joseph'.

[26] Gundry (*Matthew*, p. 30) alludes to the contrast and juxtaposition of Joseph and Herod.

1. *The Portrayal of Joseph in the Gospel of Matthew*   39

of them, went the star that they had seen at its rising, until it stopped over the place where the child was. When they saw that the star had stopped, they were overwhelmed with joy. On entering the house, they saw the child with Mary his mother; and they knelt down and paid him homage. Then, opening their treasure chests, they offered him gifts of gold, frankincense and myrrh. And, having been warned in a dream not to return to Herod, they left for their own country by another road (Mt. 2.1-12).

Though the worship of the Magi can be understood to focus the readers' attention to the majesty of the Christ, the son of David (υἱοῦ Δαυὶδ, 1.1), the savior (cf. 1.21; 2.15) and the Immanuel (Ἐμμανουήλ, 1.23), it also directs readers to Mary, who is, once again, portrayed and designated the 'mother' of the child and set in the foreground of the scene with him before whom the Magi 'paid … homage' (προσεκύνησαν αὐτῷ, 2.11).[27]

In the fourth and final pericope of the Matthean nativity, 2.13-23, concerning the flight into Egypt and the return from Egypt, Joseph reappears as the central figure in the narrative action.

Now after they had left, an angel of the Lord appeared to Joseph in a dream and said, 'Get up, take the child and his mother, and flee to Egypt, and remain there until I tell you; for Herod is about to search for the child, to destroy him.' And Joseph got up, took the child and his mother by night, and went to Egypt, and remained there until the death of Herod. This was to fulfill what had been spoken by the Lord through the prophet, 'Out of Egypt I have called my son.' When Herod saw that he had been tricked by the wise men, he was infuriated, and he sent and killed all the children in and around Bethlehem who were two years old or under, according to the time that he had learned from the wise men. Then was fulfilled what had been spoken through the prophet Jeremiah: 'A voice was heard in Ramah, wailing and loud lamentation, Rachel weeping for her children; she refused to be consoled, because they are no more.' When Herod died, an angel of the Lord suddenly appeared in a dream to Joseph in Egypt, and said, 'Get up, take the child and his mother, and go to the land of Israel, for those who are seeking the child's life are dead.' Then Joseph got up, took the child and his mother, and went to the land of Israel. But when he heard that Archelaus was ruling over Judea in place of his father Herod, he was afraid to go there. And after being warned in a dream, he went away to the district of Galilee. There he made his home in a town called Nazareth, so that what had been spoken though the prophets might be fulfilled, 'He will be called a Nazorean' (Mt. 2.13-23).

After the departure of the Magi (2.13), Joseph reappears and has another dream, which is recounted in the next brief narrative account (2.13-15). Though it may appear that Joseph's reappearance and the repeated angelic appearances present a repetition of the past, the supportive

---

[27] Luz, *Matthew 1–7* (2007), p. 114.

and threatening characters and the troubling events (2.3-4), introduced in the previous pericope (2.1-12), suggest otherwise. In fact, the Magi's interactions with Herod (2.3), the response of 'all of Jerusalem' (πᾶσα Ἱεροσόλυμα, 2.3), the dream of warning the Magi receive (2.12), aids in the reintroduction of Joseph, and with him, a new angelic revelation from God. Thus, the characters and events of the previous pericope actually disclose more of the real spiritual challenges to Joseph, Mary, and the child as well as move the story forward.[28]

Further, the reiteration of the earlier dream type (2.13-14), lends additional credibility and authority to the figure of Joseph as do his behavior and actions; demonstrating, once again, his righteousness and faith as well as his close relationship with God. At the same time, the introduction of 'Egypt' (Αἴγυπτον, 2.14) as the new destiny, and the prospect of life there, might also reconnect Joseph more directly with the patriarch Joseph, spiritually and geographically, further illuminating his role as protector of the future salvation of Israel (2.13). In fact, here, Joseph acts as did his Hebrew spiritual ancestor, the first Joseph, who brought Jacob/Israel from Canaan into Egypt, and leads Mary and the child on their own exodus from Israel, from harm's way into the security of Egypt (2.13-15).[29] Thus, again, the readers are invited to focus on the example

---

[28] Plummer (*Matthew*, p. 16) hypothesizes that the 'Magi would tell Joseph and Mary of the excitement which had been produced in Jerusalem by their visit, and Joseph would naturally think it prudent to withdraw the child from Palestine'. He believes Joseph would know enough of Herod's character to surmise that his great interest in the birth of a king of the Jews 'boded no good'.

[29] See Brown, *Birth of the Messiah* (1977), p. 216. Brown, pp. 203-204, also notes several accounts in Hebrew literature (the flight of Jeroboam from Solomon, 1 Kgs 11.40; the flight of the prophet Uriah from King Jehoiakim, Jer 26.21; the flight of the high priest Onias from King Antiochus Epiphanes, Josephus, *Ant.* XII ix 7) to document that Egypt has long been considered a refuge for the Hebrew peoples. Later, Brown (*Birth of the Messiah* [rev. ed., 1993], p. 586) asserts the the foundations of this account can be found in the obvious similarties between it and the stories of Joseph and Moses 'at the end of Genesis and the beginning of Exodus. He does not see a significant correlation between the NT Joseph and David. In this regard, see also Blomberg, *Matthew*, pp. 66-67 and Basser, *The Mind Behind the Gospels*, p. 57.

In contrast to the view that 'Joseph acts as ... the first Joseph who brought Jacob/Israel from Canaan to Egypt', see Davies and Allison, *Matthew*, I, pp. 258-64. While they acknowledge that Matthew may have been aware of numerous ancient legends with similarities to the account in 2.13-15, they believe 'the threat to the life of the young Jesus has its counterpart in tales about Moses' instead of those of the patriarch, Joseph. Bonnard(*L'Évangile selon Saint Matthieu*, pp. 29-30) and Nolland (*Matthew*, pp. 120-22) concur with this. Somewhat differently, France (*Matthew*, pp. 76-78) and Carter (*Matthew and the Margins*, p. 83) see evidence of both the Moses and Joseph traditions in 2.13-15. While Luz (*Matthew 1-7* [2007], p. 119) also feels the account in 2.13-15 may have some connection with the story of the first Joseph in Genesis, he believes, as Davies and Allison, that the 'Jewish Christian narrators of our story were especially familiar with the tradition of the rescue of the infant Moses in Egypt and Pharaoh's murder of the Israelite

of Joseph, to see him as a model for their own lives. At the same time, the pointed demarcation between Joseph and 'the child' (τὸ παιδίον) as well as between Joseph and Mary, previously acknowledged in the review of the second pericope (1.18-25) as reflective of a certain ambiguity in regard to Joseph's relationship with both 'the child' and 'his mother', is reiterated, here (2.13-14) and later (2.21-22), in the angel's specific instruction and the specific narration of his response.

Nonetheless, the introduction of a new challenge – to flee with the child and his mother from Herod and others – highlighted by the goal of the new geographical destiny of Egypt (2.13), intensifies the narrative drama and raises the interests of the readers. Having wondered how Joseph's first dilemma (1.18-25) would be resolved, they are now left to wonder how Joseph will meet this seemingly greater challenge.[30]

Accordingly, in this section of the pericope, Joseph's righteousness and faith are, once again, demonstrated, disclosing his roles as husband, father, spiritual model, and guardian of Mary and the child. In so doing, the readers learn that Joseph also fulfills the prophecy (Hos. 11.1) and the will of God, as the story of the history of salvation is further revealed (2.15). Once again, by his obedient responses to the angelic messengers, Joseph demonstrates he is both head of his young family as well as its guardian (2.13-14).[31] This is evident, directly and indirectly, in the first part of this section (2.13-15).

As the narrative moves forward it can be seen that although the readers have already learned of Herod's death (2.15), further differences between Joseph and the evil king are juxtaposed, albeit by implication, as the account of Herod's ruthless response to the Magi's deception, traditionally identified as the Massacre of the Innocents, appears in the next section of the pericope (2.16-18). Brief as it is, it does, once again, juxtapose the figures of Joseph and Herod and, additionally, sets before the readers two spiritual choices: to receive the child, the Messiah, or to fear, and even reject, him. It also further discloses (2.18) how the events of the story, including the horrific action of Herod, had been predicted by a Hebrew prophet (Jer. 31.15).

---

male children.' Nonetheless, despite these similarities, Luz thinks 'Matthew 2.13-21 is a new story.'

[30] Brown, *Birth of the Messiah* (New Updated Edition, 1993), p. 616, appears to suggest that Joseph is a 'model for fathers,' an idea that he takes from J.A. Bruce, 'The Flight into Egypt: the Dreams of Fathers', *Saint Luke's Journal of Theology* 27 (1984), pp. 287-96. Summarizing Bruce, Brown, *Birth of the Messiah* (1993) writes: 'Loyally he (Joseph) endures anxiety even though he cannot forsee where things will end; he is innovative and not immobilized by complexities; and he does his duty even though he does not fully understand the reasons.'

[31] See also Mt. 2.20-23 for a further demonstration of this role.

In the final section of this last pericope of the Matthean nativity (2.19-23), resolution comes to the challenges and obstacles Joseph has faced, showing, as before, God's care for Joseph, Mary, and the child, through angelic revelation to Joseph. In this case, two dreams are noted and introduced. Following the pattern of the dream previously encountered (1.20-25 and 2.13-15), and the visit of the angel of the Lord to Joseph in Egypt (2.19), the angel's instruction to Joseph (2.21) is virtually identical to the earlier instruction (2.13).[32] Here, the angel directs Joseph to act, and in this case, return to Israel. In response, as before, Joseph does as he has been told, and immediately rises and takes the child and his mother into the 'land of Israel' (γῆν Ἰσραήλ, 2.21).[33] Thus, Joseph takes on a new role and leads his young family on an exodus, this time, as another Hebrew spiritual ancestor, Moses, led the children of Israel, from Egypt into freedom.[34] In acting as he does, in obeying the angel's command, Joseph, again demonstrates his obedience to God's direction. In the process, he also recapitulates Israel's history by leading Mary and the child, the savior of Israel, back into a land that will, once again, offer salvation for Israel as well as the peoples of all other nations. In this case, the husband of Mary and legal father of the child leads them not to Bethlehem, where he and Mary previously resided, but to the city of Nazareth in Galilee (2.19-23).[35] Therefore, Joseph, again, demonstrates his obedience to God and his faithfulness to Mary and the child and this underscores for the readers the importance of obedience to God.

These things are also exemplified in somewhat different language in the second dream of this section (2.22), although it does bear similarities to the dream received by the Magi (2.12). In this case, upon entering the land of Israel, Joseph hears that Archelaus, the son of Herod, has

---

[32] Morris, *Matthew*, p. 47, notes that the visit of the angel of the Lord to Joseph in Egypt indicates that 'God's power and God's oversight extended to Egypt'. It also indicates that the journey and residence in Egypt has not changed Joseph's relationship with God and that he remains as spiritually close to God as before.

[33] Here is another example of how Joseph's response is often identical to his instruction from the angelic messenger. Again, in this respect, see the Greek texts of both the angelic message and the response and action of Joseph.

[34] Bonnard, *L'Évangile selon Saint Matthieu*, pp. 29-30; Green, *The Gospel According to Matthew*, p. 60; Davies and Allison, *The Gospel According to Saint Matthew*, p. 39; Gundry (*Matthew*, p. 38) and Schnackenburg (*The Gospel of Matthew*, p. 27) see parallels between the Matthean stories of Jesus and the early Hebrew stories of Moses. Davies and Allison also see this connection. See Davies and Allison, *Gospel According to St. Matthew*, vol. 1, pp. 258-64, as before (in 2.13) and p. 271 with respect to 2.21.d.

[35] See Brown, *Birth of the Messiah* (1977), pp. 216-17. He also notes (p. 214), The human instrument in this deliverance is Joseph, through his absolute obedience to the divine commands – a Joseph who has already been described as "an upright man" (1.19), i.e., a Jew totally faithful to the Law. In Matthew's mind, Jews who are true to the Law and the Prophets stand alongside the Gentile magi in accepting Jesus while the authorities reject him.

1. *The Portrayal of Joseph in the Gospel of Matthew* 43

replaced his deceased father (2.22). This discovery makes Joseph afraid (2.22); a fear that is both verified and assuaged in this final dream. While the recollection of this dream does not include specific words from an angelic figure, instruction is, nevertheless, implied by Joseph's change in direction (2.22 – he departed into the district of Galilee) and his final destiny (2.23 – he settled in the city called Nazareth), portrayed in the text. In addition, with respect to the final geographical destiny of Joseph and his family, the reader is led to see that Joseph's (and, thus, Jesus') home is to be, as Brown notes, 'Galilee of the Gentiles', a region that is suggestive of the diversity of the recipients for whom Jesus' salvation is intended, a trajectory that extends from Abraham to the gentile women in the genealogy (of Joseph and Jesus) to the Magi (the first worshippers of Jesus) to this domicile which is a fulfillment of prophetic scripture.[36]

Thus, Joseph demonstrates his obedience and faithfulness one last time, in the last verse of this chapter when, once again, he helps fulfill a prophecy about the child (2.23). Here, again, Joseph leads Mary and the child, this time to reside 'in a town called Nazareth' (εἰς πόλιν λεγομένην Ναζαρέτ) in order that 'what had been spoken through the prophets might be fulfilled' (ὅπως πληρωθῇ τὸ ῥηθὲν διὰ τῶν προφητῶν) and 'He will be called a Nazorean' (ὅτι Ναζωραῖος κληθήσεται).[37] Thus, Joseph reasserts his authority and position as *pater familias*, the active earthly head of this young family and, additionally, his role in the fulfillment of the prophecy about Jesus of Nazareth (2.23).[38]

---

[36] Brown, *Birth of the Messiah* (1977), p. 232. Thus, it is not surprising that Joseph goes to Galilee.

[37] Scholars are not agreed on the identity of this prophetic reference. With regard to the debate around 2.23, see Meyer, *Critical and Exegetical Handbook to the Gospel of Matthew*, pp. 99-100; McNeile, *Matthew*, pp. 21-22; Bonnard, *L'Évangile selon Saint Matthieu*, p. 30; Albright and Mann, *Matthew*, pp. 20-21; Hill, *Matthew*, pp. 86-88; Green, *The Gospel According to Matthew*, pp. 60-61; Tasker, *Matthew*, p. 45; Brown, *Birth of the Messiah* (1977), p. 219; Beare, *Matthew*, pp. 84-85; Bruner, The Christbook: Matthew 1-12, pp. 61-63; Allen, *Matthew*, pp.16-17; Gundry, *Matthew*, pp. 39-40; Harrington, *The Gospel of Matthew*, pp. 45-46; Blomberg, *Matthew*, p.70; Morris, *Matthew*, p. 49; Davies, *Matthew*, pp. 39-40; Hagner, *Matthew 1-13*, pp. 39-42; Garland, *Reading Matthew*, p. 31; Carter, *Matthew and the Margins*, p. 8; Mounce, *Matthew*, pp. 19-20; Schnackenburg, *The Gospel of Matthew*, pp. 27-28; See also Luz, *Matthew 1- 7* (2007), pp. 122-23 for an extensive discussion of the prophetic source Matthew may be noting. Further, Basser (*The Mind Behind the Gospels*, pp. 63-64) offers an explanation based on Rabbinic interpretative tradition.

[38] In his comments on this last pericope of the second chapter, Luz (*Matthew 1–7* [1989], pp. 142-48) notes that, as in 1.18-25, Matthew, once again, places Joseph into the center of the narrative account. In so doing, he places Joseph into both an old and a new role. As before, now in 2.13-14 and 2.19-21, Joseph continues to receive direction from the angel of God and to respond in obedience to this direction (pp. 143, 146). But, this time, in contrast to his portrayal in 1.18-25, Luz argues that Matthew does not attempt to present Joseph as a father (p. 146). Instead, Matthew presents him in a new position – that of protector and guardian – and ties this role together with his old role so

At the same time, reassurance and resolution are also conveyed in the closing words of the text, 'so that what had been spoken through the prophets might be fulfilled, "He will be called a Nazorean"' (2.23), so that the readers sense not only that one prophecy has been fulfilled but that this marks only the beginning and that more prophecies and promises will be revealed as the will of God is further disclosed in the story of the life of Jesus of Nazareth. In the process, the prominence, spiritual authority and integrity of Joseph, as well as the importance of his role as an exemplar for God's people in the present manifestation of God's salvation in Jesus, are, once again, confirmed and set before all the readers.

The final reference to Joseph occurs in Mt. 13.55, in the account of the rejection of Jesus in the synagogue in Nazareth. Here, unlike previous references, Jesus is publicly and formally identified by some residents of Nazareth as 'the carpenter's son' (ὁ τοῦ τέκτονος υἱός). The text reads:

> He came to his hometown and began to teach the people in their synagogue, so that they were astounded and said, 'Where did this man get this wisdom and these deeds of power? Is not this the carpenter's son? Is not his mother called Mary? And are not his brothers James and Joseph and Simon and Judas? And are not all his sisters with us? Where then did this man get all this?' And they took offense at him. But Jesus said to them, 'Prophets are not without honor except in their own country and in their own house.' And he did not do many deeds of power there, because of their unbelief (Mt. 13.54-58).

Although the account in Matthew's nativity narrative would have certainly led readers to believe, as has been noted, that Jesus was the legal son of Joseph, this reference constitutes the first explicit reference to Jesus as the 'son' of Joseph in this gospel.[39] Additionally, by speaking about Jesus as the 'son' of Joseph in the present tense (οὐχ οὗτός ἐστιν ὁ τοῦ τέκτονος υἱός, 13.55), the 'people in the synagogue' (αὐτοὺς, 13.54) appear to suggest Joseph's role in the life of Jesus has been of a substantial length and may be ongoing. Consequently, this reference contributes to the readers' understanding of Joseph in relationship to Jesus.

Therefore, it can be concluded that the portrayal of Joseph in Matthew as the earthly father of Jesus and the husband of Mary is, to a certain extent, complementary to his presentation as spiritual exemplar and model for the readers. This is substantiated by the focus on Joseph's heritage, authority, spirituality, righteousness, and obedience as well as his

---

that, as Moses before him, Joseph can become the obedient spiritual hero who protects the Child-Savior and his mother and leads them to freedom and safety (p. 144). Thus, Matthew places the 'thought of divine guidance and the obedience of Joseph ... in the foreground' (p. 148).

[39] This appears to verify Joseph's marriage to Mary and his fatherhood of Jesus' brothers and sisters (13.55-56).

care for his wife, Mary, and 'the child' (τὸ παιδίον), Jesus; aspects of Joseph's character which are, in one way or another, reemphasized so that the readers may have a clear sense of the identity and importance of Joseph.

2

The Portrayal of Joseph the Carpenter in the Gospel of Luke

Luke's account of the nativity and infancy of Jesus may be briefly summarized. In chapter one, the readers are introduced to accounts of the annunciation to Zechariah of the birth of John the Baptist, the annunciation to Mary of the birth of Jesus, the visitation of Mary with Elizabeth and Zechariah, the song or magnificat of Mary, and Zechariah's prophecies about John the Baptist and Jesus. In chapter two, in turn, the readers are presented the accounts of Joseph's and Mary's journey to Bethlehem, the birth of Jesus, the annunciation to the Shepherds, the adoration of the Shepherds, the circumcision and naming of Jesus, the presentation in the Temple, the return to Nazareth, and the story of the young Jesus in the temple. In addition, in the latter part of chapter three (3.23-38), the readers are introduced to a genealogy of Jesus in which it is attested that Jesus 'was the son [as was thought] of Joseph' (ὢν υἱός, ὡς ἐνομίζετο Ἰωσὴφ, 3.23). Lastly, there is one brief final reference to 'Joseph' in 4.22. Here, intriguingly, in this pericope (4.16-30), which recounts the rejection of Jesus at Nazareth, Jesus is explicitly identified by some residents of Nazareth as the son of Joseph. The readers are told: 'All spoke well of him and were amazed at the gracious words that came from his mouth. They said, "Is not this Joseph's son? (οὐχὶ υἱός ἐστιν Ἰωσὴφ οὗτος, 4.22)"'.[1]

Although many scholars have emphasized the importance of Luke's portrayal of Mary in his gospel, few have noted the significance of his portrayal of Joseph.[2] Therefore, it is essential to do so, as was done with

---

[1] This reference to Joseph in Lk. 4.22 is suggested in the parallel account in Mt.13.55 but not in the account in Mark.

[2] Numerous scholars make reference to Mary's importance. Note particularly the work of John Martin Creed, *The Gospel According to St. Luke* (London: Macmillan, 1950), p. 16; Brown, *The Birth of the Messiah* (1977), pp. 286-366; J.B. Green, *The Gospel of Luke* (Grand Rapids: Eerdmans, 1997), pp. 85-129; François Bovon, *A Commentary on the Gospel of Luke*, I (trans. James E. Crouch; Minneapolis, MN: Fortress Press, 2002), pp. 26-30, 42-65; Robert C. Tannehill, *The Narrative Unity of Luke-Acts* (Philadelpia: Fortress Press,1986), p. 134; and John Nolland, *Luke 1-9:20* (Dallas,TX: Word Books, 1989), p. 133. As previously acknowledged in the discussion of the 'History of Research', Brown, *The Birth of the Messiah* (rev. ed., 1993), p. 642, goes on to conclude, in his later

2. The Portrayal of Joseph in the Gospel of Luke

respect to Matthew's portrayal, by examining the same three issues: (1) the ways Joseph is presented and represented, (2) the respective characteristics and roles that are attributed to and associated with him and, in turn, (3) when and how he is juxtaposed with Mary, and the child, as well as other narrative figures. At the same time, in light of the paucity of research on the subject of Luke's portrayal of Joseph, it is also necessary to focus upon critical but oft neglected details such as the number of times Luke mentions Joseph by name, identifies him as the father or parent of Jesus, conjoins him with Mary as her partner and husband, and conjoins him with Mary and Jesus as husband and father, details readers would likely note. In this regard it is important to acknowledge several facts in the text that inform the portrait of Joseph. First, 'Joseph' is mentioned by name five times (1.27; 2.4, 16; 3.23; 4.22). Second, he is explicitly identified as the 'father' of Jesus two times (2.33 and 48); and in the latter reference it is Mary who uses the designation in response to Jesus. In turn, Jesus is identified as 'Joseph's son' twice (3.23; 4.22). Fourth, Joseph is specifically represented as the *de facto* father of Jesus (1.27; 2.4-7, 16-17, 22, 24, 27, 33-34, 39, 41-46, 48-51) much more than is often suggested.

The first pericope in which Joseph appears in Luke's text is 1.26-38, traditionally described as the annunciation to Mary.

> In the sixth month the angel Gabriel was sent by God to a town in Galilee called Nazareth, to a virgin engaged to a man whose name was Joseph, of the house of David. The virgin's name was Mary. And he came to her and said, 'Greetings, favored one! The Lord is with you.' But she was much perplexed by his words and pondered what sort of greeting this might be. The angel said to her, 'Do not be afraid, Mary, for you have found favor with God. And now, you will conceive in your womb and bear a son, and you will name him Jesus. He will be great, and will be called the Son of the Most High, and the Lord God will give to him the throne of his ancestor David. He will reign over the house of Jacob forever, and of his kingdom

discussion of Luke that 'Joseph will never be more than a shadow figure or speak in the Jesus story'.

Luke Timothy Johnson (*The Gospel of Luke* [Collegeville, MN: The Liturgical Press, 1991], p. 39) states that 'Luke's focus on Mary is striking not only in light of the patriarchal character of his biblical tradition (and social world) but also because it is through Joseph that Jesus receives his Davidic legitimacy "according to the flesh." At our distance, it is impossible to say whether historical reminiscence, special tradition, or Luke's predilection for presenting positive women figures (evident throughout his narrative) dictated his choice. The results, however, are clear: his narrative has exercised an incalculable influence in shaping Marian piety in subsequent Christian tradition.'

Among the few who have taken interest in Luke's portrayal of Joseph are Brown, *The Birth of Messiah* (1977), pp. 286-87, 393-94, 435-36, 440, 443-53, 471-75; Brown, *The Birth of the Messiah* (rev. ed., 1993), pp. 589, 625, 642; Green, *The Gospel of Luke*, pp. 86, 126-28, 138-40, 152-56; Bovon, *Luke*, I , pp. 43-44, 48-53, 80-86, 101, 104.

there will be no end.' Mary said to the angel, 'How can this be, since I am a virgin?' The angel said to her, 'The Holy Spirit will come upon you, and the power of the Most High will overshadow you; therefore the child to be born will be holy; he will be called Son of God. And, now, your relative Elizabeth in her old age has also conceived a son; and this is the sixth month for her who was said to be barren. For nothing will be impossible with God.' Then Mary said, 'Here am I, the servant of the Lord; let it be with me according to your word.' Then the angel departed from her (Lk. 1.26-38).

In this text the narrator recounts the visitation of 'the angel Gabriel' to Mary. However, surprisingly, the readers are not initially provided a formal introduction to Mary. Instead, they are only told that God has sent the angel Gabriel to 'a virgin' in Nazareth (Ναζαρὲθ, 1.26) who is 'engaged to a man' (παρθένον ἐμνηστευμένην ἀνδρὶ, 1.27)[3] and, then, curiously, formally introduced to the man to whom she is engaged, 'Joseph' ('Ιωσὴφ, 1.27) and his position and place within the hierarchy of his people (that he is 'of the house of David', ἐξ οἴκου Δαυίδ, 1.27); factors that inform and shape the portrayal of Joseph in Luke.[4] Thus, before the 'virgin' has been explicitly identified the readers learn of Joseph's marital and familial status (that he is 'the man' who is engaged to 'the virgin'), have been introduced to him by name, noted his position

---

[3] I.H. Marshall, *Gospel of Luke: A Commentary on the Greek Text* (Grand Rapids: Eerdmans, 1978), p. 64, believes Joseph and Mary are not living together at this point although it is certainly suggested that they have been some months later (2.4-7). At that point, Marshall (p.105) is convinced Mary 'was living with him as his wife, although the marriage had not yet been consummated (Mt. 1.25).' He adds that 'it is unlikely that she would have accompanied Joseph had she been merely betrothed to him.' William Hendriksen, *The Gospel of Luke* (Edinburgh: The Banner of Truth Trust, 1979), p. 84; Robert H. Stein, *Luke* (Nashville,TN: Broadman Press,1993) , pp. 26, 84; Darrell L. Bock, *Luke*, I (Grand Rapids: Baker Books,1994), p. 107; Judith Lieu, *The Gospel of Luke* (London: Epworth Press, 1997), p. 7, concur with Marshall. In contrast, Freed (*The Stories of Jesus' Birth*, pp. 60-66) suggests Joseph and Mary were together and that Luke believed Joseph to be the actual father of Jesus.

[4] Joseph A. Fitzmyer, *The Gospel According to Luke* (Garden City, NY: Doubleday, 1981), p. 344, points out that the name Joseph was 'widely used among Jews in the postexilic period (see Ezra 10.42; Neh 12.14; I Chron. 25.2,9).' He also suggests that Luke's Joseph, as other Josephs, attempts 'to fathom divine intention in humanly difficult situations'. However, it should be added that this only becomes evident in the second chapter of Luke's infancy narrative. In a different regard, John Nolland, *Luke 1-9:20*, p. 49 argues that 'the specific mention of Joseph and the betrothal at this point ... has produced difficulties with v. 34 ...'

With regard to the phrase, 'of the house of David,' Fitzmyer (*The Gospel According to Luke*, p. 344) notes that 'this stereotyped OT phrase (e.g. I Kgs 12.19; 2 Chr 23.3) follows immediately on the name of Joseph and expresses his Davidic lineage (also mentioned in 2.4 and 3.23).' This is in contrast to the earlier work of Alfred Plummer, *A Critical and Exegetical Commentary on the Gospel According to St. Luke* (Edinburgh: T. and T. Clark, 1896), who argues (p. 21) that it is 'impossible to decide whether these words (ἐξ οἴκου Δαυὶδ) go with ανδρι or with παρθενον or with both.'

and place within the hierarchy and spiritual history of the Hebrew peoples, and discovered that he may, as Mary, be from Nazareth; four details that help readers understand the role Joseph has within the story and his relationship to Mary and Jesus.[5]

The first detail, Joseph's marital and familial status (that he is 'engaged' to a 'virgin', 1.27a), is critical to understanding his role (as well as that of Mary's) for it informs the readers that Joseph and Mary have made a marital commitment to each other that has been publicly acknowledged (1.27). It also helps explain to them, among other things, their forthcoming response to the decree of Caesar (2.4-7) even though they have not yet become physically intimate (1.27 and 1.34), as is made clear in Mary's words, 'I know no man' (ἄνδρα οὐ γινώσκω, 1.34).[6]

Likewise, the second detail, the fact that the narrator has revealed Joseph's name (1.27a) before that of Mary's, is also noteworthy for the readers for it substantiates the importance Joseph has for the narrator.[7]

In turn, the third detail, Joseph's position and place in the hierarchy of Israel (that he is 'of the house of David', 1.27b), is also critical for it explains his role and his relationship to Jesus and Mary for readers and links him to virtually all the remaining pericopes in the text.[8] It is this 'same Davidic messianic theme', referenced in 1.26-28, that connects the second section of Luke's gospel narrative (2.1-21), the third section (2.22-38) and the rest of Luke's infancy account.[9] At the same time, the fact that it is Joseph's lineage (rather than Mary's) that is formally

---

[5] Creed (*St. Luke*, pp. 13-14) believes this initial account about the relationship between Joseph and Mary is 'wanting in cohesion'. He writes: 'Mary betrothed to Joseph, a scion of the royal line, is to bear an heir to David's throne, "of whose kingdom there shall be no end," but Mary is to bear her son, not by a man but by the power of God's Spirit. Two ideas lie here side by side, and they are not reconciled. The sonship of Jesus to Joseph is essential to the former idea, and is ruled out by the second.' Thus, he suggests that 'the first narrators who spoke of Mary as affianced or wedded to Joseph "of the house of David" may be supposed to have thought of Jesus as Joseph's son.'

[6] According to Nolland (*Luke 1-9:20*, p. 49) 'the betrothal to Joseph serves to provide (legal) Davidic ancestry for the child.' See also Craig A. Evans, *Luke* (Peabody, MA: Hendrickson Publishers, 1990), pp. 25-26.

[7] David L. Tiede, *Luke* (Minneapolis, MN:Augsburg Publishing House, 1988), p. 48, notes the brevity of the presentation of Mary at this point. Arthur A. Just, *Luke 1.1-9.50* (St. Louis, MO: Concordia Publishing House, 1997), p. 63, also alludes to this.

[8] Mark L. Strauss, *The Davidic Messiah in Luke-Acts* (JSNTS 110; Sheffield: Sheffield Academic Press, 1995), p. 117. In a similar regard, Nolland, *Luke 1-9:20*, p. 58, says '"The house of David" prepares for the Davidic descent of the child to be born.' See also Evans, *Luke*, p. 25, who states that Joseph's ancestry 'qualifies Jesus for his messianic role and makes what Gabriel says in vv.32-33 possible.' Just as well, see Brown, *The Birth of the Messiah* (rev. ed., 1993), p. 589; Lieu, *The Gospel of Luke*, p. 6.

[9] Strauss, *The Davidic Messiah in Luke-Acts*, p. 117. The theme is that 'Jesus is ... the Davidic Christ born to a descendant of David in Bethlehem, the city of David.'

acknowledged, and the fact that his lineage places him in a superior position to those of priestly lineage (Zechariah, 1.5; Elizabeth, 1.5, 43; and even Mary, 1.36), also alludes to his importance and centrality in this infancy account.[10] Thus, by giving priority to Joseph in the introduction to this pericope and revealing he is 'of the house of David', the narrator suggests to the readers that despite Mary's importance, she is not able to act as the bridge for 'the child' between the spiritual past and future of Israel and explicitly connect 'the child' to the 'house of David', as Joseph.[11] Joseph is not only the betrothed and husband of Mary but, even more, the spiritual Davidic figure who stands between King David and the one who 'will reign forever on the throne of David' as Mary is told by Gabriel in the annunciation; between God's promises in the past and those in the present and future.[12]

Finally, with respect to the fourth detail, the probable geographical location of Joseph, it is necessary to acknowledge that the initial reference to 'Nazareth' (1.26) – and the relationship it suggests between Joseph and Mary (that Joseph is from where Mary is from) – may not be immediately evident to the readers. Nevertheless, it is likely this link becomes more obvious and significant to the portrayal of Joseph, as the readers interpret further and see this reference and its connection to Joseph and Mary reiterated in the following pericopes: 2.1-7, 21-40, 41-52; 4.16-30. Thus, in summary, these four initial details help establish a foundation for the readers that enables them to understand and appreciate the role and significance of Joseph in the forthcoming pericopes in the first two chapters of Luke.

However, following the narrator's brief but revealing concentration on Joseph in the first part of v. 27, the readers' attention is redirected to Mary who is identified, not as she was first portrayed, as 'a virgin' but, now, most particularly, as 'the virgin Mary'(τῆς παρθένου Μαριάμ, 1.27b). As such, here, in these three words, and in the rest of the words of her encounter with the angel Gabriel (1.26-38), and her visit with her cousin, Elizabeth (1.39-45), and her poetic response to God in 1.46-56, readers are continually reminded of her uniqueness and importance in

---

[10] Creed (*St. Luke*, pp. 16-17) believes that 'since, according to Luke, she (Mary) is a kinswoman of Elizabeth, and Elizabeth was "of the daughters of Aaron" (v. 5), it may probably be inferred that in this cycle of stories Mary too was of Levitic descent.' See also Stein, *Luke*, p. 82 and Bock, *Luke*, I , pp. 107-108.

[11] As Creed (*St. Luke*, p. 16) states, 'It is Joseph who is of the house of David, and the claim of Jesus "to sit upon the throne of David" rests upon the Davidic descent of Joseph.' In contrast, R.C.H. Lenski, *The Interpretation of St. Luke's Gospel* (Minneapolis, MN: Augsburg Publishing House, 1971), pp. 59-61 claims Mary is a descendant of David, as does Hendriksen, *The Gospel of Luke*, p. 84.

[12] Strauss, *The Davidic Messiah in Luke-Acts*, p. 76.

the birth and life of the one she will be instructed to call 'Jesus' ('Ιησουν, 1.31).

Nonetheless, even as the readers read these narrative and poetic portrayals that emphasize the special role of Mary, they are reminded that 'Joseph of the house of David' (1.27) has a role and priority that is continually contrasted with that of 'Zechariah' (Ζαχαρίας, 1.5) and 'the division [or priestly order] of Abijah' (ἐξ ἐφημερίας Ἀβιά, 1.5) and 'of Aaron' (Ἀαρών, 1.5), with those of Levitical descent. This is repeatedly revealed through the designations and attributes associated with Mary's forthcoming child, the messiah of the house of David (who 'will be called the Son of the Most High, and the Lord God will give him the throne of his ancestor David,' 1.32; 'will rule over the house of Jacob forever, and of his kingdom there will be no end,' 1.33; who is 'the Lord' of Elizabeth, 1.43; and who is 'a mighty Savior ... in the house of his servant David,' 1.69). In this text, the 'narrator portrays Jesus as a "King to be" through the ordering of the material concerned with Davidic descent' with evidence of this found in the numerous references to David located throughout the first two chapters of Luke, beginning with the reference to 'Joseph' as being 'of the house of David' (1.27, 1.32, 1.69, 2.4, and 2.11).[13] Thus, it can be argued that each of these references, in one way or another, tie the future 'King' Jesus to Joseph, who is the source of Jesus' connection to the role of the savior and messiah of Israel. Although the readers have learned of the significance of the child to be born to Zechariah and Elizabeth, earlier in the text (1.5-26) and will learn more about this child (1.39-45 and 1.57-1.80), the text lets them know that the child for whom Joseph will act as the earthly father, will be even more important and is, in fact, 'a mighty Savior ... in the house of his servant David' (1.69).

As significant and moving as the events pertaining to Mary are for the readers, they do not diminish the importance the narrator gives Joseph in the first chapter of Luke. Thus, the first chapter prepares the readers for the elaboration of Joseph's role and relationships with Mary and Jesus in the second chapter.

As such, the readers are not surprised when Joseph assumes responsibility for Mary and her unborn child and takes them with him from the

---

[13] David Lee, *Luke's Stories of Jesus: Theological Reading of Gospel Narrative and the Legacy of Hans Frei*, (JSNTS 185; Sheffield: Sheffield Academic Press, 1999), p. 211. In contrast to this belief that Joseph is the sole source of Jesus' Davidic heritage, Plummer (*St. Luke*, p. 21) believes that 'From vv. 32 and 69 we may with probability infer that Luke regards Mary as descended from David.' However, Plummer later acknowledges that the 'repetition involved in τῆς παρθένου is in favor of taking ἐξ οἴκου Δαυὶδ with ἀνδρὶ ...' In regard to the emphasis upon Jesus' Davidic descent, see also Evans, *Luke*, p. 29.

'city of Nazareth' in Galilee to 'the city of David' in Judea in the next pericope.

> In those days a decree went out from Caesar Augustus that all the world should be enrolled. This was the first enrollment, when Quirinius was governor of Syria. And all went to be enrolled, each to his own city. And Joseph also went up from Galilee, from the city of Nazareth, to Judea, to the city of David, which is called Bethlehem, because he was of the house and lineage of David, to be enrolled with Mary, his betrothed, who was with child. And while they were there, the time came for her to be delivered. And she gave birth to her first-born son and wrapped him in swaddling cloths, and laid him in a manger, because there was no place for them in the inn (Lk. 2.1-7).

Although the additional references to 'Joseph' and the 'house of David', and 'Nazareth' (2.4), may appear redundant, they expand the initial references and clearly establish Joseph's role as the *pater familias*.[14] For, in this case, Joseph subsumes this role, takes the lead, acts as he must act, and goes where he must go. As Coleridge asserts, in this context, the narrator 'has Joseph take the initiative, with Mary not mentioned at all in v. 4. When she is mentioned in v. 5, it is as an appendix to the action, in the midst of which, initially at least, Mary remains passive. She is named, and her condition is described, but she does nothing.'[15] Thus, not only does Joseph act in response to the 'decree ... from Emperor Augustus' (2.1-2), but also because he must verify his union with Mary before the secular authorities within his country (2.3-5).[16] In addition, Joseph does what he does in order to keep Mary close to him so he may protect her (2.5-6) and the forthcoming child (πρωτότοκον, 2.5-7), and

---

[14] Once again, with regard to the portrayal of the Davidic Messiah in this gospel, see Strauss, *The Davidic Messiah in Luke-Acts*, p. 76. With respect to this reference to the 'city of David' and the house of David, Earle Ellis, *Gospel of Luke* (San Francisco: HarperCollins, 1981), p. 81, states that 'Joseph had a family as well as a tribal relationship to David.' In addition, in light of 1.39, Ellis adds (also on p. 81) that 'Mary's former home also may have been in this region'. Further, with respect to Joseph's role as *pater familias*, see Bovon, *Luke*, I, pp. 83, 85, 101, 104. M.D. Goulder, *Luke: A New Paradigm* (JSNTS 20; Sheffield: Sheffield Academic Press, 1989), p. 249, also acknowledges Joseph had this role when he notes that Luke 'knew that Roman census officials ... expected people to come and register at local towns .... Joseph, as a descendant of David, will have been required to attend at David's home-town, Bethlehem, and Mary with him ...' In turn, Johnson (*Gospel of Luke*, p. 49) sees Luke's words, 'lineage of David,' as a reference to '*patria*, which in Tob 5.12 and Jdt 8.2 appears as a subdivision of the *phyle* or tribe.'

[15] See Mark Coleridge, *The Birth of the Lukan Narrative: Narrative as Christology in Luke 1–2* (JSNTS 88; Sheffield: Sheffield Academic Press, 1993), p. 132.

[16] Strauss (*The Davidic Messiah*, pp. 108-109) believes the terms οἴκου and πατριας in 2.4 'are used (by Luke) co-referentially, both referring to Joseph's Davidic descent,' which, he adds, 'legitimizes Jesus' claim to the Davidic throne'.

reaffirm his genealogical and spiritual heritage (2.3-5).[17] Further, by his actions, Joseph confirms his role as *pater familias*.[18] Therefore, in his efforts, Joseph protects Mary and the child, substantiates his position and relationship with them, offers witness to the coming salvation of God

---

[17] With respect to Mary's appearance with Joseph for the census and Joseph's relationship with Mary, Creed, *St. Luke*, p. 33, suggests that 'Joseph and Mary are represented (in these verses) by Luke as living together. It would be strange if Mary were to travel with Joseph when she was only betrothed to him.' In turn, N. Geldenhuys, *Commentary on the Gospel of Luke* (Grand Rapids: Eerdmans, 1979), pp. 100-101, claims that 'it was not necessary' for a woman to appear at a Roman census. He believes the fact that Luke records that Joseph brought the pregnant Mary with him, suggests Joseph clearly cared for Mary and was concerned for her and the child. He hypothesizes that 'Joseph did not want to leave her behind in Nazareth, since she would probably, when the child came to be born, be treated with insult and distrust, as the people knew that she had been married to Joseph for considerably less than nine months (cf. 1.56).' See also Lenski, *The Interpretation of St. Luke's Gospel*, p. 122; Hendriksen, *The Gospel of Luke*, p. 142; Evans, *Luke*, p. 35. In partial disagreement with Geldenhuys, Marshall (*Gospel of Luke*, p. 102) argues that while Mary's presence would not have been required in 'a census' that women 'may well have been required to appear personally at 'an enrollment which determined who was to pay taxes.' He writes (p. 102): 'In Syria women of 12 years and upwards were liable to a poll tax (Ulpian, 50:15:3; Schürer, *History*, I, p. 403 n. 12), and hence they may well have been required to appear personally ...' Nolland (*Luke 1–9:20*, pp. 101, 104) concurs with this idea about the prospect of Mary's presence.

As before, Johnson (*Gospel of Luke*, p. 50) notes in 2.5, that 'Luke avoids calling Mary Joseph's wife (instead, he says, τῇ ἐμνηστευμένῃ αὐτῷ), even though the state of betrothal allowed that designation.' Nolland (*Luke 1–9:20*, p.111) believes Luke uses this word 'to suggest, in line with the Matthean tradition (1:24-25), that although they lived together they had no sexual union prior to the birth of the child that Mary was carrying.'

It should also be acknowledged that despite references to Joseph's connection to 'the house and lineage of David' that Luke's portrayal of both Joseph and Mary, in this pericope, suggests, as Johnson, *Gospel of Luke*, p. 52, asserts, that they are 'simple people who are obedient to authority. The command of the empire does not stir them to join revolt; rather they obey the decree, in contrast to Luke's mention of Judas the Galilean who revolted "at the time of the census" (Acts 5.37).' With respect to Joseph's relationship to the Roman authorities see also Marshall, *Gospel of Luke*, p. 105 and Bock, *Luke*, vol. 1, p. 204. Marshall notes that 'Joseph is portrayed as a law-abiding citizen - perhaps in deliberate contrast to the Zealots and other rebels against Rome-who in response to the imperial edict makes his way up from the comparatively low - lying countryside of Galilee to the hill-country of Judaea.'

Further, Johnson (*Gospel of Luke*, p. 52) believes Luke's account in this pericope attests that Joseph and Mary are 'among the poor of the land. However, we construe the manger and the lodge and the wrapping bands put on the baby and the visit by shepherds, there is no doubt concerning Luke's portrayal of the economic or social level of Jesus' first companions.'

[18] As Tiede (*Luke*, p. 68) acknowledges, 'Joseph is the paternal link with the house and lineage of David, and his betrothed and the unborn child are legitimated through Joseph.'

and, ultimately, acts with Mary, to fulfill the will of God with respect to this salvation.[19]

Joseph's quiet, obedient, and apparently willing response to this edict of the imperial Roman authorities is such that the readers are left with the sense that Joseph is confident that God is using Caesar Augustus as an agent of his divine plan, as Coleridge suggests. He writes: 'The authority of Caesar brings Joseph and Mary to Bethlehem, but the readers know that it is the authority of God which brings the child to birth. What begins in v. 1 is the narration of the implementation of God's plan; and this brings with it a change of subject as the initiative passes from Caesar (and Joseph) to Mary.'[20] Thus, as the readers contemplate the response of Joseph in this situation, they understand better Joseph's role as a person of deep faith. They also come to a clearer understanding of Joseph's close relationship to Mary with whom he is formally united and conjoined in ch. 2. Thus, they are not surprised that Joseph acts in conjunction with Mary in the manner that he does, particularly with respect to their relationship with the child and young boy, Jesus (2.4-7, 16, 22, 24, 27, 33, 34, 39, 41, 42, 43, 44, 45, 46, 48, 49, 50, 51).[21]

This joint action is also evident in the next pericope where Joseph's presence and union with Mary and the baby is detailed.

> And in that region there were shepherds out in the field, keeping watch over their flock by night. And an angel of the Lord appeared to them, and

---

[19] Marshall (*The Gospel of Luke*, p. 96) notes the significant differences between the birth of Jesus and that of John in his reflections on these initial verses in chapter two. Among the differences, Marshall recounts that 'the birth of Jesus ... is given a setting in world history by the reference to the census which brought Mary and Joseph to Bethlehem. It is the first hint of the cosmic significance of the birth and foreshadows the universalism disclosed in 2.32.' This difference, in turn, has implications for the readers' perception of Joseph whose role is much more significant than that of Zechariah's. As such Joseph is not only the 'legal father' of Jesus, as Marshall states, but also a special servant and witness of God 'in world history,' as Mary. With respect to these ideas, see also Green, *The Gospel of Luke*, pp. 126-27.

[20] See Coleridge, *The Birth of the Lukan Narrative*, p. 130. He suggests the narrator shares the same belief that God is using Caesar Augustus in this context. Carroll (*Luke*, pp. 64-67) concurs, noting that Luke's audience is being directed to see that 'it is God who is directing the action.' In this regard see also Evans (*Luke*, p. 35), who argues that 'Luke has framed his account in such a way that during the reign of the earth's greatest king, Caesar Augustus, the son of Joseph-a man from the line of David (v. 4), Israel's greatest king and father of the Messiah-was born.'

[21] Joseph's union and juxtaposition with Mary in this chapter, and particularly in the second half of the chapter, is quite remarkable. In sharp contrast to this understanding see Coleridge, *The Birth of the Lukan Narrative*, pp. 134-35. He writes: 'Having made his first appearance in the narrative in v. 4, Joseph disappears from the scene once Mary returns to centre stage (vv. 6-7) for the first time since 1.56.... The focus is on her alone; and she is the subject of the three verbs in v. 7. This suggests that she who has been so privileged in the first phase and to whom the initiative now passes may prove to be the one to offer the interpretation which the narrator has left to the characters.'

2. The Portrayal of Joseph in the Gospel of Luke

the glory of the Lord shone around them, and they were filled with fear. And the angel said to them, 'Be not afraid; for behold, I bring you good news of a great joy which will come to all the people; for to you is born this day in the city of David a Savior, who is Christ the Lord. And this will be a sign for you: you will find a babe wrapped in swaddling cloths and lying in a manger.' And suddenly there was with the angel a multitude of the heavenly host praising God and saying, 'Glory to God in the highest, and on earth peace among men with whom he is pleased!' When the angels went away from them into heaven, the shepherds said to one another, 'Let us go over to Bethlehem and see this thing that has happened, which the Lord has made known to us.' And they went with haste, and found Mary and Joseph, and the babe lying in a manger. And when they saw it they made known the saying which had been told them concerning this child; and all who heard it wondered at what the shepherds told them. But Mary kept all these things, pondering them in her heart. And the shepherds returned, glorifying and praising God for all they had heard and seen, as it had been told them (Lk. 2.8-20).

Although the focus of the narration appears centered upon the subjects of the shepherds, the angels' annunciation to them, and their response to the discovery of the child savior, Joseph's significance, often ignored by contemporary scholarship, is revealed to the readers in the foreground of the final scene, where he is situated, together with Mary and the child, as the shepherds approach to offer adoration (2.16-17, 20).[22]

While the readers understand that the shepherds have been directed to seek the infant 'savior' (2.11, 12, 16), they also note that 'Mary' and 'Joseph', the parents of the 'savior', are mentioned before him (ἀνεῦραν τήν τε Μαριὰμ καὶ τὸν Ἰωσὴφ καὶ τὸ βρέφος, 2.16). It is also notable in verse sixteen that in Joseph's identification and in the grammatical construction of the figures of Mary and Joseph and the baby (noted above) that the narrator portrays them as a family. The readers learn that the shepherds first 'notice Mary and Joseph, about whom the angel has said nothing, though the shepherds can hardly have failed to wonder who the parents of such a child might be; and the mention of both Mary and

---

[22] Evans (*Luke*, p. 36) thinks the account of the shepherds 'strengthens the connection between Jesus and King David' since David 'was himself a shepherd (1 Sam. 16.11), and in some of the psalms ... refers to God as a shepherd and to God's people as sheep (Ps. 23.1; 28.9; 100.3).' Luke's account also suggests that he intends to reveal more about Joseph than Coleridge, Green, Bovon and others suggest. For the remarks of Coleridge, *The Birth of the Lukan Narrative*, pp. 134-35, see previous note. Green, *Gospel of Luke*, p. 138, asserts that Joseph's role is only 'to certify Jesus' status as son of David, born in Bethlehem.' Bovon, *Luke*, Vol. 1, p. 86, virtually ignores the role of Joseph in this pericope. He makes only the briefest mention of the Carpenter, noting, 'Joseph fades into the background in v. 21.' In saying this he concurs, to a great extent, with Green's remark (*Gospel of Luke*, p. 138) that Joseph's role here is only 'to certify Jesus' status as son of David, born in Bethlehem.' Green goes on to add that following verse sixteen Luke effectively moves the Carpenter into the background.

Joseph suggests the shepherds judge them to be the parents.'[23] Thus, it is necessary to acknowledge Joseph's position with Mary and the child at this point in the narrative and to recognize that the narrator is reminding the readers that Joseph is, once again, representing himself as the father of the baby, and the husband of Mary, here, before the shepherds as well as those with whom they share their discovery; just as he represented himself before the secular authorities in the prior pericope (2.1-7).[24] It is also essential to recognize that the shepherds' offer acknowledgement *to* and *of* both parents, *both* Joseph and Mary, as well as the child, in this encounter (2.17).

At the same time, in verses seventeen and eighteen the readers learn that Joseph is (via the shepherds) a recipient of the message of the 'angel of the Lord' (2.10-12), just as Mary.[25] Consequently, the readers would all understand that Joseph is part of the group (Μαριὰμ καὶ τὸν Ἰωσὴφ καὶ τὸ βρέφος, 2.16) who responded to the shepherds and, thus, would also respond, as Mary (2.19), to the encounter with the shepherds (2.16) and to their revelations (2.17-18).[26] While it is necessary to recognize that Mary's response is the focus of the narrative in 2.19, the shepherds' preceding action (2.17-18) reveals something of Joseph's own response to these remarkable words.[27]

In the following pericope, 2.21-40, the account concerning Jesus' circumcision and presentation in the Temple, the readers learn more about the union of Joseph and Mary.

> After eight days had passed, it was time to circumcise the child; and he was called Jesus, the name given by the angel before he was conceived in the womb. When the time came for their purification according to the law of Moses, they brought him up to Jerusalem to present him to the Lord (as it is written in the law of the Lord, 'Every firstborn male shall be designated as holy to the Lord'), and they offered a sacrifice according to what is stated in the law of the Lord, 'a pair of turtledoves or two young pigeons.' Now

---

[23] See Coleridge, *The Birth of the Lukan Narrative*, p. 147.

[24] Even Stein (*Luke*, pp. 109-10) notes that here 'Joseph appears to be the father' and is present 'since the trip to Bethlehem was made due to his need to enroll in the census'.

[25] Nolland (*Luke 1-9:20*, p. 112) correctly notes that once the shepherds have seen 'the promised sign, they pay no further attention to the child. The angelic revelation is all-important, so they make known to all in the house what had been made known to them.'

[26] Fitzmyer, *The Gospel According to Luke*, p. 412; Lenski, *The Interpretation of St. Luke's Gospel*, p. 138; Hendriksen, *The Gospel of Luke*, p. 157; and Bock, *Luke,* I, pp. 221-22, recognize that Joseph as well as Mary heard the shepherds proclaim that the child would be a savior for all humanity.

[27] Goulder (*Luke*, I, p. 269) is convinced that 'Mary takes the lead over Joseph' from 2.16 until the end of the chapter and cites vv. 16, 19, 34, 51 as evidence of this. He sees this as a significant contrast in light of Luke's earlier portrayal of Zechariah and Elizabeth (1.5-25, 57-80). In these accounts Zechariah's name always appears first and he appears to be the most dominant figure.

2. The Portrayal of Joseph in the Gospel of Luke

there was a man in Jerusalem whose name was Simeon; this man was righteous and devout, looking forward to the consolation of Israel, and the Holy Spirit rested on him. It had been revealed to him by the Holy Spirit that he would not see death before he had seen the Lord's Messiah. Guided by the Spirit, Simeon came into the temple; and when the parents brought in the child Jesus, to do for him what was customary under the law, Simeon took him in his arms and praised God, saying 'Master, now you are dismissing your servant in peace, according to your word; for my eyes have seen your salvation, which you have prepared in the presence of all peoples, a light for revelation to the Gentiles and for glory to your people Israel. And, the child's father and mother were amazed at what was being said about him. Then Simeon blessed them and said to his mother Mary, 'This child is destined for the falling and the rising of many in Israel, and to be a sign that will be opposed so that the inner thoughts of many will be revealed and a sword will pierce your own soul too.' There was also a prophet, Anna the daughter of Phanuel, of the tribe of Asher. She was of a great age, having lived with her husband seven years after her marriage, then as a widow to the age of eighty-four. She never left the temple but worshiped there with fasting and prayer night and day. At that moment she came, and began to praise God and to speak about the child to all who were looking for the redemption of Jerusalem. When they had finished everything required by the law of the Lord, they returned to Galilee, to their own town of Nazareth. The child grew and became strong, filled with wisdom; and the favor of God was upon him (Lk. 2.21-40).

Here, in the first verse (2.21), the circumcision and the naming of the child, predictable matters in which Joseph and Mary, faithful and dutiful Hebrew parents, would have naturally engaged, is recounted. 'After eight days had passed, it was time to circumcise the child; and he was called Jesus, the name given by the angel before he was conceived in the womb.'[28] Since neither parent is given priority in these actions (despite the instructions given to Mary in 1.31), the readers would assume, at the very least, that Joseph and Mary cooperated with each other in the ritual of the circumcision and in the naming of the child.[29] Thus, Joseph would

---

[28] A spiritual and literary parallel to this is certainly present earlier in Luke in Zechariah's and Elizabeth's circumcision and naming of John. See Lk. 1.57-63.

[29] With regard to these two events it is very possible that Joseph took the lead, and possibly, circumcised his child since no one else is suggested in this regard (2.21), in contrast to what is stated with respect to presentation of the infant in the temple in Jerusalem (2.22-28). It is also likely, in accord with Hebrew tradition and practice, suggested in Matthew, among other places, that Joseph was also directly involved in the naming of the child. See Mt.1.21. Certainly the fact that both gospels provide the same name to be used in the naming suggests this is possible. While Carroll (*Luke*, p. 73) acknowledges the parents' obedience at this point, he does not believe it is appropriate to give emphasis to the role of either Joseph or Mary. Instead, he notes (p. 73) that 'their agency is concealed behind the passive voice' and points out that only Jesus' name is formally mentioned. See also Brown's footnote with respect to the fact that 'The parents ... are not even mentioned in the naming of Jesus (in Luke 2.21).' He writes in *Birth of*

be seen as cooperating with Mary in fulfilling the command of God mediated earlier through the angel Gabriel (1.31). Nevertheless, as Coleridge states, this verse also reveals the beginning of an important shift and transition for both the narrator and the readers. He writes:

> In v. 21, the narrator named Jesus for the first time, waiting for the characters to name the child before he himself made the move. Until that moment, the parents had been named as 'Mary' (Μαριάμ, vv. 5, 16, and 19) and 'Joseph' (Ἰωσήφ, vv. 4 and 16) throughout 2.1-21. But once Jesus is named, their names disappear from the infancy narrative, with the sole exception of v. 34 where Mary is referred to by the narrator as 'Mary his mother' (Μαριὰμ τὴν μητέρα αὐτοῦ) at a point where Simeon focuses on her specifically. Through this and the following episode the focus moves slowly but surely from the parents to Jesus; and the shift is reflected in the way the characters are named by the narrator.[30]

Although neither Joseph nor Mary are formally identified in v. 21, their union and cooperation become more explicit for the readers when the couple returns to center stage in Luke's account of the purification and the presentation in the temple and they are described as acting together ('they brought him up', ἀνήγαγον αὐτόν, 2.22).[31] Though these verses (2.22-28) do not clarify where Joseph and Mary and the child have been prior to the purification and the presentation, the readers now know they are presently in the city of Jerusalem. They also know Joseph

---

the Messiah (1977) (p. 431, n. 78): 'This is particularly curious since in 1.31 Mary was told to name the child, and we would have expected Luke to tell us that it was she who did the naming.' Luke's account (1.59-64) of the role of Zechariah in the naming of John the Baptist also adds support to the likelihood of Joseph's involvement.

[30] Coleridge, *The Birth of the Lukan Narrative*, p. 166, provides a notable insight with respect to the mention of the name of Jesus in v. 21.

[31] With respect to the translation of 'their purification', τοῦ καθαρισμοῦ αὐτῶν, 2.22, and the possibility of Joseph's involvement at this point in the narrative, see Creed, *St. Luke*, pp. 38-39; Geldenhuys, *Commentary on the Gospel of Luke*, pp. 117-18; Evans, *Luke*, p. 45; and Johnson, *Gospel of Luke*, p. 54, who believe the phrase refers to Mary or Mary and the child. Similarly, Marshall (*Gospel of Luke*, p. 116) thinks it is 'most likely that Luke has run together the cleansing of the mother and the offering of the child into one act.'

In contrast, Fitzmyer, *The Gospel According to Luke*, p. 424, argues that the 'pron., "their," must be understood to refer to Joseph and Mary because of the main verb *anegagon*, "they (i.e. his parents) brought him up."' He continues (p. 425), stating that Luke 'relates Jesus' presentation (in v. 22) to the law about the firstborn. Jesus was so designated in 2.7 and the obligation of redeeming him lay upon the parents.' The parents in this case, of course, would be Joseph and Mary. Nolland (*Luke 1-9:20*, p. 117) concurs, stating that it 'is probably best to consider that Luke speaks loosely of the purification as a family matter ...' In partial agreement with Fitzmyer and Nolland, Ellis (*Gospel of Luke*, p. 83) thinks '*their purification* (τοῦ καθαρισμοῦ αὐτῶν) may go with the following *they* (in ἀνήγαγον) and, in loose idiom, refer to Joseph and Mary', he believes the focus is upon Mary.

2. The Portrayal of Joseph in the Gospel of Luke

and Mary have come for a specific purpose, to visit the temple, the spiritual center of Israel, located in the heart of Jerusalem (2.22, 27) in order to engage in these required spiritual acts.[32] As Geldenhuys notes, here, Joseph and Mary come as a couple, to bring 'Jesus to the temple ... to consecrate Him to the service of God.'[33] As such, it is predictable when, in the fulfillment of their spiritual responsibilities (especially noted in 2.21-24), Joseph and Mary are specifically identified as 'the parents' (τοὺς γονεῖς) of the infant (2.27).[34] However, Coleridge sees additional reasons for this designation. He believes

> there are good narrative reasons for a narrator who is well aware of the virginal conception to refer to Mary and Joseph as 'the parents' nonetheless.

---

[32] With regard to these Hebrew rituals, see especially Exodus 13 and Leviticus 12. Further, note the parallel Goulder (*Luke*, I, p. 255) sees between the journey of Joseph and Mary to the temple and the earlier journey of Elkanah and Hannah (I Sam. 1.1-2.11). As he notes, 'Hannah has been the model for Mary with her humility and her Song; and just as Elkanah and Hannah went up to the temple at Shiloh and dedicated the young Samuel, so will Joseph and Mary have taken Jesus to the Jerusalem Temple to dedicate him, even though they cannot have left him there.' Ellis (*Gospel of Luke*, p. 83), in contrast with Goulder, thinks the 'analogy to Hannah's dedication of Samuel is secondary at most'.

[33] Cf. Geldenhuys, *Commentary on the Gospel of Luke*, p. 118. It is interesting and most unusual (and in concord with the writer's ideas) that in his discussion of 'the circumcision and dedication of Jesus', Geldenhuys (pp. 118-20) repeatedly pairs 'Joseph and Mary' as a couple who act in conjunction with one another. He also does this in his discussion of Jesus' time with the teachers in the temple (pp. 126-27).

[34] Robert C. Tannehill, *The Narrative Unity of Luke-Acts*, vol. I, p. 19, argues that the 'central characters' in Luke's infancy narrative 'are described as devoted to the law and to the hope of Israel's redemption (1.6: Zechariah and Elizabeth; 2.23-24, 27: Mary and Joseph; 2.25: Simeon; 2.37-38: Anna). Certainly, the readers are lead to believe that both Joseph and Mary are obedient to the law. In this regard see Lenski, *The Interpretation of St. Luke's Gospel*, pp. 139-46; Craig A. Evans, *Luke*, p. 39; C.F. Evans, *Saint Luke* (London and Philadelphia: SCM Press and Trinity Press,1990), p. 212; Bock, *Luke*, I , pp. 224-25, 234-35, 240; Tannehill, *Luke*, p. 69; Garland, *Luke*, pp. 134-35. At the same time, see Carroll (*Luke*, p. 75), who writes that this section of scripture offers 'only clarity about the fidelity of Jesus' parents to God and to the Torah.'

Steven M. Sheeley, *Narrative Asides in Luke-Acts* (JSNTS 72; Sheffield: Sheffield Academic Press,1992), p. 99, helps clarify the position and action of Joseph as well as Mary in these verses. He notes with regard to the aside in 2.23 (as it is written in the law of the Lord, 'Every male that opens the womb shall be called holy to the Lord') that this 'aside makes certain that the reader is aware that the actions of Mary and Joseph are clearly linked to their piety and obedience. The parenthetical quotation of the law serves to underscore both motifs which are present in the passage (2.21-40): the consecration of Jesus to God and the obedience of his parents to the law.'

Fitzmyer (*The Gospel According to Luke*, p. 421) concludes that the narrator's 'aim is to stress fidelity to the Mosaic Law. The new form of God's salvation comes with obedience to this Law.' He suggests (*Luke*, p. 427) that Luke's references to 'the parents' in 2.27, 41, 43 and the reference to Jesus' 'father and mother' in 2.33 and to 'your father and I' in 2.48, may indicate that the Simeon episode 'existed previously in an independent form, i.e., independent of chap.1 and its mention of the virginal conception.'

For one thing, the emphasis here is on their religious and social role rather than on them personally; and the description of them as 'the parents' captures that well. Secondly, to name them in relation to Jesus (as 'the parents' does) allows the narrator to shift the focus from them as the ones who bring Jesus to the Temple to Jesus himself as the one about whom Simeon will prophesy. At the point where the narrative will focus on Jesus for the first time, the description of them as 'the parents' looks away from Mary and Joseph to the figure of Jesus.[35]

Nonetheless, Coleridge's remarks do not diminish the fact that it is as a couple that Joseph and Mary bring the child to Simeon (καὶ ἐν τῷ εἰσαγαγεῖν τοὺς γονεῖς τὸ παιδίον, 2.27).[36] In turn, it is in the respective roles of the child's 'father' (ὁ πατὴρ αὐτοῦ) and 'mother' (ἡ μήτηρ) that Joseph and Mary marvel together (θαυμάζοντες) at the response of Simeon toward the child (2.33) and, in the same positions, that they both receive a blessing from Simeon (καὶ εὐλόγησεν αὐτοὺς Συμεών, 2.34), in the process of completing their purification and the presentation of their child before the Lord (2.22-32).[37] Although the readers, having contemplated the text up to this point, might well have believed Mary's knowledge of the uniqueness and special purpose of the child was much more substantial than Joseph's, in 2.33-34, the narrator suggests that Joseph and Mary are apparently equally 'amazed' (θαυμάζοντες) by the words of Simeon and, likewise, equally touched by his 'blessing' (εὐλόγησεν) of them; even though Simeon appears to single-out Mary for a special revelation in the second part of verse thirty-

---

[35] Cf. Coleridge, *The Birth of the Lukan Narrative*, pp. 165-66.
[36] Bock (*Luke*, I, p. 257) is emphatic in his notes on Luke 2.27 that 'Joseph functioned as Jesus' father!'
[37] A.R.C. Leaney, *A Commentary on the Gospel According to St. Luke* (New York: Harper and Brothers, 1958), p. 100, believes the reference to 'his father' in 2.33 (as well as the other references to 'his parents' in 2.27, 41, 43) suggest 'Joseph was the father of Jesus' and 'strengthens the impression that we have in this chapter (2) a source distinct from that of chapter 1.' Fitzmyer (*Luke*, pp. 428-29) acknowledges that the 'text-tradition is somewhat disturbed in this (v. 33) verse.' He feels, with respect to the subject of Joseph, that the attempt by some later scribes to replace 'his father' with 'Joseph' is 'clearly a copyist's correction, which eliminates the designation of Joseph as "his father," in view of the virginal conception of chap. 1.' In addition, Hendriksen, *The Gospel of Luke*, p. 169; Tiede, *Luke*, p. 77, and Bock, *Luke*, I, p. 246, believe Simeon's blessing is aimed at both Joseph and Mary.

Ellis, *Gospel of Luke*, p. 84, argues that both 'Matthew (1.16) and Luke recognize Joseph's fatherhood both legally and, probably following Semitic thought patterns, realistically.' Ellis believes this is indicated in light of the fact that in Luke, the 'case for Jesus' messiahship rests solidly on his Davidic heritage, and nothing is made of Mary's possible descent from the tribe of Levi'. Further, Ellis adds that 'This is not, in their (Matthew's and Luke's) thinking, inconsistent with the fact that Joseph is not Jesus' natural father. The Levirate marriage (cf. 20.28) offers a partial parallel: a son by the wife of a deceased brother is viewed as the brother's son.'

2. The Portrayal of Joseph in the Gospel of Luke

four. Further, it is also as father and mother that, having 'finished everything required of the law of the Lord', they return together to the Galilee (ἐπέστρεψαν εἰς τὴν Γαλιλαίαν), with their child, and provide for his nurture and spiritual instruction (2.39-40).[38] Thus, in this pericope, readers gain more understanding of the union and relationship of Joseph and Mary as well as more understanding of their individual roles and moral and spiritual characteristics.

Even so, in the fifth pericope, 2.41-52, the focus of the text clearly begins to shift to the figure of Jesus, the son, as more and more, he becomes the primary subject of the narration.[39]

> Now every year his parents went to Jerusalem for the festival of the Passover. And, when he was twelve years old, they went up as usual for the festival. When the festival was ended and they started to return, the boy Jesus stayed behind in Jerusalem, but his parents did not know it. Assuming that he was in the group of travelers, they went a day's journey. Then they started to

---

[38] With respect to the piety of Joseph and Mary exhibited within this fourth pericope, Fitzmyer (*The Gospel According to Luke*, p. 421) thinks that in vv. 22-24 the narrator stresses 'the fidelity of Mary and Joseph, as devout and pious Jews, to all the requirements of the Mosaic Law.' He adds, 'They carry out on behalf of Jesus all the things that Luke thought were required by that Law for the birth of a child. In these verses the Law is mentioned three times (vv. 22a, 23a, 24a), and it will be referred to later in the manifestation of Simeon (v. 27) and in the conclusion of the episode.' Evans (*Luke*, p. 39) concurs with this as does Brown, *The Birth of the Messiah* (rev. ed., 1993), p. 625.

Green's comments in *Gospel of Luke*, pp. 139-40, 152-55 are also noteworthy. Green recognizes that Luke continues to disclose examples of Joseph's obedience (as well as Mary's) which is highlighted by his and Mary's concern to 'keep the law,' noting, among other things, in his comments on the pericope of the presentation and circumcision of the child, in verses twenty-one thru forty of chapter two, that Luke 'presents Jesus' family as obedient to the Lord,' and 'unquestionably pious.' Goulder (*Luke*, I, p. 255) also recognizes this. He writes: 'The triple use of the phrases "according to the Law of Moses," "as is written in the Law of the Lord," "according to what is said in the Law of the Lord," emphasizes the piety of the family'. Here, Johnson (*Gospel of Luke*, p. 54) also agrees, although he sees five references to the 'Lord's law' in the fourth pericope (2.21-40), in 2.22, 23, 24, 27, 39. Although Green (*Gospel of Luke*, p. 139) asserts that Luke inhibits the action of Joseph in much of this narrative, he, nevertheless, recognizes that the author frames his account in this section 'by demonstrations of Mary and Joseph's obedience to God (2.21, 22, 23-24, 39).' Thus, whether inadvertently or advertently, Luke continues to enunciate the theme of Joseph's obedience throughout this pericope and well into the next. Additionally, Johnson (*Gospel of Luke*, p. 56) argues that, in this pericope (2.21-40), Luke leaves his readers with the belief that 'the Messiah will emerge from within a family and social world deeply enmeshed in the traditions of Israel'. If this is Luke's intention, does this not also suggest the importance of Joseph's role in the childhood and youth of Jesus, that this milieu in which Jesus' life has been shaped has been influenced by Joseph as well as Mary?

With regard to the location of verses thirty-nine and forty of chapter two, pertaining to the return to Nazareth, most scholars place them with this pericope because it is believed these verses both end this section and provide a transition to the next.

[39] Among others, Green (*Gospel of Luke*, p. 156) notes this shift from Joseph and Mary to Jesus.

look for him among their relatives and friends. When they did not find him, they returned to Jerusalem to search for him. After three days they found him in the temple, sitting among the teachers, listening to them and asking them questions. And all who heard him were amazed at his understanding and his answers. When his parents saw him they were astonished; and his mother said to him, 'Child, why have you treated us like this? Look, your father and I have been searching for you in great anxiety.' He said to them, 'Why were you searching for me? Did you not know that I must be in my Father's house?' But they did not understand what he said to them. Then he went down with them and came to Nazareth, and was obedient to them. His mother treasured all these things in her heart. And Jesus increased in wisdom and in years, and in divine and human favor (Lk. 2.41-52).

Nonetheless, even here, the readers discover more details of the nature of Joseph's and Mary's relationship, character, and spirituality.[40] As Green recognizes, these details, in turn, constitute a reassertion of the piety of Jesus' parents and highlight 'the place of Jesus in his family and the family of Jesus as a household that serves God'.[41] Further, as Coleridge indicates, it is significant that in 2.41-42

> the language is strongly familial. Mary and Joseph are referred to as 'his parents' ... which again defines them not in themselves but in relation to Jesus, and so stresses the bond of family. It is the parents who take the initiative, with the sole reference to Jesus being the mention of his age in v. 42. The child is backgrounded in a way that again underscores the bond of family.[42]

Thus, in this pericope, the nature of Joseph's and Mary's relationship, character, and spirituality are specifically exemplified for the readers in the disclosure of their travel with their twelve year old son to Jerusalem to celebrate the annual observance of Passover, a spiritual event that the readers are told they (2.41), 'his parents' (οἱ γονεῖς αὐτοῦ), attended 'every year' (κατ' ἔτος).[43] Moreover, their relationship, character, and

---

[40] Lenski, *The Interpretation of St. Luke's Gospel*, pp. 161-62; Brown, *The Birth of the Messiah* (1977), p. 471; Evans, *Luke*, pp. 41-42; Stein, *Luke*, p. 121; Bock, *Luke*, I, pp. 263-64; and Lieu, *The Gospel of Luke*, p. 19, see Luke's report in 2.41-42 as further indication of the piety and devotion of Jesus' parents.

In regard to v. 41 it is also important to recall Bovon's discussion in *Luke*, I, p. 104 on the fourth pericope. He notes that a few later Christian scribes amended the referent to 'his parents' (2.41), here, with the personal names, 'Joseph and Mary,' in order to distinguish the roles of Joseph and Mary. It is appropriate to acknowledge that some later Christian scribal copyists did change these Lukan referents in order to diminish the role of Joseph and remove suggestions of paternal intimacy with Jesus and romantic intimacy with Mary. See also Bruce M. Metzger, *A Textual Commentary on the Greek New Testament* (Stuttgart: Deutsche Bibelgesellschaft, 2007), p. 112.

[41] Cf. Green, *Gospel of Luke*, p. 155. See also Plummer, *St. Luke*, p. 74, who notes that 'the idea of fidelity to the Law is very conspicuous' in this pericope.

[42] Cf. Coleridge, *The Birth of the Lukan Narrative*, p. 190.

[43] Green, *Gospel of Luke*, p. 155, finds support for his belief that Jesus regularly attended Passover with his family in the work of E.P. Sanders, *Judaism: Practice and Belief*

2. The Portrayal of Joseph in the Gospel of Luke 63

spirituality are also exemplified by the narrator's representations of their continual cooperation with each other in the rest of the pericope (2.42, 43, 44, 45, 46, 48, 49, 50, 51).[44]

In addition, the readers discover a fuller and richer portrait of the relationship between Joseph and Mary with Mary's explicit reference to Joseph and herself, in conversation with her son, as 'your father and I' (ὁ πατήρ σου (καὶ) ἐγώ / κἀγώ, 2.48); an identification that reflects the character of their bond with each other as well as their child.[45] It reveals that all the prior details in the early parts of the narrative that may have appeared to distinguish and separate Mary from Joseph have not prevented them from sharing the same concerns, worries, and puzzlement in response to Jesus' absence and his behavior in the scene in the temple.[46] Additionally, Mary's identification of Joseph in this way, in this context and time, likely discloses a belief she has held and articulated with respect to Joseph (that he is Jesus' father, *de facto*) for some time,

---

(Valley Forge, PA: Trinity Press International, 1992). He writes: 'Sanders (*Judaism*, pp. 129-131 and 137) not only finds evidence that families did attend (e.g., the existence of the Court of Women at the temple; Josephus *Ant.* 11.109; Exod 12. 26-27), but also remarks, "Social reality was more important than Pharisaic debates about who attended the festivals. They were times for feasting and rejoicing, and men brought their families"' (p. 131). Sanders clarification about the meaning of the Passover for Hebrew families and the role of 'men' in this regard further elucidates the role of Joseph in this pericope. See also Brown, *The Birth of the Messiah* (1977), pp. 472-73. It is certainly possible that the appearance of Jesus before the teachers within the temple, represents, as Brown states, 'Jesus' exemplifying "Temple piety"'.

[44] Coleridge, *The Birth of the Lukan Narrative*, p. 191, sees further emphasis on the family bond between Joseph and Mary and Jesus in v. 43 of this pericope. He writes: 'Again the parents appear simply as "his parents," which underscores again the family bond and therefore the parents' role and responsibility in caring for their child.' Part of the nature of Joseph's and Mary's family is also revealed in the reference to 'their relatives and friends' (τοῖς συγγενεῦσιν καὶ τοῖς γνωστοῖς, 2.44)

[45] With respect to 2.48, Tiede (*Luke*, pp. 81-82) properly recognizes that 'the phrase *your father and I* is an appeal to authority, to filial bonds and responsibilities'. Still further, certainly Tannehill (*Luke*, p. 77) is correct, with respect to 2.48, in asserting that 'there is a play on words between "your father" (Joseph) in Mary's statement and "my father" (God) in Jesus' reply. One may also see a purposeful juxtaposition, here, made by Jesus.' However, as Tannehill (Luke, p. 77) suggests, this contrast, between 'your father' (Joseph) and 'my father' (God) does not imply an end to Jesus' relationship with Joseph (or Mary for that matter). As Luke 2.51 indicates, Jesus 'returned home with his parents' and remained 'obedient to them'. Thus, it can be assumed that his parents continue to guide and instruct Jesus and enable him to grow in 'wisdom'.

[46] As Tiede (*Luke*, p. 81) notes in his commentary on 2.41-50, both parents are worried and upset about their missing child and their 'worry, distraction, and anger ... stand in marked contrast to the composure and control' Jesus shows.

It is impossible to minimize or overlook the fact that Joseph is specifically identified by Mary as 'your father' (2.48), a unique address for Joseph in these narratives. Although Green (*Gospel of Luke*, p. 156) also alludes to the emphasis here and the significance of it, he, curiously, implies that it is an 'interchange' that Luke has 'staged'.

not only to Jesus (since he was a baby), but to others as well.⁴⁷ Further, and perhaps, most significantly, Joseph's and Mary's union and piety is also revealed in their mutual longing and search for the one who has been previously identified as 'a savior' (σωτήρ, 2.11) and will be 'the salvation of God' (τὸ σωτήριον τοῦ θεοῦ, 3.6).

At the same time, the attention of the readers is also drawn to Jesus' independence (2.43, 46, 49), his spiritual acumen (2.47), and his passionate commitment to 'the matters' of the one whom he identifies as 'my father' (πατρός μου, 2.49); factors that appear to be introduced to distinguish him from Mary as well as Joseph (2.48-50).⁴⁸ Coleridge provides insight into the narrator's understanding of Joseph at this point when he writes the following:

> More than ever, the strange action of Jesus demands interpretation; and it is Mary's question that voices the demand. The narrator styles her "his mother"... in a way that underscores anew the family bond. To the same end, the narrator also has Mary refer to Jesus as "child", thus emphasizing his relationship to his parents, and Joseph as "your father". Joseph is silent throughout, but he is given pride of place in Mary's expression, "your father and I", which as De Jonge notes is an unusual word order. The effect of the word order is to stress the phrase "your father" in reference to Joseph in order to prepare for what Jesus will say in v. 49, where that question of

---

⁴⁷ The text does not appear to offer any evidence that Mary acted in any other way. Carroll (*Luke*, p. 86) notes the importance of Mary's remark when he writes: 'Verse 48 accents Joseph's identity as father of Jesus (on Mary's lips, even: "your father and I".'

⁴⁸ Leaney (*A Commentary on the Gospel According to St. Luke*, p. 103) writes that 'Verse 48 shows that a close affection bound Joseph and Mary to Jesus, and verse 44 that they allowed him much freedom.' In contrast, Fitzmyer, *Luke*, p. 438, states that Mary's 'incomprehension' seen in 2.48, 50 'reveals that she (as well as Joseph) had much to learn' with regard to Jesus. Thus, their mutual 'incomprehension' here, along with mutual 'amazement' earlier (2.33), as well as other factors, suggests Joseph and Mary are very similar, in many respects, and share much in common with respect to their understanding of Jesus. The amazement (ἐξεπλάγησαν, 2.48) and incomprehension (αὐτοὶ οὐ συνῆκαν, 2.50) of Joseph and Mary, with respect to Jesus, also unites them. Luke asserts that both of them feel these emotions (2.48, 50). While Johnson (*Gospel of Luke*, p. 61) finds the 'incomprehension of the parents' understandable and believes it 'serves a broader literary function (of Luke),' he thinks it represents 'the first note in the theme of "ignorance" that plays such an important role in Luke–Acts. Luke shows the reader how even the most faithful of the people "did not understand" in the time of the prophet's first visitation. The reader is also reminded that just as Jesus must "progress" in wisdom, so must those who follow his story, who, like Mary, "keep these words in their heart."' Is it then difficult to believe that early and later readers would not also note the similarity and commonality between the two parents of Jesus, despite certain unique experiences of Mary?

Green (*Gospel of Luke*, pp. 156-57) argues that even the parental identities, love, piety, and obedience of Joseph and Mary, authentic as they appear, run into conflict with a stronger force within the life of Jesus in Luke's account of the young Jesus teaching in the Temple.

belonging will be cast in a quite different light. Joseph's paternity is emphasized in v. 48 in order to prepare for its transcendence in v. 49.[49]

Jesus' response to his parents through the means of two apparently rhetorical questions (τί ὅτι ἐζητεῖτέ με and οὐκ ᾔδειτε ὅτι ἐν τοῖς τοῦ πατρός μου δεῖ εἶναί με, 2.49), suggests that he is challenging them to consider that he has done what he has done, in significant part, because of their examples of faith and obedience to God. He has not acted contrary to their spiritual instruction and example but, rather, in concord it.[50] How else is one to explain why and how, following his response to his parents in this befuddling encounter that the narrator then shows Jesus following Joseph and Mary and acting in obedience to them (2.51); that in the end, their union with their son, Jesus, and his continual obedience to them is affirmed in the final words of the pericope: 'Then he went down with them and came to Nazareth, and was obedient to them...' (καὶ κατέβη μετ' αὐτῶν καὶ ἦλθεν εἰς Ναζαρέθ καὶ ἦν ὑποτασσόμενος αὐτοῖς)?[51] This last reference and the rest of the pericope

---

[49] Coleridge, *The Birth of the Lukan Narrative*, pp. 197-98. As Nolland (*Luke 1-9:20*, p. 131) sees it, 'Jesus is accused of having betrayed his parents, that is, of having betrayed the calling that was his as son of Joseph.'

[50] As Lenski (*The Interpretation of St. Luke's Gospel*, p. 168) recognizes with regard to 2.49, 'Jesus' word is misunderstood when it is thought to refuse further obedience to Joseph as Jesus' earthly father, an idea that is flatly contradicted in v.51. This obedience was part of his Father's business.' Lenski (p. 169) adds to this in his remarks about 2.51. He writes: 'He (Jesus) knew himself as the Son of the Father ... and yet, not in contradiction to but in harmony with this knowledge, he went on as a child that was obedient to Joseph and Mary.'

[51] Coleridge (*The Birth of the Lukan Narrative*, p. 208) seems to confirm this when he writes that ' At first sight it seems strange that Jesus, having just announced that he must be 'in the things of my father', should return to Nazareth with Joseph and Mary. Having proclaimed his allegiance to his heavenly father, Jesus returns to the town of the man who appears to be his father. This immediately expands the sense of what it means for him to be 'in the things of my father'. It means not only that he stay unexpectedly in Jerusalem or the Temple, but also that he return with Joseph and Mary to Nazareth. Clearly, then, it is not the location that decides what it might mean for Jesus to be 'in the things of my father'. What is decisive is that wherever he is Jesus be obedient to the will of his heavenly father; and it appears that the will of his heavenly father now is that he be obedient to the will of his parents ...' Carroll (*Luke*, p. 83) certainly concurs with this by acknowledging the reference to Jesus' obedience in Lk. 2.51 as a reference to an 'ongoing state of affairs in the household of Jesus' parents.'

Green's comments (*Gospel of Luke*, p. 156) with respect to this pericope are also quite appropriate. He remarks that Jesus' 'commitment to God's purpose' emerges and changes the central character, content, and focus of the narrative. In his fitting summary of the pericope, Green writes: 'As the scene opens, Mary and Joseph are the subjects of the action, but as it unfolds Jesus takes on the active role - for the first time in the Gospel. As the scene closes, he went to Nazareth, accompanied by them, he has become the subject of the verbs.' By adding these final words in the pericope (2.51), particularly after the awkward encounter between Jesus and his parents in the temple (2.48-50), Goulder

certainly permits the readers to understand and believe that Jesus' further youth was spent in relationship with and in obedience to Joseph as well as Mary.[52] A careful reading of this pericope also permits them to acknowledge the role Joseph played in the spiritual education of Jesus and in the ultimate destiny of Jesus.[53]

Subsequently, Joseph reappears in the genealogy of Jesus in 3.23-38. But, this reference does not add anything new to the portrait. Rather, the words that Jesus 'was the son (as was thought) of Joseph' (ὢν υἱός, ὡς ἐνομίζετο Ἰωσήφ, 3.23) both confirm what the readers have already been told (1.27 and 2.4) and reiterate earlier statements about the virginity and purity of Mary and Joseph's absence in the process of the generation of Jesus (1.26-38).[54]

(*Luke*, I, pp. 266-67) believes 'Luke has trodden a wary path which allows the reader to think well of parents and child alike ...'

[52] As Nolland (*Luke 1–9:20*, pp.132, 134) suggests, 'Jesus had not betrayed his sonship. In fact, he had no intention of dishonoring either of his sonships. Here, however, in the encounter with his distressed parents, this maturing child has set before him something of the complexity of the relationship between his identity as Son of God and as son in the family of Joseph.'

[53] Without formally acknowledging the role of Joseph in the spiritual education of Jesus, Fitzmyer (*Luke*, p. 438) observes that in 2.41-52, as in 2.22-38, this episode about Jesus 'is dominated by Jewish piety, fidelity, and respect for custom, and it goes further in emphasizing the training of the young Jewish male, and the celebration of the most important pilgrim feast in the Jewish calendar. Not only has Jesus been incorporated into Judaism and marked with the sign of the covenant (circumcision, 2.21), but he is now shown to be one trained in the Torah and its requirements and fulfilling his obligations, even in advance.' See also Ellis, *Gospel of Luke*, p. 85, who adds that 'At thirteen years of age a Jewish boy entered into the full responsibilities of adulthood. During the prior year the father (in this case, Joseph) was required to acquaint him with the duties and regulations which he was soon to assume.'

It is curious that with respect to the length of the relationship between Joseph and Jesus that Lenski (*The Interpretation of St. Luke's Gospel*, p. 169) suggests that 'Nothing further is said about Joseph. From the strong periphrastic imperfect it is fair to conclude that he lived for some years after this occurrence.'

[54] Fitzmyer's translation of this Greek phrase as 'in the minds of the people' seems most appropriate. See his text, *Luke*, p. 489.

Creed, *St. Luke*, p. 59, states 'it may be safely inferred that the circles in which the genealogies originated regarded Jesus as the son of Joseph'. See also Nolland, *Luke 1-9:20*, pp. 169, 171, and Evans, *Luke*, p. 60. Creed (*St. Luke*, p. 59) also believes ὡς ἐνομίζετο is 'an addition to cover a discrepancy with the circumstances of the conception as they had been related' in chapter one. In contrast, Marshall (*Gospel of Luke*, p. 157) writes that 'there is no inconsistency in Luke's mind between the account of the virgin birth and the naming of Joseph as one of the parents of Jesus. From the legal point of view, Joseph was the earthly father of Jesus, and there was no other way of reckoning his descent. There is no evidence that the compilers of the genealogies thought otherwise.' It is also recognized by Brown (*The Birth of the Messiah* [1977], p. 301), who states that the fact that Luke asserts that Mary can only come to bear the Christ-child with the help of 'power from the Most High' (1.35) is further confirmed in this later statement (3.23) by Luke, that 'Jesus was only the "supposed son" of Joseph'. Tiede (*Luke*, p. 96)

2. The Portrayal of Joseph in the Gospel of Luke

Lastly, there is one final reference to 'Joseph' in 4.16-30. Here, Jesus is explicitly identified by his listeners as the 'son of Joseph' in 4.22.[55] Early in this pericope, which recounts the rejection of Jesus at Nazareth (4.16-30), the readers are told: 'All spoke well of him and were amazed at the gracious words that came from his mouth. They said, "Is not this Joseph's son?"' (οὐχὶ υἱός ἐστιν Ἰωσὴφ οὗτος, 4.22). While this reference to Joseph is very brief, it is, nonetheless, important for it would provide further evidence for the readers that Joseph is formally identified by worshippers in the synagogue in his community of Nazareth as the father of Jesus and Jesus as his son. It might also explain why the members of the synagogue were amazed (ἐθαύμαζον, 4.22) and perhaps, even puzzled or troubled by the declaration of Jesus that the scriptures he had read from Isaiah had been fulfilled (πεπλήρωται, 4.21) before them.[56] After

---

agrees and feels this genealogy provides further proof 'of Jesus' legitimate paternity from David' which 'is reckoned through Joseph ...' C.F. Evans (*Saint Luke*, p. 254) likewise agrees and believes the reference in the parenthesis is from Luke and suggests only that Luke understood that 'Jesus could be "commonly presumed" to be Joseph's son.' Stein (*Luke*, p. 142) concurs with this.

Sheeley (*Narrative Asides in Luke-Acts*, p. 110) states that the 'aside in 3.23 is necessary for the reader's benefit. Certainly the reader cannot be expected to believe that Jesus is the son of Joseph, having read the story of Mary's virginal conception and coming on the heels of the baptismal christening by God. The narrator, however, makes it clear to the reader that the people with whom Jesus came into contact considered him to be the son of Joseph. The only people who knew the circumstances surrounding the conception of Jesus were those intimately involved with the family (Mary, Joseph, and perhaps Elizabeth and Zechariah and the reader). The reader is in possession of information which very few people have, and the narrator reinforces the knowledge by reminding the reader of her or his privileged position.' See also Nolland, *Luke 1-9:20*, p. 174.

It should be noted that Bovon (*Luke*, I, pp. 136-37) disagrees with this assessment. He writes: 'As for grammar, ενομιζετο ("he was considered [to be]") can be read with two very different meanings: (1) "He was considered to be Joseph's biological son" (but, I, Luke, know this is not true); (2) "He was rightfully declared to be Joseph's son" (and I, Luke, agree with this). The genealogy would tend to lose its significance if the first translation was chosen, and this detracts from its likelihood.' Goulder (*Luke*, I, p. 283), somewhat differently, insists that 'Luke's intention is clear' and that it is to assert that 'Jesus was really God's Son (1-2) and has now been assured that this is so (3.21f)...' This was the case, whatever the thoughts of others (3.21; 4.22). Ellis (*Gospel of Luke*, p. 93) appears to concur with Goulder. He writes: 'Unlike Matthew, Luke does not place the genealogy among the birth narratives but among the series of episodes attesting the messiahship of Jesus. It seems, therefore, that this messianic motif is the primary reason for listing Messiah's descent from Adam, the son of God (3.38).'

Lenski (*The Interpretation of St. Luke's Gospel*, pp. 218-20) proposes that Luke's genealogy is (unlike Matthew's) focused on Mary's ancestors.

[55] See the parallels to this in the Gospel of John (1.45 and, particularly, 6.42).

[56] Plummer (*S. Luke*, p. 125) thinks this 'question is ... a summary' of the 'scepticism' of the members of the synagogue. Likewise, Nolland (*Luke 1-9:20*, p. 199) thinks 'Luke's narrative requires that these words express an objection to Jesus' claims'. Lenski, *The Interpretation of St. Luke's Gospel*, p. 254; Evans, *Saint Luke*, p. 273, and Bock, *Luke*, vol. I, p. 414, agree with Plummer and Nolland. Taking a somewhat different approach,

all, Jesus was one of them; as they supposed and believed, 'the son of Joseph'. However, it would probably not be completely clear to the readers if the question about Joseph's relationship to Jesus, constructed as it is, suggests Joseph is alive.

Alessandro Falcetta, 'The Call of Nazareth: Form and Exegesis of Luke 4:16-30,' in *Cahiers de la Revue Biblique* (Paris: J. Gabalda, 2003), pp. 53, 56, and 57, argues that the 'question of the Nazarenes' in 4.16-30 'focuses on the identity of the father of Jesus'. Their 'blindness consists in the inability of seeing beneath the surface of what they think they know: Jesus' apparent origin does not match his words.' Falcetta believes the disbelief of the Nazarenes is 'one stage' of 'the lengthy process of recognition of Jesus' identity' which he is convinced is a 'major Lukan theme'.

In contrast, Creed (*St. Luke*, p. 67) believes the question need not express more 'than surprise'. In turn, Evans (*Luke*, p. 71) believes it actually expresses 'pleasant surprise'. Likewise, Tannehill (*Luke*, p. 93) does not think this question is meant 'to denigrate Jesus but to point out that he is a hometown boy'. Lieu (*The Gospel of Luke*, p. 33) concurs with this.

3

The Portrayal of Joseph the Carpenter in the Gospel of John

While the portrayal of Joseph in the Gospel of John is not as detailed and substantial as the portrayals found in the Gospels of Matthew and Luke, it still offers two explicit references to 'Joseph' in which Jesus is identified as the 'son of Joseph' (υἱὸν τοῦ Ἰωσὴφ, 1.45; ὁ υἱὸς Ἰωσήφ, 6.42); references that both intrigue and challenge readers. Though John's Gospel begins with a prologue that extends back into eternity, readers are only introduced to Joseph in the context of the beginning of Jesus' ministry. Thus, by the time the readers encounter the figure of Joseph in the narrative of John, they have already been told that Jesus is 'the Word' (ὁ λόγος, 1.1), 'was with God' (ἦν πρὸς τὸν θεόν, 1.1), 'was present with God in the beginning' (ἦν ἐν ἀρχῇ πρὸς τὸν θεόν, 1.2), and that 'through him all things came into being' (πάντα δι' αὐτοῦ ἐγένετο, 1.3). At the same time, they have also been told that Jesus was the 'Word' (ὁ λόγος, 1.1, 14) that 'became flesh' (σὰρξ ἐγένετο, 1.14) and 'dwelled among us' (ἐσκήνωσεν ἐν ἡμῖν, 1.14) and is the 'only begotten God' (μονογενὴς θεός, 1.18), the divine son of God. Even further, the readers have been told that Jesus is 'the Lamb of God' (ὁ ἀμνὸς τοῦ θεοῦ, 1.29, 36) 'who takes away the world's sin' (ὁ αἴρων τὴν ἁμαρτίαν τοῦ κόσμου, 1.29). At the same time, he has also been identified as 'the son of God' (ὁ υἱὸς τοῦ θεοῦ, 1.34), 'Rabbi' (ῥαββί, 1.38), 'the Messiah' (τὸν Μεσσίαν, 1.41), and 'Christ' (Χριστός, 1.41), designations that largely direct readers to the divine character of Jesus' person and draw their attention to his close and special relationship with God.[1] Therefore, when they are introduced to the assertion that Jesus is the 'son of Joseph' (υἱὸν τοῦ Ἰωσήφ, 1.45), the readers are both challenged to contemplate

---

[1] These designations are also followed, after the initial introduction of Joseph, with other important designations for Jesus, including 'King of Israel', that further emphasize Jesus' divine character.

the role and significance of Joseph as well as expand their perceptions of Jesus.² The text reads:

> The next day Jesus decided to go to Galilee. He found Philip and said to him, 'Follow me.' Now Philip was from Bethsaida, the city of Andrew and Peter. Philip found Nathanael and said to him, 'We have found him about whom Moses in the law and also the prophets wrote, Jesus son of Joseph of Nazareth.' Nathanael said to him, 'Can anything good come out of Nazareth?' Philip said to him, 'Come and see.' When Jesus saw Nathanael coming toward him, he said of him, 'Here is truly an Israelite in whom there is no deceit! Nathanael asked him, 'Where did you get to know me?' Jesus answered, 'I saw you under the fig tree before Philip called you.' Nathanael replied, 'Rabbi, you are the Son of God! You are the King of Israel! Jesus answered, 'Do you believe because I told you that I saw you under the fig tree? You will see greater things than these.' And he said to him, 'Very truly, I tell you, you will see heaven opened and the angels of God ascending and descending upon the Son of Man' (Jn 1.43-51).

In this first reference to Joseph, Philip, a recent follower of Jesus, tells Nathanael, a prospective disciple, that he has 'found him about whom Moses in the law and also the prophets wrote, Jesus son of Joseph from Nazareth (ὃν ἔγραψεν Μωϋσῆς ἐν τῷ νόμῳ καὶ οἱ προφῆται εὑρήκαμεν, Ἰησοῦν υἱὸν τοῦ Ἰωσὴφ τὸν ἀπὸ Ναζαρέτ, 1.45).'³ As such, Philip's identification of Jesus as 'son of Joseph' and 'from Nazareth', coming as it

---

² In this regard, see R. Alan Culpepper, *The Gospel and the Letters of John* (Nashville, TN: Abingdon, 1998), p. 124, where he writes: 'Since so much attention has been given to Jesus' origin from God in the prologue (of John), the reader cannot miss the contrast' between the earlier designations of the narrator about Jesus and Philip's declaration that Jesus is the 'son of Joseph from Nazareth'.

³ B.F. Westcott, *The Gospel According to St. John* (Grand Rapids: Eerdmans, 1881, Reprinted 1981), p. 26, translating Ἰησοῦν υἱὸν τοῦ Ἰωσὴφ τὸν ἀπὸ Ναζαρέτ, 1.45 as 'Jesus of Nazareth, the son of Joseph', states that 'Philip describes the Lord by the name under which He would be commonly known'. See also Rudolf Schnackenburg, *The Gospel According to St. John,* vol. I (New York: The Seabury Press, 1980), p. 315 and Andreas J. Kostenberger, *John* (Grand Rapids: Baker Academic, 2004), p. 80. In his later more detailed text on the Gospel of John, B.F. Westcott, *The Gospel According to St. John: The Greek Text with Introduction and Notes* (London: John Murray, 1908), p. 54, notes Philip's declaration that he has 'found him about whom Moses in the law and also the prophets wrote, Jesus son of Joseph from Nazareth indicates that he 'recognised in One whom he knew as truly man, the fulfillment of all the promises of Scripture.' This, according to Westcott (*The Gospel According to St. John*, p. 54), stands in 'contrast' to the response in 6.42. See also F.F. Bruce, *The Gospel of John* (Grand Rapids: Eerdmans, 1983), pp. 59–60; Andrew T. Lincoln, *The Gospel According to Saint John* (London and New York: Continuum, 2005), p. 120.

It is interesting that Jesus is identified as the 'son of Joseph' in two encounters around the Sea of Galilee, some distance from Nazareth (1.43-45; 6.24, 59). This may suggest Jesus was often identified as the 'son of Joseph'. In addition, it is also fascinating that the reference to 'Nazareth' in this pericope is the first in this Gospel (1.45, 46; 18.5, 7; 19.19).

does after repeated words about Jesus' divinity and representations of his divine capacity, would likely surprise the readers.[4]

Further, having been clearly and repeatedly informed of the divine nature of Jesus, these words challenge the readers to consider his human character, and particularly, the historical and familial relationships and realities pertaining to Jesus.[5] As they learn of Jesus' associations with 'Joseph' and 'Nazareth', they are reminded that just as Jesus was the 'Word' (ὁ λόγος, 1.1, 14), the 'only begotten God' (μονογενὴς θεός, 1.18), the divine son of God, he was also 'the Word' that 'became flesh' (σὰρξ ἐγένετο, 1.14) and 'dwelled among us' (ἐσκήνωσεν ἐν ἡμῖν, 1.14); that he was relationally attached as a 'son' (υἱὸν) to a particular person, a father, in the history of his life, named, 'Joseph', as well as attached to a physical and historical place, named, 'Nazareth'.[6] With respect to the

---

[4] See F. Godet, *Commentary on the Gospel of John*, vol. I (New York: Funk and Wagnalls, 1886), p. 333; Rudolf Bultmann, *The Gospel of John: A Commentary* (Philadelphia: The Westminster Press, 1971), pp. 103-104; Hermann N. Ridderbos, *The Gospel according to John: A Theological Commentary* (trans. John Vriend; Grand Rapids: Eerdmans, 1997), p. 88. Somewhat differently, J. Ramsey Michaels, *New International Biblical Commentary: John* (Peabody, MA: Hendrickson Publishers, 1989), p. 39, believes Philip's 'startling bit of news' to Nathanael includes the fact that Jesus 'son of Joseph', the one who is 'the Messiah' is, as Nathanael, a 'fellow Galilean'.

[5] E.M. Sidebottom, *The Christ of the Fourth Gospel* (London: SPCK, 1961), p. 97, believes the two references to Jesus as the 'son of Joseph' are important referents to his humanity. He states that Jesus' humanity 'is emphasized more obviously and deliberately here [in John] than in the synoptics. His origin and name are stressed: "They said, Is not this Jesus, the son of Joseph, whose father and mother we know? How can he now say, I have come down from heaven? Philip tells Nathanael, We have found him of whom Moses in the Law and the prophets wrote -Jesus of Nazareth, the son of Joseph"'. J. Ramsey Michaels, *The New International Commentary on the New Testament: John* (Grand Rapids: Eerdmans, 2010), p. 128 disagrees. He writes: 'Even without birth narratives, they (the readers) would have known that "son of Joseph" and "Son of God" are not contradictory terms. "The Word came in human flesh," after all (v.14), and "son of Joseph" is as legitimate expression as any for "human flesh." As to the virgin birth, the term "son of Joseph" neither implies nor excludes it, as the birth narratives in Matthew and Luke both recognize.'

[6] J.H. Bernard, *A Critical and Exegetical Commentary on the Gospel According to St. John* (Edinburgh: T. and T. Clark, 1928), p. 62, argues that 'it is certain that the author of the Fourth Gospel did not regard Jesus as a "son of Joseph"; for him Jesus was μονογενὴς θεός.' Similarly, C.K. Barrett, *The Gospel According to St. John* (London: SPCK, 1955), p. 153, concurs that it 'is in accord with his (John's) ironical use of traditional material that he (John) should allow Jesus to be ignorantly described as "son of Joseph" while himself believing that Jesus had no human father.' This perspective appears similar to that of R.H. Lightfoot, *St. John's Gospel* (Oxford: Clarendon Press, 1956), p. 103, who states that 'Here' (in 1.45) 'the words ('son of Joseph') are used by one called indeed to be a disciple and prepared to see the promises of the O.T. fulfilled in Him, but as yet without the deeper understanding of His Person.' In this regard, see also Schnackenburg, *St. John*, vol. I, p. 315 and Kostenberger, *John*, pp. 80-81. In contrast, Raymond Brown, *The Gospel According to John*, pp. i-xii (Garden City, NY: Doubleday, 1966), p. 82, states that the designation ' "Jesus, son of Joseph" is the normal way of distinguishing this

association of Jesus with Nazareth in John, it is also important to note that he is later identified as 'the Nazarene' (τὸν Ναζωραῖον) in Jn 18.5 and 7 and (ὁ Ναζωραῖος) in 19.19. As such, in these references to 'Joseph' and 'Nazareth', readers are introduced to a tension within the narrative evoked by the dual portrayals of Jesus as both the divine son of God (illustrated by the particular references to the divine character of Jesus, noted in the first chapter as well as the following chapters) and the earthly son of Joseph, both the son of the One who transcends earth and the world and the son of one who is part and parcel, of the earth and the world, of Joseph and of Nazareth.[7]

And yet the readers already know, from what they have read in the text about the identity of Jesus, that God has chosen to reveal his salvation through this particular historical and human figure. Thus, they know more than Nathanael, before he responds to Philip's declaration with the skeptical question, 'Can anything good come out of Nazareth?' (ἐκ Ναζαρὲτ δύναταί τι ἀγαθὸν εἶναι, 1.46).[8] As such, the readers are not astonished when Jesus surprises Nathanael by disclosing that he has

---

particular Jesus from others of the same name at Nazareth ...' and believes this holds true for the use of this phrase in 6.42 as well. For a similar assessment, see also D.A. Carson, *The Gospel According to John* (Grand Rapids: Eerdmans, 1991), p. 159. Additionally, Bultmann (*The Gospel of John*, p. 104) correctly notes that 'Joseph's fatherhood' is not disputed within the text. See also Ernst Haenchen, *John 1: A Commentary on the Gospel of John* (Philadelphia: Fortress Press, 1984), p. 166.

Bultmann (*Gospel of John*, p. 104) also states that the reference to 'Jesus' origins in Nazareth' is also not 'modified by the assertion that he was born in Bethlehem.' Several other scholars acknowledge the association of the village of 'Nazareth' with Jesus and recognize that reference to it is not found in either literature before John (in the Old Testament, Hebrew Scriptures) or contemporary literature (the Talmud or Midrash or current pagan narratives and apologetics). See especially the work of R.H. Lightfoot, *St. John's Gospel*, p. 103; Lindars, *The Gospel of John*, p. 118; Schnackenburg, *St. John*, vol. I, p. 315; F.F. Bruce, *The Gospel of John*, p. 60; George R. Beasley-Murray, *John* (Word Biblical Commentary; Waco, TX: Word Books, 1987), p. 27; Herman N. Ridderbos, *The Gospel according to John: A Theological Commentary*, p. 88; Kostenberger, *John*, p. 81; Lincoln, *Gospel According to Saint John*, p. 120.

[7] Edwyn Hoskyns, *The Fourth Gospel* (London: Faber and Faber, 1947), p. 182, confirms the presence of this tension by stating 'Philip is still satisfied with the assertion that Jesus, the son of Joseph and the man from Nazareth, is the Christ who was foretold by Moses and by the prophets of Israel ...' Bultmann (*The Gospel of John*, p. 104) also highlights this tension. He writes that 'the offence of the Messiah's coming from Nazareth belongs, as the Evangelist understands it, to the offence of the incarnation of the Logos. No attempt is made to give a rational defence. Nathanael is simply told: "Come and see!"' Lincoln (*Gospel According to Saint John*, p. 120) also alludes to this tension.

[8] Ridderbos (*The Gospel according to John*, p. 88) points out that Nathanael's 'objection concerned Nazareth as Jesus' place of origin (he does not mention Jesus' father) ...' In this regard, see also C.H. Dodd, *Historical Tradition in the Fourth Gospel* (London: Cambridge University Press, 1963), p. 311 n. 1, who notes that 'Nathaniel ... is clearly thinking of an individual known, as was usual, by name and patronymic, and the fact that he comes from Nazareth makes it unlikely that he can amount to much.'

3. *The Portrayal of Joseph in the Gospel of John* 73

foreknowledge of Nathanael's location and identity (1.47-48). Thus, the connection of Jesus to 'Joseph' and 'Nazareth' helps the readers comprehend the disbelief of Nathanael; a disbelief that gives way to unbridled faith in the confession of this 'true Israelite' that Jesus is 'the Messiah' and the 'King of Israel' (1.49).

Several chapters later, in 6.41-51, Jesus' relationship to Joseph is again addressed.

> Then the Jews began to complain about him because he said, 'I am the bread that came down from heaven.' They were saying, 'Is not this Jesus, the son of Joseph, whose father and mother we know? How can he now say, 'I have come down from heaven?' Jesus answered them, 'Do not complain among yourselves. No one can come to me unless drawn by the Father who sent me; and I will raise that person up on the last day. It is written in the prophets, 'And they shall all be taught by God.' Everyone who has heard and learned from the Father comes to me. Not that anyone has seen the Father except the one who is from God; he has seen the Father. Very truly, I tell you, whoever believes has eternal life. I am the bread of life. Your ancestors ate the manna in the wilderness, and they died. This is the bread that comes down from heaven, so that one may eat of it and not die. I am the living bread that came down from heaven. Whoever eats of this bread will live forever; and the bread that I will give for the life of the world is my flesh' (Jn 6.41-51).

In this second reference to Joseph, in contrast to the first in ch. 1, the readers discover that a group, identified as 'the Jews' (οἱ Ἰουδαῖοι, 6.41), a group with a different perspective than that of the early followers of Jesus (1.35-51), exhibited earlier in the text, also acknowledge the relationship between Jesus and Joseph (6.42).[9] In the apparent context of a synagogue in the town of Capernaum on the Sea of Galilee (6.24, 29), the readers are told that the members of this group explicitly identify Jesus as 'the son of Joseph' (ὁ υἱὸς Ἰωσήφ, 6.42).[10] Further, their additional comments ('whose father and mother we know, οὗ ἡμεῖς οἴδαμεν

---

[9] Bernard (*Gospel According to St. John*, pp. 202-203) believes 'the Jews' are 'natives of Galilee and acquainted with the household at Nazareth.' Hoskyns, *The Fourth Gospel*, p. 296, asserts that the 'paternity of Jesus is ... well known to the Jews in the synagogue at Capernaum ...' In this regard, see also Schnackenburg, *St. John*, vol. II, p. 49. Somewhat differently, Barrett (*Gospel According to St. John*, pp. 244-45) believes John 'alludes' to Jesus' virgin birth in 6.41-51, suggesting that 'if the objectors had known the truth about Jesus' parentage they would have been compelled to recognize that it was entirely congruent with his having come down from heaven.' Michaels, *John*, p. 110, argues that Jesus' identity as 'son of Joseph' verifies, in this second pericope, that the divine, the true 'manna' is the 'flesh-and-blood person who stands before them–Jesus the son of Joseph. Jesus does not merely give bread ... He is that bread; in all that he says and does ...'

[10] Cf. Bruce, *Gospel of John*, p. 155. In contrast to Jesus' identification in 1.45 as 'son of Joseph' (υἱὸν τοῦ Ἰωσήφ), here, Jesus is identified as 'the son of Joseph' (ὁ υἱὸς Ἰωσήφ) in 6.42. Barnabas Lindars, *The Gospel of John* (London: Marshall, Morgan, and Scott, 1972), p. 117, recognizes this additional qualification as an attempt to offer 'fuller detail'

τὸν πατέρα καὶ τὴν μητέρα, 6.42), expand this second assertion and verify Joseph's position as Jesus' father as well as his marriage and relationship to Jesus' mother (6.42) for readers.[11] Indeed, by speaking of Joseph in the present tense, they suggest to the readers that Joseph's role in the life of Jesus is ongoing and has been of a substantial length.[12] And, yet, as in the protest of Nathanael, the readers see that the protest of the members of this group, of 'the Jews', as they are identified, is based on the fact that they do acknowledge Jesus' father and mother to be the real earthly parents of Jesus.[13] Still further, this group highlights their protest for the readers by adding the question, 'How can he *now* say, "I have come down from heaven."?' (πῶς νῦν λέγει ὅτι ἐκ τοῦ οὐρανοῦ

---

about Jesus' human background. He believes 'these details are necessary' for the later dialogue in the pericope. In addition, see Judith Lieu, 'Anti-Judaism, the Jews, and the Worlds of the Fourth Gospel,' in Richard Bauckham and Carl Moser, eds., *The Gospel of John and Christian Theology* (Grand Rapids: Eerdmans, 2008), p. 176, who believes Jesus' statement in 4.22 that 'salvation is from the Jews,' is informative for 6.42. While this seems a real possibility, could it not also be the case that both the references to Jesus as 'son of Joseph' in 1.45 and 6.42 suggest or even verify this idea of 4.22?

Still further, Carson, *Gospel According to John*, pp.159-60, agrees with Barrett (see earlier note) that the narrator uses irony in the use of 'son of Joseph' but only with respect to its use, here, in 6.42.

Additionally, Michaels (*John* [2010], p. 384) points out that in the Gospel of John "Capernaum ... is as much Jesus' home as Nazareth ...' Thus, one might conclude that the individuals criticizing Jesus at this point might well have encountered his parents at his home in Capernaum or, more likely, in synagogue in Capernaum.

[11] It is also important to note that this is the first and only reference to the mother of Jesus in these two pericopes.

[12] Michaels (*John* [2010], p. 383, n. 5) intriguingly notes that 'Jesus could have been known by reputation as "son of Joseph," even by those not personally acquainted with his father or mother, suggesting that Jesus might well have been sometimes addressed as "Jesus, son of Joseph" or "Jesus bar Joseph" as well as as "Jesus of Nazareth." He adds (p. 384, fn.6) that although 'the absence of Jesus' father ... at the Cana wedding (2.1) and at Capernaum afterward (2.12) suggests that he was probably dead by this time ... "the Jews" claim to "know" (ἡμεῖς οἴδαμεν) both the father and the mother, as if both are still alive.'

[13] J. Marsh, *Saint John* (London: Penguin, 1983), p. 304, summarizes the objection of the members of this group by stating that 'since Jesus' parentage is known (and normal?) it cannot be the instrument of any divine revelation: for natural process is natural process.' Haenchen (*John*, p. 292) concurs and adds that the narrator 'assumes ... that Jesus as a true man, had an earthly father and mother; he further assumes that this does not deny that he came from God. It is not said that one encountered this opinion only among "Jews"; it is possible that the Evangelist also knew Christians for whom the acceptance of a human father for Jesus was not compatible with their Christology as, for example, those represented in Matthew and Luke.' In this regard, see also Michaels, *John* (2010), pp. 383-84.

καταβέβηκα, 6.42).[14] Thus, these who protest Jesus' claim find it impossible to acknowledge, as the readers realize, that it is also possible for Jesus to have come out of heaven, for God to reveal the salvation of humanity 'in history', through the very 'man, whose father and mother they know …'[15] After all, as the readers would probably admit, the kind of divinity claimed for Jesus, is not usually manifested in the very humble and ordinary context in which Jesus appears to have emerged.[16]

Thus, the repetition of this designation and identification of Jesus in this second reference, coming as it does after even more revelations of the divinity of Jesus (in chs. 3, 4 and 5), heightens the interest of the readers and, again, draws their attention to Jesus' connection and relationship with Joseph. At the same time, this reaffirmation of the relationship by this second reference to Jesus as 'the son of Joseph' (ὁ υἱὸς Ἰωσήφ, 6.42) and by the further assertion, previously noted, that Joseph is 'the father' (τὸν πατέρα, 6.42) of Jesus, leads readers both to appreciate the person of Joseph and comprehend better the extent and significance of his role in the life of Jesus. In turn, the specific representations of Joseph in 1.45 and 6.42, also remind readers of the dual nature of the person of Jesus (that he is both human and divine). In the process, these portrayals also lead readers to recall the historical and physical character of Jesus' life, ministry, suffering, resurrection, and salvation that the narrator details. Therefore, in the end, these particular representations of Joseph (as well as the representations of the mother of Jesus) enlarge and enhance Jesus' portrayal.

Additionally, it may not be without significance that the mother of Jesus is not identified by name within the prior pericopes noted or anywhere in John's narrative. She is mentioned in several passages as 'the mother of Jesus' (ἡ μήτηρ τοῦ Ἰησοῦ, 2.1, 3), 'his mother' (ἡ μήτηρ αὐτοῦ, 2.5, 12; 19.25), 'mother' (μητέρα, 6.42), and 'your mother' (ἡ

---

[14] Leon Morris, *The Gospel According to John* (Grand Rapids: Eerdmans, 1971), p. 371 believes that the use of 'now' in 6.42 should be interpreted as follows: '"Now" means "after all the years He has lived like anyone else."'

[15] Bultmann, *The Gospel of John*, p. 229. Lincoln, *Gospel According to Saint John*, p. 230, also recounts an important point with respect to 6.42. He writes that 'The evangelist and those whom he represents want to maintain the paradox of the incarnation in which both perspectives (divine and human) on Jesus' origins are true, because he is the divine Logos who has become flesh. The Jewish opposition to such Christian claims insisted that the earthly perspective was sufficient to categorize Jesus.'

[16] Jerome H. Neyrey, S.J., *The Gospel of John* (Cambridge: Cambridge University Press, 2007), p. 126, n. 179, points out that 'Encomia and bioi in antiquity begin by noting gender, generation, and geography; noble people necessarily come from noble poleis (not Nazareth) and from noble families and parents (not peasant laborers), but, of course, the crowd does not know that Jesus' geography is the heavenly world and that God is his Father.'

μήτηρ σου, 19.27) but is never identified by name, as Joseph is.[17] Nonetheless, her portrayal in the later account of the passion in John raises questions about the actual significance the absence of her name would ultimately have for the readers. In 19.25-27, the narrator relates an encounter between the dying Jesus, the 'disciple whom he loved' and Jesus' mother that has a bearing upon the portrayal of Joseph in this gospel. Beginning in v. 25, John writes:

> Meanwhile, standing near the cross of Jesus were his mother, his mother's sister, Mary the wife of Clopas, and Mary Magdalene. When Jesus saw his mother and the disciple whom he loved standing beside her, he said to his mother, 'Woman, here is your son.'[18] Then he said to his disciple, 'Here is your mother.'[19] And, from that hour the disciple took her into his own home (Jn 19.25).

It would have been difficult for the readers not to be affected by the words of Jesus in this encounter and not to be led to serious reflection upon them. The impact and effect of this scripture on the perception, understanding, and representation of the mother of Jesus (and, in turn, on the perception, understanding, and representation of Joseph) has been profound. In particular, the words, 'Behold, your mother' (ἴδε ἡ μήτηρ σου, 19.27) spoken by the dying Jesus to 'the disciple whom he loved', invites readers to reflect and speculate upon the future role and significance of the mother of Jesus. In addition, these words also suggest that the mother of Jesus had already achieved a special position within the Johannine community. Thus, it is likely that the poignancy and content of this account would assume a priority even over the earlier affirmations of the role of Joseph for the readers. Although, as has been acknowledged, Joseph is the first of Jesus' parents to be introduced to the readers (1.45), and the only one named, with the mother of Jesus being introduced shortly thereafter (2.1, 3, 5, 12), and both being referenced together later (6.42), the readers' eyes are drawn to Jesus' other parent at this point in the narrative. For it is the mother of Jesus who is the last parent to appear in the narrative and her appearance (19.25-27), amplified by Jesus' words to and about her (λέγει τῇ μητρί· γύναι, ἴδε ὁ υἱός

---

[17] Morris (*John*, p. 178), who chooses to 'comment on the absence of any mention of Joseph' in the context in which the mother of Jesus is first mentioned in the Gospel of John, in 2.1,3, 5, 12, is one of the few scholars who raise this issue.

The fact that the mother of Jesus is not mentioned by name in the Gospel of John does not suggest that she is unimportant for the narrator. Alan Culpepper, *Anatomy of the Fourth Gospel* (Philadelphia: Fortress Press, 1983), pp. 133-34, along with others, has acknowledged the significance of the mother of Jesus in this Gospel. However, he has put this significance in proper perspective.

[18] Here, the Greek text ἴδε ὁ υἱός σου literally reads, 'Behold, your son.'

[19] Similarly, here, the Greek text ἴδε ἡ μήτηρ σου literally reads, 'Behold, your mother.'

σου. εἶτα λέγει τῷ μαθητῇ· ἴδε ἡ μήτηρ σου, 19.26b-27), enhances her character and role in this Gospel.

Thus, the narrator emphasizes the importance of Joseph to the readers in order that they may understand Jesus' humanity (1.45; 6.42), and raises the prospect that Joseph may still be present for part of the ministry of Jesus (6.42).[20] Nevertheless, the absence of Joseph from the narrative in 19.25-27 strongly suggests that he has expired by the time of Jesus' crucifixion.

Conclusion: The Canonic Portrayals of Joseph the Carpenter

Having offered a careful reading of these three canonic narratives, what portraits emerge to which later narrators and artists would have access to inform their own work? This conclusion seeks to make these canonic portraits clear.

In Matthew, they would find a portrayal of Joseph that depicts his unusual relationship to Mary and to her child – where he is represented as her husband but not identified as the biological father of her child (1.16). This portrait reveals the fear and anguish that gripped him when he discovers that Mary, his betrothed, was pregnant (1.18-19); how these troubles led him to prayer, sleep, and how in this time an angel of God spoke to him, reassuring him, directing him to accept the child of Mary, and to name him, thus claiming this child as his own (1.20-21). They would learn that Joseph not only believes what the angel of God has told him but follows God's directions, not only accepting Mary and the child, but also abstaining from sexual intimacy with her for a certain period, and naming the child 'Jesus' (1.24-25).

The portrait also reveals a Joseph to whom God continues to speak directives through dreams, directives which Joseph always, without question, obeys to the letter, with identical language often occurring in both the command and the description of Joseph's obedience. Such obedience is seen in the account of the second dream where Joseph is directed to take Mary and the child and flee to Egypt, a command Joseph fulfills exactly (2.13-15), remaining faithfully in Egypt until his next divine encounter that appears to take a couple of years in narrative time (2.14-15). This obedience, spirituality, and care for his family are also underscored in the account of his third dream (in 2.19-21), when he is directed to return with Mary and the child to the land of Israel. As Matthew relates, Joseph obeys God's command in this dream as well (2.21).

---

[20] As such, while Joseph has literary and narrative significance, it is curious that he never actually appears within the text, as does the mother of Jesus. So, in essence, it could be said that with respect to Joseph in this gospel narrative, we have a characterization without a character.

However, on this occasion Joseph's obedient response is delayed by what he hears – Archelaus is 'ruling over Judea in place of his father Herod' – which makes him 'afraid to go there' (2.22). At this point he is warned in yet another dream (2.22-23) to go to the district of Galilee. Apparently, discerning his way from there, Joseph takes the family to the city of Nazareth that, though not divinely directed in the text, nevertheless, fulfills the words of the prophets. Thus, it may be suggested that it is Joseph's spiritual discernment that leads him to choose a new location, Nazareth in Galilee, which is not only within the land of Israel to which God had directed him but also the exact place he must reside in order to fulfill the destiny of his son according to the words of the prophets (2.22-23).

One more reference to Joseph occurs in 13.54-58, which relates the rejection of Jesus in his family's synagogue in Nazareth. This last reference to Joseph in Matthew is the only place where Jesus is described, in the present tense, as the 'son' of Joseph (13.55). Significantly, this designation is made by the very people with whom Jesus has lived and who have known his family, the 'people in the synagogue' in Nazareth (13.54). The passage suggests Joseph's role in the life of Jesus has been of a substantial length and may even be ongoing, providing further substantiation of the role and significance Joseph. Thus, Matthew presents Joseph as a very prominent figure who plays the important roles of father, husband, protector, and guide in the earliest period of the life of Jesus. In his focus upon Joseph's heritage, authority, spirituality, righteousness and obedience, Matthew emphasizes Joseph's importance within this narrative.

At the same time, Matthew portrays Joseph as a spiritual exemplar who both listens for God's direction (1.18-20; 2.13, 19-20, 22) and obeys God's directions, as the text reveals (1.24-25; 2.14-15, 21, 22-23). As a result, later writers and artists would find Matthew's portrayal of Joseph provides them with a substantial source for developing their perceptions of the person and character of Joseph.

A careful reading of Luke reveals that Joseph is held in high esteem in this narrative. From the earliest references in ch. 1, in which he is identified as the 'betrothed' of Mary and as a member of the 'house of David' (1.27), the portrait reveals a Joseph formally identified before Mary is formally introduced (1.27). The introduction of Joseph's lineage and the emphasis on connections between Joseph and the messiah of the house of David (1.32, 69), reveal the priority Joseph has over those associated with the priestly orders of 'Abijah' and 'Aaron' (1.5), including Mary. The portrait not only underscores Joseph's heritage (1.27, 32, 69; 2.4-7) and its significance for Jesus' identity and role, but also emphasizes Joseph's righteousness, obedience, and parental affection and concern. Later interpreters and artists would find further evidence of respect for

Joseph in ch. 2, where he is formally portrayed as *pater familias*, the *de facto* father of Jesus and the husband of Mary, who first publicly acknowledges his relationship with Mary (and, thus, with the child she will bear) in the act of registration (2.1-5) and then provides safety for her and the child (2.6-7). Subsequently, they would see the esteem shown to Joseph and his importance in the roles he plays as witness and protector when shepherds come to see the savior (2.1-20).

Further substantiation of the high regard given Joseph would be seen when Joseph joins with Mary in bringing the child for circumcision (2.21), presenting him in the temple (2.22-38), where the portrait reveals that Joseph is Jesus' 'parent' (2.27) and 'father' (2.33). Even more signs of this respect toward Joseph are found in the references to Joseph and Mary taking Jesus to the festival of Passover (2.41-43), in the search for Jesus in the temple in Jerusalem (2.44-50), and in the instruction of Jesus as a child and youth (2.51-52), where, again, Joseph is directly identified as Jesus' 'parent' (2.41, 43) and 'father' (2.48).

Later narrators and artists are offered one brief final detail of this portrait of Joseph in a reference to 'Joseph' in 4.22.[21] In this pericope (4.16-30), which recounts the rejection of Jesus at Nazareth, Jesus is explicitly identified by some residents of Nazareth as 'Joseph's son' (4.22), once again, highlighting Joseph's role as Jesus' father. Luke presents Joseph as a prominent figure in his narrative although Mary is more dominant. In the process, he makes it clear that Joseph has significant roles and, acts as father, husband, protector, and guide in the earliest period of the life of Jesus.

Luke places great emphasis upon the relationship between Joseph and Mary and offers specific scenes in which they seem to act as a couple, as husband and wife, in their efforts to obey God, follow the law, and protect and guide their son (2.4-7, 16-18, 21-24, 27-34, 39-40, 41-43, 44-50, 51). While there is an emphasis upon the importance of Joseph's heritage, Joseph's righteousness and obedience are represented as something he shares with his wife, the mother of his adopted child. As a result, later writers and artists would find Luke's portrait of Joseph to be a foundation upon which they could base their own representations of Joseph.

John's portrait of Joseph, although brief, would also inform later writers' and artists' understanding of Joseph for it confirms his role as the 'father' of Jesus by offering two explicit references to 'Joseph' in which Jesus is identified as the 'son of Joseph' and Joseph is identified as the

---

[21] This is the one 'final detail' that appears to add more to the portrayal of Joseph. Of course, as was noted earlier, 'Joseph' is mentioned in the geneaology found in Luke 3. However, the reference here simply confirms what the readers have already been told and reiterates earlier statements about the virginity and purity of Mary and Joseph's absence in the process of the generation of Jesus.

'father' of Jesus, 1.45 and 6.42. Joseph's significance is also highlighted in this narrative. The Johannine portrait of Joseph also reveals that the nature of his relationship with Jesus was once the subject of community discussion (6.41-51). The Johannine portrait indicates that Jesus was believed to be the 'son of Joseph' and of Mary. But it also may imply (in light of the question raised about Jesus) that Joseph was still alive at the beginning of Jesus' ministry for in the apparent context of a synagogue in the town of Capernaum on the Sea of Galilee (6.24, 29), the readers are told that the members of this group explicitly identify Jesus as 'the son of Joseph' (6.42). Their additional comments ('whose father and mother we know', 6.42), expand this second assertion and further verify Joseph's position as Jesus' father as well as Joseph's marriage and relationship to Jesus' mother (6.42). By speaking of Joseph in the present tense, they suggest to the readers that Joseph's role in the life of Jesus may be ongoing and likely has been of a substantial length.

An appreciation for and knowledge of these canonic portraits of Joseph makes the task of tracing his effective history in literature and art possible, for it provides a basis by which later developments can be assessed. With these portraits in mind, this study turns its attention to portraits of Joseph revealed in later narratives.

Part III

The Response of Later Christian Writers and Their Communities to the Canonic Portrays of Joseph

Following the creation of the New Testament Gospels in the first century, additional narratives were created over the next several centuries, both to defend the nascent faith and to articulate certain perspectives in regard to the virginity of Mary and the divinity of Jesus. It is to these narratives that this study now turns for four of them, namely, the Infancy Gospel of James, the Infancy Gospel of Thomas, the History of Joseph the Carpenter, and the Gospel of Pseudo-Matthew, also contain representations of Joseph the Carpenter. Thus, the main concern of Part III will be to track the development of the Joseph tradition as it appears in these non-canonic narratives.[1]

Formal analysis of the four non-canonic narratives will be organized according to the approximate respective chronology of each narrative. Thus, the first narrative to be reviewed will be the Infancy Gospel of James. This examination will then be followed by analyses of the Infancy Gospel of Thomas, the History of Joseph the Carpenter, and the Gospel of Pseudo-Matthew.

In order to understand the response of these later Christian writers and their communities to the canonic portrayals of Joseph, consideration will first be given to the issues of the date, provenance, language, stability of the text, history of translation and dissemination, availability and accessibility, purpose, and content of each non-canonic narrative, to the extent to which they can be ascertained.

---

[1] With respect to the importance of these texts for understanding the history of interpretation and influence of the New Testament portrayals of Joseph, C. Philip Deasey, 'St. Joseph in the English Mystery Plays', PhD dissertation (Washington: Catholic University of America, 1937), p. 5, asserts that they are the 'ultimate source of the popular medieval conception of Joseph'. In a similar spirit, Marjory Bolger Foster, 'The Iconography of St. Joseph in Netherlandish Art, 1400-1550', PhD dissertation (Lawrence, KS: University of Kansas,1978), p. 9, correctly notes that 'From the point of view of the iconography of St. Joseph the fact that Joseph is treated at much greater length in the Apocrypha than in the authentic Gospels is a primary factor in understanding the influence of these writings on this image.'

Second, attention will be directed to the characterization of Joseph; to the particular way(s) he is portrayed within the text. This will include consideration of the varied details each narrative reveals with respect to the following: Joseph's age, his physical features and characteristics, demeanor, and posture; his proximity to Mary and the Christ-child; his physical position and location within the particular event or scene in which he is portrayed (i.e. within the narrative background or foreground of the image); the roles and actions in which it appears he engaged; and the different ways he and Mary are juxtaposed as complementary or contrasting figures.

Third, consideration will be given to the level of autonomy the narrator's work reveals in relationship to earlier canonic and non-canonic narrative accounts, as appropriate; to the role earlier canonic and non-canonic portrayals of Joseph (narrative and artistic) may or may not have played in the portrayal of Joseph in each non-canonic narrative, i.e. to the uniqueness of the portrayal of Joseph in each of these texts.

Fourth, an effort will be made to determine if and how a specific narrator received or assimilated canonic as well as earlier non-canonic narratives; if he/she may have created their own non-canonic portrayals of Joseph independent of received (and certainly later) non-canonic texts; and if and how a specific narrator may have been influenced by prior visual representations of Joseph.

Fifth, the focus will then turn to the perceptions and beliefs the narrators of the non-canonic texts and their respective ecclesiastical communities held about Joseph.

Sixth, and finally, a summary will be offered of the development of the *Wirkungsgeschichte* of the canonic portrayals of Joseph found in each non-canonic narrative along with an evaluation of the similarity and dissimilarity this portrayal discloses with respect to the canonic portraits of Joseph in Matthew, Luke, and John. At the same time, it will be determined if the representation of Joseph in each non-canonic narrative reveals evidence of a pattern or trajectory that largely affirms and enhances his portrayal and role found in the canonic accounts or evidence of a pattern or trajectory that largely dismisses and diminishes this portrayal.

4

The Portrayal of Joseph in the Infancy Gospel of James

Introduction

With few exceptions, most scholars think the Infancy Gospel of James (hereafter identified as IGJames) was composed in the second half of the second century CE, some time around or after 150.[1] They usually base this conclusion on two factors. The first is found in the narrative of the church father, Origen, in his Commentary on Matthew (in his reference in 10.17 to Mt. 13.55), in what most believe to be a 'certain reference' to IGJames.[2] The second factor consists of the 'apologetic concerns that drive much of the narrative'.[3] By this time, if not before this narrative was composed, Jewish and pagan writers had started to raise serious questions about the divinity of Jesus through attacks upon his virtue and that of his mother.[4] These attacks inevitably led to a variety of apologetical

---

[1] Most scholars believe the Infancy Gospel of James was written in the second half of the second century CE. See Harm Reinder Smid, *Protevangelium Jacobi: A Commentary*. Apocrypha Novi Testamenti 1 (Assen: van Gorcum, 1965), p. 24; J.K. Elliott, *The Apocryphal New Testament*, p. 49; and Ronald F. Hock, *The Infancy Gospels*, pp. 11-12.

[2] With respect to this first factor see Bart D. Ehrman and Zlatko Pleše, *The Apocryphal Gospels: Texts and Translations* (Oxford and New York: Oxford University Press, 2011), p. 32. They note that Origen states that 'James was the son of Joseph from a previous marriage, claiming that this is taught either in "the Gospel of Peter" or the "Book of James," the latter of which, he says, stresses the ongoing virginity of Mary. As the latter is a key theme of the Protevangelium (the Infancy Gospel of James), there is little doubt that Origen is referring to our text.' Smid, *Protevangelium Jacobi: A Commentary*. Apocrypha Novi Testamenti 1, pp. 22-24; Elliott, *The Apocryphal New Testament*, p. 49; and Hock, *The Infancy Gospels*, p. 11, concur with this point. Smid, *Protevangelium Jacobi: A Commentary*. Apocrypha Novi Testamenti 1, pp. 22-24, and Elliott, *The Apocryphal New Testament*, p. 49, believe additional support for dating this narrative in the second half of the second century CE can be found in the writings of Clement of Alexandria, in his *Stromateis* 7.16.93.

[3] This quote from Ehrman and Pleše, *The Apocryphal Gospels*, p. 35, summarizes the second factor that leads to this conclusion.

[4] One of the most noted attacks was executed by Celsus, the pagan philosopher. In his work (found in Origen's, *Contra Celsum* 1.28-39), he argued that the divinity of Jesus was a fabrication because, as Ehrman and Pleše recount (*The Apocryphal Gospels*, p. 35),

responses from the Christian community in this period and many scholars believe IGJames is one of these.[5]

But in contrast to their reflections on the date of the text, scholars offer little definitive with respect to the provenance of this text. While some postulate a possible location in Syria, only Elliott offers explicit evidence for this hypothesis.[6] He believes this may be suggested since IGJames, the Odes of Solomon, and Ignatius (*ad Eph.* 19) seem to share the idea that Mary's virginity was 'virginity *in partu*'.[7] However, most scholars are reluctant to suggest more than some location within the Greek east of the Roman Empire.[8]

In light of the large reservoir of early Greek manuscripts of IGJames, few question that the original language was Greek.[9]

But there is some dispute about the shape and completeness of the text for even the 'earliest full manuscript, Bodmer V, ... demonstrates that enormous textual alterations have been made in the course of the transmission'.[10] Further, as Ehrman and Pleše assert, any search 'for an ostensible original is complicated by the circumstance that the Protevangelium gives clear signs of being based on yet earlier sources available to the author.'[11] Nevertheless, the editor of the best available edition of IGJames, E. de Strycker, and IGJames scholars, Hock and Elliott, believe the vocabulary and literary style of the present texts allude to 'an original unity of the text ...'[12]

Nonetheless, the multiplicity of extant manuscripts of this work alone suggest that the thoughts and beliefs articulated in this narrative were shared by members of other early Christian communities throughout eastern Christianity. Thus, various forms of the manuscript would have

---

'Jesus came from the lower class, that his parents were poor and not of royal blood, that his "father" was a common laborer (a carpenter), and that his mother had to spin for a living. Moreover, the circumstances of his birth were highly suspect: his mother, according to Celsus, had been seduced by a Roman soldier and given birth out of wedlock.'

[5] This led to numerous apologetical treatises by Christians, including that of Origen who, in his *Contra Celsum*, defended both the virtue and virginity of Mary and the divinity of Jesus.

[6] See Elliott, *The Apocryphal New Testament*, p. 49. Smid, *Protevangelium Jacobi*, p. 22, makes the same claim but offers no evidence for this hypothesis.

[7] Elliott, *The Apocryphal New Testament*, p. 49.

[8] Most scholars believe the origin remains elusive. In this regard see especially Hock, *The Infancy Gospels*, pp. 12-13, and Ehrman and Pleše, *The Apocryphal Gospels*, p. 35. They believe there is not enough evidence to warrant a conclusion in this regard.

[9] See Hock, *The Infancy Gospels*, pp. 28-30.

[10] See Ehrman and Pleše, *The Apocryphal Gospels*, p. 33.

[11] See Ehrman and Pleše, *The Apocryphal Gospels*, p. 33.

[12] See Hock, *The Infancy Gospels*, pp. 13-14; Elliott, *Apocryphal New Testament*, p. 50; Ehrman and Pleše, *The Apocryphal Gospels*, p. 33.

either been available to artists and artisans, as well, or, at least, available to others around them who would have read it aloud or shared with them. Evidence of this may be found in the fact that there are over one hundred extant Greek manuscripts as well as numerous translations in other eastern Christian languages as Syriac, Ethiopic, Georgian, Sahidic, Old Church Slavonic, and Armenian in which IGJames appears.[13] Subsequently, this confirms the widespread dissemination and popularity of this narrative in this part of Christendom.[14] This is the case despite the efforts of Jerome and his followers to limit the dissemination of IGJames in the fifth and sixth centuries, especially in western Christianity.[15] Moreover, it is also critical to remember that within a century or two a substantial portion of IGJames emerged in the West, in the non-canonic narrative of the Gospel of Pseudo-Matthew.[16] This narrative incorporated and elaborated significant portions of IGJames (including many of the ideas about Joseph that were initially introduced in IGJames) and was also quite popular. Thus, it became a means through which IGJames' portrait of Joseph could be perpetuated.

The Purpose of the Infancy Gospel of James

Although the title attributed to this narrative might suggest it is very similar to the canonic Gospels, it takes little time for the readers to discover this is not the case. For in contrast to these earlier narratives, IGJames consists of accounts that reflect its author's desire to venerate Mary and address challenges and questions about her and the origin of her child raised by critics of the early Christian movement; very different narrative accounts from those found in the earlier gospels. This is seen not only in those chapters where she is the only or dominant subject (6-7, 11-12) but also in those chapters where her character either influences or determines the content and movement of much of the narrative (1-5, 8-10, 13, 14-15, 16-17, 18-20, 22, 23).[17] Therefore, even a cursory

---

[13] See Elliott, *The Apocryphal New Testament*, p. 48; David R. Cartlidge and J. Keith Elliott, *Art and the Christian Apocrypha* (London and New York: Routledge, 2001), p. 3.

[14] Hock, *The Infancy Gospels*, pp. 27-28; Luigi Gambero, *Mary and the Fathers of the Church: The Blessed Virgin Mary in Patristic Thought* (San Francisco: Ignatius Press, 1999), p. 35; Cartlidge and Elliott, *Art and the Christian Apocrypha*, pp. 3, 21.

[15] See Ehrman and Pleše, *The Apocryphal Gospels*, pp. 31-32. It is important to recall, as Hock (*The Infancy Gospels*, p. 27) notes, that IGJames 'did not face official rejection' in eastern Christianity.

[16] See Ehrman and Pleše, *The Apocryphal Gospels*, pp. 31-32; Hock, *The Infancy Gospels*, p. 27.

[17] The author of this narrative has been variously identified as James, the step-brother of Jesus (see Mk 6.3), James the Less (see Mk 15.40), son of Alphaeus and one of the twelve apostles of Jesus, or an unknown pseudonymous Christian narrator. However, few would suggest he was the step-brother of Jesus in light of his lack of knowledge of

review of IGJames reveals that Mary is the most important character in this narrative. Thus, from its very first chapter, the readers learn this text is more akin to an 'encomiastic history' or 'recitation' of praise than a 'gospel', that its primary interest is with Mary and the nature of her relationship with the other characters in the narrative, including Joseph.[18] Accordingly, the narrative concerns presented to the readers are largely different from those of the earlier gospels.[19]

Palestinian geography and Hebrew tradition and religious practice. Filas (*Joseph: The Man Closest to Jesus*, p. 25) suggests the author may be identified as 'the apostle James the Less-the first bishop of Jerusalem'. Nonetheless, there is no proof for this. Most scholars conclude, as Smid (*Protevangelium Jacobi*, pp.12-14) contends, that this narrator 'hides himself behind a great man of the apostolic time', notably, James 'the brother of the Lord' (see IGJames 25.1-4) in order to give authority to his account and remains hidden to modern interpreters. In this regard, see also Elliott, *The Apocryphal New Testament*, p. 49; Hock, *The Infancy Gospels*, pp. 9-11.

With respect to the subject of the author's purposes, see especially, Smid, *Protevangelium Jacobi*, pp. 14-19; Elliott, *The Apocryphal New Testament*, pp. 50-51; Hock, *The Infancy Gospels*, pp. 11-12 and 15-20; Lienhard, *St. Joseph in Early Christianity*, p. 8; Gambero, *Mary and the Fathers of the Church*, pp. 40-41; Elliott, *A Synopsis of the Apocryphal Nativity and Infancy Narratives*, p. ix.

[18] Hock (*The Infancy Gospels*, pp. 15-20) argues that it is this literary genre that best describes the narrative form found in IGJames.

[19] As such, in the process of reading IGJames, they learn several key details about Mary that shape her portrait. First, the readers learn that Mary was born of very rich and righteous parents, named Joachim and Anna, who were members of the twelve tribes of Israel (1.1-3; 2.1). Second, they discover that Mary was named by her mother (5.10) and her life dedicated to God (4.2; 7.1). Then, they are told that at the occasion of her first birthday, the high priests blessed her and prophesied that her name would be 'on the lips of future generations forever' (6.6-7, 9). In addition, the readers learn that Mary has been kept pure since her birth by her parents (6.4-5) and the priest of the Lord's temple (8.2), and that during her time in the temple she was 'raised in the Holy of Holies', 'fed by heavenly messengers', and 'danced for them' (8.2; 13.7; 15.11-12).

Further, they come to understand that she is a 'virgin of the Lord' (9.7; 10.2-4), who has been repeatedly acknowledged by many to be chosen by the Lord for a special purpose (7.7-8; 11.2, 5, 7-8; 12.2, 5; 13.6-7; 14.5-6; 15.11-12). In turn, they are also told that the Lord (through a sign) has selected Joseph to take her into his care and protection (8.7-8; 9.7, 11). Still further, the readers also learn that Mary is the antithesis of Eve (13.5 and 14.6), has prophetic ability (17.8-9) and sometimes appears to function in the role of Joseph's 'mistress' or 'lady', upon whom he obediently waits (9.7-8, 11-12; 17.10-11; 18.1-2; 19.1-16).

Thus, in sum, IGJames seems to suggest several things with respect to Mary. First, it reveals that she has always been a virgin and never had intimate contact with a man. Second, it discloses that Mary is a person of deep spirituality and righteousness who regularly receives special communications from 'a heavenly messenger' and 'the messenger of the Lord' (11.1-7). Third, IGJames represents her as a unique figure who has been chosen by God to 'disclose his redemption to the people of Israel during the last days' (7.7-8) and give birth to the one who is to be the savior of the world (11.8; 14.6). Fourth, the readers are led to believe that Mary is able to fulfill these purposes without the assistance of anyone one else (except God). As such, they seem led to the conclusion that Mary, and Mary alone, is the real mother and earthly parent of the child, and that she, and she alone, will have the roles of bringing 'redemption to the people of Israel'

4. The Portrayal of Joseph in the Infancy Gospel of James

Nonetheless, IGJames offers a very distinctive portrait of Joseph which warrants exploration.[20]

The Characterization of Joseph in the Infancy Gospel of James

'Joseph' is mentioned by name 21 times in IGJames.[21] However, the first references to Joseph do not occur until ch. 8, notably, in the account in chs. 8 and 9, in which 'James' details the selection of Joseph to be the guardian of Mary.

Here, the readers learn that Joseph has been married, is a widower, is an obedient follower of the Lord, has 'sons', is 'an old man' and is a builder of 'houses' (8.7, 9; 9.8, 12; 13.1).[22] Further, the readers also learn that Joseph has 'been chosen ... to take the virgin of the Lord' into his 'care and protection' (9.7, 11) and has only reluctantly agreed to take her as a result of his sense of spiritual obligation and 'fear' (9.9, 11). Thus, by implication and by the clarification of the high priest and the narrator (see the difference between 8.8, and 9.7, 11 for the different descriptions of the relationship between Joseph and Mary), it is suggested that Joseph has no real personal or romantic interest in Mary and, for this reason, will not become her husband.[23]

These first details about Joseph place him in sharp juxtaposition to what the readers are told about Mary: that she is also unmarried, is a very 'young woman', and a very special person, a 'virgin of the Lord' (8.3-9;

(7.8) and of having intimate familial contact with the child (11.7-8; 14.6; 17.11; 19.15-16) and act as his sole caregiver and caretaker (21.10-11; 22.3).

[20] Therefore, summaries of both the outline of IGJames and of the portrayal of Mary give readers insights into the larger literary context in which an early narrative portrait of Joseph is found as well as insights into the dynamics of the principal character with whom Joseph is often engaged and juxtaposed (8.6–9.12; 13.1–14.8; 15.1–16.8; 17.1–19.17; 21.1-12).

[21] Several scholars have briefly acknowledged the portrayal of Joseph in the Infancy Gospel of James, in one way or another, but have not explored the matter in depth. See Smid, *Protevangelium Jacobi*, p. 185, who does not explore the matter but recognizes the number of times 'Joseph' is identified by name in his 'Index Verborum'. In addition, see Foster, 'The Iconography of St. Joseph in Netherlandish Art, 1400-1550', pp. 9-19; Hock, *The Infancy Gospels*, pp. 24-25; J.K. Elliott, *The Apocryphal Jesus: Legends of the Early Church* (Oxford: Oxford University Press, 1996), pp. 44-46; Lienhard, *St. Joseph in Early Christianity*, pp. 7-9.

Additionally, several scholars have commented on James' portrayal of Mary. See the following scholarly texts: Smid, *Protevangelium Jacobi: A Commentary*; Elliott, *The Apocryphal New Testament: A Collection of Apocryphal Christian Literature in an English Translation*; Hock, *The Infancy Gospels*; Lienhard, *St. Joseph in Early Christianity*; Gambero, *Mary and the Fathers of the Church: The Blessed Virgin Mary in Patristic Thought*; and J.K. Elliott, *A Synopsis of the Apocryphal Nativity and Infancy Narratives*.

[22] Citing the translation of Hock, *The Infancy Gospels*, pp. 47, 49, 55.

[23] Citing the translation of Hock, *The Infancy Gospels*, p. 49.

9.7, 8).[24] Similarly, the detail that Joseph's primary responsibility is 'to take the virgin of the Lord' into his 'care and protection' (9.7, 11), further distinguishes him from the virgin, illuminates his character, and suggests roles and actions he will take with respect to Mary and the forthcoming child.[25]

Even so, following IGJames' introduction of Joseph in this account in chs. 8 and 9, the readers' attention is redirected to Mary and to the accounts of her selection to help create the temple veil (ch. 10), of the annunciation of the messenger of the Lord to her about the child she will bear (ch. 11), and of her visit with her relative, Elizabeth. In the process, Mary's virtue, purity, virginity, and uniqueness (10.2-4; 11.2-3, 7-9; 12.2, 5-6) are reiterated for the readers. As a result, they become further aware of the distinctions between Joseph and Mary that, in part, prepare them for Joseph's later actions and interactions with her and the child and the other characters in the narrative.

In the next section in which Joseph is mentioned, in chs. 13 and 14, additional distinctions are drawn as the readers learn of Joseph's return to Mary (9.12), of his discovery of Mary's pregnancy, of his reproach towards himself and her (13.1-10) and of the annunciation of the messenger of the Lord to Joseph in a dream (14.1-8). They see that, upon discovering Mary is pregnant, Joseph initially blames himself for what has transpired (13.1-3). As such, Joseph questions and discloses his own spiritual limitations and raises the genuine possibility that he has done something wrong. Joseph asks, 'What sort of face should I present to the Lord God? What prayer can I say on her behalf since I received her as a virgin from the temple of the Lord God and did not protect her?' (13.2-3).[26]

At the same time, in his struggle to understand what has taken place, Joseph also imagines Mary may be to blame and levels accusations against her by questioning her purity, saying, 'Why have you brought shame on yourself, you who were raised in the Holy of Holies and fed by a heavenly messenger?'(13.5-7) or questions her truthfulness, saying, 'Then where did the child you're carrying come from?'(13.9).[27] Such accusations against the one who has been lauded for her virtue and purity and even described herself as one whom 'every generation on earth will congratulate' (12.6), poignantly disclose the substantial differences between Joseph and Mary, and may temporarily cast him in a further negative light.

---

[24] Citing the translation of Hock, *The Infancy Gospels*, pp. 47, 49.
[25] Citing the translation of Hock, *The Infancy Gospels*, p. 49.
[26] Citing the translation of Hock, *The Infancy Gospels*, p. 55.
[27] Citing the translation of Hock, *The Infancy Gospels*, pp. 55, 57.

4. The Portrayal of Joseph in the Infancy Gospel of James 89

Nonetheless, the readers may have some sympathy for Joseph for they know he has not been told what Mary has been told, he has not had the spiritual revelations and experiences she has had. They may also see in his struggle a deep desire to do the right thing, to be in right relationship with God, disclosed in his own profound reflections:

> If I try to cover up her sin, I'll end up going against the law of the Lord. And if I disclose her condition to the people of Israel, I'm afraid that the child inside her might be heaven-sent and I'll end up handing innocent blood over to a death sentence. So what should I do with her? (I know) I'll divorce her quietly (IGJames 14.2-4).[28]

Concurrently, Joseph's spirituality is also seen in the event of the annunciation and dream, in ch. 14, which brings him reassurance. It reminds the readers that Joseph's inclination to follow and obey the Lord, remains, despite his moral and spiritual limitations and is manifested in Joseph's willingness to both receive and respond positively to the annunciation of the 'messenger of the Lord' (14.5).[29] This account also discloses that, following the annunciation and dream, Joseph is able to offer praise to 'the God of Israel', and return to his proper role as the protector and guardian of 'the girl' Mary and her savior son, 'Jesus' (14.6-7); actions that reassure the readers that Mary's purity and virginity has been maintained and that he has not had sexual relations with her or entered into a familial or marital relationship with her.[30]

Further, the readers learn even more about Joseph in chs. 15 and 16 where Joseph and Mary are conjoined, presented as a spiritual couple who must face, together, spiritual judgments, accusations, and tests. Thus, just as the readers imagine the issue of Mary's pregnancy has been resolved, they discover Joseph and Mary face another crisis – (that they are accused by the high priest and his assistants of having had sexual relations). Consequently, Joseph and Mary find themselves pitted, together, against those who are supposed to represent the highest standards of piety and righteousness within their spiritual community.

First, the high priest questions Mary, asking, among other questions, 'Mary, why have you done this?' (15.10). In response, Mary responds strongly, saying, 'As the Lord God lives, I stand innocent before him. Believe me, I've not had sex with any man', (15.13) a statement that not only absolves Joseph and reaffirms his righteousness but also reaffirms

---

[28] Citing the translation of Hock, *The Infancy Gospels*, p. 57.
[29] Citing the translation of Hock, *The Infancy Gospels*, p. 57.
[30] Citing the translation of Hock, *The Infancy Gospels*, p. 57. Several of the verses in chs. 13 and 14 parallel Mt. 1.18-25 and are based upon verses in this canonic pericope, namely IGJames 13.1 (Mt. 1.18); IGJames 14.2, 3 (Mt. 1.19); IGJames 14.5 (Mt. 1.20); IGJames 14.6 (Mt. 1.21); IGJames 14.7-8 (Mt. 1.24-25). But the rest of the verses in these chapters are unparalleled in the canonic Gospels.

that she remains both pure and a virgin.[31] Next, the high priest questions Joseph. He, in turn, responds similarly, saying, 'As the Lord lives, I am innocent where she is concerned' (15.15). However, the high priest continues his attack upon Joseph, asserting the Carpenter has lied, had his 'way with her', had not 'humbled himself before God [so his imagined child might be blessed]', and not revealed his action 'to the people of Israel', a statement that suggests Joseph bears a responsibility to 'the people of Israel' as well as to Mary and her child (15.16-17). Intriguingly, in reaction to the priest, Joseph is 'silent' (15.8).

Finally, in an attempt to substantiate his conviction that Joseph and Mary have lied to him the high priest says, 'I'm going to give you the Lord's drink test, and it will disclose your sin clearly to both of you'(16.3).[32] This he administers, first to Joseph, by making him drink the water, and then, by sending 'him into the wilderness' (16.4).[33] Subsequently, the high priest does the same with Mary. However, they both return unharmed (16.4-6). As such the moral and spiritual character of both figures, Joseph and Mary, is reaffirmed. So the readers are told,

> everybody was surprised because their sin had not been revealed. And so the high priest said, 'If the Lord God has not exposed your sin, then neither do I condemn you.' And he dismissed them. Joseph took Mary and returned home celebrating and praising the God of Israel (IGJames 16.6-8).[34]

Thus, once again, Joseph is able to act as a witness to the piety, purity, and virginity of Mary; a role, curiously, that Mary, through her actions in these chapters, also fulfills with respect to his character.

Next, following the account of their exoneration by the high priest and Joseph's and Mary's joyful return to their shared home (16.7-8), the readers are offered an account of the birth of Jesus (17.1–19.17). In the process, the distinctions between Joseph and Mary are further accentuated in these three chapters by the immediate disclosure that Joseph is uncertain about how he will 'enroll' Mary in response to an 'order ... from Emperor Augustus that everybody in Bethlehem of Judea be enrolled in the census' (17.1-4).[35] The readers are told that Joseph has no concern about the enrollment of his 'sons', but has serious questions about how Mary should be enrolled, questions which reiterate for the readers the significant chronological and familial distinctions between Joseph and Mary (17.1-3).[36] Thus, through the revelation of Joseph's own words and struggle to define precisely his relationship to Mary

---

[31] Citing the translation of Hock, *The Infancy Gospels*, p. 59.
[32] Citing the translation of Hock, *The Infancy Gospels*, p. 61.
[33] Citing the translation of Hock, *The Infancy Gospels*, p. 61.
[34] Citing the translation of Hock, *The Infancy Gospels*, p. 61.
[35] Citing the translation of Hock, *The Infancy Gospels*, pp. 61, 63.
[36] Citing the translation of Hock, *The Infancy Gospels*, pp. 61, 63.

(17.2-3) and the description of Joseph's activities with respect to the journey to Bethlehem (17.2-11), the readers are reminded that Joseph is most appropriately described as Mary's caretaker and protector, as one whose primary responsibilities relate to Mary's and her unborn child's safety, comfort and protection, responsibilities he appears to share, at this point, with his unnamed son and his second son, Samuel (17.5–18.2).[37]

In addition, in this propitious time, the readers discover that Joseph can express care, in part, by engaging in self-reflection out of concern for Mary (17.7), as well as by engaging in conversation with Mary (17.6-11) that facilitates a soteriological declaration by the virgin (17.9). This may be an allusion to Luke 2.34 and may refer to the joy that will be forthcoming for those who believe in the child Mary carries and the sorrow for those who do not.[38] Thus, in the process, Joseph helps Mary along the journey toward Bethlehem (17.5, 10) and is sensitive to her needs (17.5, 7, 11).[39]

In turn, Joseph's sensitivity and care are further highlighted following Mary's specific request for help as she approaches the time of the birth of her child (17.10). In response, readers learn that Joseph finds shelter (in 'a cave', 18.1) for her in which she will have 'privacy' (17.11) and insures this by stationing 'his sons to guard her (18.1)'.[40]

Subsequently, Joseph leaves to find 'a Hebrew midwife' who he believes will be necessary to help Mary with the birth (18.2).[41] On his way, Joseph is a recipient of a revelatory experience, a dramatic vision that he recounts in first-person, in which he and other people and animals, and all nature appear to stand still, suspended in time (18.2-11).[42] Among other things, it is an account that reminds readers of Joseph's piety and spirituality, and his responsiveness (previously demonstrated in his reception of a messenger of the Lord in the night) to new revelation from God. It also discloses Joseph's capacity, previously acknowledged, to be a witness to the supernatural and miraculous power of God. Further, it

---

[37] Citing the translation of Hock, *The Infancy Gospels*, pp. 49, 61, 63, 65.

[38] Citing the translation of Hock, *The Infancy Gospels*, p. 63. See also Hock's commentary on the reference to the 'two peoples' in 17.9, *The Infancy Gospels*, p. 63.

[39] Citing the translation of Hock, *The Infancy Gospels*, p. 63.

[40] Citing the translation of Hock, *The Infancy Gospels*, pp. 63, 65.

[41] Citing the translation of Hock, p. 65. Additionally, it should be noted that in chapter seventeen, IGJames begins his narration of the events surrounding the birth of Jesus (which he details in chapters seventeen through twenty-four) which has some parallel to the pericope of Lk. 2.1-7. Of these chapters, chapters seventeen and eighteen of James reveal parallels with verses in this Lukan pericope, notably in IGJames 17.1 (Lk. 2.1), IGJames 17.2-3 (Lk. 2.3, 5), and IGJames 17.10–18.2 (Lk. 2.6-7). In contrast, as noted with respect to chs. 13 and 14, the rest of the verses of this chapter are without parallel in the canonic portraits.

[42] Citing the translation of Hock, *The Infancy Gospels*, p. 65.

suggests he might understand that his vision reflects something momentous. However, Joseph's ongoing search for a mid-wife and his apparent conviction the child has not yet been born (19.6, 9-11), following his vision, seems to infer Joseph does not fully comprehend the meaning of his vision and the revelation it offered.[43] In addition, Joseph's physical separation from Mary and the child during the time of the birth highlights a real distinction between them, illuminated not only by means of the two distinct physical locations (Joseph – on the road and Mary – in a cave), in which they are envisioned by the readers but also by the distinctive emotional and spiritual locations in which the readers probably imagine them (Joseph – preoccupied by his search for someone to help Mary and thus, separated from Mary and the child and the experience of the birth-and Mary – caught up in the profundity and miracle of the birth of her own child).

These distinctions, in turn, are similarly confirmed in the account of Joseph's encounter and dialogue with 'a Hebrew mid-wife' (19.1-9).[44] Once Joseph has clarified he is 'an Israelite' who is 'looking for a Hebrew midwife' the readers are further reminded that Mary is not his wife (19.6-9), in Joseph's own words. In response to the mid-wife's query about the identity of Mary, Joseph says:

> She is Mary, who was raised in the temple of the Lord; I obtained her by lot as my wife. But she's not really my wife; she's pregnant by the holy spirit (IGJames 19.8-9).[45]

Then, he invites the midwife to follow him to the site of the birth, saying, 'Come and see', the last words Joseph speaks in the narrative (19.11). There she and Joseph enter the cave (19.12-13). Upon doing so, they encounter 'an intense light' (19.15) that shortly recedes and reveals 'the infant' and 'his mother Mary' (19.16).[46] However, strangely, Joseph, unlike the midwife, does not formally respond to this miraculous event, and virtually disappears from the story; suggesting to readers that he is no longer necessary to the narrative.[47] Further, Joseph's disengagement highlights Mary's independence and autonomy (she did not really

---

[43] Cited according to the translations of Hock, *The Infancy Gospels*, p. 67.
[44] Citing the translation of Hock, *The Infancy Gospels*, p. 67.
[45] Citing the translation of Hock, *The Infancy Gospels*, p. 67.
[46] Citing the translation of Hock, *The Infancy Gospels*, p. 67.
[47] There is one final reference to Joseph in IGJames. In 21.1-12, the readers learn of the arrival of certain 'astrologers' and the 'great uproar' their arrival and questions about 'the newborn king of the Judeans' raise. They are also informed that this takes place as Joseph is 'about ready to depart to Judea', and occurs in the village of Bethlehem (21.1-2). In this regard see the translation of Hock, *The Infancy Gospels*, p. 71. Although Mary is mentioned in two verses in the rest of IGJames' narrative (22.3-4; 25.4), there is no mention of Joseph or allusion to him after 21.1.

need Joseph in order to have this child), the limitations of Joseph's significance and role, and the priority given Mary within IGJames.

The Infancy Gospel of James and the History of Effects

A close reading of the text of IGJames reveals a lack of allusion to most of the canonic references related to Joseph. In fact, a comparison of the references to Joseph in the canonic Gospels with those in IGJames reveals that only references to Joseph in Mt. 1.18-21, 24-25 and in Lk. 2.1, 3, 5, 6-7 appear in IGJames and that these are limited to chs. 13, 14, 17 and 18.[48] This comparison also suggests that the purpose of these canonic references is largely to enhance Mary's own position and role in the narrative. This, in turn, helps explain why Joseph's portrayal in IGJames is limited in the ways that it is; so much so that even his primary roles as caretaker and protector of Mary and her child are significantly restricted.

Thus, this portrait of Joseph provides additional details and characterizations that, among other things, set Mary and her child apart from the other characters, highlight her virtues and holiness, and signify her distinction and special relationship with Jesus. At the same time, in the process, this portrait also expands the image of Joseph with additional details and characterizations that significantly alter his role in relationship to Mary and Jesus. As such, the portrait of Joseph in IGJames responds to the literary challenges of the *Leerstellen*, 'gaps in the narrative' and the *Unbestimmtheitsstellen*, 'places where things are unclear', raised by the canonic Gospels by providing more information about the nature and character of Joseph's relationship to Mary and Jesus as well as the significance of the figure of Mary.[49] In the process, the narrator of IGJames provides an intriguing portrayal of Joseph.

---

[48] It is notable that IGJames does not include or adapt the following texts from the gospel nativity and infancy narratives that represent Joseph in a very positive light, especially, Mt. 2.13-15 (the 'Escape to Egypt') and 2.19-23 (the 'Return from Egypt') and Lk. 1.26-27 (the 'Announcement that a virgin [Mary] is engaged to a man whose name was Joseph), 2.21-38 (the 'Naming and Presentation of Jesus in the Temple'), 2.39-40 (the 'Return of Joseph, Mary, and Jesus to Nazareth'), and 2.41-52 (the 'Boy Jesus in the Temple'). It is also noteworthy that IGJames also does not include or adapt the three additional pericopes, namely, Mt. 1.1-17 (the 'Genealogy of Jesus the Messiah') and Lk. 2.8-20 (the 'Visitation of the Shepherds') and 3.23-38 (the 'Genealogy of Jesus'). As such, the exclusion of these nine canonic texts also alters the image of Joseph for the readers of IGJames because it excludes key portions of the canonic representations of Joseph the Carpenter.

[49] See Smid, *Protevangelium Jacobi*, p. 14 and Elliott, *A Synopsis of the Apocryphal Nativity and Infancy Narratives*, p. ix. In regard to the importance of considering these literary challenges in reviewing the *Wirkungsgeschichte* of biblical narratives, see Wolfgang Iser, quoted in John F.A. Sawyer, 'The Role of Reception Theory,' p. 8.

The Distinctiveness of the Portrait of Joseph in the Infancy Gospel of James

Therefore, the effect of this narrative upon the image and perception of Joseph, formally recognized by few scholars, must also be acknowledged. While this distinct portrait, in one respect, enlarges Joseph's canonic portrayal, it also significantly transforms it, as particular details found in IGJames suggest.[50] These include, among others, new information about Joseph's age – (that he was a very old man, who felt embarrassed to be associated with such a young 'girl') and his marital and familial history – (that he had been previously married, had lost his wife to death and already had two sons). They also include new information about the history of Joseph's relationship with Mary – (that he had known her since she was twelve and had taken her from the Temple and been responsible for her care and protection and was her caretaker and guardian; not her husband). They also indicate that from the perspective of the narrator of IGJames, Joseph's primary roles, with respect to Mary and the child, are those of caretaker, protector, and witness, as was highlighted at the time of Joseph's reception of Mary (9.7 and 9.11). At those times Joseph's presence, observation, and response confirm Mary's key characteristics, especially, her purity and virginity (9.7; 13.1–14.8; 15.1–16.8; 17.1–18.2; 18.3–11; 19.1–15).

Thus, IGJames establishes its distinction from the canonic Gospels with respect to Joseph by responding to the literary challenges of the *Leerstellen* and the *Unbestimmtheitsstellen*, raised by these earlier Gospels, by providing more information about Joseph. Accordingly, it can be concluded that the portrayal of Joseph in IGJames offers a substantial reservoir of information about the development of the *Wirkungsgeschichte* of the Joseph tradition in the second century CE.

The Narrator's and the Narrator's Community's Perceptions and Beliefs about Joseph in the Infancy Gospel of James

The outline, organization, and content of IGJames (with its heavy emphasis on the birth and childhood of Mary and her virginity and purity) suggest that the primary concern of the narrator and his/her community is to offer veneration to Mary. Thus, they are not very concerned with the character of Joseph and seek to ensure that his presence (which they know is necessary) and his role (which is kept subsidiary in most scenes) in the narrative do nothing to detract from Mary or to diminish their portrait of her as holy, pure, and virginal. Consequently, they construct a clear wall between Joseph and Mary, as well as Joseph and Mary's child,

---

[50] Hock, *The Infancy Gospels*, pp. 24-25; Lienhard, pp. 7-9.

that is exemplified by the representation of Joseph as a very elderly figure who has been previously married and fathered adult children. At the same time, they heighten this wall by portraying Joseph as a reticent character who prefers to deal with Mary at arms-length and appears quite disengaged from her child. Accordingly, from the beginning until the end of the narrative, very strict limits on his overall position in the narrative and upon the nature and character of his relationship with Mary and the child shape his portrait in IGJames. Thus, it can be concluded that the narrator and the narrator's community believed Joseph was an ancillary figure whose significance needed to be carefully represented and always limited in relationship to Mary and her child.

5

The Portrayal of Joseph the Carpenter in the Infancy Gospel of Thomas

Introduction

Many scholars also believe the Infancy Gospel of Thomas (abbreviated in this study as IGThomas) was composed in approximately the same period, between c.150 and 225 CE.[1] Reasons for this conclusion vary but center primarily on two convictions, clearly summarized by Ehrman and Pleše: first, that early Christians would have early generated stories about the childhood of Jesus in order to fill-in gaps about his life present in the canonic birth narratives in Matthew and Luke and, second, that the church father, Irenaeus, writing in the middle to late second century CE, appears to document the presence of a prominent story found in IGThomas.[2]

There is also significant, if not complete, consensus with respect to the original language of the text which most scholars believe was Greek.[3]

The provenance of this narrative, in contrast, is much harder to ascertain. Opinions about this seem only united in the idea that it most likely

---

[1] Most scholars believe IGThomas was written in this time range. See Hock, *The Infancy Gospels*, p. 91; Lienhard, *St. Joseph in Early Christianity*, pp. 7 and 9-10; Tony Chartrand-Burke, 'The Infancy Gospel of Thomas: The Text, is Origins, and its Transmission', PhD dissertation (Toronto: University of Toronto, 2001), p. 408; J.K. Elliott, *A Synopsis of the Apocryphal Nativity and Infancy Narratives*, p. xiii; Reidar Aasgaard, *The Childhood of Jesus*, p. 2; Ehrman and Pleše, *The Apocryphal Gospels*, p. 5.

[2] Ehrman and Pleše, *The Apocryphal Gospels*, pp. 5-6. They believe that the story 'where the young Jesus confronts and confounds a potential teacher by explaining to him the mysteries of the alphabet (see ch. 14) – is attested already in the writings of Irenaus from around 180 CE (*Adv. Haaer.* 1.20.1) and in the *Epistula Apostolorum* (ch. 4), which dates possibly several decades earlier.' Additional support for these convictions can be found in the work of Hock, *The Infancy Gospels*, pp. 91-92 and Aasgaard, *The Childhood of Jesus*, pp. 14 and 167-68.

[3] Hock, *The Infancy Gospels*, pp. 99-101; Ehrman and Pleše, *The Apocryphal Gospels*, pp. 4-5.

originated in a Christian community somewhere close to a rural proximity in the 'Greek East of the Roman Empire'.[4]

However, the most problematic issue with regard to IGThomas centers around the shape and size of the text. For, as Ehrman and Pleše note, the extant 'Greek manuscripts that contain the account differ radically from one another, with entire chapters missing from some witnesses and present in others'.[5]

Nonetheless, this problem did not inhibit the spread of much of this narrative. This is indicated, in part, by the fact that the IGThomas 'is found in a considerable number of manuscripts, both Greek and versional'.[6] While there are only fourteen separate manuscripts of this infancy gospel in Greek, the narrative is much more common 'as part of larger story collections', and it is through this kind of format that the IGThomas was often disseminated.[7] The number and diversity of the manuscripts in other languages is quite substantial and includes texts in Latin, Syriac, Armenian, Ethiopic, Arabic, Georgian, Slavonic and several other European and Slavic languages.[8] Aasgaard's discussion on the dissemination of the narrative is quite illuminating and highlights the fact that it would have been available and accessible to a wide variety of peoples in many different geographical locales. He writes:

> The diversity of languages into which the material was spread and the fairly high manuscript number in some versions attest to IGT's broad appeal. The quick and broad dissemination of the short form also supports this. Already in the third to fourth centuries it had spread from Greek to Latin (West) and Syriac (East), and was by the fifth to sixth centuries known in Armenian and Georgian (North-East) and Ethiopic (South). And it was well-known in reworked and combined forms in Irish and Arabic in the seventh to early eighth centuries.[9]

Certainly these numbers and the diversity of the texts confirms this narrative was both widely circulated and very popular.[10] Thus, Aasgaard

---

[4] Hock (*The Infancy Gospels*, pp. 91-92) suggests the former and concludes the latter. With respect to Hock's suggestion that IGThomas emerged within a rural context, see especially Aasgaard, *The Childhood of Jesus*, pp. 187-91. In regard to his belief that this narrative was a creative product of eastern Christianity, see Aasgaard, *The Childhood of Jesus*, p. 181 and Ehrman and Pleše, *The Apocryphal Gospels*, p. 5.

[5] Ehrman and Pleše, *The Apocryphal Gospels*, p. 3.

[6] Aasgaard, *The Childhood of Jesus*, p. 180. Significant study of the manuscripts has been detailed in Chartrand-Burke, 'Infancy Gospel', pp. 101-33, 245-64, 277-88.

[7] Aasgaard, *The Childhood of Jesus*, p. 181.

[8] Aasgaard, *The Childhood of Jesus*, pp. 181-85.

[9] Aasgaard, *The Childhood of Jesus*, pp. 184-85.

[10] Aasgaard, *The Childhood of Jesus*, pp. 184-85. Ehrman and Pleše, *The Apocrpyhal Gospels*, p. 3, also acknowledge its popularity. At the same time, the dissemination and popularity of the Infancy Gospel of Thomas with its foci that include significant attention to the nature of the relationship between Jesus and Joseph, may help explain later positive

concludes that there 'is no sign that the material was the reserve of some special theological milieu; rather, it appears to have been embraced and forwarded by early Christianity at large.'[11] And, yet, there is no direct evidence that the portrayals of Joseph in this narrative, as the strong, compassionate, and engaged parent and father of Jesus, were adopted by later Christian writers and artists. Nonetheless, Joseph's portrait in the IGThomas represents an important literary witness to the development of the *Wirkungsgeschichte* of the Joseph tradition.

The Purpose of the Infancy Gospel of Thomas

As was the case with respect to IGJames, it is also the case in regard to this second non-canonic narrative that the title attributed to this document might suggest it is very similar to the canonic Gospels. However, readers quickly discover that this is not the case for IGThomas consists of new stories about the character and life of Jesus between the ages of five and twelve years and make 'known the extraordinary childhood deeds of our Lord Jesus Christ' (1.1).[12] But it does more than just relate these 'deeds', as Ehrman and Pleše, recognize. These stories serve, as

---

representations of Joseph and portrayals of his relationship with Jesus as well as less positive and even negative portrayals.

With respect to the possible influence of the Infancy Gospel of Thomas on art, there appears to be only limited evidence that (unlike the influence of the Infancy Gospel of James) it exercised much influence on the creation and shaping of Christian art. While certain 'elements' – such as the presentation of Jesus as a 'young miracle worker' and a 'deliverer from sickness and death' – represented in its narrative may be found in later art and some specific parallels may be drawn between the Infancy Gospel of Thomas and 'a few artistic depictions ... in eleventh-to-fifteenth century material, its influence upon later art appears slight. See Aasgaard, *The Childhood of Jesus*, pp. 169 and 173. In this regard, also see Cartlidge and Elliott, *Art and the Christian Apocrypha*, pp. 106-16.

[11] Aasgaard, *The Childhood of Jesus*, p. 185.

[12] The exception to this is the story in the final chapter, ch. 19, of IGThomas which is a rendition of the account of Jesus in the temple found in Lk. 2.41-52. Chartrand-Burke, 'The Infancy Gospel of Thomas', pp. 397-98 and Aasgaard, *The Childhood of Jesus*, p. 129, both believe the narrator of this apocryphal gospel did not see a need to reinterpret the nativity accounts in the canonic gospels. Rather the narrator had other concerns, especially the concern to provide an account of the childhood of Jesus not found in the canonic Gospels.

See also Hock, *The Infancy Gospels*, p. 105. Hock (*The Infancy Gospels*, p. 99) bases his translation, which covers pp. 104-43, upon the Greek text of Tischendorf A, the present 'standard text for translations and studies' of this narrative although he has incorporated some changes he deems appropriate (p. 101). Chartrand-Burke, 'The Infancy Gospel of Thomas', pp. 305-11, believes the Elijah and Elisha narratives were possibly examples and sources for the narrator of the Infancy Gospel of Thomas. As Aasgaard (*The Childhood of Jesus*, p. 9) notes, Chartrand-Burke thinks 'the problematic features (of this "gospel") such as Jesus' cursing can be explained on this basis, since such activity is also attributed to them (Elijah and Elisha)'.

those of other ancient biographers, 'to adumbrate the outstanding features of their (protagonists') personalities that came to full expression in deeds during their adulthoods.'[13] Further, IGThomas, in sharp contrast to IGJames, also reveals significant details about the nature and character of the relationship between Joseph and Jesus, who are explicitly and implicitly identified as 'father' and 'son', while providing only limited information about the nature and character of the relationship between Mary and Jesus. Therefore, IGThomas offers much additional detail that expands the portrait of Joseph.

The Characterization of Joseph in the Infancy Gospel of Thomas

A brief summary of the IGThomas suggests the priority given to Joseph. Organized, in part, on the basis of four chronological stages within the childhood of Jesus (at ages five, seven, eight, and twelve), the narrator relates the development of Jesus, during this period, in nineteen chapters.[14] In the first chapter readers are briefly introduced to the author who identifies himself as 'Thomas the Israelite' and claims to be addressing his words to 'all my non-Jewish brothers and sisters' in order 'to make known the extraordinary childhood deeds of our Lord Jesus Christ ...' (1.1).[15]

Next, they are introduced to a long selection of stories that they are told took place when Jesus was five-years-old, and which span several chapters and detail Joseph's relationship with Jesus in this period (2.1–10.4). This lengthy selection begins with three accounts of the divine power exhibited by Jesus. This set of stories about the powers of Jesus are then followed by a lengthy series of three related narratives, in 6.1–8.4, that detail Joseph's attempts to have the teacher Zacchaeus instruct Jesus and Jesus' reactions to these attempts; all of which proved futile. Afterwards, two miracle stories are presented, in 9.1–10.4, in which, once again, Jesus brings healing to people. But, Joseph is not featured in either of these. Subsequently, the readers are introduced to a smaller selection of stories, covering events when Jesus was six and eight in which he performed miracles for his own family. These stories are found in 11.1–13.4.[16] They, in turn, are followed by other attempts by Joseph to find instruction for Jesus in 14.1–15.7. Once again, Joseph's attempts initially end in failure. However, resolution over this matter is finally

---

[13] Ehrman and Pleše, *The Apocryphal Gospels*, p. 6.

[14] There is considerable debate about which text is the closest to the original text of this narrative. Extensive discussion of this can be found in Chartrand-Burke, 'The Infancy Gospel of Thomas', pp. 134-244. However, as noted, for the purposes of this examination, the Greek text of Tischendorf's A , used by Hock, is followed here.

[15] Citing the translation of Hock, *The Infancy Gospels*, p. 105.

[16] Citing the translation of Hock, *The Infancy Gospels*, p. 129.

reached when, in Joseph's last attempt to find instruction for his son (15.1-7), Jesus demonstrates to the teacher, a 'close friend' of Joseph's that 'already he's full of grace and wisdom' (15.6).[17] Thus, the teacher tells Joseph that Jesus is not in need of instruction and asks him 'to take him back home' (15.6).[18] Afterwards, the readers are then presented a series of three additional miracle stories in which Jesus saves his brother James from a deadly snake bite (16.1-2), brings a child back to life before a 'crowd of onlookers' (17.1-4), and does the same with a man who has fallen from the top of a building (18.1-3).[19] Finally, in the last chapter, 19.1-13, they encounter a representation of the Lukan account of Jesus in the temple in which his mother, notably, has a more prominent role than Joseph. Nevertheless, as this summary indicates, Joseph is given priority as the 'father' and parent of Jesus throughout this narrative.

However, few scholars have formally acknowledged Joseph's importance in the IGThomas or examined his portrayal in detail.[20] Thus, in order to achieve a better understanding of the evolution and history of reception of the early gospel portrayals of Joseph, it is necessary to examine his portrayal in the IGThomas and give it appropriate consideration. Having briefly addressed the issues of the date, provenance, language, purpose, and content of this narrative, it is now appropriate to turn to the characterization of Joseph within it.

Joseph is referred to by name 31 times (2.4, 5; 3.3, 4; 4.4; 5.1, 4; 6.1, 2, 3, 4, 13, 14; 7.4, 11; 12.3; 13.2 [2], 3, 4; 14.1, 2, 5 [2]; 15.1, 2, 5, 6, 7; 16.1; 17.1). In addition, the readers also find Joseph described as 'Jesus' father' (2.4; 13.1) and 'his (Jesus') father' (12.1; 13.2, 4).[21] Additionally, they learn that Jesus also identifies Joseph as 'my father' (6.4) and, throughout the narrative, responds to Joseph as his father. Similarly, Jesus is identified by others, in conversation with Joseph, as 'your [Joseph's] boy' (2.4; 3.4) and is later described as 'his [Joseph's] child' (5.1; 15.7).[22] The focus of IGThomas upon the relationship between Joseph and Jesus

---

[17] Citing the translation of Hock, *The Infancy Gospels*, p. 137.

[18] Citing the translation of Hock, *The Infancy Gospels*, p. 137.

[19] Citing the translation of Hock, *The Infancy Gospels*, pp. 137, 139.

[20] Two scholars have reflected on select aspects of the role of Joseph in the Infancy Gospel of Thomas, namely, Hock (*The Infancy Gospels*, pp. 85-90) and Aasgaard (*The Childhood of Jesus*, pp. 56, 58, 60-61, 64, 66, 75, 76-79, 108, 109, 110, 112, 157-58, 163), but neither has engaged in a thorough examination of his portrayal. In turn, others have only briefly acknowledged the role of Joseph in the Infancy Gospel of Thomas. In this regard, see Foster, 'The Iconography of St. Joseph in Netherlandish Art, 1400-1550', pp. 9-19; Lienhard, *St. Joseph*, pp. 7, 9-10; Chartrand-Burke, 'The Infancy Gospel of Thomas', p. 400.

[21] Hock, *The Infancy Gospels*, pp. 107, 129, 131[3].

[22] Hock, *The Infancy Gospels*, pp. 107, 109, 111, 113, 137. There are also further allusions to Joseph being the father of Jesus. See ('you have such a boy' and 'teach him to bless and not curse'), 4.4 and ('You have a bright child ...'), 6.2.

5. *The Portrayal of Joseph in the Infancy Gospel of Thomas* 101

is further highlighted by the fact that the first reference to the mother of Jesus does not occur until 11.1 and little interest is shown in her relationship with Jesus.[23]

The first references to Joseph in IGThomas occur early in the narrative, in 2.1-7 and 3.1-4, in two related episodes about the miraculous powers of Jesus at age five. Here, Joseph is introduced to the readers as 'Joseph, Jesus' father' (2.4) and Jesus is identified as 'your boy' (2.4).[24] Thus, their relationship as father and son is confirmed. Within a short time it is also demonstrated for the readers when Joseph responds to the complaint of 'a Jew' that Jesus 'has violated the sabbath' (2.4).[25] Revealing his own adherence to the sabbath, and his responsibility for Jesus' behavior, Joseph quickly approaches Jesus and shouts, 'Why are you doing what's not permitted on the Sabbath?'(2.5).[26]

This episode is followed by a related one in 3.1-4 in which the readers learn of Jesus' confrontation with a young boy ('the son of Annas the scholar', 3.1) that makes the young boy wither away.[27] Shortly afterwards the parents of the young boy gather their 'withered' son and bring him to Joseph, accusing him and saying: 'It's your fault – your boy did all this' (3.4).[28]

These two stories are, in turn, connected to two accompanying accounts in chs. 4 and 5 (4.1-5.6), that also reveal the amazing powers of the five-year-old Jesus. In the first account Jesus is walking in his village when, as the readers learn, 'a boy ran by and bumped him on the shoulder' (4.1).[29] Angry at the boy's act, the young Jesus tells him that he will not 'continue' his journey (4.1); a declaration that is followed by the boy's collapse and death.[30] However, Jesus' actions also lead the 'parents

---

[23] In 11.1 and several other places, she is referred to as 'his mother' (11.1, 3, 4; 14.5; 19.6, 11[2]). Similarly, she is identified as 'the mother of this child' in 19.8. Finally, she is identified by name, but surprisingly, only once, at the end of the document, as 'his mother Mary' (19.6).

Joseph and Mary are only conjoined and directly engaged with one another within the narrative on two occasions, in 14.5 and in the account of 19.1-12. Further, they are only referred to together, as 'his parents', on a few occasions (19.1, 2, 11).

With regard to the specific designations and titles attributed to characters within the holy family, it is also interesting to note that Jesus is sometimes referred to as 'the child' (6.11, 15, 16; 7.1; 8.1, 3; 10.4; 12.1[2]; 13.2, 3, 4; 14.1, 2, 5; 15.1, 2, 7; 17.2; 19.2) or 'this child' (6.3,9[2]; 7.3, 4, 9; 13.4; 15.6; 17.4; 18.3; 19.8) or even 'this boy' (4.3) in the narrative; a designation that appears to set him apart from other children as well as the adults in the text.

[24] Hock, *The Infancy Gospels*, p. 107.
[25] Hock, *The Infancy Gospels*, p. 107.
[26] Hock, *The Infancy Gospels*, p. 107.
[27] Hock, *The Infancy Gospels*, p. 107.
[28] Hock, *The Infancy Gospels*, p. 109.
[29] Hock, *The Infancy Gospels*, p. 109.
[30] Hock, *The Infancy Gospels*, p. 109.

of the dead boy' (4.4), as others before (3.4), to approach Joseph and blame him for Jesus' actions. In the process, they issue an ultimatum to Joseph with respect to his family's residence within the village and tell Joseph what he must do. They say: 'Because you have such a boy, you can't live with us in the village or else teach him to bless and not curse. He's killing our children!'(4.4)[31] Thus, through these stories, the readers are informed that those living in the village with Joseph believe he is the father of Jesus (2.4; 3.3, 4). They treat Joseph as though (and apparently he, alone) is responsible for his child's behavior, and suggest that Joseph is responsible for teaching Jesus to use his powers for the good of others (2.4; 3.4). The assumption behind the ultimatum of the dead child's parents appears to be that if Joseph will 'teach' (4.4) Jesus to use his powers in positive ways ('to bless and not curse', 4.4) that his family may be able to continue to reside in the village.[32]

In light of this the readers are likely not surprised when Joseph summons Jesus and confronts the five-year-old 'in private' and says: 'Why are you doing all this? These people are suffering and so they hate and harass us' (5.1).[33] Jesus, in turn, responds to Joseph's protest by promising that he will 'keep quiet for your sake' (5.2).[34] Even so, the readers discover that despite his promise, Jesus quickly abandons this commitment and causes 'the parents of the dead boy' to become blind (4.4; 5.2).[35] As a result, this exacerbates the situation and leads Joseph to get angry and grab Jesus' ear (5.4). As a result, Jesus lashes out at Joseph and says: 'It's one thing for you to seek and not find; it's quite another for you to act this unwisely' (5.5), a statement that might lead readers to imagine Jesus is suggesting that Joseph lacks understanding of his son's role and purpose.[36] The limits of Joseph's spiritual understanding and the limits of his relationship with Jesus also appear to be implied in Jesus' words to Joseph: 'Don't you know that I don't really belong to you?' (5.6).[37]

Thus, Jesus appears to draw a line, separating himself from Joseph, while suggesting there are real limitations to Joseph's fatherhood. At the same time, Jesus' next words, 'Don't make me upset' (5.6), seem to assert his dominance over Joseph.[38] Therefore, as the account in ch. 5 draws to an end, the readers perceive that a certain tension has emerged between Joseph and Jesus. As such, in these two accounts they learn more

---

[31] Hock, *The Infancy Gospels*, p. 109.
[32] Hock, *The Infancy Gospels*, p. 109.
[33] Hock, *The Infancy Gospels*, p. 111.
[34] Hock, *The Infancy Gospels*, p. 111.
[35] Hock, *The Infancy Gospels*, pp. 109, 111.
[36] Hock (*The Infancy Gospels*, p. 111) acknowledges in his note that this quote is from a text that 'has ... problems' and 'is far from secure'.
[37] This question also seems to foreshadow Jesus' later remark in 19.7.
[38] Hock, *The Infancy Gospels*, p. 111.

5. The Portrayal of Joseph in the Infancy Gospel of Thomas   103

about the nature of the relationship between Joseph and Jesus and the challenges Joseph faces as he attempts to 'father' and 'parent' the child Jesus.

As the narration unfolds at the beginning of ch. 6, Jesus' behavior evokes awe as well as sympathy from the figure of a teacher named, Zacchaeus. On the one hand, Zacchaeus' initial private reaction to Jesus, in which he says to himself, 'He is just a child and saying this!' would remind the readers of some of the villagers' prior attitude toward Jesus and might not surprise them (5.3; 6.1).[39] On the other hand, filled with sympathy for Joseph's dilemma, Zacchaeus summons the troubled father, saying, 'You have a bright child, and he has a good mind ... I'll teach him everything he needs to know so as not to be unruly'(6.2).[40] In light of Jesus' prior behavior the readers may well understand Joseph's skepticism about Zacchaeus' offer (6.2) and would likely empathize with Joseph's warning to Zacchaeus that 'No one is able to rule this child except God alone' (6.3).[41] Further, their sense of the challenge facing Joseph would intensify even more with the bold declaration Jesus directs toward his prospective teacher, Zacchaeus.

> If you wish to be a perfect teacher, listen to me and I'll teach you wisdom that no one else knows except for me and the one who sent me to you. It's you who happen to be my student ... (IGThomas 6.6-7).[42]

Nonetheless, the readers would likely comprehend Joseph's decision to accept Zacchaeus' offer to teach Jesus (an offer that will play out within this long cycle of stories in 6.1–8.4), in part, in light of earlier demands of his fellow villagers who insisted Jesus be taught how to use his knowledge and power for good (4.4; 6.2, 14).[43] So the readers may well interpret Joseph's effort as both natural and logical, the kind of thing that the parent of Jesus may well be expected to do in order to attempt to harness and discipline the amazing prowess of his child. However, Zacchaeus is unsuccessful and after a short time he asks Joseph to 'take him (Jesus) back to your house' (7.11).[44]

Following this account and the introduction of Jesus' mother, Joseph reappears in chs.12 and 13, in the context of two miracle stories.[45] Here,

---

[39] Hock, *The Infancy Gospels*, p. 113.
[40] Hock, *The Infancy Gospels*, p. 113.
[41] Hock, *The Infancy Gospels*, p. 113.
[42] Hock, *The Infancy Gospels*, pp. 113, 115.
[43] Hock, *The Infancy Gospels*, pp. 109, 113, 115.
[44] Hock, *The Infancy Gospels*, pp. 121, 123.
[45] Before Joseph reappears in the narrative, the mother of Jesus is introduced to the readers. Chapters 11–13 offer an account of Jesus's miraculously helping a member of his family. In this case the readers are told how a six-year-old Jesus is miraculously able to bring water to 'his mother' (11.1). In addition to learning of the help he provides his mother, they also learn of her affection for him demonstrated in her response to Jesus'

intriguingly, there is no evidence of the prior tension between Joseph and Jesus. Instead, in both stories, Joseph joyfully welcomes and responds to the amazing powers of his child. In the first account, the now eight year old, assists Joseph, who is sowing, and his assistance results in a crop so large that Joseph and Jesus are able to provide for all the poor in their village (12.1-4).[46]

In the second story, in ch. 13, Jesus miraculously resolves a problem his father has created in his poor carpentry of a bed for a rich man. Joseph has cut one of the boards for the bed too short. In his fear, Joseph turns to Jesus who miraculously expands the size of the board in order that it might properly fit the bed and satisfy Joseph's customer (13.1-4).[47] Thus, in these stories the readers witness a new level of cooperation between Joseph and Jesus that leads the child to help his father in ways that not only benefit Joseph (13.1-4) but those in their village who once wished them ill (12.1-4). They also witness, in these two accounts, something of a role reversal. While Joseph still takes the lead in matters, Jesus offers assistance, through his miraculous powers, that substantially enhances the efforts of Joseph (13.1-4). In the first story this is seen in the immense harvest produced from Jesus' simple sowing of 'one measure of grain' (12.1) that is so great that it enables Joseph to feed 'all the poor in the village' (12.3).[48]

The next set of references to Joseph (in chs. 14 and 15), also relate attempts by Joseph to find a teacher to instruct Jesus. In the first episode, detailed in 14.1-5, Joseph takes Jesus to a new teacher with the hope that his son will respond to instruction.[49] But, the new teacher rapidly tires of Jesus' unresponsiveness and hits Jesus 'on the head' (14.4).[50] In response, the readers learn that 'Jesus got angry and cursed' the teacher who 'immediately lost consciousness and fell face down on the ground' (14.4).[51] Afterwards, Jesus returns 'to Joseph's house' where Joseph, upset by the actions of his son, instructs his mother not to 'let him go outside, because those who annoy him end up dead' (14.5).[52]

However, matters take a different turn in the second episode in 15.1-7 when 'a close friend' of Joseph's tells him: 'Send the child to my

miracle, for 'once she saw the miracle that had occurred, [she] kissed him'(11.4). At the same time, they may have began to discern that 'his mother' has some comprehension of how special Jesus is and how important his life will become, for they are told that having witnessed Jesus' miracle, 'she kept to herself the mysteries that she had seen him do' (11.4).

[46] Hock, *The Infancy Gospels*, p. 129.
[47] Hock, *The Infancy Gospels*, p. 131.
[48] Hock, *The Infancy Gospels*, p. 129.
[49] Hock, *The Infancy Gospels*, p. 133.
[50] Hock, *The Infancy Gospels*, p. 133.
[51] Hock, *The Infancy Gospels*, p. 133.
[52] Hock, *The Infancy Gospels*, p. 135.

5. *The Portrayal of Joseph in the Infancy Gospel of Thomas*   105

schoolroom. Perhaps with some flattery I can teach him his letters' (15.1).[53] At this point, following all his attempts to provide instruction for his child, Joseph's words of caution to his friend, 'If you can muster the courage, brother, take him with you' (15.2), reveal that he is at his wits' end.[54] Accordingly, the readers would understand the surprise of Joseph when, after some time, the teacher tells Joseph, upon his approach to the classroom, 'Brother, please know that I accepted this child as a student, but already he's full of grace and wisdom. So, I'm asking you, brother, to take him back home' (15.6).[55] In turn, they would also comprehend Joseph's pleasure and relief once he hears Jesus' response to the words of the teacher: 'Because you have spoken and testified rightly, that other teacher who was struck down will be healed' (15.7).[56] For this response of Jesus suggests that after much effort and worry, the matters of Jesus' education and behavior appear to have finally been positively resolved. Thus, Joseph was able to take 'his child' and go home, as the teacher recommended (15.7).[57]

There are only two brief references to 'Joseph' in chs. 16 and 17.[58] The first is the story of another miraculous healing by Jesus. This time, Jesus heals another son of Joseph (who is curiously introduced for the first time at this point within the narrative) identified only as 'his (Joseph's) son James', who may be somewhat older than Jesus who, in this case, is described as 'the child Jesus' (16.1).[59] In turn, in ch. 17, there is only a brief mention of the father of Jesus in which reference is made to 'an infant in Joseph's neighborhood' becoming 'sick' and dying (17.1).[60]

Finally, the last set of references to Joseph occurs in the final chapter of IGThomas, ch. 19. Here, in this representation of the event of Jesus in the temple, the readers discover an emphasis upon 'his mother Mary' (19.6-11), an emphasis the readers have not encountered in prior portions of the narrative, not even in the earlier portrayal of her in ch. 11 (11.1-4).[61] At the same time they also discover that the role of Joseph has changed. He is no longer the sole or primary parent juxtaposed with Jesus in the narrative. Rather, in this last account, he is conjoined with

---

[53] Hock, *The Infancy Gospels*, p. 135.
[54] Hock, *The Infancy Gospels*, p. 135.
[55] Hock, *The Infancy Gospels*, pp. 135, 137.
[56] Hock, *The Infancy Gospels*, p. 137.
[57] Hock, *The Infancy Gospels*, p. 137.
[58] Hock, *The Infancy Gospels*, p. 137.
[59] Hock, *The Infancy Gospels*, p. 137.
[60] Hock, *The Infancy Gospels*, p. 137.
[61] Hock, *The Infancy Gospels*, pp. 127, 129, 143. See also Hock, *The Infancy Gospels*, pp. 127, 129 for three references to her as 'his mother' in 11.1-4.

Mary (as he was briefly conjoined with her in 14.5) and formally identified, with her, as one of Jesus' 'parents' (19.1, 2, 11).[62] In turn, in this context, it is also the case that the readers realize that Joseph now fulfills his parental responsibilities in conjunction with Mary rather than independent of her; as was largely the case in the previous eighteen chapters.[63]

So IGThomas ends with a shift from an extensive focus upon Joseph to a brief but important focus upon Mary in the final pericope of the last chapter of the narrative. Nonetheless, even the inclusion of Mary and the attention given her at the end, does not diminish either the prominence or priority given to Joseph within the IGThomas.

Therefore, the importance of this narrative upon the image and perception of Joseph, must be acknowledged. For the examination of the portrayal of Joseph within the IGThomas reveals that this portrayal does expand the canonic portrayals of him and does so largely in very positive ways. This is seen in the numerous additional details related in the accounts of interaction between Joseph and Jesus, as well as in their respective and mutual interactions with others within this narrative.

Subsequently, readers recognize that Joseph's role is much more substantial than Mary's, and that, as has been documented in innumerable

---

[62] Hock, *The Infancy Gospels*, p. 133. In the reference in 14.5 Joseph seems to control the situation and direct the behavior of Mary. In contrast, in 19.6-11, Mary seems to control the dynamics of the interaction with Jesus and, at least in some respects, direct the behavior of Joseph. See also Hock, *The Infancy Gospels*, pp. 141, 143.

[63] See especially 19.1-4 in Hock, *The Infancy Gospels*, p. 141. In the second half of ch. 19, in 19.6-13, the readers note a special emphasis on the role of Mary and her relationship with Jesus as well as an affirmation of the unique character of Jesus. It reads: 'His mother Mary came up and said to him, "Child, why have you done this to us? Don't you see, we've been worried sick looking for you." "Why are you looking for me?' Jesus said to them. 'Don't you know that I have to be in my father's house?" Then the scholars and the Pharisees said, "Are you the mother of this child?" She said, "I am." And they said to her, "You more than any woman are to be congratulated, for God has blessed the fruit of your womb! For we've never seen nor heard such glory and such virtue and wisdom." Jesus got up and went with his mother and was obedient to his parents. His mother took careful note of all that had happened. And Jesus continued to excel in learning and gain respect. To him be glory for ever and ever. Amen' (19.6-13).

Thus, among other things, at the very end of this narrative, the readers are reminded of the importance of Mary in the life of Jesus through both her words and actions as well as those of 'the scholars and the Pharisees' (19.6-10). For in this encounter Mary's intimate role in relationship to Jesus is further acknowledged and enhanced for the readers. Prior to this pericope, aside from the brief account in chapter eleven, Mary has remained largely behind the scenes in the story. However, in this account she is brought to the foreground of the narrative in a new way and clearly affirmed for the readers in the following words of 'the scholars and the Pharisees' who say: 'You more than any woman are to be congratulated, for God has blessed the fruit of your womb!'(19.10)

Additionally, Mary is kept in the foreground in 19.11 where, again, special emphasis is placed upon 'his mother' as the readers are instructed that: 'Jesus got up and *went with his mother* and was obedient to his parents.'

references to him within the IGThomas, he has a much more significant presence in most of the narrative. In turn, the usual relegation of Jesus' 'mother' to simple domestic tasks (11.1-4; 14.5; aside from 19.1-13) and her limited appearance within the text, further confirms the idea that she 'leaves a much fainter impression than Joseph'.[64] At the same time, the fact that the primary responsibilities (particularly with respect to his behavior and education) for parenting Jesus are left to Joseph is also probably quite telling for the readers of this narrative and instructive with respect to the proper role of fathers in the care of their children.[65] Thus, the readers (and, perhaps, particularly male readers), might well perceive Joseph as an exemplar and model for them in their own parenting. Subsequently, it seems fair to conclude that the expansion and elaboration of Joseph's role and his relationship with Jesus offers significant data about the transformation that is taking place in the development of the Joseph tradition of Matthew, Luke, and John.

The Infancy Gospel of Thomas and the History of Effects

A comparison of the portrayal of Joseph in the canonic gospels with the representation of Joseph in IGThomas, leads to the conclusion that their influence is largely limited to the inclusion of significant portions of Lk. 2.41-52 in the final chapter of the document, ch. 19. While it is clear that there is a dependence upon this canonic pericope, it is also clear that there are significant differences between the earlier and later texts, differences that start to emerge after verse four of chapter nineteen.[66] One of the most striking is the change evident in the response of the temple teachers to Jesus. In Lk. 2.47, the readers are told: 'all who heard him were amazed at his understanding and answers'. In contrast, in IGThomas, 19.5, the miraculous character of Jesus' remarks to the temple teachers is suggested.[67]

---

[64] Aasgaard, *The Childhood of Jesus*, pp. 109-10. Aasgaard (p. 109) suggests that 'Joseph ... emerges (in this narrative) as a very lifelike figure.' He goes on to add that 'Mary and Joseph each have their distinctive profiles, which very much mirror ancient thinking. Stated in modern terms: Mary has the role of a supporting and protecting mother, Joseph of a controlling and advising father. But ... Joseph emerges as far more important for his (Jesus') socialization ...' (p. 110).

[65] Aasgard (*The Childhood of Jesus*, p. 66) believes this is appropriate. He writes: 'In keeping with ancient practice, Joseph as *paterfamilias* emerges as having primary responsibility for Jesus' upbringing.'

[66] Some of these differences were suggested in the earlier discussion of chapter nineteen.

[67] Hock, *The Infancy Gospels*, pp. 141.

At the same time, significant differences appear in the second half of ch. 19, in 19.6-13.[68] Here, in 19.6-13, in IGThomas, in contrast to what is found in Lk. 2.48-52, the readers note a special emphasis on the role of Mary and her relationship with Jesus, as was highlighted in the discussion of ch. 19.[69] Thus, among other things, at the very end of this narrative, the readers are reminded of the importance of Mary in the life of Jesus through both her words and actions as well as those of 'the scholars and the Pharisees' (19.6-10); words and actions that represent formal changes in the canonic account upon which this pericope is based, Lk. 2.48-52.[70] These changes include, first, the change from the Lukan words, "When his parents saw him they were astonished', where there is an emphasis on both parents of Jesus to 'His mother Mary came up' (19.6), which puts the focus on one parent.[71] Second, these changes include the insertion of a highly positive encounter between 'the scholars and the Pharisees' in the temple with Mary in regard to her and her relationship to Jesus which further highlights her significance for the readers (19.8-10).[72] Subsequently, they also include the special attention given to Mary in 19.11. In Lk. 2.51 readers were told: 'Then he (Jesus) went down with them (Joseph and Mary) and came to Nazareth and was obedient to them.' Still, in the account in IGThomas, special significance is placed upon 'his mother', as the readers are instructed that: 'Jesus got up and went with his mother and was obedient to his parents' (19.11).[73]

Finally, it should be noted that examples of the influence of the canonic Gospels can also be found, among other references and allusions, in the regular mention of the main characters of Joseph (including a fascinating reference and discussion of his work as 'a carpenter', 13.1-4), Jesus, and Mary, repeated use of the name, Zacchaeus (6.1–8.3) as well as a single reference to Annas (3.1).[74]

Nonetheless, having acknowledged these examples, it can be concluded, as was the case with IGJames, that a close reading of the text of the IGThomas reveals that it has little interest in the canonic references related to Joseph.[75] As such, it is not surprising that a comparison of the references to Joseph in the canonic Gospels with those in IGThomas

---

[68] Hock, *The Infancy Gospels*, pp. 97-98, in contrast, does not see 'significant departures' from the Lukan text.
[69] Hock, *The Infancy Gospels*, p. 143.
[70] Hock, *The Infancy Gospels*, p. 143.
[71] Hock, *The Infancy Gospels*, p. 143.
[72] Hock, *The Infancy Gospels*, p. 143.
[73] Hock, *The Infancy Gospels*, p. 143.
[74] Hock, *The Infancy Gospels*, p. 98.
[75] It is notable that IGThomas does not include or adapt numerous references to Joseph in Matthew, Luke and John that reveal aspects of Joseph's nature and character found in these canonic texts but instead appears satisfied to focus on its own particular concerns with respect to Joseph.

reveals that only the specific New Testament references and allusions to Joseph in Mk. 6.3, Mt. 13. 55 and Lk. 2.41-52 appear in IGThomas and that these references are limited to chs. 13, 16, and 19.[76]

The Distinctiveness of the Portrait of Joseph in the Infancy Gospel of Thomas

Thus, in conclusion, this infancy gospel offers a portrait of Joseph that stands in some tension with the earliest gospel portrayals. This is evident in additional elements to the 'characterization' of Joseph that stretch the parameters of the conception and image of the Carpenter in early Christianity. Among these is the fact that in this gospel, Joseph is a very active father who continually engages with Jesus. This, in itself, puts IGThomas in sharp contrast with IGJames for whom Joseph has little to offer. Further, as Hock notes, this new role for Joseph is made even more intriguing by the fact that he is often at odds with his son and must regularly discipline him. And yet, it is in this context of the continuous engagement of Joseph with Jesus that this non-canonic narrative reveals a much fuller picture of Joseph that presents him as a caring, patient, thoughtful, conciliatory, and loving father who embodies the characteristics of a 'good' father.[77] As such, the portrayal of Joseph in IGThomas (as the portrayal of Joseph in IGJames), responds to the literary challenges of the *Leerstellen*, 'gaps in the narrative' and the *Unbestimmtheitsstellen*, 'places where things are unclear', raised by the canonic Gospels by providing more information about the nature of Joseph's relationship with Jesus and the role Joseph played in Jesus' earthly family.[78] In the process, it provides its own thought-provoking and paradigmatic portrayal of Joseph.

---

[76] Further, this comparison also suggests that the desire of the narrator of IGThomas to respond both to the need for knowledge and information about the childhood of Jesus and to provide guidance to parents and children through the models of Joseph and Jesus in these accounts made him less inclined to use extensive references from the canonic narratives. In turn, it may also help explain why Joseph's portrayal in IGThomas is as extensive as it is. At the same time, it also seems to explain Chartrand-Burke's suggestion in 'Completing the Gospel: *The Infancy Gospel of Thomas* as a Supplement to the Gospel of Luke', in *The Reception and Interpretation of the Bible in Late Antiquity: Proceedings of the Montreal Colloquium in Honour of Charles Kannengiesser* (Leiden and Boston: Brill, 2008), pp. 101-17, that the author builds his new text, in part, upon the foundations of the Gospel of Luke and, most notably, specific narrative patterns informed by Luke, especially by the narrative found in Lk. 2.41-52.

[77] Hock, *The Infancy Gospels*, pp. 86-90.

[78] See Elliott, *A Synopsis of the Apocryphal Nativity and Infancy Narratives*, p. ix.

The Narrator and the Narrator's Community's Perceptions and Beliefs about Joseph the Carpenter in the Infancy Gospel of Thomas

For these reasons, in light of the priority given to Joseph and the ways in which he is characterized and represented in IGThomas (aside from the brief attention directed to Mary), it is evident that the narrator and the narrator's community held Joseph in high regard and believed he was an essential and positive figure in the childhood of Jesus. By presenting Joseph as the primary parent and the most prominent adult in the narrative, they offer a more complete portrait of Joseph that not only depicts him in multiple roles but also sheds more insight into the breadth and depth of his personal relationship with Jesus. Thus, in this account, Joseph can be understood as a caring and loving character as well as a disciplinarian; as one who seeks the best for his child as well as one who insists his child respects their neighbors; as a real, nurturing father. As a result, the narrator and the narrator's community indicate that they believe Joseph's primary role, above all others, was that of *pater familias*.

6

The Portrayal of Joseph the Carpenter in the History of Joseph the Carpenter

Introduction

Having examined two early non-canonic narrative portrayals of Joseph in IGJames and IGThomas, consideration is now directed toward a third, later narrative that, interestingly, bears the name of the primary character of this study in its traditional title: the History of Joseph the Carpenter (hereafter abbreviated as HJC). It appears to stand in a period between the composition of the Infancy Gospel of Thomas and the Gospel of Pseudo-Matthew. Morenz,[1] James,[2] and Bienert,[3] and Elliott[4] believe HJC may be dated as early as the fourth or fifth century, around two to three hundred years after the compositions of IGJames and IGThomas, but only Elliott provides specific support for this suggestion. However, Elliott also thinks that it may be dated later since its focus is on the glorification of Joseph and this would appear to be more appropriate to a later period when 'saints' days' were observed.[5] Ehrman and Pleše concur and go so far as to state that the text was 'likely composed ... in the late sixth or early seventh century.'[6] They believe this range of dates is more likely because the account of Joseph's death is 'strikingly similar in

---

[1] Siegfried Morenz, *Die Geschichte von Joseph dem Zimmermann* (Berlin: Akademie-Verlag, 1951), p. 112, believes some of the narrative may have been written as early as the third quarter of the fourth century.

[2] Similarly, Montague Rhodes James (*The Apocryphal New Testament* [Oxford: Clarendon Press, 1953], p. 84) states that the History of Joseph the Carpenter may have been written in 'the fourth century'.

[3] Likewise, Bienert ('The Relatives of Jesus', p. 484) concurs with this range of dates when he states that this document 'presumably originated ... about 400 ...'

[4] Elliott (*The Apocryphal New Testament*, p. 111) also concurs, noting that the 'existence of the book in both main Coptic dialects is one of the arguments that have been put forward in favour of a fourth-fifth century date for its composition'. In addition, Elliott notes that the 'millenarian teaching of ch. 26' and 'other eschatological teaching' may also support dating the text to this period.

[5] Elliott (*The Apocryphal New Testament*, p. 111) acknowledges that others have argued for a later date because the 'purpose [of the book] appears to be 'to glorify Joseph's feast day' and this may suggest a later period 'when saints' days were observed ...'.

[6] Ehrman and Pleše, *The Apocryphal Gospels*, p. 158.

form and content to various sixth-and seventh-century Coptic accounts of the passing of the Virgin Mary ...'.⁷ Therefore, a period of composition that extends from around 350 to 625 CE seems most appropriate.

In regard to the provenance of the narrative, scholars also appear to believe this 'history' originated, as IGJames and the IGThomas, in a location within eastern Christianity.⁸ Although the precise origin remains a matter of debate, it appears that the HJC may have been composed in Egypt.⁹ This seems likely, for three reasons. First, parallels appear to exist between some of the teachings about death in this narrative and comparable teachings found in accounts about the death of the Virgin Mary in other Coptic literature.¹⁰ Second, an Egyptian origin may also be suggested by the early presence of this text in the two main Coptic dialects; in toto in the Bohairic dialect and in fragments in the Sahidic dialect.¹¹ Finally, the fact that 'the cult' of St. Joseph 'was long confined to Egypt'

---

⁷ Ehrman and Pleše, *The Apocryphal Gospels*, p. 158.

⁸ See the discussions offered by James, *The Apocryphal New Testament*, p. 84; Bienert, 'The Relatives of Jesus', p. 484, and Elliott, *The Apocryphal New Testament*, p. 111. It may also be the case that the references to the 'congregation of the virgins' (ch. 26) and 'the church of the virgins' (ch. 26) as well as the reference to Jesus' promise to 'every poor man' that poverty and sudden death shall end in his family if he names a son 'Joseph' (ch. 26), suggest that this text originated in a wider Christian community that contained both celibate and non-celibate Christian groups. There is certainly significant evidence of the presence of celibate Christian communities in Egypt during the period in which this text was likely written. In this regard, see *The Desert Fathers* (trans. Helen Waddell; New York: Vintage Books, 1998). In this regard also see Ehrman and Pleše, *The Apocryphal Gospels*, p. 158. They note that 'All four manuscript witnesses of the Sahidic version, now randomly distributed in three major European collections, originate from the same locale-the library of the White Monastery in Upper Egypt.'

⁹ Morenz (*Die Geschichte von Joseph dem Zimmermann*, p. 110) argues that despite arguments to the contrary, he believes there can be no question that HJC originated in Egypt. James, *The Apocryphal New Testament*, p. 84, is also quite clear about his position. He states unequivocally that HJC 'is an Egyptian book.' Bienert, 'The Relatives of Jesus', p. 484, also seems to agree when he states that this text 'presumably originated in Egypt ...' Elliott (*The Apocryphal New Testament*, p. 111) also thinks Egypt is the likely location. Again, see Ehrman and Pleše, *The Apocryphal Gospels*, pp. 158-59.

¹⁰ In this regard, see James, *The Apocryphal New Testament*, p. 84, who argues that the narrative is filled with 'picturesque and highly Egyptian descriptions of death', and that the 'lamentations of Joseph and his prayers find many parallels in the literature of Christian Egypt, and especially in the Coptic accounts of the death of the Virgin.' See also Elliott, *The Apocryphal New Testament*, p. 111, who concurs with respect to James' ideas about the 'teaching on death' and the 'parallels in the Coptic accounts of the death of the Virgin.' This is also acknowledged in Ehrman and Pleše, *The Apocryphal Gospels*, p. 158.

¹¹ Morenz, *Die Geschichte von Joseph dem Zimmermann*, pp. 88-96, acknowledges that the Coptic language of the earliest extant texts suggests it origin was Egypt. Further, see James, *The Apocryphal New Testament*, p. 84. Additionally, see Elliott, *The Apocryphal New Testament*, p. 111, who states that an Egyptian origin is likely since the earliest manuscripts of HJC are found in the two main dialects of the Coptic language Bohairic and Sahidic.

6. The Portrayal of Joseph in the History of Joseph the Carpenter

may also support an Egyptian provenance.[12] While these factors raise the likelihood of this hypothesis, they do not appear able to resolve the question of the narrative's origin completely.

Scholars are also divided with respect to the issue of the original language of the text. Ehrman and Pleše, believe the text was initially composed in a Coptic dialect and most likely, Sahidic, although an early complete copy is lost.[13] In contrast, Morenz and Elliott believe a Greek text lies behind the Coptic ones.[14]

However, there appears to be little dispute about the basic integrity of the shape and size of the text as it is found in its three different linguistic redactions of Bohairic, Sahidic, and Arabic.[15]

Further, while proof of interest in the text of HJC is found in the early presence of HJC in texts of two of the main Coptic dialects, Bohairic and Sahidic, and in its presence in early Arabic texts, and in the existence of a later Latin translations, there is no extant evidence that it was disseminated beyond the region of Egypt and its neighboring areas. This, in turn, indicates that it was not widely available or accessible and was probably not known to the larger Christian community outside these confines or familiar to many writers, artists, and artisans beyond these areas. Additionally, there is no explicit evidence that this narrative was incorporated into a later Gothic, Medieval, or Renaissance texts as parts of IGJames, the GPM, and other early Christian non-canonic texts were. Still further, there is also no evidence that any other writer or theologian within this period of time came to share the same passion, found in HJC, to glorify the life of Joseph and to celebrate his feast day for some centuries. Thus, it seems difficult not to conclude that what must have been created or intended as a theological correction or as an attempt to provide balance to the emphasis typically placed upon Mary, failed to meet its objective.[16] Finally, with respect to the importance and significance of HJC, it must be acknowledged that important and significant as it was and remains for the study of the evolution of the portrayal of Joseph in the early centuries of the Christian church, its influence appears to have been diminished as time has passed.

---

[12] James, *The Apocryphal New Testament*, p. 84.

[13] Ehrman and Pleše, *The Apocryphal Gospels*, pp. 158-59. They find support for their argument for the priority of a Coptic (and probably Sahidic text) in the work of Lefort, Giamberardini, and Boud'hors.

[14] Morenz, *Die Geschichte von Joseph dem Zimmermann*, pp. 88-96, makes a detailed argument that concludes that the earliest text of HJC was in Greek. Elliott (*The Apocryphal New Testament*, p. 111) concurs, stating that 'the original language is likely to have been Greek …'

[15] Ehrman and Pleše, *The Apocryphal Gospels*, pp.158-59.

[16] In this regard, see Elliott, *The Apocryphal New Testament*, p. 111.

The Purpose of the History of Joseph the Carpenter

The general purpose of this text, as with the earlier two non-canonic texts, is to fill gaps the narrator and his community believe that the canonic accounts did not fill. In this case, in contrast to the others, the main concern is to focus on Joseph and to relate much more information about his life and death, as well as his relationship with Jesus.

The History of Joseph the Carpenter consists of a prologue and 32 chapters. In the prologue, the readers are informed that the narrative is entitled, 'This is the departure from the body of our father Joseph, the carpenter, the father of Christ according to the flesh' (prologue).[17] In addition, they are told that the source or author of this account is Jesus himself, who told this story about 'the life of my father Joseph, the blessed old carpenter' to his 'disciples' on 'the Mount of Olives' (ch.1).[18] Subsequently, in chs. 2–11, the readers learn from Jesus, himself, several details about Joseph's origins, vocations, marriage, biological family, first contact with Mary, registration of Mary and Jesus in Bethlehem, presence during the birth of Jesus, the family's eventual residence in Nazareth of Galilee, and Jesus' life with Joseph and Mary and Joseph's youngest children, Judas and James the Less (ch. 11).[19] Following this, they are informed by Jesus about the last days and death of Joseph in an extensive recollection that lasts for most of the rest of the narrative (chs. 10; 12–29).[20] In the process, they also discover more details about Joseph's life. In the final three chapters, 30–32, the readers learn about the response of the 'apostles' of Jesus who heard 'these things from our Savior' (ch. 30) and of their reiteration to Jesus of his commission to them, that

> When I ... send you to preach the holy Gospel, preach also my beloved father Joseph; and again, Speak these words of life in the testament of his departure from the body; and again, Read the words of this testament on the feast days and on the sacred days ... (HJC 30).[21]

Thus, as the narrative draws to a close, the readers are reminded that Joseph remains an important figure in the life of the Christian community and in the story of the gospel of Jesus Christ.

---

[17] This first English reference in the text is dited in the translation of Ehrman and Pleše, *The Apocryphal Gospels*, p. 163.

[18] Citing the translation of Ehrman and Pleše, *The Apocryphal Gospels*, p. 163. In contrast, these earlier non-canonic accounts suggest they were authored by early apostolic sources (James, the brother of Jesus, and the disciple, Thomas).

[19] Citing the translation of Ehrman and Pleše, *The Apocryphal Gospels*, p. 169.

[20] Citing the translation of Ehrman and Pleše, *The Apocryphal Gospels*, pp. 169, 171-89.

[21] Citing the translation of Ehrman and Pleše, *The Apocryphal Gospels*, p. 189.

The Characterization of Joseph in the History of Joseph the Carpenter

In HJC, the readers discover substantial details about Joseph's significance, background, character and faith (and beliefs), relationship with Jesus (and relationship with Mary), and his role as a model and help for others within the larger contemporary Christian community that shape the portrait of Joseph in this narrative. Hints of this emerge from the very beginning of the narrative, with the introduction of its title and prologue that invite readers to consider the role and the significance of Joseph and his position within the larger Christian story and gospel.[22] Through the title, the prologue, and the first chapter the readers are introduced to some of the aforementioned details about Joseph that are addressed in later parts of the text.[23] Thus, they learn that Joseph is a very important figure whose death and life offer meaning and hope for them ('words of life', ch. 30), even in their present lives.[24] Second, because he is identified within the title as 'our father', it is also suggested that Joseph should be recognized and acknowledged as a spiritual father for all Christians (prologue).[25] Third, at the same time, by means of the phrases, 'the holy old man' and 'the blessed old carpenter' and similar phrases, the readers are introduced to specific characteristics of this figure (that he is 'holy', 'blessed,' and 'old') that will repeatedly inform their perception and understanding of the figure of Joseph (prologue and ch. 1).[26] Finally, by means of the word 'carpenter', the readers are informed of Joseph's primary vocation (prologue and ch. 1).[27] Thus, these initial references, found in the title, prologue, and ch. 1, suggest Joseph's significance, set the tone, and introduce subjects that will be addressed throughout the narrative.

It can be assumed that the readers have these things in mind when they turn to ch. 2, where the focus is largely on Joseph's past. Since Jesus is presented as the source of this information, readers are likely not surprised that they are provided a host of details. Thus, it is not unexpected

---

[22] Citing the translation of Ehrman and Pleše, *The Apocryphal Gospels*, p. 163.

[23] The English translation of the prologue found in the translation of Ehrman and Pleše, *The Apocryphal Gospels*, p. 163, reads: 'This is the departure from the body of our father Joseph, the carpenter, the father of Christ according to the flesh, who lived one hundred and eleven years, and whose entire life our Savior related to the apostles on the Mount of Olives. The apostles, for their part, wrote down these words and deposited them in the Library at Jerusalem. And the day when the holy old man laid down the body was the twenty-sixth day of the month of Epiphi, in the peace of God.'

[24] Citing the translation of Ehrman and Pleše, *The Apocryphal Gospels*, p. 189.

[25] Citing the translation of Ehrman and Pleše, *The Apocryphal Gospels*, p. 163.

[26] Citing the translation of Ehrman and Pleše, *The Apocryphal Gospels: Texts and Translations*, p. 163.

[27] Citing the translation of Ehrman and Pleše, *The Apocryphal Gospels*, p. 163.

to learn that Joseph was 'from a city called Bethlehem ... the city of King David' (ch. 2) and was acknowledged to be a 'son of David' (chs. 6, 7, and 17).[28] Further, in light of what they had been told in the title, prologue, and ch. 1, they are not surprised to discover that Joseph was 'well versed in the knowledge and craft of carpentry' (ch. 2).[29] The fact that Joseph is most often identified as a 'carpenter' and given the full appellation 'Joseph the Carpenter' (title, prologue, ch. 1, and ch. 30), indicates this is his primary vocation.[30]

Jesus also reveals that following the family's return from Egypt that they settled in Nazareth, also an ancestral residence, where Joseph would remain, work, and be buried, 'next to his parents' (chs. 27 and 29). Here, Joseph, again, 'worked at the craft of carpentry and we lived from the work of his hands' (ch. 9).[31] The readers also learn details about Joseph's earlier life not suggested in the title and prologue. These include that Joseph was 'forty' before he married (ch. 14) and was married for 'forty-nine years' (ch. 14) to a woman who 'died' (chs. 2 and 14).[32] Further, they learn that Joseph fathered six children, 'four male sons and two female daughters' (ch. 2), with this woman.[33]

Accordingly, as a result of this information and other details, they are led to understand that Joseph was quite old before he met Mary.[34] However, despite his age, around the time of the death of Joseph's wife, the priests in Jerusalem begin to contemplate what they would do about the future care of Mary, who was a 'virgin' (chs. 3, 4, and 5), 'good and blessed in every manner' (ch. 3), and had lived in the temple for several years (ch. 3).[35] Subsequently, the readers learn that Mary was 'received' (ch. 4) by Joseph into 'his house' (ch. 4).[36] Thus, the readers witness a specific example of Joseph's righteousness in his response to the priests (and to God).

---

[28] Citing the translation of Ehrman and Pleše, *The Apocryphal Gospels*, pp. 165, 167, 175.

[29] Citing the translation of Ehrman and Pleše, *The Apocryphal Gospels*, p. 165.

[30] Citing the translation of Ehrman and Pleše, *The Apocryphal Gospels*, pp. 163, 189-91.

[31] Citing the translation of Ehrman and Pleše, *The Apocryphal Gospels*, p. 169.

[32] Citing the translation of Ehrman and Pleše, *The Apocryphal Gospels*, pp. 173, 165. The sons were named Judas, Joset, James and Simon; the daughters, Lysia and Lydia.

[33] Citing the translation of Ehrman and Pleše, *The Apocryphal Gospels*, p. 165.

[34] Joseph is identified as 'old' (see the prologue and ch. 4, as well as references to his old age in chs. 7, 8, 10, 12, 15[2], 17, 18[2], 19, 22, 25, 27, and 30). Certainly, part of the reason for the stress on Joseph's age is to further the idea that he is so much older than Mary that it would be inconceivable to think he might be physically intimate with her.

[35] Citing the translation of Ehrman and Pleše, *The Apocryphal Gospels*, p. 165.

[36] Citing the translation of Ehrman and Pleše, *The Apocryphal Gospels*, p. 167.

6. The Portrayal of Joseph in the History of Joseph the Carpenter

Yet, once Mary was established in Joseph's home he 'took to the road to work in carpentry' (ch. 4).[37] Joseph's immediate departure following Mary's arrival, as well as the disclosure of her age ('twelve', ch. 3) and unavailability for sexual intimacy (she is described as pure and virgin), would imply to the readers that the relationship between Joseph and Mary was not like that of a married couple, even though she has been identified as Joseph's 'betrothed' (chs. 2 and 3).[38] However, Joseph's familial commitment to Mary and Jesus is emphatically demonstrated when, upon his arrival in Bethlehem for the registration required by Emperor Augustus, Joseph 'had his name recorded by the scribe: "Joseph, the son of David, and Mary his wife, and Jesus his son are of the tribe of Judah."'[39]

Following the birth of Jesus, Joseph remained with Mary, Jesus, Judas, and James the Less and lived and acted as the real father of Jesus until Jesus reached eighteen or nineteen years of age (chs. 9, 11, 12, and 15) and, Joseph, the age of 'one hundred and eleven years' (chs. 15 and 29) of age.[40]

Additional hints about Joseph's character and faith emerge early when Jesus describes Joseph as 'the blessed old carpenter' (ch. 1), 'a righteous man' (ch. 2), 'this righteous man' (ch. 2), 'the good old man' (chs. 4, 7, 21), 'the guileless Joseph' (ch. 5), 'the blessed old man' (chs. 9, 15, 24), 'the blessed old man Joseph'(chs. 18 and 30), and 'the righteous old man' (ch. 22).[41] Therefore, readers are left with no doubt that Joseph is a 'righteous' person.

Further, they discover that Joseph's commitment to his primary vocation of carpentry and 'the Law of Moses' (chs. 2 and 9) was so high that he 'never ate bread he did not earn' (ch. 9) and, in fact, 'was working at the craft of carpentry until the day he fell sick with the illness of which he was to die' (ch. 29).[42]

The readers also learn more information about Joseph's faith through the means of particular beliefs he appears to hold. With regard to his theological convictions, they learn that he believes in God, believes he can turn to God in times of fear and need (chs. 5-9 and 13), and believes that God addresses him directly in dreams (ch. 6) and in other ways, and that he is obligated to obey God and follow God's directions (chs. 7, 8, 9).[43]

---

[37] Citing the translation of Ehrman and Pleše, *The Apocryphal Gospels*, p. 167.
[38] Citing the translation of Ehrman and Pleše, *The Apocryphal Gospels*, pp. 165-67.
[39] Citing the translation of Ehrman and Pleše, *The Apocryphal Gospels*, p. 167.
[40] Citing the translation of Ehrman and Pleše, *The Apocryphal Gospels*, pp. 169-73.
[41] Citing the translation of Ehrman and Pleše, *The Apocryphal Gospels*, pp. 165, 167, 177, 185.
[42] Citing the translation of Ehrman and Pleše, *The Apocryphal Gospels*, pp. 165, 169, 189.
[43] Citing the translation of Ehrman and Pleše, *The Apocryphal Gospels*, pp. 167-69, 171.

This becomes evident in Jesus' recollection of his conception and the response this evoked in Joseph. Recounting this event, Jesus states that upon discovering Mary was pregnant, Joseph initially 'planned to dismiss her secretly' (ch. 5).[44] Even so, as Jesus recalls, within a short time, 'in the middle of the night', in the midst of his 'grief', 'Gabriel, the archangel of joy', appeared to Joseph and spoke to him in a dream (chs. 5 and 6).[45] Having heard what God wanted him to do, the readers learn that Joseph relinquishes his fear, consents to 'take Mary' (ch. 6) as his 'wife' ('your wife', ch. 6, a designation first made in the reference to Mary as Joseph's 'wife' in ch. 2) and reassures Mary that he will bind himself to her in order to protect her and her child from social ostracism.[46] Thus, the example of Joseph's righteousness is exemplified by his openness to God in the midst of his great anxiety, his trust that God will help him, and his willingness to do what God requires, despite the difficulty involved.

In chs. 8, 9, and 10, Jesus reveals one example after another of Joseph's efforts to be *pater familias*, to take care of Mary and him and to provide for their protection.[47] As a result, Jesus discloses, once again, the breadth of Joseph's openness to God, trust of God, and willingness to obey God.

In turn, in the account of Joseph's prayer that follows in ch. 13, the readers gain more insight into Joseph's faith and spirituality as he openly addresses God as the 'God, the Father of all mercy and the God of all flesh' (ch. 13).[48] Unabashedly addressing the One he also calls 'the Lord of my soul, body, and spirit' Joseph asks God to send the angel Michael to comfort and guide him (ch. 13).[49] Also desirous of God's mercy, Joseph prays in a manner reminiscent of the psalmists when he adds 'O God who judges everyone with equity and righteousness, let now your mercy, my Lord, become my solace; for you are the fountain of all good. Yours is the glory forever and ever' (ch. 13).[50]

But they also learn that, in sharp contrast to his prior prayer in the temple, here, Joseph, feeling even closer to his forthcoming death, engages in a prayer of woes, of lamentation about his physical and spiritual condition (ch. 16).[51]

---

[44] Citing the translation of Ehrman and Pleše, *The Apocryphal Gospels*, p. 167.
[45] Citing the translation of Ehrman and Pleše, *The Apocryphal Gospels*, p. 167.
[46] Citing the translation of Ehrman and Pleše, *The Apocryphal Gospels*, pp. 165, 167.
[47] Citing the translation of Ehrman and Pleše, *The Apocryphal Gospels*, pp. 167-69. These chapters detail the registration of Joseph and Mary in the time of Augustus Caesar, the birth of Jesus in a cave, the flight to Egypt, the residence there, and the eventual return of Joseph, Mary, and Jesus to Nazareth in Galilee.
[48] Citing the translation of Ehrman and Pleše, *The Apocryphal Gospels*, p. 171.
[49] Citing the translation of Ehrman and Pleše, *The Apocryphal Gospels*, p. 171.
[50] Citing the translation of Ehrman and Pleše, *The Apocryphal Gospels*, p. 171.
[51] Citing the translation of Ehrman and Pleše, *The Apocryphal Gospels*, pp. 173-75.

In ch. 17, after Joseph's prayer of lamentation (which Jesus seems to have heard), Jesus goes to Joseph and seeks to comfort him. Upon Jesus' arrival, Joseph cries out, 'Hail many times, my beloved son. Behold, my soul has rested within me a little when I heard your voice' (ch. 17).[52] It is at this point that Joseph begins to disclose his personal beliefs about Jesus, revealing his convictions that Jesus is divine, saying, 'You are truly God, you are truly the Lord …' (ch. 17).[53]

In addition to learning details about Joseph's significance, background, and character and faith, the readers also discover more about Joseph's relationship with Jesus. By repeatedly acknowledging Joseph as 'Joseph my father', 'my father Joseph' or 'my father' (in chs. 2, 3, 4[2], 11, 12, 15[3], 17, 18[2], 21[4], 22[4], 25, 26, 27, 28, 29, 31), 'my father according to the flesh' (chs. 2 and 17), and 'my beloved father Joseph' (chs. 14, 17[2], 24, 25, 26[2], 30), Jesus challenges the readers to understand that he had a real familial, substantive, and extensive relationship with Joseph, as any son might with any father.[54] In the context of that relationship, Jesus demonstrated great respect and love toward Joseph, just as he did toward Mary (ch. 11).[55] Thus, the readers understand that Joseph's relationship with Jesus and Joseph's parenting of him were critical to his growth and development. Jesus describes growing up in the following way: 'And I called Mary my mother and Joseph my father, and I obeyed them in everything they told me. I never contradicted them, but I loved them dearly' (ch. 11).[56]

While much is revealed about the depth and breadth of the relationship between Joseph and Jesus in the first half of HJC, much is also disclosed in the second half of the text. Here, the readers discover that Jesus made specific and significant efforts to reassure his father of the wonderful salvation of God that awaited him beyond his earthly life (chs. 17–19, 21–22, 26).[57] In turn, they learn that during this time, Jesus invited others, including Mary, and the biological children of Joseph, and the

---

[52] Citing the translation of Ehrman and Pleše, *The Apocryphal Gospels*, p. 175
[53] Citing the translation of Ehrman and Pleše, *The Apocryphal Gospels*, p. 175.
[54] Citing the translation of Ehrman and Pleše, *The Apocryphal Gospels*, pp. 167, 169, 173-79, and 185-91. In this regard, one of the most striking revelations in this narrative is that Joseph 'has his name recorded by the scribe: "Joseph, the son of David, and Mary his wife, and Jesus his son are of the tribe of Judah"' (ch.7).
[55] Citing the translation of Ehrman and Pleše, *The Apocryphal Gospels*, p. 169.
[56] Citing the translation of Ehrman and Pleše, *The Apocryphal Gospels*, p. 169. See also mention of Jesus' obedience to Joseph on p. 189 of this translation (in ch. 30 of the narrative).
[57] Citing the translation of Ehrman and Pleše, *The Apocryphal Gospels*, pp. 175-81, 185-87.

villagers and neighbors of Joseph in Nazareth to express their grief and love and respect for him freely and openly (chs. 18–20, 24, 25, 27).[58]

Subsequently, the readers note even more the passion and care Jesus shows Joseph as he approaches death, the amazing human tenderness and spiritual intimacy between them, the continual substantiation that they are father and son, highlighted in many ways by the depth of love that Jesus exhibits, the poignancy of Joseph's relationship with Jesus, both as Joseph is dying and after his death (chs. 18–29).[59] This is particularly evident in chs. 18–29. From the time of Joseph's last hours to his burial, Jesus assumes care for the one he calls 'my father' and displays in one example after another his intimacy with and love for Joseph (ch. 18).[60] Perhaps to their surprise, the readers discover that Mary, likely moved to comfort Joseph, rises to assist Jesus in his efforts with his father. In response, Jesus invites his 'beloved mother Mary' to 'go inside to the blessed old man Joseph', which she does (chs. 18–19).[61] Further, they learn that Jesus sat 'at his (Joseph's) head' and 'held his hands and his knees for a long while, as he (Joseph) looked at me (Jesus)' and begged Jesus, saying, 'Do not let me be taken away!' (ch. 19).[62] In addition, they discover that Jesus' actions evoked responses from Mary and led Mary to touch Joseph's feet (chs. 19 and 20).[63] Finding Joseph's feet cold, Jesus summoned Joseph's sons and daughters and told them to 'Get up and speak with your father; for this is the time to speak ...' (ch. 20).[64] As a result, Joseph's biological children respond and join together with Jesus and Mary, and mourn and weep along with them; an event, accentuated by Jesus' last words in the chapter: 'I, too, and Mary, my virgin mother, cried with them, for surely the hour of death was come' (ch. 20).[65] Thus, at this point in the narrative, the readers are left with an image of a dying Joseph surrounded by *all* the different members of his family.

In chs. 21–23, the readers learn how Jesus stayed with Joseph (whom Jesus identifies as 'my father' several times in chs. 21[4] and 22[4]) in his last waking moments and 'reprimanded the Devil and those who were with him' and 'raised a prayer to my Father of many mercies' on behalf

---

[58] Citing the translation of Ehrman and Pleše, *The Apocryphal Gospels*, pp. 177-79, 184-85, 187. In this regard, one of the distinct features revealed in this narrative are examples in which Mary demonstrates significant affection towards Joseph (similarly to some of the actions of her son). These examples not only disclose new things about Mary's relationship with Joseph but also provide information about Mary's relationship with Joseph's biological children (chs. 4, 11, 18–20, and 24).

[59] Citing the translation of Ehrman and Pleše, *The Apocryphal Gospels*, pp. 177-89.

[60] Citing the translation of Ehrman and Pleše, *The Apocryphal Gospels*, p. 177.

[61] Citing the translation of Ehrman and Pleše, *The Apocryphal Gospels*, pp. 177-79.

[62] Citing the translation of Ehrman and Pleše, *The Apocryphal Gospels*, pp. 177-79.

[63] Citing the translation of Ehrman and Pleše, *The Apocryphal Gospels*, pp. 177-79.

[64] Citing the translation of Ehrman and Pleše, *The Apocryphal Gospels*, p. 179.

[65] Citing the translation of Ehrman and Pleše, *The Apocryphal Gospels*, p. 179.

of Joseph (chs. 21 and 22).⁶⁶ Turning to his heavenly Father on behalf of Joseph, his earthly father, Jesus prays:

> My Father and the Father of all mercies, the Father of truth, the eye that sees, the ear that hears, hear me, your beloved Son, as I beseech you for the work of your hands, namely my father Joseph: send me a great choir of angels, and Michael the steward of goodness, and Gabriel the herald of light, that they may walk with the soul of my father Joseph ... And be merciful toward the soul of my father Joseph as it is ascending to your holy hands, for this is the hour when he needs mercy (HJC 22).⁶⁷

Afterwards, Jesus reports that

> The angels took his soul and wrapped it in finest linen packages ... And, I made Michael and Gabriel watch over his soul ... and the angels sang before it until they delivered it to my good Father (HJC 23).⁶⁸

Following this, Jesus 'brought down his (Joseph's) eyes and tried to close them and his mouth' (ch. 24).⁶⁹

Then 'a host of angels' came and took up 'the blessed body of my father Joseph' (ch. 25). Subsequently, Jesus 'laid his hands upon his (Joseph's) body and promised him many things, and assured him that 'all will be well with you' (ch. 26).⁷⁰ After offering this reassurance, Jesus makes six further promises to Joseph and, by implication, to those reading the text, that he will keep if certain stipulations are met by Christian worshippers on the day in which Joseph's life is remembered (ch. 26).⁷¹

Next, the readers learn of Jesus' final time with the body of Joseph, and how the 'dignitaries of the town came' and took the body of Joseph 'out to the tomb' where his 'parents' were buried (ch. 27).⁷² However, as Jesus is recounting their action, it evokes memories for him of 'the day when he (Joseph) had traveled with me down to Egypt and the great torments he had suffered because of me' (ch. 27).⁷³ Reflecting upon this thought led Jesus to lie upon Joseph's body and weep 'over him for a long while' and, once again, reveal both Jesus' humanity and his deep affection for his earthly father (ch. 27).⁷⁴

In light of Jesus' obvious affection and love of his earthly father, as well as Joseph's own character and faith, the readers are invited by Jesus to consider Joseph as a model for their own lives, both as spiritual father

---

⁶⁶ Citing the translation of Ehrman and Pleše, *The Apocryphal Gospels*, pp. 179-81.
⁶⁷ Citing the translation of Ehrman and Pleše, *The Apocryphal Gospels*, p. 181.
⁶⁸ Citing the translation of Ehrman and Pleše, *The Apocryphal Gospels*, pp. 181-83.
⁶⁹ Citing the translation of Ehrman and Pleše, *The Apocryphal Gospels*, p. 183.
⁷⁰ Citing the translation of Ehrman and Pleše, *The Apocryphal Gospels*, p. 185.
⁷¹ See Ehrman and Pleše, *The Apocryphal Gospels*, pp. 185-87.
⁷² Citing the translation of Ehrman and Pleše, *The Apocryphal Gospels*, p. 187.
⁷³ Citing the translation of Ehrman and Pleše, *The Apocryphal Gospels*, p. 187.
⁷⁴ Citing the translation of Ehrman and Pleše, *The Apocryphal Gospels*, p. 187.

and exemplar. Specifically, from the beginning of the narrative, they are asked to consider Joseph as their 'father' ('our father', prologue) and, as Jesus' disciples, to 'listen' (and take seriously) what Jesus says about 'the life of ... Joseph' (ch. 1). Further, they are directed by Jesus to show honor and respect to Joseph's life by participating in his 'memorial day' and taking very specific ethical actions on this 'day' in his memory (ch. 26).[75] These actions, include making 'an offering' and placing 'it in your shrine' on this day; giving 'bread into the hand of a poor person in your name'; giving 'a cup of wine into the hand of a stranger, a widow, or an orphan on your memorial day'; and copying 'the book of your departure from the body and all the words that have come forth from my mouth today ...' (ch. 26).[76] Provision is also made for the very poor in the community. If 'a poor person' fathers 'a son and names him Joseph, glorifying your name' then Jesus promises that 'no famine or pestilence will happen in that house because your name dwells in it' (ch. 26).[77]

Finally, on the basis of the apostles' personal report that Jesus directed them to 'preach also my beloved father Joseph' when, under the 'power' of 'the Advocate, the Holy Spirit' I 'send you to preach the holy gospel' (ch. 30), the readers are likewise enjoined to do just as the apostles and show appropriate honor to Joseph in the ways described.[78]

The Portrait of Joseph in the History of Joseph the Carpenter and the History of Effects

A comparison of the references to Joseph in the nativity and infancy accounts in the canonic Gospels with those in HJC reveals that specific references to Joseph and events associated with Joseph in the pericopes of Mt. 1.18-25, 2.13-15, and 2.19-23, appear in HJC. Relative to their appearances in this non-canonic narrative, the first evidence of the influence of Matthew seems present in Jesus' description of Joseph as 'a righteous man' and his reference to his betrothal to Mary (ch. 2); references present in Mt.1.18, 19.[79] Subsequent evidence is found in Jesus' account of Joseph's discovery of Mary's pregnancy, in ch. 5 of HJC.[80] Here, the text appears dependent on the earlier representation of Joseph's doubt about Mary, found in Mt.1.19 for it reads: 'And when she was three months pregnant, the guileless Joseph came from the place where he worked in carpentry and found my virgin mother pregnant.

---

[75] Citing the translation of Ehrman and Pleše, *The Apocryphal Gospels*, p. 185.
[76] Citing the translation of Ehrman and Pleše, *The Apocryphal Gospels*, p. 185.
[77] Citing the translation of Ehrman and Pleše, *The Apocryphal Gospels*, p. 187.
[78] Citing the translation of Ehrman and Pleše, *The Apocryphal Gospels*, p. 189.
[79] Citing the translation of Ehrman and Pleše, *The Apocryphal Gospels*, p. 165.
[80] Citing the translation of Ehrman and Pleše, *The Apocryphal Gospels*, p. 167.

6. *The Portrayal of Joseph in the History of Joseph the Carpenter* 123

Disturbed and fearful, he planned to dismiss her secretly' (ch. 5).[81] This, in turn, is closely followed by an account of the annunciation to Joseph in ch. 6.[82] It also seems to have a significant reliance upon the early portrayal of this annunciation found in Mt. 1.20-24.[83] Further evidence of the influence of Matthew also appears present in chs. 8 and 9.[84] Here, there are accounts of the flight into Egypt and the arrival of Joseph, Mary, and Jesus in Nazareth in Galilee that appear dependent upon the earlier representations of these events in Mt. 2.13-15 and 2.19-23.[85] In addition, Joseph's later confession about his distrust of Mary, following the disclosure of her pregnancy in HJC also seems to depend, in part, upon the earlier account of the doubt of Joseph and the annunciation to him found in Mt. 1.19-21 (ch. 17).[86]

Finally, mention should also be made of Jesus' account of the burial of Joseph in ch. 27 of HJC for this text also includes a brief reference by Jesus to the 'great torments' Joseph endured on Jesus' account during the flight into Egypt, found in Mt. 2.13-15.[87] Thus, there appear to be several ways in which Matthew directly and indirectly informed HJC.[88]

A similar comparison of the references to Joseph in the nativity and infancy accounts of the Gospel of Luke with those in HJC reveals that Luke has a more limited influence upon this later narrative. It appears that only one specific reference is clearly dependent upon Luke: that found in ch. 7.[89] Here, there are references to the census of 'Augustus', the 'order' for 'all the inhabited world' to 'be registered', for 'each person' to go to 'his city', Joseph's obedient response ('the good old man also went'), and the birth of Jesus in 'Bethlehem' (ch. 7) that appear to parallel ones in Lk. 2.1-7.[90]

A comparison of the references to Joseph in the non-canonic IG-James with those in HJC reveals that specific non-canonic allusions to Joseph and events associated with Joseph in IGJames 7.4, 8.1-9, 9.1-8, 11-12 and 18.1, appear in HJC. The first evidence of the influence of IGJames appears in ch. 2 of HJC, where references to Joseph's previous marriage and his children by another woman, appear to parallel earlier

---

[81] Citing the translation of Ehrman and Pleše, *The Apocryphal Gospels*, p. 167.
[82] Citing the translation of Ehrman and Pleše, *The Apocryphal Gospels*, p. 167.
[83] Citing the translation of Ehrman and Pleše, *The Apocryphal Gospels*, p. 167.
[84] See Ehrman and Pleše, *The Apocryphal Gospels*, p. 169.
[85] Citing the translation of Ehrman and Pleše, *The Apocryphal Gospels*, p. 169.
[86] See Ehrman and Pleše, *The Apocryphal Gospels*, p. 175.
[87] Citing the translation of Ehrman and Pleše, *The Apocryphal Gospels*, p. 187.
[88] In addition to the formal references noted, there are also several allusions to Matthew's narrative.
[89] See Ehrman and Pleše, *The Apocryphal Gospels*, p. 167. However, there is likely an allusion to Lk. 2.51 in the reference in the HJC (ch. 11) to Jesus living with his parents 'in full obedience of childhood'.
[90] Citing the translation of Ehrman and Pleše, *The Apocryphal Gospels*, p. 167.

references in IGJames 8.7-9 and 9.8.[91] This is closely followed by another short reference to Joseph as a 'widower' and a more extensive reference to Mary's status in the temple prior to her marriage to Joseph in ch. 3; references that seem to parallel earlier ones in IGJames 8.3-4 and 8.7-9.[92] Additional evidence of the influence of IGJames may also appear in ch. 4. Here, there is a reference to Joseph's selection by 'lot' to receive Mary, a reference to Joseph's departure from Mary after her reception into his home; references that seem to parallel earlier ones in IGJames 8.7-9, 9.7, 11-12.[93] A fourth reference to IGJames 8.7-9 may also be present in the references to Joseph's prior marriage in ch. 14.[94] Thus, the influence of IGJames appears likely in the texts although it does not appear to be as significant as that of Matthew.

In turn, a comparison of the references to Joseph in the non-canonic IGThomas with those in HJC suggests this non-canonic text had minor influence on it. The most that can be said is that allusions to chs. 16, 17, and 18 of IGThomas may be present in chs. 11 and 17 of HJC.[95] Thus, these numerous references from earlier Christian narratives, found within HJC, indicate that it clearly stands within the effective history of Joseph.

The Distinctiveness of the Portrait of Joseph in the History of Joseph the Carpenter

The distinctiveness of the portrayal of Joseph in HJC is revealed in at least seven different ways.

First, it is disclosed by the fact that Joseph is the primary subject of this narrative and by the fact that the book discloses Joseph's own thoughts, feelings, and words. These are often found in Jesus' revelations of Joseph's own confessions, prayers, and testimonies, about his person and character.

Second, it is also revealed by the frequency with which his name is referenced – 58 times – (prologue, chs. 1, 2 [4], 3, 4 [4], 5, 6 [2], 7 [2],

---

[91] See Ehrman and Pleše, *The Apocryphal Gospels*, p. 165.
[92] Citing the translation of Ehrman and Pleše, *The Apocryphal Gospels*, p. 165.
[93] Citing the translation of Ehrman and Pleše, *The Apocryphal Gospels*, pp. 165-67.
[94] See Ehrman and Pleše, *The Apocryphal Gospels*, pp. 171-73.
[95] Again, see Ehrman and Pleše, *The Apocryphal Gospels*, pp. 169, 175-77. Morenz, *Die Geschichte von Joseph dem Zimmermann*, p. 117, does concur that the influence of IGThomas may be found in ch. 17 of HJC. Reference to Joseph's 'son James' in ch. 11 may depend upon the earlier witness in ch. 16 of IGThomas that James was the son of Joseph. The reference to the resurrection of the young 'boy' who had been bitten by the serpent in ch. 17 of HJC may also suggest a parallel with the account of Jesus' healing of James following a viper bite in ch. 16 of IGThomas and the narrative of Jesus' resurrection of a dead infant in ch. 17 of IGThomas.

8, 9, 11 [2], 12, 14, 15[3], 17 [3], 18 [4], 19, 20[3], 21[4], 22 [4], 24 [4], 25 [2], 26 [3], 28, 29, 30 [2], and 31).[96]

Third, it is also seen, as previously noted, in the fact that Joseph is identified by Jesus as 'Joseph my father', 'my father Joseph' or 'my father' (in chs. 2, 3, 4[2], 11, 12, 15[3], 17, 18[2], 21[4], 22[4], 25, 26, 27, 28, 29, and 31), 'my father according to the flesh' (chs. 2 and 17), and 'my beloved father Joseph' (chs. 14, 17[2], 24, 25, 26[2], and 30), as well as 'our father' (prologue) and the 'father' of all the followers of Jesus.[97]

Fourth, the distinctiveness of this particular portrayal of Joseph is also indicated by the fact that most of the narrative (particularly those parts pertaining to the elucidation of the character, role, words, and actions of Joseph), is disclosed through the words of Jesus (chs. 2–31).

Fifth, it is also seen by the fact that, in this text, Jesus proclaims in explicit and detailed ways how he 'will also bless in the celestial offering' all those 'who will provide an offering and deposit it in your shrine on your memorial day' as well as do other things to commemorate the life of Joseph (ch. 26).[98] Indeed, it is striking that Jesus promises Joseph that explicit and particular veneration of Joseph on the particular day in which his life is remembered will lead believers (and by implication those reading the text) to receive several particular blessings and rewards from Jesus, himself (ch. 26).[99]

Sixth, the distinctiveness of the portrayal of Joseph in this text is indicated by the fact that this text explicitly directs readers to offer specific veneration to Joseph in their present lives (ch. 26) and to tell the story of Joseph's life (ch. 30).[100] Therefore, each of these factors within the narrative lead to the expansion of the readers' perception of Joseph as well as reinforce the initial ideas that Joseph is their 'father' and one whom they should imitate and venerate.

Seventh, the special character of this portrait of Joseph in HJC is also found in the fact that this text, as earlier non-canonic narratives, also responds to the literary challenges of the *Leerstellen*, 'gaps in the narrative' and the *Unbestimmtheitsstellen*, 'places where things are unclear', raised by the canonic Gospels by providing more information about Joseph. The HJC does this in large part, as has been noted, by providing new and substantial details about Joseph's significance, background, work, character

---

[96] Citing the translation of Ehrman and Pleše, *The Apocryphal Gospels*, pp. 163-91.
[97] Citing the translation of Ehrman and Pleše, *The Apocryphal Gospels*, pp. 163, 169, 173, 175-81, 185-91.
[98] Citing the translation of Ehrman and Pleše, *The Apocryphal Gospels*, pp. 185-87. As Morenz, *Die Geschichte von Joseph dem Zimmermann*, p. 107, acknowledges, the primary purposes of the narrative seem to be to promote the importance of the figure of Joseph and to encourage celebration of his festival.
[99] See Ehrman and Pleše, *The Apocryphal Gospels*, pp. 185-87.
[100] See Ehrman and Pleše, *The Apocryphal Gospels*, pp. 185-87, 189-91.

and faith, relationship with Jesus and role as a model and help for others within the larger contemporary Christian community.[101] Thus, it offers a portrait of Joseph that not only stands in some tension with the earliest canonic images of Matthew, Luke, and John and the portrayals offered by IGJames and the IGThomas, but contributes further information about the characterization of Joseph. Among the critical elements in this information are the facts that in this narrative Joseph is clearly and unabashedly portrayed as the earthly father of Jesus and as an integral figure in the life of Jesus, and is understood to be so important and special in the life of Jesus that his life is represented as an essential feature in the message of the Christian faith and offered as a holy exemplar for Christians.

In conclusion, this portrait of Joseph in HJC provides additional details and characterizations that accentuate the close relationship shared by Joseph and Jesus as well as Joseph's virtues and holiness. Thus, HJC provides a unique, exemplary, and evocative portrayal of Joseph that warrants serious consideraton.

The Narrator's and the Narrator's Community's Perceptions and Beliefs about Joseph the Carpenter in the History of Joseph the Carpenter

Finally, consideration must be given to the beliefs and practices of the community in which HJC arose. In this regard, it seems fair to conclude that this community was one in which Joseph was held in very high esteem for this appears to be substantiated in at least five ways. It is, perhaps, first, indicated in the early words of the prologue of the narrative which reveal not only that Joseph the Carpenter is the primary subject but that he is also understood to be *a* spiritual father ('our father', prologue), if not *the* spiritual father of the community.[102] Second, proof of this high level of esteem and of the 'fatherhood' of Joseph may also be seen in the fact that Jesus (the Lord and Savior of the community) narrates most of this account of Joseph and, in the process, repeatedly identifies Joseph as 'father', 'my father' and 'my beloved father', and is unabashed in his respect and affection for the man. Third, substantiation of this respect for Joseph can also be seen in the fact that in the process of relating an amazing array of stories and details about Joseph, Jesus always seems to remind the readers of Joseph's spirituality, his love of God, and of his love of Jesus, himself. Fourth, the community's great appreciation of Joseph also seems to be exemplified by this community's veneration of Joseph with an annual celebration during their liturgical

---

[101] Among other new and distinctive details, HJC provides an enlarged portrait of the relationship between Joseph and Mary.

[102] Citing the translation of Ehrman and Pleše, *The Apocryphal Gospels*, p. 163.

6. *The Portrayal of Joseph in the History of Joseph the Carpenter* 127

year, as well as with a set of further times in which Joseph is also remembered.[103] Fifth, this very high esteem for Joseph also seems to be indicated by Jesus' promises to him, in Jesus' declarations toward the end of the narrative that this explicit adoration of Joseph on the particular day in which his life is remembered, will lead believers (and by implication those reading the text) to receive particular blessings and rewards from Jesus, himself (chs. 26 and 30).[104]

In addition, it should also be recognized that this explicit focus upon Joseph and clear desire to respect and revere him (while at the same time still acknowledging the significance and priority of Mary), may suggest that this community seeks to establish some semblance of parity between the earthly parents of Jesus, in both the narrative of the community and in the worship and liturgy of the community; something not found in all early Christian communities.[105]

Consequently, it should be noted that the narrative sheds some insight on the beliefs of the community with respect to the roles of Jesus and Mary. This seems evident in light of the dominance Jesus retains (and in light of the ongoing significance of Mary) in the text, even when (and, perhaps, notably, when) he is the channel for innumerable details about Joseph and, also, in light of the significance Joseph retains, even in relationship to Jesus and Mary. Similarly, the community's beliefs in the humanity and divinity of Jesus and in the perpetual virginity and purity of Mary also appear to be exhibited, among other ways, by Jesus acting as the narrator (and in the process providing readers with an extensive collection of his own words as well as those of Joseph) and by the confessions and professions of Joseph. This could suggest that the members of this community share central beliefs that also appear to be held by additional Christian communities, including, to some extent, by the earlier communities of IGJames and IGThomas.[106]

---

[103] See Ehrman and Pleše, *The Apocryphal Gospels*, pp. 185-87, 189-91. It is in the context of these declarations that it is disclosed that this community celebrated a 'memorial day' for Joseph, and also 'read the words of this testament (this narrative of the History of Joseph the Carpenter) on the feast days and on the sacred days', apparently references to both a specific time and a set of times when explicit and specific honor was shown to Joseph within the community from which this narrative arose (chs. 26 and 30).

[104] Again, see Ehrman and Pleše, *The Apocryphal Gospels*, pp. 185-87, 189-91.

[105] As Ehrman and Pleše remark (*The Apocryphal Gospels*, p. 157), this narrative functions as 'a kind of Christian midrash on the canonic infancy narratives ...'

[106] By offering a text that is posited as representing the actual memory and words of Jesus, the community of the HJC, appears to assert it has possession of a scripture and written witness that is of similar and, possibly, equal merit to that of the gospel witnesses of Mark, Matthew, Luke, and John. This may also suggest that this community is older than some scholars have suggested and may have existed in a place and time in which there was still some debate about the extent of the New Testament canon.

7

The Portrayal of Joseph the Carpenter in the Gospel of Pseudo-Matthew

Introduction

The fourth and final non-canonic narrative to be examined is entitled: the Gospel of Pseudo-Matthew (hereafter abbreviated as GPM). Possibly the most influential non-canonic narrative of the nativity and youth of Jesus, it was likely composed between 500-800 CE.[1]

Scholars are reluctant to suggest a specific geographical provenance of GPM. But, in light of the language of most of the early extant manuscripts, they seem willing to conclude that it originated somewhere in the Latin west, was initially composed in Latin, and was possibly adapted from IGJames by an individual associated with 'monastic orders'.[2]

A redacted work, GPM, is primarily based upon IGJames (chs. 1–17 are adapted from this earlier text) and as such, served to introduce this earlier Greek and eastern Christian non-canonic text to medieval Europe.[3] But additional sources for the remaining chapters (chs. 18–24)

---

[1] J. Gijsel, *Libri de Nativitate Mariae: Pseudo-Matthaei Evangelium Textus et Commentarias*, vol. IX (Corpus Christianorum, Series Apocryphorum, Brepols-Turnhout: Association pour 'étude de la littérature apocryphe chrétienne, 1997), p. v, adheres to the title C. Tischendorf gave this work. He notes that 'the attribution of the work to the Evangelist Matthew is the second step in the tradition and the primitive title was probably "Nativity of Mary".' He dates the origin of the text to the early seventh century (p. v), although he adds that it may be dated as early as the middle of the sixth century and as late as the end of the eighth century. In turn, Ehrman and Pleše (*The Apocryphal Gospels*, p. 75) seem to concur with Gijsel's date, by saying that 'he makes a convincing argument that the text was produced in the first quarter of the seventh century …' James (*The Apocryphal New Testament*, p. 70) states that the text dates to the eighth or ninth century. Elliott (*The Apocryphal New Testament*, p. 86) concurs with James in this volume but gives an earlier date (of the 6th to the 7th century) in another volume, (*A Synopsis of the Apocryphal Nativity and Infancy Narratives*, p. xiv). Further, preferring earlier dates, Foster ('The Iconography of St. Joseph in Netherlandish Art, 1400-1550', p. 9) dates Pseudo-Matthew to the middle of the sixth century and Filas, *Joseph: The Man Closest to Jesus*, p. 26, dates it to the fifth century.

[2] Ehrman and Pleše, *The Apocryphal Gospels*, pp. 73-75.

[3] The translation noted and followed in this study is that offered by Ehrman and Pleše, *The Apocryphal Gospels*, pp. 73-113. As Ehrman and Pleše acknowledge (*The Apoc-*

may include an earlier edition of the Arabic Infancy Gospel or a similar text.[4] The inclusion of this previous non-canonic literature, especially portions of IGJames (which had been deemed heretical by the influential fifth century church father, Jerome) constitutes a most curious literary resurrection that can only be completely comprehended if the theological agenda, disclosed early in the narrative, is understood. While Tischendorf did include further chapters (25–42) in his nineteenth-century edition of GPM, even he separated them from the rest by identifying them as 'altera pars'.[5] Ehrman and Pleše believe the additional chapters (25–42) found in three of Tischendorf's four manuscripts of GPM constitute a clear addition to the text that was appended some years after their present translation was composed.[6] They believe it constitutes a 'Latin reworking of the Infancy Gospel of Thomas'.[7] Thus, they have not included it. Most contemporary scholars concur with them on this matter. Gijsel believes chs. 25–42 should not be included in modern editions of the manuscript because they are not present in the best and earliest manuscript families, notably A and P.[8] Also Mary Clayton agrees. She writes:

> The last part (the part based on the *Infancy Gospel of Thomas*) is clearly not part of the original text of *Pseudo-Matthew* and is not included in Gijsel's edition, but was included in Tischendorf in his very influential edition, with the label "Pars Altera". It was added to the text at the stage of the Q redaction, dated probably to the eleventh century, and is not found in the earlier manuscript families, A and P.[9]

Thus, most scholars see the text as a finished work that is encompassed in chs. 1–24 and was composed by 800 CE. For this reason, the parameters of this study will only focus on the representation of Joseph found in these chapters in GPM that most scholars believe were written by this date.

---

ryphal Gospels, p. 75), their translation gives 'the original introduction (from the P recension) followed by the best attested form of the text (the A recension)'. Thus, in their English translation, the narrative is not 'attributed ... to Matthew but to James (pp. 74-75)'. Subsequently, 'the epilogue of the Protevangelium (IGJames) has, in effect, become the prologue of Pseudo-Matthew (p. 75)'.

[4] Elliott, *A Synopsis of the Apocryphal Nativity and Infancy Narratives*, p. xiv.
[5] Ehrman and Pleše, *The Apocryphal Gospels*, p. 74.
[6] Ehrman and Pleše, *The Apocryphal Gospels*, p. 74.
[7] Ehrman and Pleše, *The Apocryphal Gospels*, p. 74.
[8] Gijsel, *Libri de Nativitate Mariae : Pseudo-Matthaei Evangelium Textus et Commentarias*, vol. IX, pp. v-vii.
[9] Mary Clayton, *The Apocryphal Gospels of Mary in Anglo-Saxon England* (Cambridge and New York: Cambridge University Press, 1998), pp. 18-23.

With respect to the availability of this text, it can be concluded that the multiplicity of the extant manuscripts of GPM in at least one hundred and eighty existing Latin manuscripts as well as numerous versions and adaptations in other western Christian languages as Old French, Anglo-Norman, German, Old English, suggests the texts would have been accessible to a variety of peoples through a variety of means – both oral and written.[10]

Further, the reach and inspiration of GPM can be seen in Hrosvitha's late tenth-century versed legend, Maria; the later tenth or eleventh century non-canonic narrative, the Gospel of the Birth of Mary – with which GPM appears to have been frequently associated; as well the eleventh- and twelfth-century Old English translations of GPM, and numerous shorter complementary English texts, including the early fourteenth century English Holkham Picture Bible.[11] At the same time, both GPM and compositions containing parts of both texts were often used to influence the liturgy of particular medieval Christian celebrations, notably, 'the most important Mariale holiday of the ninth century', the Assumption of the Virgin and, in the twelfth and thirteenth centuries on the liturgical celebrations of the 'Nativity', the 'Conception', and 'the celebration of St. Anne'.[12]

Gijsel notes further that it was also incorporated into a versified 'written history' for the first time in the latter part of the twelfth century and that 'the definitive version' appears in Godfrey of Viterbo's, Pantheon.[13] It also inspired two additional twelfth century books of poems in German by Wernher of Augsburg and Konrad von Fußesbrunnen.[14] Gijsel adds that it is also likely that Old French and Anglo-Norman 'poems on the miracles of the Jesus child' (that 'are adaptations of chapters 18–22 from the Pseudo-Matthew') were also created toward the end of the thirteenth century.[15] In turn, GPM provided inspiration for the mid-

---

[10] See Elliott, *The Apocryphal Jesus: Legends of the Early Church*, p. 48; Gijsel, *Pseudo-Matthaei Evangelium Textus et Commentarias*, pp. 22-34; M. Clayton, *Apocryphal Gospels of Mary*, pp. 1-5; Cartlidge and Elliott, *Art and the Christian Apocrypha*, pp. 3, 21.

[11] Several scholars have noted the influence of the GPM, particularly during the medieval period. See James, *The Apocryphal New Testament*, p. 79; Foster, 'The Iconography of St. Joseph in Netherlandish Art, 1400-1550', pp. 10-17; Gijsel, *Pseudo-Matthaei Evangelium Textus et Commentarias*, pp. 22-34, 266; Clayton, *The Apocryphal Gospels of Mary in Anglo-Saxon England*, pp. 2, 23, 153; Elliott, *The Apocryphal New Testament*, pp. 84-86, 120; Elliott, *A Synopsis of the Apocryphal Nativity and Infancy Narratives*, pp. xiv-xv.

[12] Gijsel, *Pseudo-Matthaei Evangelium Textus et Commentarias*, pp. 24-25.

[13] Gijsel, *Pseudo-Matthaei Evangelium Textus et Commentarias*, p. 26.

[14] Gijsel *Pseudo-Matthaei Evangelium Textus et Commentarias*, p. 28, records the name of the 'three book poem' by Wernher as *Driu liet von der maget* and the poem by Konrad von Fußesbrunnen as *Kindheit Jesu*.

[15] Gijsel, *Pseudo-Matthaei Evangelium Textus et Commentarias*, pp. 28-29.

thirteenth century hagiographical work by the French author, Jacques of Voragine, known as the *Golden Legend*.[16]

With respect to the later influence this portrait of Joseph had on contemporary and later representations of Joseph, M.R. James, well states the importance and influence of this narrative. He writes:

> The real importance of Pseudo-Matthew lies not so much in the stories which it preserves, as in the fact that it was the principal vehicle by which they were known in the Middle Ages and the principal source of inspiration to the artists and poets ... It is upon this text that the many vernacular versions for the most part depend; and by this that the pictures of the Rejection of Joachim's offering, his meeting with Anne at the Golden Gate, the Presentation of the Virgin, the Repose in Egypt, and the few that we have of the Infancy Miracles, are inspired.[17]

In turn, following the idea of M.R. James, it could be added that GPM was also the inspiration for the many 'pictures' of Joseph that likewise appear in later Christian literature and art.

Accordingly, it can be argued that the portrayal of Joseph in GPM, represents an important literary witness to the *Wirkungsgeschichte* of the New Testament representations of Joseph the Carpenter in the early medieval period.

The Purpose of the Gospel of Pseudo-Matthew

Even a cursory reading of the text reveals that beliefs and ideas, found in IGJames, that explicitly venerate Mary have been incorporated and placed in the first several chapters (1–8) of GPM as well as in the rest of the text.[18] Thus, as was the case with IGJames, from its very first chapter,

---

[16] Gijsel, *Pseudo-Matthaei Evangelium Textus et Commentarias*, pp. 29-34.

[17] James, *The Apocryphal New Testament*, p. 79.

[18] As the translation of Ehrman and Pleše, *The Apocryphal Gospels*, pp. 73-89, reveals, the readers encounter clear evidence of the veneration of Mary from the very beginning of the narrative. First, they learn that Mary is distinguished from Joseph as well as others by the designation, 'holy Mary' (prologue, p. 79). Second, they discover that Mary is held in the highest esteem by people from all walks of life, from 'all the people of Israel' to prominent church leaders and authorities and was, early on, distinguished from other human beings by her demeanor and actions (chs. 1–8, pp. 79-89). Thus, the readers see that even before her birth it is said that 'This one will be the temple of God and the Holy Spirit will rest within her, and she will be blessed above all holy women, so that no one will be able to say that there has ever been anyone like her, nor will there be anyone like her after her (GPM 3).'

Third, the narrative also reveals that even before she was born, her life was dedicated solely to God (ch. 2, pp. 79-81) and that this dedication has been affirmed by her in her declaration that 'It is not possible for me to know a man or for a man to know me' (ch. 7, pp. 87-89); a statement that is reaffirmed, implicitly and explicitly, before and after the introduction of Joseph (ch. 8, pp. 89-93). Fourth, the GPM also discloses that Mary is a person of deep spirituality and righteousness who regularly engages in prayer and

the readers learn that this text is more similar to an 'encomiastic history' or 'recitation' of praise than a 'gospel'; that its primary interest lay with Mary and the nature of her relationship with the other characters in the narrative (including Joseph and Jesus) as well as her relationship with the readers of the narrative.[19] Nonetheless, the portrait of Joseph offered in this text warrants exploration and documentation as the three previous non-canonic narratives.

The Characterization of Joseph in the Gospel of Pseudo-Matthew

While several scholars have formally acknowledged and examined the portrayal of Mary in this narrative, only a few have given appropriate consideration to the significance of the portrayal of Joseph in this narrative.[20] Thus, a close examination of this narrative is necessary and warranted. Consequently, having briefly addressed the issues of the date,

---

praise to God and is aided and fed by angels of the Lord (ch. 6, p. 87). In turn, fifth, they read that she is also described, even in comparison with the other virgins in the temple of the Lord as 'more perfect in virtue'(ch. 6, p. 87). Sixth, the narrative also reveals her spiritual and miraculous powers, which the readers discover include the capacity to both speak with angels but to get them to care for her 'as to a most esteemed loved one' (ch. 6, p. 87). Similarly, seventh, it also discloses her ability to heal, so easily that it is said that 'any sick person who touched her was immediately restored to health by her' (ch. 6, p. 87). Eighth, and finally, this gospel also teaches the readers that with the advent of the life of Mary, God instituted 'a new arrangement ... since she has vowed to God to remain a virgin' for life (ch. 8, p. 89).

[19] Hock (*The Infancy Gospels*, pp. 15-20) argues that it is most appropriate to identify IGJames as 'encomiastic' literature. In light of the apparent purpose and content of the GPM, and the similarities it shares with regard to much of its purpose and content, it seems that it could also be categorized this way.

The focus on Mary is certainly evident in the translation of Ehrman and Pleše, *The Apocryphal Gospels*, pp. 73-113. With respect to the subject of the author's purposes, see especially, Filas, *Joseph: The Man Closest to Jesus*, pp. 26, 31-34; Foster, 'The Iconography of St. Joseph in Netherlandish Art, 1400–1550' , p. 10; Gijsel, *Pseudo-Matthaei Evangelium Textus et Commentarias*, pp. 16-34; Clayton, *The Apocryhal Gospels of Mary in Anglo-Saxon England*, pp. 18-23; Lienhard, *St. Joseph in Early Christianity* , pp. 7-10; Elliott, *The Apocryphal New Testament: A Collection of Apocryphal Christian Literature in an English Translation*, p. 85; Elliott, *A Synopsis of the Apocryphal Nativity and Infancy Narratives*, p. ix.

[20] Several scholars have commented on Pseudo-Matthew's portrayal of Mary. See the following scholarly texts: Filas, *Joseph: The Man Closest to Jesus*, pp. 26, 31-34; Gijsel, *Pseudo-Matthaei Evangelium Textus et Commentarias*, pp. 16-34, 348-472; Clayton, *The Apocryhal Gospels of Mary in Anglo-Saxon England*, pp. 18-23; Lienhard, *St. Joseph in Early Christianity*, pp. 7, 9-10; Elliott, *The Apocryphal New Testament*, p. 85. In contrast, Gijsel, *Pseudo-Matthaei Evangelium Textus et Commentarias*, pp. 348-472, offers some discussion of the role and portrayal of Joseph in his notes that accompany his new translation of the Gospel of Pseudo-Matthew. In addition, note that the portrayal of Joseph in this text (along with other apocryphal texts) is also examined in C. Philip Deasey, 'St. Joseph in the English Mystery Plays', pp. 4-15. Further, see Filas, *Joseph: The Man Closest to Jesus*, pp. 26, 31-34. He offers a succinct summary of the portrayal of Joseph in the Gospel of

7. The Portrayal of Joseph in the Gospel of Pseudo-Matthew 133

provenance, language, purpose, and content of the GPM, it is now appropriate to turn to the characterization of Joseph within this narrative.

'Joseph' is mentioned by name in GPM 42 times. The initial references to Joseph are found in the first words of James, who writes: 'I, James, son of Joseph the carpenter, ... have carefully recorded everything I have seen with my own eyes that occurred at the time of the birth of the holy Mary and of the Savior' (prologue). So, from the very beginning the readers have some sense that Joseph will have some import since he is identified as the father of the narrator. However, they must wait until ch. 8 to discover this for Joseph does not reappear in the narrative until the time comes for Mary to be 'given' by the priests of the temple to a male guardian and he, as a member of 'the tribe of Judah' and one who is 'old' and without a wife, is considered a candidate (ch. 8).[21] But, because he is 'an old man' Joseph is initially ignored in this selection process (ch. 8).[22] Nevertheless, following the visitation of 'the angel' of the Lord to the high priest and his direction to him to reconsider Joseph, the high priest calls Joseph forward to receive his branch, which the high priest had previously placed in 'the holy of holies' (ch. 8).[23] Subsequently, the readers learn that once Joseph responds and takes 'the branch', that it becomes clear that Joseph is the choice of God for 'immediately from the tip of the branch a dove emerged, brighter than snow, very beautiful, and after flying a long time around the top of the Temple, it went up to the heavens' (ch. 8).[24]

Nevertheless, the readers are further informed that, following the priests' command to Joseph to take Mary, he protests, saying, 'I am an old man and I have sons: why are you handing this little girl over to me' (ch. 8)?[25] Nonetheless, his sense of obligation to God, his tribe, the priests, and the people of Israel leads him to become 'her guardian' for a period of time (ch. 8).[26] However, uncomfortable with the situation,

---

Pseudo-Matthew in these pages and refers to this text in relationship to his discussion of Joseph (which has an explicit doctrinal perspective) at several other points. In turn, Foster, 'The Iconography of St. Joseph in Netherlandish Art, 1400–1550', pp. 9-19, also offers a fairly comprehensive summary of the portrayal of Joseph in the Gospel of Pseudo-Matthew. In contrast, most other scholars make either no mention or only brief mention of the portrayal of Joseph within this non-canonic narrative. In this regard, see Elliott, *The Apocryphal Jesus: Legends of the Early Church*, pp. 44-46; Clayton, *The Apocryphal Gospels of Mary in Anglo-Saxon England*, pp. 18-23; Lienhard, *St. Joseph in Early Christianity*, p. 10; Elliott, *The Apocryphal New Testament*, pp. 84-86; Elliott, *A Synopsis of the Apocryphal Nativity and Infancy Narratives*, pp. xiv-xv.

[21] Citing the translation of Ehrman and Pleše, *The Apocryphal Gospels*, pp. 89-93.
[22] Citing the translation of Ehrman and Pleše, *The Apocryphal Gospels*, p. 91.
[23] Citing the translation of Ehrman and Pleše, *The Apocryphal Gospels*, p. 91.
[24] Citing the translation of Ehrman and Pleše, *The Apocryphal Gospels*, p. 91
[25] Citing the translation of Ehrman and Pleše, *The Apocryphal Gospels*, p. 91.
[26] Citing the translation of Ehrman and Pleše, *The Apocryphal Gospels*, pp. 91, 93.

Joseph asks the high priest to provide 'several virgins' who can serve as 'her companions' and give 'comfort' to her (ch. 8).[27] The high priest does (ch. 8).[28] But, not even this act is enough to prevent Joseph from keeping a significant distance between himself and Mary. As the readers learn, shortly after 'Joseph received Mary into his home, along with the five other virgins', he decided he had to leave and went off to work (as a carpenter) 'in Capernaum' (chs. 8 and 9).[29]

Thus, through the means of repeated references to Joseph's familial status and old age, in chs. 8 and 9, it is suggested that Joseph and Mary have very little in common and, by implication, very little to draw them close to one another, either emotionally or physically. In the process, the readers are led to believe that a substantial wall exists between Joseph and Mary that will shape their developing relationship and, among other things, preserve her righteousness, purity, and virginity (and, thus, ultimately, the divinity of the forthcoming child).

This wall only appears to grow in chs. 10 and 11, as the readers learn of Joseph's returning, after 'nine months' and his discovery of her pregnancy (ch. 10).[30] For the discovery of Mary's pregnancy evokes immense anxiety inside Joseph and convinces him that either Mary has abandoned her commitment to her virginity or some man has taken advantage of her and forced himself upon her (ch. 10). Yet, his suspicions and feelings are immediately challenged by 'the virgins who were with Mary', who attempt to assuage Joseph's doubt and grief (ch. 10).[31] Testifying to the purity and righteousness of Mary's character, they tell Joseph that they know 'no man has ever touched her' and suggest 'an angel of the Lord has made her pregnant'(ch. 10).[32] But, their words do not appear to diminish his grief and fear. This only occurs after 'an angel of the Lord' appears to him 'in his sleep' and offers him reassurance (ch. 11).[33] Only this encounter leads Joseph to respond positively, to give thanks to God, to return to conversation with 'Mary and the virgins' (at which point he apologizes to Mary for suspecting her of sin), and to return to his role as her 'guardian' (ch. 11).[34] In addition, through these actions (his thanks to God, his apology to Mary, and his resumption of his role as guardian), Joseph also confirms what the virgins with Mary had earlier confirmed: that she has not had sexual relations with any man (ch. 11). As such, he

---

[27] Citing the translation of Ehrman and Pleše, *The Apocryphal Gospels*, p. 93.
[28] Citing the translation of Ehrman and Pleše, *The Apocryphal Gospels*, p. 93.
[29] Citing the translation of Ehrman and Pleše, *The Apocryphal Gospels*, p. 93.
[30] Citing the translation of Ehrman and Pleše, *The Apocryphal Gospels*, p. 93.
[31] Citing the translation of Ehrman and Pleše, *The Apocryphal Gospels*, p. 95.
[32] Citing the translation of Ehrman and Pleše, *The Apocryphal Gospels*, p. 95.
[33] Citing the translation of Ehrman and Pleše, *The Apocryphal Gospels*, p. 95.
[34] Citing the translation of Ehrman and Pleše, *The Apocryphal Gospels*, p. 95.

also gives witness that Mary's purity and virginity have been maintained.[35]

Even so, as the narrative moves forward, into ch. 12, the readers may begin to wonder if Joseph's fears, demonstrated in the previous two chapters, were not warranted. For within a short time, they discover that Joseph and Mary must both face charges that they have had sexual relations. Joseph is the first to face accusations. Presuming Joseph has had intimacy with Mary, the priests declare: 'If you had not done her violence, she would have remained a virgin to this day' (ch. 12).[36] Yet, their verbal accusation is met by Joseph's vow that he has 'never even touched her' (ch. 12).[37] Nevertheless, still convinced of Joseph's guilt, the high priest, Abiathar, tells Joseph, 'As the Lord lives, now I will make you drink the water of the Lord's drinking, and your sin will immediately be revealed' (ch. 12).[38]

At the same time, the readers learn that Mary is 'brought to the Temple' and before her relatives and the priests, directed by the 'priests, her parents, and her relatives' to confess her sin (ch. 12).[39]

After this, the events surrounding the administration of the water test to Joseph are described and it is revealed that, in the end, 'no sign of sin appeared in him' (ch. 12).[40] Accordingly, the readers are told that 'all the priests, and ministers and people' absolved Joseph (ch. 12).[41]

Then, the readers' attention is redirected to Mary who is told to 'confess who has seduced you' (ch. 12).[42] However, Mary defends her righteousness and immediately and fearlessly approaches 'the altar of the Lord', drinks 'the water of drinking' and walks round the altar 'seven times' (ch. 12).[43] Still some doubt her. Thus, Mary, again, declares her purity and reasserts her vow to remain a virgin her whole life.[44] This, in turn, leads the people to 'begin kissing her knees, asking her (as Joseph had earlier) to forgive their evil suspicions' (ch. 12).[45]

Further distinctions between Joseph and Mary are disclosed to the readers in chs. 13 and 14. Among other things, Joseph's role is significantly diminished in the account of the journey to Bethlehem (ch. 13). This becomes evident following Joseph's response to a vision Mary has

---

[35] Citing the translation of Ehrman and Pleše, *The Apocryphal Gospels*, p. 95.
[36] Citing the translation of Ehrman and Pleše, *The Apocryphal Gospels*, pp. 95, 97.
[37] Citing the translation of Ehrman and Pleše, *The Apocryphal Gospels*, p. 97.
[38] Citing the translation of Ehrman and Pleše, *The Apocryphal Gospels*, p. 97.
[39] Citing the translation of Ehrman and Pleše, *The Apocryphal Gospels*, p. 97.
[40] Citing the translation of Ehrman and Pleše, *The Apocryphal Gospels*, p. 97.
[41] Citing the translation of Ehrman and Pleše, *The Apocryphal Gospels*, p. 97.
[42] Citing the translation of Ehrman and Pleše, *The Apocryphal Gospels*, p. 97.
[43] Citing the translation of Ehrman and Pleše, *The Apocryphal Gospels*, p. 97.
[44] Citing the translation of Ehrman and Pleše, *The Apocryphal Gospels*, p. 97.
[45] Citing the translation of Ehrman and Pleše, *The Apocryphal Gospels*, p. 99.

had (ch. 13). Having scolded her, he finds himself confronted by a beautiful angelic boy, who, 'dressed in bright clothing', both questions Joseph's criticism of Mary's vision and explains her vision (ch. 13).[46] His criticism of Joseph and his interpretation of Mary's vision would suggest that Joseph does not have a comparable spiritual capacity to that of Mary and the angelic boy. This impression is reinforced by the fact that following his interpretation, the angelic boy seems to subsume the role of Joseph who, in essence, disappears from this account. As such, the readers see the angelic boy take the lead in guiding and directing Mary in the rest of the account (ch. 13).[47] Similarly, they witness him commanding Mary to get down off the animal and go into the cave. In turn, they see that she does as the angelic boy says, and goes on to give birth to the child *sans* Joseph, who has gone to find midwives (ch. 13).

Following the birth of the child, Joseph returns with one midwife whom he believes Mary might need for her 'medicine', but Mary is largely unresponsive to Joseph's efforts (ch. 13).[48] Joseph's spiritual limitations are further disclosed for readers when, following his announcement to Mary that the midwife has arrived, he tells her to 'not smile', an expression that, again, reflects his lack of understanding about the nature of Mary's purity and virginity (ch. 13).[49]

Still, the readers find Joseph and Mary conjoined in chs. 14 and 15 and acting together in ways that reveal their mutual righteousness and spirituality. Joseph's and Mary's actions (from their entering Bethlehem on the sixth day to their circumcising and offering of the child on the eighth day) are repeatedly described as actions they take together (although Joseph is sometimes identified as taking the lead in the actions). Thus, as they enter Bethlehem, it is said that 'he (Joseph) entered Bethlehem' and that 'he spent seven days' there (ch. 15).[50] Then, the readers are told that 'he brought the child to the Temple of the Lord' (ch. 15).[51] Nonetheless, the fact that Joseph and Mary are both engaged in these actions reemerges in reference to Jesus' circumcision and the offering of him to God (ch. 15). Specifically, the readers are told that 'when the child received circumcision, they (Joseph and Mary) offered up for him a pair of turtledoves and two young doves' before God and Simeon and Anna (ch. 15).[52]

Yet, following the conjoined action of Joseph and Mary in these events, in the narration of the visit and adoration of the magi, the focus

---

[46] Citing the translation of Ehrman and Pleše, *The Apocryphal Gospels*, p. 99.
[47] Citing the translation of Ehrman and Pleše, *The Apocryphal Gospels*, p. 99.
[48] Citing the translation of Ehrman and Pleše, *The Apocryphal Gospels*, p. 101.
[49] Citing the translation of Ehrman and Pleše, *The Apocryphal Gospels*, p. 101.
[50] Citing the translation of Ehrman and Pleše, *The Apocryphal Gospels*, p. 103.
[51] Citing the translation of Ehrman and Pleše, *The Apocryphal Gospels*, p. 103.
[52] Citing the translation of Ehrman and Pleše, *The Apocryphal Gospels*, p. 103.

shifts to Mary and the child.[53] For as the magi went into the house where the child was 'they found the child Jesus sitting on Mary's lap' (ch. 16).[54] Nonetheless, this shift is modified by the fact that when the magi 'opened their treasures', they 'presented expensive gifts to Mary *and* Joseph' (ch. 16).[55]

Afterwards, Joseph's importance is reasserted in ch. 17, in the account of the massacre by Herod. The readers discover that the day before the massacre of all the male children was to begin, 'Joseph was warned by the angel of the Lord', to take 'Mary and the child and go, take the desert route to Egypt' (ch. 17).[56]

Following the stories of Joseph's second dream and the massacre of the young children by Herod, in ch. 17, much more is revealed about Joseph and Mary in chs. 18–24, which offer accounts of their journey in Egypt. Among other things, the readers learn, in ch. 18 that Joseph did exactly as directed by the angel (in ch. 17) and took Mary and the child and entered Egypt. At the same time, three other developments took place that changed the dynamics of the account. First, the readers are told that 'three male servants' and 'one female servant' have joined Joseph and Mary and the child Jesus for the journey and were, in fact, already with them in the cave where they were resting (ch. 18).[57] Second, they are informed that frightening 'dragons' are also present with them in the cave (ch. 18).[58] Third, they are further startled by the unexpected response of the child Jesus to the dragons, who, they are told, 'roused himself, got to his feet, and stood' before the dragons (ch. 18).[59] The response of the dragons is perhaps even more startling for amazingly they adored the child and 'worshiped him' (ch. 18).[60] Joseph's and Mary's response to all this was quite natural for they were both afraid the dragons might 'harm the child' (ch. 18).[61] However, Jesus' response to Joseph's and Mary's fear and the response of the dragons to him, might well take the readers aback.

Nonetheless, it was likely that Jesus' bold action as well as the behavior of the beasts towards them diminished Joseph's and Mary's fear as they continued on their journey in ch. 19. Certainly, as they traveled on,

---

[53] This is particularly evident in ch. 16 in the emphasis on Joseph's significance in the entrance to Bethlehem and in bringing Jesus into the Temple of the Lord.
[54] Citing the translation of Ehrman and Pleše, *The Apocryphal Gospels*, p. 105.
[55] Citing the translation of Ehrman and Pleše, *The Apocryphal Gospels*, p. 105.
[56] Citing the translation of Ehrman and Pleše, *The Apocryphal Gospels*, p. 105.
[57] Citing the translation of Ehrman and Pleše, *The Apocryphal Gospels*, pp. 105, 107.
[58] Citing the translation of Ehrman and Pleše, *The Apocryphal Gospels*, p. 107.
[59] Citing the translation of Ehrman and Pleše, *The Apocryphal Gospels*, p. 107.
[60] Citing the translation of Ehrman and Pleše, *The Apocryphal Gospels*, p. 107.
[61] Citing the translation of Ehrman and Pleše, *The Apocryphal Gospels*, p. 107.

Joseph and Mary saw the 'great reverence' the dragons, lions, and leopards showed them (ch. 19).[62] Learning this, the readers may well feel led to contemplate their own thoughts and feelings not only toward the child Jesus but also toward those who travel with him, most particularly toward Joseph and Mary.

Additional contemplation upon the roles and characters of Joseph and Mary may emerge as the readers learn of the events 'on the third day' of the journey into Egypt (ch. 20).[63] According to GPM, having grown 'weary' from her extensive journey, and spotting a large palm tree where she might find shelter, Mary 'wanted to rest awhile in its shade' (ch. 20).[64] In response 'Joseph hastened to lead her to the palm and he had her descend from the donkey' (ch. 20).[65] Here, Joseph assumes the kind of role the readers would imagine he should assume (though he seemed to be kept from doing so earlier) as he gently and lovingly cares for the woman who had recently delivered a child and been entrusted to him. But, the limits to Joseph's ability are shortly revealed in his response to her request for fruit from the (tall) palm for her to eat. Joseph says:

> I am surprised that you are saying this, when you can see how high the palm is. You are thinking of the fruit of the palm; but I am thinking about the water that we no longer have in our skins; we have nowhere to replenish them to quench our thirst (GPM 20).[66]

Clearly, Joseph cannot simply pull the branches of the tree down to the ground. Nonetheless, the readers immediately note that the child Jesus can and does. Once again, asserting his power, the child addresses the tree and says, 'Bend down, O tree, and refresh my mother from your fruit' (ch. 20).[67] Later, in turn, Jesus, responding to Joseph's concern, demonstrates further power and commands the palm tree to 'open up from your roots the hidden springs, that water may flow from them to quench our thirst' (ch. 20).[68] Thus, as a result of Jesus' words, Mary, Joseph, and the others, are fed and refreshed and the readers (as well as the travelers) are able to comprehend further the divinity and power of the child Jesus (which is especially highlighted for the readers in this section, in chs.18-20, of the GPM).[69]

The same conclusion may also be drawn with respect to the role of Jesus in ch. 21, where, he, again, addresses the palm tree and announces

---

[62] Citing the translation of Ehrman and Pleše, *The Apocryphal Gospels*, p. 107.
[63] Citing the translation of Ehrman and Pleše, *The Apocryphal Gospels*, p. 107.
[64] Citing the translation of Ehrman and Pleše, *The Apocryphal Gospels*, pp. 107, 109.
[65] Citing the translation of Ehrman and Pleše, *The Apocryphal Gospels*, p. 109.
[66] Citing the translation of Ehrman and Pleše, *The Apocryphal Gospels*, p. 109.
[67] Citing the translation of Ehrman and Pleše, *The Apocryphal Gospels*, p. 109.
[68] Citing the translation of Ehrman and Pleše, *The Apocryphal Gospels*, p. 109.
[69] Citing the translation of Ehrman and Pleše, *The Apocryphal Gospels*, p. 109.

that one of its branches will 'be taken by my angels and planted in the paradise of my Father' (ch. 21).[70] Here, curiously, as before, his role is stressed, while the roles of his fellow travelers (including Joseph and Mary) are only alluded to with the plural pronoun, 'they' (ch. 21).[71] In the process, Jesus' faith and spirituality is contrasted with that of his fellow travelers (including Joseph and Mary), whom the readers are told have let 'fear' overtake their 'hearts' (ch. 21).[72]

Following this chapter, the final reference to Joseph in GPM occurs in the first part of the next chapter, ch. 22. Here, the readers are informed that at a later time, while the group was traveling further within Egypt, Joseph complains to Jesus about the terrible heat they are experiencing within the desert and asks if the group could travel another way (ch. 22). In response, Jesus tells Joseph 'Do not fear, Joseph; I will shorten the stages along the way for you, so that you will reach your humble abode in this single day, when it would normally take you thirty days of haste' (ch. 22).[73] Just as Jesus makes this promise, the readers learn that Joseph and Mary and their fellow travelers sense themselves being miraculously transported 'toward the mountains of Egypt and its plains', and shortly afterwards, 'they entered one of the cities, called Sohennen' (ch. 22).[74]

Subsequently, after this last reference to Joseph by Jesus in the first part of ch. 22, the emphasis of the narrative is upon the prominence of Mary and the child Jesus. This continues in chs. 23 and 24.

The Portrait of Joseph in the Gospel of Pseudo-Matthew and the History of Effects

A close reading of the text of GPM reveals some similarities between this narrative and the Gospels of Matthew and Luke. In fact, a comparison of the references to Joseph in the canonic Gospels with those in GPM reveals that several references to Joseph (Mt. 1.18-20, 24-25; 2.1-12, 13-15 as well as Lk. 2.1-7 , 21-38) are represented or alluded to in GPM and that these references occur in chs. 10, 11, 13, 14, 15, 16, and 17.[75] However, careful analysis of their use suggests that even Joseph's primary roles of guardian of Mary and her child and witness, articulated in the canonic Gospels, are significantly restricted in GPM in order to enhance Mary's own position and role. In this regard, it is notable that

---

[70] Citing the translation of Ehrman and Pleše, *The Apocryphal Gospels*, p. 109.
[71] Citing the translation of Ehrman and Pleše, *The Apocryphal Gospels*, p. 109.
[72] Citing the translation of Ehrman and Pleše, *The Apocryphal Gospels*, p. 109.
[73] Citing the translation of Ehrman and Pleše, *The Apocryphal Gospels*, p. 111.
[74] Citing the translation of Ehrman and Pleše, *The Apocryphal Gospels*, p. 111.
[75] Citing the translation of Ehrman and Pleše, *The Apocryphal Gospels*, pp. 93, 95, 99, 101, 103, 105.

GPM does not include or adapt the following texts from the Matthean and Lukan nativity and infancy narratives that represent Joseph in a very positive light: Mt. 1.1-17 (the 'Genealogy of Jesus the Messiah'); 2.19-23 (the 'Return from Egypt'); Lk. 1. 26-27 (the 'Announcement that a virgin [Mary] is engaged to a man whose name was Joseph'); 2.39-40 (the 'Return of Joseph, Mary, and Jesus to Nazareth'); 2.41-52 (the 'Boy Jesus in the Temple'); 3.23-38 (the 'Genealogy of Jesus'). As was noted in previous comparisons between the canonic Gospels and specific non-canonic texts, the exclusion of these passages, in this case, seven canonic pericopes, alters the image of Joseph for the readers of GPM because it excludes key portions of the canonic representations of Joseph the Carpenter.

At the same time it is also important to consider the influence IGJames had on GPM. Its influence has been duly noted by several scholars and is particularly evident in chs. 1–17.[76] In this regard, once again, a close reading of GPM reveals some very significant similarities between this narrative and IGJames. In fact, a comparison of the references to Joseph in IGJames with those in GPM reveals that several references to Joseph in IGJames (chs. 9, 13, 14, 15, 16, 17, 19, 20, 21, and 22) are represented or alluded to in GPM and that these references occur in chs. 8, 10, 11, 12, 13, 16, and 17.[77]

Therefore, it can be concluded that this portrait of Joseph provides additional details and characterizations that, among other things, set Mary and her child apart from him as well as other characters by highlighting her virtues and holiness, and signifying her uniqueness and special relationship with Jesus. On the one hand, the GPM expands the image of Joseph in the canonic Gospels, in part, by providing these additional details and characterizations of Joseph through the disclosure of new stories and accounts. Accordingly, this narrative does respond to the literary challenges of the *Leerstellen*, 'gaps in the narrative' and the *Unbestimmtheitsstellen*, 'places where things are unclear', raised by the canonic gospels by providing more information about the nature of Joseph's character and his relationship with Mary and Jesus. On the other

---

[76] James (*The Apocryphal New Testament*, pp. 70. 73) says IGJames is used in the first seventeen chapters and thinks it 'is in all likelihood the sole source ...' However, he goes on to add that 'there are many omissions and amplifications' in the GPM. Elliott (*The Apocryphal New Testament*, pp. 84-85), in turn, agrees that IGJames is an important source in the first seventeen chapters. In addition, he also mentions certain differences between the two documents and notes that 'Pseudo-Matthew embellishes PJ(IGJames) by including the circumcision and purification'. In this regard, see also Gijsel, *Libri de Nativitate Mariae: Pseudo-Matthaei Evangelium Textus et Commentarias*, vol. IX, pp. v-vii.

[77] See these references to Joseph in the GPM in Ehrman and Pleše, *The Apocryphal Gospels*, pp. 89, 91, 93, 95, 95, 97, 99, 101, 103, 105.

7. The Portrayal of Joseph in the Gospel of Pseudo-Matthew 141

hand, these additional details and characterizations often highlight Joseph's elderly character and physical impediments as well as his spiritual and emotional limitations, factors that invariably diminish his role and significance in relationship to Mary and Jesus. Nonetheless, in the process of relating the events it recounts, and building and expanding upon the foundation of IGJames, the GPM testifies to the ongoing development and evolution of the *Wirkungsgeschichte* of the Matthean, Lukan, and Johannine portrayals of Joseph the Carpenter.

The Distinctiveness of the Portrait of Joseph the Carpenter in the Gospel of Pseudo-Matthew

The Gospel of Pseudo-Matthew reveals significant distinctions between the background, characteristics, and actions of Joseph, on the one hand, and those of Mary, on the other hand, with these distinctions repeatedly disclosed and highlighted. Desiring to construct a large wall between Joseph and Mary, GPM presents Mary, from the very beginning, as someone who is substantially different from both Joseph and all the other human beings with whom she associates and has contact. This is indicated in dramatic and profound ways by the fact that she is addressed as 'the holy Mary', even before the narrative formally begins (prologue).[78] However, as the readers learn, this title is but a reminder and sign of aspects of her person and character that will be revealed to them throughout the remaining portions of GPM. So it is that as they read beyond the prologue they discover, as has been acknowledged, that Mary is held in the highest esteem by people from all walks of life. So it is that this title suggests, as the readers come to discern, that Mary is 'more perfect in every virtue' (ch. 6) and spirituality, so much so that 'no one will be able to say that there has ever been anyone like her, nor will there be anyone like her after her' (ch. 3).[79] So it is that they learn from the narrative that even angels feed and care for her, and the sick find her touch makes them well (ch. 6).[80] So it is that they come to understand that, in and through her virginal life, God has instituted 'a new arrangement … since she has vowed to God to remain a virgin' (ch. 8).[81] As with the prior non-canonic narrative representations that have been examined, it is also the case that GPM adds to the portrait of Joseph that was offered in the canonic Gospels. In the process, it responds, in its own way, to what it perceives to be the literary challenges of the *Leerstellen*, 'gaps in the narrative' and the *Unbestimmtheitsstellen*, 'places

---

[78] Citing the translation of Ehrman and Pleše, *The Apocryphal Gospels*, p. 79.
[79] Citing the translation of Ehrman and Pleše, *The Apocryphal Gospels*, pp. 87, 83.
[80] Citing the translation of Ehrman and Pleše, *The Apocryphal Gospels*, p. 87.
[81] Citing the translation of Ehrman and Pleše, *The Apocryphal Gospels*, p. 89.

where things are unclear', with regard to Joseph, raised by these earlier Gospel narratives, by providing 'additional' information about him. Accordingly, GPM provides a distinctive and important portrayal of Joseph that warrants serious consideraton.

The Narrator's and the Narrator's Community's Perceptions and Beliefs about Joseph the Carpenter in the Gospel of Pseudo-Matthew

Next to the exceptionally youthful and virtuous image of Mary presented in GPM, the readers see an image of Joseph who they discover, in a variety of ways, is almost everything Mary is not. Among other things, the readers are informed early in the narrative that he is 'an old man'; a characteristic highlighted by the fact that they are also told, directly and indirectly, that he is not only 'an old man', but also a person who has grandsons who are older than Mary (ch. 8).[82] Thus, very quickly, his substantial age difference from Mary, as well as his marital and familial history (that he has had a wife with whom he has had relations that have led to the birth of children) set him apart from the fourteen year old virgin whose 'guardian' he is supposed to become (ch. 8).[83] At the same time, this juxtaposition is also sharpened by the fact that Joseph is a less than enthusiastic participant in the matters in which God has asked him to be engaged; is a person who, though faithful to God, is reluctant to be involved with Mary and has some serious doubts about what is to transpire. Therefore, it is this early portrayal of Joseph and juxtaposition of Joseph and Mary that informs and shapes his representation throughout the rest of the text.

In turn, the details of GPM also indicate that Joseph's primary roles, with respect to Mary and the child, are believed to be those of guardian and witness, as was highlighted at the time of Joseph's reception of Mary and at those times where Joseph's presence, observation, and response confirm Mary's key characteristics, especially, her purity and virginity.[84] As such, it seems safe to assume that both the portrayal of Joseph and the veneration and praise offered Mary in this narrative reflect thoughts and beliefs of the spiritual community from which it arises.

---

[82] Citing the translation of Ehrman and Pleše, *The Apocryphal Gospels*, p. 91.
[83] Citing the translation of Ehrman and Pleše, *The Apocryphal Gospels*, pp. 89, 91.
[84] Citing the translation of Ehrman and Pleše, *The Apocryphal Gospels*, p. 95.

Conclusion: The Non-Canonic Portrayals of Joseph the Carpenter in Early Christian and Early Medieval Literature

Analysis of these portrayals of Joseph has revealed that several later literary interpreters continued to be interested in the character and role(s) of Joseph. This may be documented in at least two ways. First, evidence that Joseph remains a major character and continues to evoke substantial interest within the later narratives is corroborated by the fact that Joseph is frequently acknowledged and mentioned in each of the four narratives examined (mentioned by name 21 times in IGJames; 31 times in IGThomas; 58 times in HJC; 42 times in GPM). Second, each of the respective narrators relate substantive information about both their perceptions of Joseph's character and their beliefs about the nature of his relationships with Mary and Jesus, going to some effort to craft their portrayals of Joseph.

This examination of the four non-canonic narratives has also revealed that Christians in different communities felt they had the theological warrant to expand and contract the portrayals of Joseph in the Matthean, Lukan, and Johannine gospels for their own theological and apologetical reasons (particularly in order to clarify the nature of the relationships between Joseph and Mary and Joseph and Jesus).[85] It appears that these later narrators interacted with the New Testament portrayals of Joseph in at least four different ways that document the development of the reception history of the early gospel portrayals of Joseph in these non-canonic texts.

The first way in which the later narrators interacted with these early narrative portrayals documents their response to representations of Joseph based upon specific canonic events in which he was explicitly featured. There are numerous examples of this type of composition and they include representations of Joseph, especially in the scenes of the Annunciation to Joseph and First Dream of Joseph, the Journey to Bethlehem, and the Nativity. The second way documents their engagement with portrayals of Joseph that are based upon one specific canonic event which, interestingly, did not explicitly feature Joseph; notably, the event of the Adoration of the Magi.[86]

The third way substantiates their engagement with canonic accounts that may infer events not described and imply the direct participation of Joseph; notably, the event of Joseph Taking Mary into His Home (or of

---

[85] This was likely motivated by a desire to emphasize and defend particular theological convictions such as the virginity and purity of Mary as well as the divinity of Jesus.

[86] It is both intriguing and curious that narrators (and their communities) deemed it important to portray this scene and to include Joseph in it although there is not an explicit canonic record of his presence.

Joseph Taking Guardianship of Mary). This event was not directly recounted in the canonic records. But, the extant non-canonic narrative portrayals of it suggest that some Christians believed the canonic narratives alluded to it. Thus, these first three ways seem to have their inspiration and foundation primarily in canonic scenes.

In contrast, the fourth way in which they responded to the earlier canonic portraits of Joseph was by creating representations of Joseph either based upon the narrator's and/or community's beliefs or upon one or more earlier non-canonic narrative accounts (in one of the four extant non-canonic narratives reviewed) in which Joseph is explicitly featured. While it is evident that these specific examples are not based upon the early gospel portrayals of Joseph, they nonetheless document important responses to the them and so constitute a significant part of their reception history. Among these examples are found two large narratives, IGThomas and HJC, that present a substantial amount of new information and new scenes related to the character of Joseph and, largely, his relationship with Jesus. The first text, IGThomas, is focused primarily on depictions of the child Jesus interacting with his father, Joseph. The second narrative, HJC, is mainly concerned with stories of Jesus about the life, fatherhood, character, and last days of Joseph, information Jesus related to his disciples on the Mount of Olives. Representations of Joseph in scenes of the Water Test, Joseph's Search and Discovery of a Mid-wife or mid-wives, other scenes of Joseph Leading the Holy Family to Egypt, and the Greeting of the Holy Family by Afrodisius in Sotina on their Flight into Egypt, are also found in these later Christian narratives. Thus, these numerous and variegated portrayals of Joseph provide concrete evidence of the various way(s) in which the later Christians related, integrated, and supplemented the earliest canonic portraits of Joseph as well as canonic nativity and infancy accounts.

This investigation has revealed three areas of theological and literary agreement between these texts: a belief in the divinity of Jesus, a belief in the purity and perpetual virginity of Mary, and a belief in the right of their Christian communities to contract and expand the canonic accounts in order to accomplish their particular theological goals. For example, although the HJC places a strong emphasis on the role and significance of Joseph in the life and moral and spiritual development of Jesus, this emphasis does not diminish its concern simultaneously to show particular deference and veneration toward Mary. Despite such theological lines of agreement, they do not overshadow the significant differences visible between the documents.

This analysis of these non-canonic portrayals of Joseph also suggests that they reveal at least two trajectories: these later narrators seemed inclined to expand the Matthean, Lukan, and Johannine portraits of Joseph in ways that affirmed and enhanced Joseph's character and role, on the one hand, or seemed inclined to contract them in ways that diminished or weakened his figure, on the other hand. Evidence of these two tendencies or inclinations – either to expand or contract the canonic portraits – appears abundant in the variety of narrative characterizations of Joseph. These suggest that the characterization of Joseph's roles could also substantially vary and that some narrators believed it more fitting to portray him in certain roles. While these roles were suggested, if not based upon prior ones, found in the Matthean, Lukan, and Johannine portrayals, some of them were emphasized much more than others.

Similarly, related to the variation in roles, is the variation also found in the characterization and description of Joseph's relationship with Mary and Jesus. The different portrayals of Joseph clearly indicate that some narrators felt it was appropriate to place Joseph in close proximity to Mary and Jesus (as the early gospel narratives imply), while others felt it was more appropriate to place Joseph some distance from Mary and Jesus (as some non-canonic accounts imply).

While it may not be possible to date exactly the beginning of these tendencies or to track precisely the trajectories of these tendencies, it seems tenable that the former, the first trajectory (the one inclined to expand the canonic portraits of Joseph in ways that enhanced the meaning of the earliest gospel portrayals of Joseph), likely emerged at least by the latter half or last quarter of the second century CE and is clearly visible in IGThomas. HJC appears to move along the same theological trajectory in regard to Joseph as IGThomas.

As the prior narrative and literary analysis has shown, these two narratives clearly and repeatedly expand the role of Joseph and increase his significance. These expansions include an emphasis on Joseph's connection to the line of David, the annunciation and spiritual dreams, the care and protection of Mary and the child, the direction and guidance of Mary and the child, his relationship with God, and his relationship with Mary and the child. In the case of these two narratives, with respect to the representation of Joseph, the focus seems primarily to be two-fold: first, to highlight and emphasize the significance and role of Joseph during the period of Jesus' childhood (as seen in IGThomas) and, second, to highlight and emphasize the significance and role of Joseph throughout his relationship with Jesus, up to the period of Joseph's death and Jesus' young adulthood (as seen in HJC).

As the first, the second trajectory appears to have emerged in roughly the same period, in the latter half of the second century. However, initially manifested in IGJames, it appears inclined to minimize the canonic portraits of Joseph in ways that diminish or weaken the meaning and value of the Matthean, Lukan, and Johannine portraits. In light of the many similarities between IGJames and GPM (created between the beginning of the sixth century and the beginning of the ninth century), it appears that GPM moves along much the same theological trajectory in regard to Joseph as IGJames. As the prior narrative and literary analysis of IGJames and GPM has shown, these two narratives clearly and repeatedly dissipate the role of Joseph and diminish his significance. This is manifested in the efforts of both IGJames and GPM largely to ignore or depreciate Joseph's connection with the line of David, the annunciation and spiritual dreams, the care and protection of Mary and the child, the direction and guidance of Mary and the child, his relationship with God, and Joseph's relationship with Mary and the child (disclosed in Matthew and Luke).[87] In the case of these two narratives, the focus seems primarily to highlight and emphasize Mary's purity and virginity and the connection of these characteristics to her relationship to Jesus. However, the reworking and reshaping of the character of Joseph and his relationship with Mary and Jesus in these two narratives also suggests that they have other purposes that include an intent largely to contract and diminish the role and significance of Joseph in the stories of the nativity and childhood of Jesus. Thus, as in IGJames, so in GPM, a clear effort is seen to depreciate the canonic portraits of Joseph in ways that seriously limit their value and significance.

These two trajectories represent two theological and aesthetical schools of thought. One school documents the positive representation of Joseph as important and essential and as in no way, threatening or diminishing the virginity and purity of Mary or the divinity of Jesus. The other places priority on Mary and Jesus and believes it must limit and diminish the role of Joseph. From this perspective every effort is made to enhance their images, especially the ideas of the virginity and purity of Mary and the divinity of Jesus, even if such efforts should minimize the significance and role(s) of Joseph.

Accordingly, it may be concluded that these four later non-canonic narratives reveal both the existence of different historical attempts to define Joseph and the existence of different historical perceptions of Joseph and his role(s) in the Christian story in the first several hundred years of Christianity. Spread over a set period of time (at least over the period between c. 150 and 800 CE), these later narratives also disclose the existence of an ongoing struggle within the broader Christian community of how to respond to the canonic portraits of Joseph in light of certain theological and apologetical concerns. Together, these narratives provide numerous details about the development of the *Wirkungsgeschichte* of the canonic representations of Joseph from the early Christian to the early medieval periods; details that witness to the emergence of two very different perspectives about Joseph.

---

[87] It is this position (that limited the role of Joseph and minimized his existence) that eventually 'won the day' in most places in later years.

Part IV

The Response of Later Christian Artists and Their Communities to the Canonic Portrayals of Joseph

Having documented the various responses to the portraits of Joseph in Matthew, Luke, and John in the representations of Joseph in IGJames, the IGThomas, the HJC, and the GPM, composed between c. 150 CE and 800 CE, and discovered the presence of two different trajectories within the development of the *Wirkungsgeschichte* of the Joseph tradition, attention is now turned to further responses found in eighteen distinct artistic portrayals of Joseph, created between c. 300 CE and 800 CE in order to determine if they also reveal evidence of these two trajectories.[1]

However, in contrast to these earlier analyses of canonic and non-canonic Christian literature in Parts II and III, that were organized according to the approximate respective chronology of each narrative, in Part IV, this review will begin with some remarks about the beginnings of Christian art and issues that must be addressed with respect to the rise of Christian art. Thus, with the help of certain scholars, an effort will be made, in this prefatory discussion, to come to some general conclusions about the different communities with which artists may have associated; how artists may have received or assimilated canonic as well as non-canonic texts related to narrative portrayals of Joseph; if they developed their own non-canonic representations of Joseph independent of received (and, certainly, later) non-canonic texts; and if they may have been influenced by prior visual portrayals of Joseph.

The formal examination of eighteen art portrayals that include portraits of Joseph will follow and will be organized according to five specific iconographic themes found in canonic or non-canonic literature. The first images to be examined will be representations of the First Dream of Joseph and the Annunciation to Joseph that will be reviewed in Chapter 8. These will be followed by compositions of the four other

---

[1] While 47 portrayals of Joseph from this period have been located and identified, it is believed that the 18 portrayals that will be examined in this study are representative of both the quality and the diversity of these works and represent a fair sampling for the hypotheses set forth in this book.

themes, notably, the Water Test (in Chapter 9), the Journey to Bethlehem (in Chapter 10), the Nativity (in Chapter 11), and the Adoration of the Magi (in Chapter 12).

Subsequently, consideration will first be given to the subject, date, and provenance of each work, as well as these matters can be determined.[2]

Second, attention will be directed to the way and manner in which Joseph is portrayed and characterized in each composition. In this regard, as with the narratives, the focus will be directed to: the age of Joseph; his physical features, characteristics, demeanor, and posture; his proximity to Mary and the Christ-child; his physical position and location within the particular composition (i.e. within the background or foreground of the image); the roles and actions in which he appears to be engaged; and, finally, to the different ways Joseph and Mary are juxtaposed as complementary or contrasting figures. As a result, attention will also be given to the independence the artist's work reveals between itself and possible canonic and non-canonic literary referents; its substantial or minimal difference from possible narrative referents; the distinctiveness of the representation of Joseph found in these artistic works.

Third, an attempt will be made, with regard to each work of art, to ascertain if and how a specific artist/artisan may have received or assimilated canonic as well as non-canonic texts; if he/she developed their own non-canonic representations of Joseph independent of received (and, certainly, later) non-canonic texts; and if the artist was influenced by prior visual portrayals of Joseph.

Fourth, in light of the information gleaned from the analysis of these initial three concerns, consideration will be directed to the perceptions and beliefs these specific art works suggest their creators and their respective ecclesiastical communities, patrons, commissioners or guilds, appear to have held with respect to Joseph.

Fifth, and finally, consideration will be given as to whether or not a portrayal of Joseph reveals evidence of a trajectory that largely affirms and enhances the portrayal and role of Joseph found in the canonic accounts or evidence of a trajectory that largely dismisses and diminishes this portrayal and role. This certainly seems possible for, as Harvey has

---

[2] Although the provenance of certain objects can be determined with relative certainty, that is not the case with others, as O.M. Dalton, *Catalogue of the Ivory Carvings of the Christian Era*, pp. xliii-xliv, notes in his remarks on ivory compositions. As previously noted, Dalton (p. xliv) acknowledges it is 'often very difficult to date (ivories) with precision or assign (them) to any particular locality'.

recognized, 'images of the Bible ... engage a specific text and, more often, a particular aspect of it.'³

The Beginnings of Christian Art and the Reception and Assimilation of Canonic and Non-Canonic Texts by Artists in the Early Christian and Early Medieval Periods

Any study of the literary and artistic reception history of a narrative character from the New Testament must begin with the recollection of the historical and political context in which Christianity developed. It should be remembered that as rapid as the Christian movement spread in the first two centuries of the Common Era the context in which it grew was one in which it was both often outlawed and persecuted. However, an indication of the end of this situation came with Constantine's decision to lift sanctions against Christians in the western portion of the empire in 306 CE. This policy permitted Christians 'to practice their religion unhindered' and also provided for 'the immediate restoration of property earlier confiscated from the Church'.⁴ Further, this effort was complemented in the spring of 311 CE, when Emperor Galerius (one of the most vigorous persecutors of the Christians) issued his Edict of Toleration. In this Edict, issued but days before his death, Galerius not only ended the formal persecution of Christians but also ordered 'the restoration of places of worship so that Christians might again gather ...'⁵ Thus, Galerius opened the door for eastern Christians to begin to feel they could worship and express their convictions in a more open and public way.⁶ This act was amplified in February 313, when the new co-emperors, Constantine in the West and Licinius in the East,

---

³ John Harvey, *The Bible as Visual Culture: When Text Becomes Image* (Sheffield: Sheffield Phoenix Press, 2013), p. 10.
⁴ Jonathan Bardill, *Constantine, Divine Emperor of the Christian Golden Age* (Cambridge and New York: Cambridge University Press, 2011), pp. 133, 271.
⁵ Bill Leadbetter, *Galerius and the Will of Diocletian* (Oxford and New York: Routledge, 2009), p. 225. It was posted a few days after his death on April 30, 311 in Nicomedia, the eastern and most important capital of the Roman Empire at the time. Part of the motivation of Galerius was his desire to get the Christians on his side. Thus, he concluded this Edict by directing 'Christians to pray to their God on his behalf and for that of the empire'.
⁶ This text of the Edict of Toleration is found in Lactantius, *Of the Manner in which the Persecutors Died* in *ANF*, 2nd series, vol. 7 (Peabody, MA: Hendrickson, 2004), p. 315. A lengthy explanation of Galerius' attitude toward the Christians can be found in Leadbetter, *Galerius and the Will of Diocletian*, pp. 221-26.

agreed on a policy by which Licinius would extend to Christians in Asia Minor, Syria, Palestine, and Egypt the privileges that Christians in the West had possessed by law since 306 under Constantine ...[7]

Prior to this period a not insignificant amount of Christian worship was conducted in secret, usually in private homes.[8] As a result, most Christian art was limited to very small objects and images painted in underground catacombs. The images painted in the catacombs, cemeteries of the early Christians, have been documented in extensive detail.[9] Less has been said about 'small-scale Christian art' that was probably

---

[7] Bardill, *Constantine, Divine Emperor of the Christian Golden Age*, p. 133, explains that the identification of this policy as 'the Edict of Milan' is 'misleading'. He notes that there is 'no evidence that any edict was issued in that city'. However, he acknowledges that a text of the 'agreed policy' is 'preserved in two versions: a letter sent by Licinius to the governor of Bithynia in June 313, which is preserved in Latin by Lactantius; and another document posted in Caesarea some time later, which reads more like an edict and is preserved in Greek by Eusebius'. A copy of the purported 'edict' from Licinius can be seen in Lactantius, *Of the Manner in which the Persecutors Died* in *ANF*, 2nd series, vol. 7, p. 320. A contemporary translation of these two texts, mentioned by Bardill, is found in Lactantius' *Persecutors*, 48.2-12, pp. 70-73 (quoted in G. Clarke, 'Christianity in the First Three Centuries: Third-Century Christianity,' in A.K. Bowman, P. Garnsey, and A. Cameron [eds.], 2005, *Cambridge Ancient History*, pp. 589-671) and Eusebius, *Church History* 10.5.2-14, pp. 322-32.

Having acknowledged this agreement, it should also be noted, as Thomas F. Mathews, *The Clash of Gods* (Princeton: Princeton University Press, 1993), p. 3, reports, that Licinius ultimately broke his commitment to this new policy and to Constantine and began 'purging Christians from the ranks of government and army, a move that provided Constantine with the pretext for taking up arms against him'. See Mathews' detailed discussion of this on pp. 3-11.

[8] Bardill, *Constantine, Divine Emperor of the Christian Golden Age*, p. 247.

[9] Several scholars address the subject of the early beginnings of Christian Art. In this regard, see W.F.Volbach, *Early Christian Art: The Late Roman and Byzantine Empires from the Third to the Seventh Centuries* (trans. Christopher Ligota; New York: Harry N. Abrams, Inc.,1961); Pierre du Bourguet, *Early Christian Painting* (trans. Simon Watson Taylor; New York: The Viking Press, 1965); André Grabar, *Christian Iconography:A Study of Its Origins* (trans. Terry Grabar; Princeton: Princeton University Press, 1968); André Grabar, *Early Christian Art: From the Rise of Christianity to the Death of Theodosius* (trans. by Stuart Gilbert and James Emmons; New York: Odyssey Press, 1968); Pierre du Bourguet, *Early Christian Art* (trans. Thomas Burton; New York: Reynal & Company in association with William Morrow & Company, Inc., 1971); Gertrud Schiller, *The Iconography of Christian Art*, vol. I; Kurt Weitzmann, (ed.), *The Age of Spirituality: Late Antique and Early Christian Art, Third to Seventh Century* (New York: The Metropolitan Museum of Art, 1979); John Lowden, *Early Christian and Byzantine Art* (London and New York: Phaidon Press, 1997); Robin M. Jensen, *Understanding Christian Art* (London and New York: Routledge, 2000); Neil Macgregor and Erika Langmuir, *Seeing Salvation: Images of Christ in Art* (New Haven and London: Yale University Press, 2000); Matilda Webb, *The Churches and Catacombs of Early Christian Rome* (Brighton: Sussex Academic Press, 2002); Jeffrey Spier (ed.), *Picturing the Bible: The Earliest Christian Art* (New Haven and London:Yale University Press, 2009).

'portable' and used in private worship by some early Christians.[10] Writing about these small artistic works, Lowden notes that

> The church historian and biographer of Constantine, Eusebius, Bishop of Caesaria in Palestine (d. 340), commented: 'I have examined images of the apostles Peter and Paul and indeed of Christ himself preserved in painting: presumably men of old were heedlessly wont to honour them thus in their houses.' His reference to 'men of old' implies that he believed such practices went back well before the time of Constantine.[11]

Thus, early in their history at least some Christians engaged in the creation and use of artistic images.

Therefore, it is not surprising that following the recognition Christianity received through the actions of Constantine, Galerius, and Licinius that many more and larger Christian works of art and architecture were created.[12] Several of these were commissioned by Constantine who 'not only built new churches throughout the empire, helping to compensate for the damage of the persecutions, but also endowed a number of them generously'.[13] Others were also created by affluent Christians and groups of Christians who finally felt free to express openly and boldly their devotion to God. Certainly included in these creations were images of portraits of one or more members of the holy family.

Unfortunately, only a limited number of Christian artifacts remain from the first centuries of the early Christian period. Nonetheless, those that are extant provide important insight into both the theological beliefs and perceptions of the early Christian community, including insight into early beliefs and perceptions about Joseph the Carpenter. For, along with the numerous canonic and non-canonic narratives created within this time that presented portraits of members of the holy family and expressed varying levels of interest, appreciation, and even devotion toward Jesus, Joseph, and Mary, there are also early artistic representations on sarcophagi, mosaics, ivory plaques, book covers, and other artifacts that reveal similar things.[14] Therefore, it is the intention of this chapter and the following chapters in this section of the thesis to examine and document the different levels of appreciation toward Joseph found in eighteen different early Christian and early medieval artistic portrayals in order to

[10] Lowden, *Early Christian and Byzantine Art*, pp. 56-57.
[11] Lowden, *Early Christian and Byzantine Art*, pp. 56-57.
[12] This was particularly true following Constantine's sanction of the religion, after 325.
[13] Bardill, *Constantine, Divine Emperor of the Christian Golden Age*, p. 248.
[14] Some time ago, M. Charles Murray, 'Art and the Early Church', *Journal of Theological Studies* 28 (1977), pp. 304-45, appropriately argued that the time had arrived in Christian scholarship 'that the monuments of the Church should be put back into the context of church history alongside the literary remains in order to arrive at a more rounded estimate of matters of fact in the early Church.'

establish more understanding of the reception history of the canonic portrayals of Joseph. But, first, some reflection must be given to the world of Christian artists/artisans in the early Christian and early medieval periods and to the issue of their reception and assimilation of canonic and non-canonic texts.

An exact picture of the world of the artists in the early Christian and early medieval periods is very hard to discern. Few textual accounts related to art in these periods remain and so one must rely upon what can be gleaned about the content, function, purpose, design, materials, date, and social, ecclesiastical, and geographical contexts, in order to discover pieces of evidence that can give insight into the world of these early creators and the various influences that could have, and sometimes did, inform and shape their work.

The 'communities' with which the artist had association could include monasteries or other ecclesiastical groups, guilds, ateliers, or private or public patrons. However, this is difficult to determine because there are scant references to such 'communities' and artists were not known to leave discernible signatures or marks, as later artists.[15] Thus, much about the nature and character of artists associations and communities remains elusive. Still, some clues (and, in some cases, very specific clues) can be discovered by considering two different factors: the size and the function of the work and asking the appropriate questions related to these factors. While it may not be possible to achieve a definitive answer in all cases it is still appropriate to ask, with respect to the size of the artistic creation, if the work appears to have required the effort of an individual artist/artisan or the efforts of a group of artists/artisans. Similarly, with regard to the function of an artistic work, it is reasonable to ask both for whom it may have been created (an individual or a family or a larger group) and for what purpose it was made (ecclesiastical or secular). The prospective answers to these questions will be noted as they are found in later examinations of the artistic compositions with which this study is concerned.

At the same time, the scholar must also face the fact that there appears to be little direct evidence about how artists/artisans received or assimilated canonic and non-canonic Christian texts. This has led Cassidy,

---

[15] While it can be assumed that some artists/artisans worked alone (perhaps with the aid of an apprentice or assistant), it can be also be assumed that others did not and, instead, affiliated with a guild or workshop and worked together and shared and borrowed ideas. They are believed to have existed in major cities before the rise of Christianity so they would likely have continued. Certainly some artistic projects required this; necessitated a team or guild of workers in order to complete specific elaborate projects, particularly after Constantine's recognition of Christianity and his commitment to use the treasury of the state to restore, build, and enhance innumerable Christian architectural structures.

Part IV. *The Response of Later Christian Artists and Their Communities* 153

among others, to caution modern scholars to be careful in their attempts to substantiate the level of influence ancient texts had upon artists/artisans in this period 'since artists rarely if ever adhere scrupulously to a text even on those occasions when they have recourse to one ...'[16] As Cassidy continues,

> It was not for their learning that they earned reputations. The proper object of their talents was to represent the characters and events of history, mythology, and religion in ways that were visually compelling ... Only occasionally would artists have had to resort directly to written sources, or receive from the oft-cited but rarely sighted humanist or theologian detailed instructions about the subjects they were expected to represent. For most commissions they would have drawn from a common fund of oral lore and pictorial tradition ... But, mostly, their acquaintance with the stories would have been acquired in less deliberate, non-literary ways. And, left to his own devices, the artist's sense of what was important ... would have as much to do with the pictorial possibilities of the narrative ...[17]

However, while there is some validity to Cassidy's perspective, it does not tell the whole story.

Writing about the use of texts in Greco-Roman society and specifically, about their use in Christian communities, Gamble, offers clues about how artists/artisans could come to receive and assimilate different texts.[18] In his study, he provides important insight into the social and cultural world of early Christians and the different types of exposure they had to early Christian literature; insight that is suggestive of the social and cultural context in which artists/artisans lived and worked. Acknowledging the estimate that literacy in the Greco-Roman world was probably seldom higher than 10-15% of the population, Gamble argues that it, nonetheless, cannot be concluded that the lack of literacy inhibited Christians from familiarity with early Christian texts. As he has noted, it must be acknowledged in light of the documentary evidence that does exist that

---

[16] Brendan Cassidy, 'Introduction : Iconography, Texts and Audiences', in Brendan Cassiday (ed.), *Iconography at the Crossroads* (Princeton, NJ : Index of Christian Art, Princeton University Press, 1993), pp. 9-10. Similar caution has been expressed by David Cartlidge, 'Which Path at the Crossroads? Early Christian Art as Hermeneutical and Theological Challenge', in Julian V. Hills (ed.), *Common Life in the Early Church: Essays Honoring Graydon F. Snyder* (Harrisburg, PA: Trinity Press International, 1998), pp. 357-72; Robin Jensen,'Giving Texts Vision and Images Voice: The Promise and Problems of Interdisciplinary Scholarship', in Julian V. Hills (ed.), *Common Life in the Early Church: Essays Honoring Graydon F. Snyder* (Harrisburg, PA: Trinity Press International, 1998), pp. 344-56.

[17] Cassidy, 'Iconography, Texts, and Audiences', pp. 7-8.

[18] Harry Y. Gamble, *Books and Readers in the Early Church* (New Haven and London: Yale University Press, 1995).

all ancient reading was reading aloud and that much of it occurred in public, quasi-public, and domestic settings where those listening might include semiliterate and illiterate as well as the literate ... Most Christian texts were meant to speak to the whole body of the faithful to whom they were read. These writings envisioned not individual readers but gathered communities and through public, liturgical reading they were heard by the whole membership of the church.[19]

So illiteracy or semi-literacy did not inhibit Christians (including Christian artists) 'from becoming familiar with Christian texts'.[20] Indeed, as Gamble argues, it is the case that

> Those who were drawn to Christianity were intensively schooled in its literature, especially scripture. The extended catechetical process by which converts came into the church concentrated, at least from the second century onward, upon doctrinal and moral instruction. It certainly did not include learning to read or write, but it did include close familiarization with Christian scripture. Further, an essential element of Christian liturgical gatherings was the reading of scripture. In the early centuries scripture was not read in snippets but in long segments ... With such regular and lengthy readings, followed by their homiletical exposition, Christians who could not read nevertheless became conversant with the substance of scriptural literature an also with other texts that were occasionally read in the setting of worship.[21]

Therefore, 'the limited extent of individual literacy ... had little adverse effect on the ability of Christians generally to gain a close acquaintance with Christian literature'.[22] This is particularly relevant for comprehending the access artists/artisans had to Christian literature for as Gamble, building upon the work of Meeks, recounts,

> The most typical members of the Christian groups (in the first centuries of the Christian movement) were free craftspeople, artisans, and small traders, some of whom had attained a measure of affluence, ... had the resources to travel, and were socially mobile.[23]

Thus, he reminds scholars that artists/artisans were often in the very center of places and people where they would in fact have had repeated accessibility to the stories and accounts of the canonic and non-canonic narratives.

Further, there is documentary evidence from three particular Christian sources in the late fourth and early fifth centuries, Paulinus of Nola,

---

[19] Gamble, *Books and Readers in the Early Church*, pp. 39-40.
[20] Gamble, *Books and Readers in the Early Church*, p. 8.
[21] Gamble, *Books and Readers in the Early Church*, p. 8.
[22] Gamble, *Books and Readers in the Early Church*, pp. 8-9.
[23] Gamble, *Books and Readers in the Early Church*), p. 5. See Wayne Meeks, *First Urban Christians* (New Haven and London: Yale University Press, 1983).

Part IV. *The Response of Later Christian Artists and Their Communities* 155

Prudentius of Rome, and an anonymous source that artists/artisans could also be exposed to these narratives through the means of the theological criteria and programs of their lay and ecclesiastical patrons and other theological figures (that certainly incorporated selections from canonic and non-canonic texts). Thus, this represents another way in which they could be exposed to these narratives. Certainly an example of this is evident in the poem of Paulinus, a wealthy Christian patron, written to his friend, Nicetas, a bishop of Remesiana. In describing a set of fresco scenes from the Hebrew scriptures that he had had created in a basilica (and in other surrounding buildings) he had endowed near the tomb of St. Felix near Nola (in the southern Italian province of Campania), Paulinus discloses not only his own involvement in the designs and compositions of Christian artists/artisans who worked for him but also his desire to shape the beliefs of the 'peasant' Christians around him.[24] He also reveals his wish to give them access to the stories and teachings of the scriptures in a 'faithful' and 'clear' way. Writing to Nicetas, Paulinus says:

> Now I desire thee to see the paintings on the porticoes decorated with a long series and to take the slight trouble of bending they neck backwards, taking stock of everything with head thrown back. He who on seeing this recognizes Truth from the idle figures, feeds his faithful spirit with a by no means idle image. For the painting contains in faithful order everything that Moses wrote in five books ...

> It may be asked how we arrived at this decision, to paint, a rare custom, images of living beings on the holy houses.

> Hark and I will attempt briefly to expound the causes. What crowds the glory of St. Felix drives hither, is unknown to none; the majority of the crowd here, however, are peasant people, not devoid of religion but not able to read. These people, for long accustomed to profane cults, in which their belly was their God, are at last converted into proselytes for Christ while they admire the works of the saints in Christ open to everybody's gaze ...

> Therefore it seemed to us useful work gaily to embellish Felix' houses all over with sacred paintings in order to see whether the spirit of the peasants would not be surprised by this spectacle and undergo the influence of the coloured sketches which are explained by inscriptions over them, so that the script may make clear what the hand has exhibited ...[25]

---

[24] Caecilia Davis-Weyer, *Early Medieval Art 300-1150: Sources and Documents* (Toronto: University of Toronto Press, 1986), pp. 17-18.
[25] Davis-Weyer, *Early Medieval Art 300-1150*, pp. 18-19. Davis-Weyer took this translation from Paulinus of Nola, *Carmina* XXVII, 512-95 in Rudolf Carel Goldschmidt, *Paulinus' Churches at Nola* (Amsterdam: N.V. Noord-Hollandsche Uitgevers Maatschappij, 1940), pp. 61-65.

Impassioned and involved as Paulinus was in the numerous artistic projects in and around Nola, it is not surprising to know that more evidence of his involvement in the design and composition of illustrations in other Christian basilicas and churches can be found.[26] Consequently, it is easy to concur with Davis-Weyer when she states that Paulinus 'was as much the author of the iconographic programs as of the poems which accompanied them and took an equal pride in both.'[27]

A similar desire to offer guidance and direction about the nature and character of illustrations in Christian basilicas and churches (and in the process to provide further accessibility the Christian scriptures) may be present in a poem written by the Roman Christian poet, Prudentius, entitled, *Lines to be Inscribed under Scenes from History*.[28] As Davis-Weyer states, the poem, written around 400, 'may have been either a blueprint for or a reminiscence of the inside of a basilica or large church in which one side of the walls of the nave were illustrated with images from themes and subjects in the Hebrew scriptures and the other side with images from themes and subjects in the Christian scriptures.[29] Since 'the title of Prudentius' poem suggests that its verses were composed as inscriptions' it is certainly possible that he used this poem to offer not only actual texts to accompany specific portrayals but explicit content for the representations. In some of the lines of his poem that are focused on the birth of Jesus, Prudentius reveals his choices of narrative themes and subjects (and his particular interpretations of specific texts from Luke and Matthew) which he believes artists/artisans should illustrate.

XXV. THE ANGEL GABRIEL IS SENT TO MARY

The coming of God being at hand, Gabriel comes down as a messenger from the Father's throne on high and unexpectedly enters a virgin's dwelling. 'The Holy Spirit,' he says, 'will make thee with child, Mary, and thou shalt bear the Christ, thou holy virgin.'

---

[26] Davis-Weyer, *Early Medieval Art 300-1150*, pp. 20-23, includes a second letter in her compendium that Paulinus wrote to a friend in Tours, Sulpicius Severus, in 403. In it, Paulinus describes his desires to provide a theological program of illustrations for other churches. Davis-Weyer took this translation from Paulinus of Nola, *Epist.* 32, chs. 10-14, 17 in Rudolf Carel Goldschmidt, *Paulinus' Churches at Nola* (Amsterdam: N.V. Noord-Hollandische Uitgevers Maatschappij, 1940), pp. 61-65.

[27] Davis-Weyer, *Early Medieval Art 300-1150*, p. 20.

[28] Davis-Weyer, *Early Medieval Art 300-1150*, pp. 25-33. Davis-Weyer took this translation from the Loeb Classical Library volume on Prudentius, *Lines to be Inscribed under Scenes from History*, trans. H.J. Thompson (Cambridge, Mass. and London: Harvard University Press and Heinemann, 1953) II, pp. 346-71.

[29] Davis-Weyer, *Early Medieval Art 300-1150*, p. 25.

XXVI. THE CITY OF BETHLEHEM

Holy Bethlehem is the head of the world, for it brought forth Jesus from whom the world began, himself the head and source of all beginnings. This city gave birth to Christ as man, yet this Christ lived as God before the sun was made or the morning star existed.

XXVII. THE GIFTS OF THE WISE MEN

Here the wise men bring costly gifts to the child Christ on the virgin's breast, of myrrh and incense and gold. The mother marvels at all the honours paid to the fruit of her pure womb, and that she has given birth to one who is both God and man and king supreme.

The third and earliest extant example of specific instructions about Christian illustrations can be found in four pages of fragments from an illuminated Bible from the community of Quedlinburg, Germany. Composed by an anonymous Christian between 350 and 410, the manuscript contains Old Latin (Old Itala) selections from the text of Kings in the Hebrew scripture. The manuscript presents alternating pages so that the scripture can be found on one page and illustrations (of the text) on the corresponding page. What makes this particularly important for this study, as Davis-Weyer reveals, is that a considerable amount

> of the color has fallen off, revealing instructions for the painter written underneath. They tell him not only what elements to include in his painting, but at the same time furnish him with a summary of the story. The completeness of the instructions seems to indicate that the painter was expected to follow them without further recourse to a prototype.[30]

Three examples from these instructions indicate the explicit nature of the instructions with which artists/artisans could be faced.

> Make Saul by the oak and his servant and three men who talk to him, one carrying three kids, one three loaves of bread, one a wineskin.

> Make prophets, one with a cithara, another with a flute, the third one with a drum, and Saul prophesying and his servant with a harp.

> Make where the prophet Samuel and Saul meet in Mapha and talk to the people ...

> Make where King Saul begs the angry prophet that they may pray God for him and pleads his ignorance.[31]

Despite the fact that only a small portion of this illuminated text remains, there should be little doubt that the kind of direct instructions

---

[30] Davis-Weyer, *Early Medieval Art 300-1150*, p. 24.

[31] Davis-Weyer, *Early Medieval Art 300-1150*, pp. 24-25. Davis-Weyer took the selection she uses from H. Degering and A. Boeckler, *Die Quedlinburger Itala Fragmente* (Berlin: Cassiodor Gesellschaft, 1932), pp. 66-67, 69-72, 74-75.

witnessed here were not also given in the rest of the manuscript in order to facilitate its illustration. Thus, in light of these extant instructions (and the numerous others that can be assumed to have once existed), the anonymous author leaves little question about what he/she believes the artists/artisans should do. Certainly, these three examples indicate that the anonymous writer and Paulinus, and probably Prudentius, held particular ideas about which canonic characters should be portrayed as well as how they should be portrayed and believed their iconographic agenda (which consistently included references to specific canonic scriptures) was appropriate for the artists/artisans to follow.

Additionally, it is hardly likely that these three diverse sources were the only Christian patrons/commissioners to offer such guidance and direction. Rather, their witness suggests that others likely provided similar instruction for theological portrayals, including instruction for different portrayals of themes/subjects related to the birth and childhood of Jesus. Still further, the early date and the organization of the theological and aesthetic programs offered by these individuals suggests they were probably not the first to provide such prescriptions.

However, it is much easier to discern if artists developed their own non-canonic representations of Christian themes and characters and, specifically, of Joseph, independent of canonic (and, certainly later) non-canonic texts. Although it was certainly the case that canonic and non-canonic narratives served as referents for artists as they developed the different themes and the characters within them for their various audiences, even a cursory review of the eighteen compositions to be examined in the forthcoming chapters suggests artists were inclined to act in an independent fashion and spirit.[32] Harvey acknowledges one example of this 'independence' in his discussion of 'conflation' in Christian art.[33]

> Precedents for representing biblical stories, themes, and characters in the guise of periods, places, and persons remote from their original historical context date back to the beginnings of Christian art. It represents an example of conflation: the practice of fusing biblical stories with the artist's vision of their contemporary world.[34]

Thus, as he goes on to note and as is evident in the images in this study, artists were inclined to bind 'the image of the biblical narrative to a specific time and place'.[35] This led them to be inclined to dress, as it

---

[32] This appears to be the case whether or not it can be determined that an artist acted on his/her own or in cooperation with a guild/workshop or at the direction/commission of a private patron– an individual or family members – or an ecclesiastical patron – a pope or church administrator or an ecclesiastical community – church or monastery.

[33] Harvey, *The Bible as Visual Culture: When Text Becomes Image*, pp. 32-37.

[34] Harvey, *The Bible as Visual Culture: When Text Becomes Image*, pp. 32.

[35] Harvey, *The Bible as Visual Culture: When Text Becomes Image*, pp. 33.

Part IV. *The Response of Later Christian Artists and Their Communities* 159

were, biblical characters and subjects in the 'clothes, architecture, and artefacts contemporary to the artist' and his/her cultural context.[36] Therefore, it is not surprising, in light of the period and locales of the works examined in this study, to find biblical characters dressed in Roman attire in Graeco-Roman architectural settings, as will be noted in future discussions. Harvey believes this allowed artists to create compositions that became 'grounded in the present', in their own particular worlds.[37]

Parallel, and related as canonic and non-canonic texts and early Christian and early medieval art may be on some levels, the art created from the narrative is never simply a copy or reproduction of the text. Rather, it often represents characters and events as well as the interpretation of these things in different ways from a canonic or non-canonic narrative. So it is that in the process of creating their work of art, the artist not only creates his/her own interpretation of the subject/theme and the characters within it but their own independent account; an account that has narrative, historical, and aesthetic integrity in and of itself, and provides an important record of early Christian perception and belief with regard to many matters – including the understanding of Joseph. In fact, it can be said that the artist tells 'more' because he/she addresses issues such as the 'characterization' and 'proximity' of the characters in different ways and has the ability in the composition(s) created to address more directly and succinctly the issues of the size of characters, their proximity to each other, their relationship to each other, the roles they play, the context of their actions, and other details.[38] In many respects, they speak, in a different language and, as an example, by their simple positioning of a character, can often tell us quite a bit about both him/her and their relationships with the other characters. Thus, the artistic works from the period provide complimentary and parallel data and evidence that goes far beyond being ancillary or supplementary.

It is also easier to substantiate the influence of prior visual representations of other Christian themes and portrayals of Joseph. In many respects, early Christian and early medieval art are part and parcel of Roman and Greek classical art which provided the aesthetic environment in which the former arose. So it is inevitable as one looks closely at the different works under examination in this study that evidence of this environment and of the adaptation of specific artistic patterns and

---

[36] Harvey, *The Bible as Visual Culture: When Text Becomes Image*, p. 36.
[37] Harvey, *The Bible as Visual Culture: When Text Becomes Image*, p. 36.
[38] Harvey, *The Bible as Visual Culture: When Text Becomes Image*, p. 35, explains these additions of the artist, in part, by noting that the 'inclusion of representations of these places and relics, putatively thought to have been the actual places and things at the time, would have imparted to the works an aura of historical veracity.'

themes can be found in some degree or another. This must be acknowledged, as Grabar states, for

> at the beginning of the Christian experiment in iconography, the inspiration could have only come from the art of other religions or from profane art ... The makers of Christian images could not have been ignorant of the multifarious figurations that surrounded them, nor could they have escaped being to some degree influenced by them. One could say ... that Christian iconography was born in this epoch thanks to the exceptional growth of figurative art in the Roman Empire.[39]

The hard truth of this, Grabar continues,

> can be verified by observation of certain of the most general and frequent features of Christian images: the presentation of the human figure, its common accessories, and the architecture or furnishings that surround the figure.[40]

Subsequently, he adds,

> it was actually because of this that the new, Christian images they (Christian artists/artisans) created were understandable to their contemporaries, and therefore effectively achieved the ends intended.[41]

Therefore, this influence must be acknowledged. Yet, it is also the case that as the Christian movement grew in power and prestige and came into a clearer sense of its own identity that it was able to define itself in more distinctive ways with much more ease because they 'had only to trace a few new features and details to transform an image of a type common in that period into a Christian image, ... into one that evoked a Christian thought or a historical event charged with Christian meaning.'[42]

What is more surprising (and will become manifest as this study progresses) is that Christian artists/artisans and even secular or pagan artists/artisans engaged in work for Christians, exercised the kind of interpretive and stylistic independence from each other that they did. With the exception of certain patterns (found in representations of the

---

[39] Grabar, *Christian Iconography: A Study of Its Origins*, p. xliii. Grabar (p. xliii) goes on to add that 'any particular image of any period of history contains its share of motifs common to the society that produced it – commonplaces, in truth – just as a written text or any verbal expression, contains words and locutions of current usage.' In just the same way, he continues (p. xliii), 'the bases upon which the original Paleo-Christian images were founded ... found expression entirely, almost uniquely, in the general language of the visual arts and with the techniques of imagery commonly practiced within the Roman Empire from the second to the fourth century'.

[40] Grabar, *Christian Iconography: A Study of Its Origins*, pp. xlv-xlvi.

[41] Grabar, *Christian Iconography: A Study of Its Origins*, p. xlvi.

[42] Grabar, *Christian Iconography: A Study of Its Origins*, p. xlvi.

Part IV. *The Response of Later Christian Artists and Their Communities*   161

Journey to Bethlehem and the Adoration of the Magi), they exercised significant independence with respect to their artistic creations, including those of concern in this analysis, the First Dream of Joseph and the Annunciation to Joseph, the Water Test, the Journey to Bethlehem, the Nativity, and the Adoration of the Magi. Thus, they were largely independent not only of the canonic and non-canonic narrative referents that informed the particular themes with which they were engaged but also significantly independent of the work of earlier artists/artisans and of prior visual portrayals, even with regard to the portrait of Joseph.

8

Portraits of Joseph in Compositions of the First Dream of Joseph and the Annunciation to Joseph

The first canonic theme to be considered is the First Dream of Joseph and the Annunciation to Joseph. It is well documented in canonic and non-canonic narratives that have been reviewed in Parts II and III and can be found in Matthew 1, IGJames 14, HJC 6, and GPM 11. The theme is also well-documented in early Christian and early medieval art, and illustrated, in this analysis, in four representative compositions, made of different materials (marble, mosaic, and ivory) that include portraits of Joseph from the fourth, fifth, and sixth centuries.

The first composition, found on a fourth-century Gallic sarcophagus lid, features a reclining Joseph. Its importance and the importance of other representative sarcophagi in this study are indicated for three reasons. First, as Anna Taggart notes, these sarcophagi from the later Roman Empire 'document an unbroken evolution of relief style ... to the Early Christian world of the fourth century, which is not otherwise attested'.[1] Second, they also offer very early representations of the birth and infancy of Jesus of Nazareth. Third, and most important for this analysis, they appear to present early representations of Joseph, if not the earliest extant representations of Joseph.[2] Thus, these sarcophagi constitute significant sources for the documentation of the *Wirkungsgeschichte* of the Matthean, Lukan, and Johannine portrayals of Joseph in the periods with which this study is concerned.[3] Consequently, they warrant careful review and analysis in order to determine what information they may provide about early Christian perceptions of the person and role of Joseph.

---

[1] Anna McCann Taggart, *Roman Sarcophagi in The Metropolitan Museum of Art* (New York: Metropolitan Museum of Art, 1978), p. 20.

[2] Seitz, *Die Verehrung des hl. Joseph in ihrer geschichtlichen Entwicklung bis zum Konzil von Trient dargestellt*, pp. 71-72.

[3] Wilpert, *I Sarcofagi Cristiani Antichi*, vol. III, suppl., pp. vii–viii, only speaks briefly about the specific subject of the 'representations of Saint Joseph' in sarcophagi. His analysis is significantly shaped by his assumption that in 'the first three centuries Roman artists' did not present the figure of Joseph in scenes of the nativity of Jesus in order to avoid the appearance that Joseph may have been Jesus' father. So Wilpert is convinced (p. vii) that portrayals of Joseph can only be found in the fourth century and beyond.

8. *Portraits in the First Dream of Joseph and the Annunciation to Joseph* 163

Figure 1
Sarcophagus, Arles, *First Dream of Joseph and Annunciation to Joseph*, Gallic, Fourth Century, Musée de l'Arles Antique, Arles, France

Introduction

While some scholars have suggested that the various sarcophagi and sarcophagi fragments found in southern Gaul around Arles and other French cities were products of Roman workshops or artists, located some distance away, this is not a necessary conclusion. In light of the history and significance of its Christian population in and around Arles, the fact it was encircled by graveyards, and the accompanying demand they would have for the creation of sarcophagi, by this time, it is more likely that this area would have come to have its own independent artists and workshops.[4] Further, the very personal nature of this art and the

---

[4] However, this does not negate the prospect that their artistic sensibilities had been formed by Roman artisan and workshops.

Arles became a critical Roman seaport and political and military center in the first century CE following the decision of its leaders to side with Julius Caesar in his victorious fight against Pompey. This led both J. Caesar and later Roman rulers to bestow their blessings and monies upon the city for an arena, an amphitheatre, a substantial cryptoporticus (subterranean galleries) and numerable monuments, several of which remain. These gifts and its location and prominence also enabled Arles to become an important Roman political center. They certainly also helped Arles to become a center of Christian activity and life. Substantiation of this can be documented by the fact that the city's Christian population was guided by several important early Christian leaders, including, Saint Trophimus, Saint Honore, and Saint Hilary and the fact that it was sometimes the site for critical Christian councils in the early Christian period, including the famous

circumstances surrounding a request for the creation of such works, and the fact that most clients for these works were people of means, would require that the sarcophagus sculptor or the director of the atelier of sculptors have some personal contact with the individual or family of the deceased in order that they might properly accommodate their wishes.[5] Thus, it is likely that this art was part of the creation of an anonymous Gallic sculptor who, whether by direction or choice, created this composition of the *First Dream of Joseph and the Annunciation to Joseph*, illustrated in Figure 1, and now located in the Musée de l'Arles Antique, Arles, France.

The Characterization of Joseph in Figure 1

In this image Joseph, dressed in an exomis, lies reclined on a bed with his legs crossed and his right hand supporting his head as if he is in a state of contemplation or sleep, against the backdrop of an architectural structure that represents Joseph's residence.[6] To his right, a figure, dressed in a Roman toga stands at the edge of Joseph's bed and extends his right hand toward him, as if he is addressing him. With his left hand, this angelic figure holds an object (possibly a scroll) that may contain the message he brings to Joseph with respect to the veiled female figure that stands to the right of the angel. Wilpert believes this is suggested (and at least part of the content of the message implied) by the 'presence of a

---

council of 314 (that dealt with the issue of Donatism) which was supervised by Constantine (in competition with the northern Gallic Christian centers of Vienne and Lyon). Further information about the importance of Arles in the early Christian movement can be found in Charles Herbermann, 'Archdiocese of Aix' and 'Le Puy', *Catholic Encyclopedia* (New York: Robert Appleton, 1913), n.p.

[5] Sarcophagi can be found in marble, stone, alabaster, terracotta, and lead. Having noted the materials and forms used in these sarcophagi, it is highly likely that the extant Christian sarcophagi (as is the case with the extant pagan sarcophagi) that will be examined in this survey, probably represents work done for wealthy Christians (a minority of the Christian population) rather than that constructed for 'average' Christians. Many Christians would have had only modest financial means. Giovanni Battista de Rossi, James Spencer Northcote, and William R. Brownlow, *Roma Sotterranea* (London: Longmans, Green, Reader, and Dyer, 1869), p. 296, acknowledges that 'the sarcophagus was an expensive article, and the mass of the Christian community was composed of the poor'. Taggart (*Roman Sarcophagi*, p. 27) also confirms this. She writes that 'Plain, purely functional coffins had long been used by the poorer classes'. Thus, their sarcophagi would have probably been made of wood or may have only consisted of a thick cloth wrapping.

[6] This piece is featured in Wilpert, *I Sarcofagi Cristiani Antichi*, vol. I, plate XX.1. His discussion of the image is found in *I Sarcofagi Cristiani Antichi*, vol. I, p. 23. In addition, in *I Sarcofagi Cristiani Antichi*, vol. III, Supplement, p. VII, he argues that the 'people' found in Figures 6 and 7 (from the city of Le Puy-en-Velay) of this essay are also present in Figure 1 (Arles) 'with some variations …'

veiled woman' and by her location, just to the right of the angelic figure.[7] It is this individual character (who Wilpert identifies as Mary) that he is convinced 'determines the scene' and suggests that the angel is directing Joseph to 'take home the Virgin'.[8] Consequently, in light of the formulation of this composition of the *First Dream of Joseph* and the specific characterization of Joseph in it, it is obvious that the sculptor has created a portrayal that has incorporated certain characters and aspects of the canonic narrative in Mt. 1.18-26. Yet, at the same time, with this narrative offering no physical description of Joseph, and few other illustrative details, the artist has had to create his/her own representation in marble, significantly distinct from the textual canonic narrative and, in the process, a new and probably unique portrait of Joseph and composition of the *First Dream of Joseph*. Additionally, although this theme is also found in the narrative account of IGJames 14 (which may have been known to the creator of this work), there is no explicit evidence within the design of this composition to substantiate that this sculptor assimilated material from this or any other non-canonic texts. Further, there is no extant evidence to indicate that this composition of the *First Dream of Joseph* and the portrait of Joseph it offers bears any relationship to any earlier or later representations of the same theme. Thus, the value and integrity of his/her work as an independent witness from the fourth century to the Christian story is evident. It is, perhaps, most manifest in the fact that it provides significant illustrative details that are not found in the text of Mt. 1.18-26. For, unlike this canonic narrative portrayal, this later artistic composition illustrates the size and dress of Joseph and the other characters, places them in very specific physical positions in relationship to each other, and notably includes the figure of Mary, whom it seems the sculptor has inserted with the angelic messenger in order to highlight the specific directions the messenger has given to Joseph and the fact that these directions require an immediate response from Joseph.

The Artist's and the Artist's Community's Perceptions and Beliefs about Joseph in Figure 1

While the client(s) who sought to purchase this sarcophagus likely conferred with a particular sculptor or the director of a workshop of carvers in order to make sure certain wishes were met with regard to the style and design of the resting place of their loved one, it was likely the artist who created and executed the specific design seen here. Consequently, it was this specific artist who portrayed Joseph as he is portrayed here, in

---

[7] Wilpert, *I Sarcofagi Cristiani Antichi*, vol. I, p. 23.
[8] Wilpert, *I Sarcofagi Cristiani Antichi*, vol. I, p. 23. Wilpert believes the 'artist added (this) to make this' a clearer composition.

a very positive light, as a character of equal size to the other characters in the composition and as the figure both the angelic messenger and Mary turn to with expectation and hope.

Therefore, it can be said that this positive portrait of Joseph in this relief carving in this fragment of a sarcophagus, likely created in or around Arles, in southern France, in the fourth century, is an example of a work that enhances the Matthean portrayal of Joseph and substantiates the presence of a trajectory that affirms Joseph's significance in the Christian story.

Figure 2
Mosaic, *Annunciation to Mary and First Dream of Joseph and Annunciation to Joseph*, Roman, Fifth Century, Santa Maria Maggiore, Rome, Italy

Figure 3
Mosaic, *First Dream of Joseph and Annunciation to Joseph*, Roman, Fifth Century, Santa Maria Maggiore, Rome, Italy (detail of fig. 2)

Introduction

Much more is known about the provenance, history, and date of Figure 3, showing the right side of the larger conflated portrayal of the *Annunciation to Mary and First Dream of Joseph and Annunciation to Joseph* found in Figure 2.

Shortly after the decision of the Council of Ephesus in 431 CE to designate Mary *theotokos*, 'mother of God', Bishop Sixtus III of Rome, decided to construct a church in her honor, a magnificent architectural structure that still stands on the Esquiline Hill in Rome, the Basilica of Santa Maria Maggiore.[9] Inside this structure, in the nave, in the upper sections of the triumphal arch that frames the main altar and the apse behind it, is a group of large conflated fifth-century mosaics that reveal the wishes of Sixtus III.[10] A most impressive spiritual and artistic cycle,

---

[9] Although he officially identified himself as the Bishop of Rome in the formal dedication he had inscribed in the middle of the mosaics on the triumphal arch, he was identified as the successor to Peter, and thus the Pope of the Christian church, by many within Christendom. He was consecrated as pope in July 31, 432 and remained in this office until his death in August 19, 440. Seitz, *Die Verehrung des hl. Joseph in ihrer geschichtlichen Entwicklung bis zum Konzil von Trient dargestellt*, p. 76, believes these mosaics constitute 'a glorification of the Ephesian dogma of the dignity of the Mother of God, Mary'.

The Basilica of Santa Maria Maggiore is one of four 'major' or 'papal' basilicas in Rome. It is also known as the Liberian Basilica because it is believed to have been constructed on or near the site of this earlier basilica, constructed c. 360, that was commissioned by Pope Liberius who was consecrated pope in 352 and remained in office until his death in 366. The apex of Sixtus' work as a creator of Christian churches in the holy city, his designation of the Basilica and influence upon the mosaic narratives within it constituted not only an acknowledgment of Mary's particular role in Christian *Heilsgeschichte* but also a window into his and others' perceptions and beliefs about the events of the nativity and the early childhood of Jesus and the roles of the main actors, including Joseph the Carpenter.

The importance of these mosaics is also affirmed by Suzanne Spain, 'The Program of the Fifth Century Mosaics of Santa Maria Maggiore', PhD dissertation (New York: New York University, 1968), p. 3, who writes that 'The figurative cycles of Santa Maria Maggiore are not only the oldest extant, but they appear to have been the first examples of such a decorative scheme in a Roman Christian basilica. The decision to so embellish a church thus constitutes an innovation in church design and a modification of ecclesiastical policy.'

[10] Sixtus III commissioned and paid for the construction of this basilica as is indicated in the dedication he had prepared in the mosaic circle located in the center of the triumphal arch. The Latin reads: 'XYSTUS EPISCOPUS PLEBI DEI'. It can be translated: 'Sixtus the Bishop to the people of God'. As such, it seems appropriate to conclude that this dedication verifies his approval and imprimatur upon both the content and design of these mosaics. Thus, there should be little question that he was also involved, to some extent in decisions about the theological content and aesthetic composition of these mosaics. Lawrence Nees, *Early Medieval Art*, Issue 5970 (New York and London: Oxford University Press, 2002), pp. 88-89, thinks the dedication suggests even more. He believes this 'dedicatory inscription' is a declaration by Sixtus III that he is both 'builder' and 'political leader', a role and position that Nees argues Sixtus had taken by assuming

it offers pictorial representations of narrative scenes from the first century canonic gospels of Matthew and Luke, with non-canonic elements, as well as a scene from a later and familiar non-canonic Christian text. In order, on the left side of the arch, from top to bottom, are found images of the *Annunciation to Mary and the First Dream of Joseph and the Annunciation to Joseph*, the *Adoration of the Magi*, the *Mothers of Bethlehem Pleading before Herod for Their Children* (also identified as *the Massacre of the Innocents*) and the *Sheep before the Gates of Jerusalem*, some of which include important representations of Joseph the Carpenter.[11] On the right side of the arch, in order, from top to bottom, are found images of the *Presentation in the Temple and the Second Dream of Joseph and the Second Annunciation to Joseph*, the *Adoration of the Magi*, the *Greeting of the Holy Family by Afrodisius at Sotinen in Egypt during the Flight into Egypt* (the scene from a non-canonic Christian gospel) and the *Sheep before the Gates of Bethlehem*, some of which also include important portrayals of Joseph the Carpenter.[12] Finally, in the center of the arch, are found images of Peter and

a 'traditionally imperial responsibility and prerogative' and beginning the construction of this large basilica in the first place.

[11] The *Annunciation to Joseph* can also be designated as the *First Dream of Joseph*, as is sometimes suggested.

[12] In light of the broader artistic context in which the portrayal of the *Second Dream of Joseph* is featured within this mosaic cycle, notably just above the representation of the *Greeting of the Holy Family by Afrodisius at Sotinen in Egypt during the Flight into Egypt*, it seems reasonable to suggest this portrayal of a dream of Joseph is based upon the second dream recounted in Matthew 2.13-15 rather than one of the two later dreams in 2.19-21, 22.

Although few examples of cycles of Christian images from this early period remain, this pictorial cycle of biblical and non-canonic scenes of the nativity and early childhood of Jesus in Santa Maria Maggiore was probably one of many extant in the first several centuries of Christianity. Lowden (*Early Christian and Byzantine Art*, pp. 52-56) states this, while noting that 'so little survives' and adds that their 'ubiquitous' presence and their purpose is suggested in written Christian sources, notably in the writing of the fifth century saint, Neilos of Sinai, and his contemporary, the Roman poet Prudentius. Lowden writes: 'The ascetic Saint Neilos (Nilus) of Sinai (d.c.430) ... is reported to have given the following advice: "Represent a single cross in the sanctuary ... Fill the Holy Church on both sides with pictures from the Old and New Testaments, executed by an excellent painter, so that the illiterate who are unable to read the Holy Scriptures may, by gazing at the pictures, become mindful of the manly deeds of those who have genuinely served the true God, and may be roused to emulate their feats".' Further, Lowden, p. 56, recounts that the Christian 'Roman poet Prudentius composed around 400 AD a series of verses on Old and New Testament subjects that read as though they could have been intended to accompany a church decoration of this sort [of the sort mentioned by Neilos].' In her translation of the Latin poems of Prudentius, Sister M. Clement Eagan, *Prudentius* (Washington, DC: Catholic University of America Press, 1962), pp. xiii-xiv, identifies this series of verses as the *Dittochaeon* or *Tituli Historiarum*. She asserts that it consists of 'forty-nine hexameter quatrains on Old and New Testament scenes' and 'is generally attributed to Prudentius'. Continuing, Eagan notes that 'The quatrains were probably intended as inscriptions for mosaics or frescoes in some basilica, and may have been inspired by the epigrams of Pope Damasus and the verses composed by Paulinus of

8. Portraits in the First Dream of Joseph and the Annunciation to Joseph

Paul as well as images of the symbols of the four evangelists, situated to the right and left of a circle in which are found images of 'the apocalyptic throne and the Book of the Seven Seals'.[13] Beneath these images is the Latin dedication of Sixtus III.[14] Therefore, it is evident that the nature, construction, and context of Figure 2 is much more elaborate and complex.

In contrast to Figure 1, the second composition of the theme of the *First Dream of Joseph and the Annunciation to Joseph*, represented in Figure 3, is a very public liturgical work, explicitly designed through a commission of Pope Sixtus III, to inspire and encourage the numerous ecclesiastical leaders and laity who regularly visited and worshipped in this fifth-century sanctuary of Santa Maria Maggiore. Further, it is a much more complex work, not only because this theme is conflated with that of the *Annunciation to Mary*, and this large conflated composition is but one of several mosaic representations in a series on the birth and childhood of Jesus, but also because this composition is a more dynamic and elaborate work, with many more characters and much more action.

The first of the mosaics in this series in which Joseph figures, Figure 2 is located in the upper left section of the triumphal arch. A rare if not unique representation, it features and juxtaposes two literary scenes that are seldom portrayed together: the angelic encounter with Mary and the angelic encounter with Joseph the Carpenter; the annunciation to Mary by the angel, Gabriel, from Lk. 1.26-38, with that of the annunciation to Joseph by an 'angel of the Lord' during a dream, from Mt. 1.20-24.[15] Moreover, it is not only this conflation that is rare but also the way and manner in which the two scenes are brought together in this mosaic.

Nola to accompany pictures in churches'. However, a review of a translation of these inscriptions of Prudentius [found in a translation of this list in Caecilia Davis-Weyer, *Early Medieval Art 300-1150*, pp. 25-33] reveals no reference to Joseph the Carpenter. Nonetheless, the evidence of the present mosaic cycle, sponsored and endorsed by Sixtus III, certainly suggests it was acceptable to include elements found in non-canonic accounts in artistic portrayals within churches.

[13] While there has been some dispute about what this throne actually signifies, Matilda Webb's interpretation seems appropriate. See Webb, *The Churches and Catacombs of Early Christian Rome*, pp. 63-64.

[14] See note 10 above for the details on this dedication. With respect to the selection of the scenes in the mosaic it is curious, as Spain, 'The Program of the Fifth Century Mosaics of Santa Maria Maggiore', p. 105, notes that there is no nativity scene although there is a scene of the non-canonic 'Aphrodisius incident'.

[15] This event takes place within a large pericope (Mt. 1.18-25) in which additional subjects are addressed including the conception and birth of Jesus, the relationship of Joseph to Mary, the doubt and initial resolution of Joseph, the acceptance of Mary and the Child, and the naming of Jesus. These two scenes are relatively close to each other in Tatian's *Diastessaron* and Augustine's *Harmony*.

The Characterization of Joseph in Figure 3

While the primary literary characters of Joseph and 'the angel of the Lord' are found in the Matthean narrative (1.20, 24), this composition of the *First Dream of Joseph* clearly includes more characters and details than the narrative provides and reveals that the creator of this composition and portrait of Joseph has gone to great lengths to create a new and intriguing representation of this theme that, as the work of the sculptor of Figure 1, sets it apart from the narrative in the ways the dream of Joseph is portrayed, the annunciation by the angel is presented, and Joseph is characterized.

Certainly part of the uniqueness of the characterization of Joseph's dream in this composition is found in the fact, as Seitz observed, that, here, Joseph is portrayed as a heavily 'robust man ...' who appears alert and spiritually engaged, standing and awake, with a staff (a scepter?) in his left hand, with eyes wide open, as he is approached.[16] At the same time, curiously, he has his right arm raised and appears to point his right hand toward himself, as if to suggest that he questions that the angels seek him. In addition, in this portrayal he is not approached by one angel but two who, with their right hands raised, appear to address and direct him with an announcement from God (as the other angels address and direct Mary). Joseph is also distinguished by the fact that he appears, as Seitz asserts, to have just emerged from a 'temple-like building' ('a house of prayer'), 'where he has shared his concerns with God'.[17] Joseph seems to share the same relative height and weight and age of Mary, despite the special position reserved for her on a throne. As early as the writing of IGJames (c.150–175 CE), there is a strong effort to present Mary as a young adolescent or maiden and to present Joseph as a very elderly figure: an effort realized in many later Christian images and writings. Yet, here, Joseph and Mary are represented as being close in age.[18]

It is also evident that there is a significant contrast between Joseph's dress and Mary's. Although both appear in Roman attire (as are the

---

[16] Seitz (*Die Verehrung des hl. Joseph in ihrer geschichtlichen Entwicklung bis zum Konzil von Trient dargestellt*, pp. 76-77) has suggested this object may be seen as a scepter.

[17] Seitz, *Die Verehrung des hl. Joseph in ihrer geschichtlichen Entwicklung bis zum Konzil von Trient dargestellt*, pp. 76-77. Mary, in contrast to Joseph, sits upon a throne. There, she is surrounded by other figures. One angelic figure appears to her right. Her attention appears to be focused upon him and he, in turn, seems to be addressing her. At the same time, two other angelic figures appear to her left who seem to be in conversation with each other. In addition, two other spiritual figures, both seemingly focused upon Mary, appear above her: a descending white bird (which may symbolize the overshadowing of the Holy Spirit upon her – mentioned in Lk. 1.35) and a flying angel.

[18] In this regard, note that Seitz, *Die Verehrung des hl. Joseph in ihrer geschichtlichen Entwicklung bis zum Konzil von Trient dargestellt*, p. 76, believes the portrayal of Joseph in these mosaics suggests he is 'between 30 and 40 years'. It is interesting that Seitz does not speculate on the age of Mary. She does appear to be slightly younger than Joseph.

adult-looking angelic figures that approach them with outstretched arms and hands), Joseph's dress suggests he has a less prominent role than Mary. He appears in a 'Dalmatika, a tunic that covers the knees with two drapes cascading down from the shoulders, over which a pallium is wrapped'.[19] It is the type of dress that might be customary for a prominent citizen of the Empire or of a member of the court of the Emperor. However, significant as this is, it is not the same as the dress of Mary who appears dressed in an 'imperial Roman costume', as an empress on a throne, in a fashion similar to representations of earlier Roman and Oriental images of the Egyptian goddess, Isis, as well as the images of Roman and Byzantine empresses.[20] Thus, in these ways, the mosaicist reveals that he/she feel free to offer an interpretation that is significantly independent of the actual words of the text in Mt. 1 (as well as those in the text of Lk. 1) in order to highlight more explicitly the importance and place of Joseph within this specific encounter as well as within the larger story of the nativity and infancy of Jesus.

In addition, there are also signs of pagan and imperial influence that confirm, as Gertrude Schiller notes, in her discussion of the form of the

[19] Seitz, *Die Verehrung des hl. Joseph in ihrer geschichtlichen Entwicklung bis zum Konzil von Trient dargestellt*, p. 76.

[20] As Seitz notes, in *Die Verehrung des hl. Joseph in ihrer geschichtlichen Entwicklung bis zum Konzil von Trient dargestellt*, p. 76, 'Mary appears ... like the mother of a divine king, like a queen herself, as her exquisite clothing and a following of angels indicate ...' Spain, 'The Program of the Fifth Century Mosaics of Santa Maria Maggiore', pp. 115-19, argues, that 'the Joseph in the Annunciation scene is an outrageous interpolation', the result of an elaborate restoration, and has replaced 'another figure' who she later claims to be Abraham (pp. 136-39). She compares the artistry and composition of the angelic messengers with that of Joseph and, on this basis, insists the present figure of Joseph must be a later interpolation. Among other things, she says Joseph is: 'a blocky figure, stubby and short-legged' who 'stands on small misshapen feet set on the border of the mosaic field' (p. 116). Later, in 'The Program of the Fifth Century Mosaics of Santa Maria Maggiore', pp. 126-27, she discusses the 'imperial' type of Mary in some detail. See also Thomas F. Mathews and Norman Muller, 'Isis and Mary in Early Icons', in Maria Vassilaki (ed.), *Images of the Mother of God* (Hants, UK and Burlington, VT: Ashgate, 2005), pp. 3-9. They recount that 'Isis has been called both the "Mother of God", meaning the mother of the divine Horos (Harpocrates) and the "Great Virgin". By Late Antiquity Isis has become the most widely venerated divinity of the Graeco-Roman world as she was gradually identified with the most popular and most powerful goddesses of the whole Mediterranean, from the Magna Mater to Aphrodite (Venus) to Tyche (Fortuna).' Mathews and Muller believe the early Christians associated many of the physical, contextual, and theological attributes of Isis (such as her throne and halo) to Mary in order 'to demonstrate that she (Mary) was equal to, and indeed replaced, the ancient Mother of God'. However, the influence of images of Roman and Byzantine empresses is also evident in interpretations of Mary in early Christian frescoes of the *Adoration of the Magi*, notably in the fourth century Catacomb of Sts. Mark and Marcellian and the late third century Catacomb of Priscilla, located in Rome. Nees (*Early Medieval Art*, issue 5971, p. 90) notes that the costume of Mary is an imperial Roman costume that brings to mind 'the costume worn by the contemporary Empress, Galla Placida'.

mosaic series, the influence of prior visual iconographies, not from earlier Christian work, in this case, but from imperial work. For in this mosaic series,

> The story of Christ's childhood is not told chronologically in the form of a narrative sequence, rather those scenes are chosen which demonstrate the divinity of the Child and the dawn of the era of salvation for the whole world. This intention is in keeping with the hieratic style of the work, which derives from the court art of the time. Dependent upon this art too are the triumphal arch as such and the arrangement of the pictorial registers, also the ceremonial of homage, individual figural types, attributes and the dress of the Virgin. Christian art of the fifth and sixth centuries took over these existing artistic premises and gave them new meaning. It used the forms of imperial art primarily when prominence had to be given to the divinity of Christ and to his new world-dominion. This represents a protest against the deification of the imperial office, for as people looked upon the divinity of Christ in familiar pictorial formula, so gradually veneration of the emperor faded from their minds.[21]

Furthermore, there is no evidence of the presence of material from any non-canonic textual source in this particular artistic portrayal of Joseph, other than the evidence also found in the narrative of Matthew. Thus, it is evident that the creators of this ecclesiastical work did develop their own non-canonic representation of Joseph largely independent of received (and, certainly, later) non-canonic texts. In the process, whether by their own choice or the choice of Pope Sixtus or one of his ecclesiastical administrators, a decision was made to create this positive portrayal of Joseph and conjoin it with a very positive portrayal of Virgin Mary in a conflated work that retold, in a unique way, the textual narratives of both of their annunciations in the context of a much larger work dedicated to the Virgin Mary.

The Artists' and the Artists' Community's Perceptions and Beliefs about Joseph in Figure 3

Although it is possible that a single mosaicist or the head of an atelier of mosaicists was commissioned by Pope Sixtus III to design and execute

---

[21] See Schiller, *The Iconography of Christian Art*, I, pp. 26-d27. Lowden, *Early Christian and Byzantine Art*, pp. 52-56, also acknowledges the significance of these fifth century mosaic images in Santa Maria Maggiore. The significance of this mosaic cycle is also recognized in several additional studies on the Basilica of Santa Maria Maggiore. See especially Richard Krautheimer, 'S. Maria Maggiore', in *Corpus Basilicarum Christianarum Romae,* Vol.3 (Vatican City: Pontifico istituto di archeologia Cristiana,1937-1980), pp. 1-60; the later article by Suzanne Spain, 'The Promised Blessing: The Iconography of the Mosaics of Santa Maria Maggiore', *The Art Bulletin* 61 (1979), pp. 518-40; Joanne Deane Sieger, 'Visual Metaphor as Theology: Leo the Great's Sermons on the Incarnation and the Arch Mosaics at S. Maria Maggiore', *Gesta* 26 (1987), pp. 83-91.

8. Portraits in the First Dream of Joseph and the Annunciation to Joseph

the large mosaic series in the triumphal arch in the basilica of Santa Maria Maggiore of which this composition of the *First Dream of Joseph* is a part, it is more likely that the work was completed by a Roman guild/atelier of mosaicists who were known for their skilled craft. As Spain has recognized, determination of the artist(s) involved in the creation of these mosaics is complicated by the fact that significant portions of the iconography of the triumphal mosaics are 'unique', in particular, 'the Annunciation and Adoration of the Magi differ in composition and iconography from other illustrations of the same theme'.[22] This fact and the fact, which Spain later acknowledges, that there is a 'paucity of surviving monuments from this 75 to 100 year period' makes, as she states 'any attempt at comparative analysis futile and inconclusive. The stylistic relationship of mosaic monuments in this period and the geographical origins of style remain elusive.'[23]

Nevertheless, the role of Pope Sixtus III in the conception and development of the sanctuary in which this composition of the *First Dream of Joseph* and the portrait of Joseph lies can be established in part. Sixtus III commissioned and paid for the construction of this basilica as is indicated in the dedication he had prepared in the mosaic circle located in the center of the triumphal arch that was previously mentioned.[24] As such, it seems appropriate to conclude that this dedication verifies his approval and imprimatur upon both the content and design of these mosaics.[25] Thus, there should be little question that he was also involved, to some extent, in decisions about the theological content and aesthetic composition of these mosaics. Lawrence Nees, writing in *Early Medieval Art*, thinks the dedication suggests even more. He believes this 'dedicatory inscription' is a declaration by Sixtus III that he is both 'builder' and 'political leader', a role and position that Nees argues Sixtus had taken by assuming a 'traditionally imperial responsibility and prerogative' and beginning the construction of this large basilica in the first place.[26] Spain concurs, adding,

> The figurative cycles of Santa Maria Maggiore are not only the oldest extant, but they appear to have been the first examples of such a decorative scheme in a Roman Christian basilica. The decision to so embellish a church thus

---

[22] Spain, 'The Program of the Fifth Century Mosaics of Santa Maria Maggiore', p. 38.
[23] Spain, 'The Program of the Fifth Century Mosaics of Santa Maria Maggiore', p. 41.
[24] Again, see n. 10 in this chapter.
[25] The apex of Sixtus' work as a creator of Christian churches in the holy city, his designation of the Basilica and influence upon the mosaic narratives within it constituted not only an acknowledgment of Mary's particular role in Christian *Heilsgeschichte* but also a window into his and others' perceptions and beliefs about the events of the nativity and the early childhood of Jesus and the roles of the main actors, including Joseph the Carpenter.
[26] Nees, *Early Medieval Art*, Issue 5970, pp. 88-89.

constitutes an innovation in church design and a modification of ecclesiastical policy.[27]

Along with this decision, the configuration of the different themes, including that of the *First Dream of Joseph* and the portrait of Joseph found within this portrayal, reveals that Sixtus III gave permission to the mosaicists contracted for this ecclesiastical project, to exhibit substantial liberty in their execution of the whole series of mosaics. In conclusion, it can be said that this portrait of Joseph in this mosaic composition that they created, in a monumental series that related the birth and childhood of the Savior of the Christian faith, set in a basilica dedicated to the Virgin Mary and created as a result of an important commission by Pope Sixtus III, is an example of a work that enhances the Matthean portrayal of Joseph. It provides more substantiation of the presence of a trajectory that affirms Joseph's significance in the Christian story even though it is part of a larger tribute that affirmed the Council of Ephesus' declaration that Mary was theotokos.

Introduction

The third portrait of Joseph to be reviewed is found in a composition in the upper part of a conflated panel (Figure 4) featured in the famous sixth century ivory cathedra created for Archbishop Maximianus of Ravenna. This image of the *First Dream of Joseph and the Annunciation to Joseph* (Figure 5) is conjoined with a second representation of Joseph, the *Journey to Bethlehem* (which will be examind later in this study), illustrated in the lower portion of the panel that features Figure 5.[28] Unlike the prior elaborate portrayal in Figure 3, this configuration in Figure 5 is simple and conveys only part of the narrative account found in Mt.1.20-26: that an angelic figure came to Joseph while he slept. Another important source for this study, this ivory carving is an example of both a later interpretation of this Matthean account and of one of many Christian ivories that document of the *Wirkungsgeschichte* of the canonic portrayals of Joseph in the early Christian and early medieval periods.[29]

---

[27] Spain, 'The Program of the Fifth Century Mosaics of Santa Maria Maggiore', p. 3.

[28] G.W. Morath, *Die Maximianskathedra in Ravenna: Ein Meisterwerk christlich-antiker Reliefkunst* (Freiburg: Herder, 1940), pp. 40-41, discusses the two carvings in this panel in some detail.

[29] John Lowden, 'The Word Made Visible: The Exterior of the Early Christian Book as Visual Argument', in William E. Klingshirn and Linda Safran (eds.), *The Early Christian Book* (Washington: The Catholic University of America Press, 2007), p. 47, affirms the importance of Christian ivories when he acknowledges that 'the early Christian book cover was ... a locus for public affirmation of orthodox belief'. Accordingly, it is not surprising that Lowden argues on pp. 46-47 that 'the characteristic iconography of a five-part diptych, those themes - including the Protevangelium scenes – common

8. Portraits in the First Dream of Joseph and the Annunciation to Joseph 175

Figure 4
Ivory Plaque, *First Dream of Joseph and Annunciation to Joseph and the Journey to Bethlehem*, Cathedra for Archbishop Maximianus of Ravenna, Byzantine, 546-556, Archiepiscopal Museum, Ravenna, Italy

While ivory carvings from this period have been referred to as part of the 'minor arts', Williamson correctly notes that they provide a critical and informative source for 'the stylistic and iconographic changes that occurred' in the period 'between 500-1050' because 'little monumental

---

to all examples, imply that the images were intended to affirm the broad significance and meaning of the gospel texts'.

Figure 5
Ivory Plaque, *First Dream of Joseph and Annunciation to Joseph*, Cathedra for Archbishop Maximianus of Ravenna, Byzantine, 546-556, Archiepiscopal Museum, Ravenna, Italy (detail of fig. 4)

sculpture of the highest quality' of this time remains.[30] The forms of the Christian ivories that are extant suggest that these works of art were usually carved in relief on a flat square or rectangular plaque that was mounted on ivory or wooden boards in order to serve as a cover for a bible or liturgical text (as is the case with many of the objects that will be reviewed in this study).[31] While the diptych form or 'their derivatives', namely, 'book covers and devotional panels' constituted the 'most important of all ivory carvings', panels were also carved for other private and public objects, including, as shall be seen in this analysis, a box or

---

[30] Paul Williamson, *An Introduction to Medieval Ivory Carvings* (London: Her Majesty's Stationary Office, 1982), p. 5, highlights the importance of the ivory carvings of this period. Although Dalton (*Catalogue of the Ivory Carvings*, p. xxvii) does refer to ivory carving as 'the minor art' he concurs with Williamson's claim by noting that 'very frequently the carver is found to have studied the works of sculptors in marble and bronze, reproducing their style and quality as far as his narrow limits allowed'. However, Dalton goes on to acknowledge that there were times when the ivory carvers provided inspiration for the sculptors. He adds, p.xxvii: 'More rarely, he (the ivory carver) has himself provided the models for the greater work, and thus exercised a most important influence over the development of the arts in Europe.'

[31] Lowden, 'The World Made Visible: The Exterior of the Early Christian Book as Visual Argument', pp. 45-46, believes 'the primary function of such covers was display'. This 'display' could be manifested temporarily 'when the book was carried processionally during the liturgy' or for a longer period 'when the book was set up on an altar' and 'displayed open with the covers ... toward the viewers'. The latter display permitted, among other things, 'a narrative or progressive reading of the two (carved images) together, from left to right'.

8. Portraits in the First Dream of Joseph and the Annunciation to Joseph 177

casket or even a chair in order to express the faith of the believer.[32] Thus, these artistic creations provided another means of relating key narrative accounts of the Bible and other early Christian texts, including accounts pertaining to the birth and infancy of Jesus. As such, it is not surprising to find depictions of many of the canonic scenes (as well as the non-canonic scene of the *Water Test*), represented in early Christian and early medieval ivories, which, in turn, incorporate and detail portrayals of Joseph.

Therefore, this conflated ivory image in Figure 4, with its portrayal of Joseph, sheds further light on perceptions of him within this early period.[33]

The Characterization of Joseph in Figure 5

In this composition of the *First Dream of Joseph* in Figure 5 the character of Joseph is again, as in Figure 3, represented as a bearded figure who is dressed in a Roman toga.

Found in the upper portion of the panel, a double-winged angel approaches a reclined Joseph while he sleeps on an elongated pallet. With a staff in his left hand, the angel leans toward Joseph, touching his bed with the same hand. At the same time, the angel extends his right hand toward the sleeping figure, suggesting he is presenting a message to Joseph.[34]

Thus, in this portrayal, the artist offers an abbreviated composition of the *First Dream of Joseph*; the most abbreviated of the representations of this theme offered in this study. While it indicates a basic dependence upon the story found in Matthew 1, in light of the presence of the two main characters of Joseph and the angel and the representation of the event as an event that occurred while Joseph was asleep, there are no

---

[32] Dalton (*Catalogue of the Ivory Carvings of the Christian Era*, pp. xix-xxi) discusses the importance of ecclesiastical diptychs and book covers and devotional panels in some detail. For his discussion of boxes or caskets and furniture see pp. xxii-xxiii. The rarity of ivory ecclesiastical book covers in the first several centuries of Christianity is also discussed by J.A. Szirmai, *The Archaeology of Medieval Bookbinding* (Aldershot: Ashgate, 1999), pp. 7-10, 15-16, 40-41, 48-49, 78-81, 127-30 and in Paul Needham, *Twelve Centuries of Bookbindings: 400-1600* (New York and London: The Pierpont Morgan Library and Oxford University Press, 1979), pp. 3-29.

[33] For the purposes of this study, the dates and origins attributed by most specialists to the extant ivories that are examined, have been followed. Nevertheless, as has been noted, as Dalton, *Catalogue of the Ivory Carvings of the Christian Era*, pp. xliii-xliv, acknowledges it is 'often very difficult to date (ivories) with precision or assign (them) to any particular locality'. Few ivories provide inscriptions that would help in this regard.

[34] Since this scene appears in the same panel as the scene of the *Journey to Bethlehem*, found in the lower portion, it might be assumed that this angel is both directing Joseph to accept Mary and the child she is carrying and instructing him to take them to Bethlehem.

indications to suggest the artist has assimilated information from a non-canonic literary source. Rather, the very simplicity of the carver's effort indicates he/she wishes to acknowledge that Joseph plays a central role and is presented as both a recipient of God's attention and communication; as one, set apart and chosen to play a special role in this story.

The Artists' and the Artists' Community's Perceptions and Beliefs about Joseph in Figure 5

The presence of the carved monogram of Archbishop Maximianus, found in the front center of the cathedra, directly above the representation of John the Baptist, certainly serves as an imprimatur on the work and indicates his approval of its content, including the nature and character of the compositions of Joseph.[35] Accordingly, one must acknowledge the role of the Archbishop and the hierarchy associated with the church and ecclesiastical community in Ravenna. Likewise, the carved monogram may also suggest that Maximianus acted as the patron for the creation of this piece and possibly suggested the theological outline of the piece: the priority given to the four Gospel writers and John the Baptist, and the emphasis placed upon key themes in the birth and early childhood of Jesus (that includes the specific inclusion of Joseph the Carpenter in every representation of these themes) and key themes in the life of Joseph of Genesis.

Thus, while it is certainly conceivable that this panel (as the rest of the panels from the cathedra that are included in this thesis) was created and carved by artists associated with a monastic community in or near Ravenna, another possibility exists, as Williamson suggests.[36] Reflecting upon the generosity and patronage of Emperor Justinian I (527- 565 CE), he states that the cathedra may have been a gift from the Emperor and, in light of its 'unsurpassed quality ... must have come from the metropolis Constantinople'.[37] However, the evidence of the monogram of the Archbishop on the cathedra lends more credibility to the idea that it was commissioned by him and made in Ravenna. In any event, without additional information, it is impossible to ascertain the specific community in which this work originated.

Nonetheless, it can be confirmed that this artistic creation of the *First Dream* stands on its own, as an independent work of art, as can be seen in the differences that exist between this Ravenna or Byzantine artist's sixth century illustration of this biblical theme and the illustrations created by the earlier artists/artisans in the fourth and fifth centuries.

---

[35] Paul Williamson, *An Introduction to Medieval Ivory Carvings*, pp. 8-9.
[36] Paul Williamson, *An Introduction to Medieval Ivory Carvings*, pp. 8-9.
[37] Paul Williamson, *An Introduction to Medieval Ivory Carvings*, p. 8.

8. Portraits in the First Dream of Joseph and the Annunciation to Joseph   179

Finally, its broader artistic context must also be taken into account. This ivory plaque is one of several compositions found in an extensive group of ivory-carved panels that were prepared in order to decorate a cathedra for Archbishop Maximianus of Ravenna between 546 and 556 CE.[38] While it is possible that this cathedra may have been created and designed as a throne for Maximianus, its size and fragility suggest it may instead have had another function.[39] As Lowden states, 'It is difficult to imagine that such a fragile object could have been intended for a bishop actually to sit on, since it has no underlying wooden structure that would have absorbed the stresses, only the ivories themselves.'[40] In attempting to discern its 'real purpose', Lowden hypothesizes that it may have been designed as 'a conspicuous symbol of the power of the see of Ravenna' and as such, possibly even 'envisaged as becoming itself a precious relic'.[41] In making this argument Lowden opens the door to the proposals of Wedoff that this cathedra may have been used as an altar upon which a large copy of the Gospels or the Bible was placed, following the liturgical procession by the Archbishop and his attendants at the beginning of worship and that the primary purpose of this throne and the images attached to it was to provide 'witness' to the incarnation of the Christ.[42] Thus, it can be concluded that it was a piece created for regular

---

[38] The ivory panels in the cathedra of Archbishop Maximianus in Ravenna are discussed in detail in B.Wedoff, 'Word and Witness: A Reevaluation of the Function, Form, and Imagery of the Cathedra of Maximian', MA thesis (Dekalb, IL: Northern Illinois University, 2009). Earlier important works include: Carlo Cecchelli, *La cattedra di Massimiano ed altri avorii romano-orientali* (Roma: La Libreria dello Stato, 1936-44); Morath, *Die Maximianskathedra in Ravenna: Ein Meisterwerk christlich-antiker Reliefkunst* ; P.A.Waddy, 'The Cathedral of Maximian and Other Sixth-Century Ivories from Constantinople', MA thesis (New Orleans, LA: Tulane University, 1965). Shorter discussions of this cathedra are also found in J. Natanson, *Early Christian Ivories* (London: Alec Tiranti Ltd), pp. 30-32; Lowden, *Early Christian and Byzantine Art*, pp. 116-18.

[39] Lowden, *Early Christian and Byzantine Art*, p. 116. The cathedra measures 22 (W) x 59 (H) inches.

[40] Lowden, *Early Christian and Byzantine Art*, p. 116.

[41] Lowden, *Early Christian and Byzantine Art*, p. 116.

[42] Wedoff, 'Word and Witness: A Reevaluation of the Function, Form, and Imagery of the Cathedra of Maximian' (unpublished), hypothesizes in her abstract that 'the form, material, portability, and decoration (imagery)' of this particular cathedra suggests 'it may have served an alternative … function to that of a bishop's chair', that it may well have been used 'as a platform on which to display a sacred Gospel book for Christian veneration'. As she notes in her initial discussion of the portrayal of the four evangelists, on p. 41, 'The mere presence of the evangelists on the throne directly associates the chair with the Gospels. Each evangelist holds a Gospel book marked with a Greek cross, recalling his role in the divine plan as a documenter of Christ's life and works. The figures gesture, as if in the act of preaching the news of the Gospel. This particular representation of the evangelists is unique in that the hand of each evangelist holding the Gospel is veiled in reverence, an artistic choice that affirms the importance of the Gospel stories, but also the sanctity of the physical texts themselves.' She goes on to note that Morath, *Die Maximianskathedra*, p. 86, 'mentioned that clergy, including bishops would veil their hands

public view. Now located in the Museo Arcivescovile in Ravenna, the cathedra features a variety of series, including a series of five vertical panels of portraits of the four apostles and John the Baptist (with the Baptist situated in the center) in the front of the cathedra; a series of ten horizontal panels that relate the story of Joseph from Genesis on both sides of the throne; and a series of five different two-sided vertical panels (originally there were eight two-sided panels and six one-sided panels) that recount the birth and life of Jesus from the gospels on the interior and exterior of the back of the cathedra.[43]

There are five ivory panels that presently decorate the interior of the backrest of the cathedra, the most visible section aside from the series of the apostles and the Baptist. They relate the following canonic and non-canonic events of the birth and infancy of Jesus: the *First Dream of Joseph and Annunciation to Joseph*, the *Water Test*, the *Journey to Bethlehem*, the *Nativity and the Healing of the hand of Salome* and the *Adoration of the Magi*.[44] Thus, the very position of these narrative images on the front of the cathedra, including beside the image in Figure 5 featured here those found in Figures 8 and 11, suggests their priority for the patron and the carver(s) and the importance they place upon the figures and the events portrayed within these carved representations.

Consequently, this portrayal of Joseph, visible in Figure 5, in the context of all these other positive representations of Joseph from the cathedra of Maximianus, provides more proof of the presence of a trajectory

---

when touching both the Eucharistic bread and the Gospel book not only to demonstrate their unworthiness but also in order to express the importance of the sacred objects'. Later, in her conclusion (on p. 92), Wedoff summarizes her findings by stating: 'The imagery ... emphasizes not only the Gospel narrative and symbolism of the New Law, but also the physical text of the Gospel itself, and witnesses to the miraculous stories therein. The combination of factors surrounding the cathedra suggests that the object ... may have been employed to display the Gospel text to designate the presence of Christ. In identifying a chair owned by a bishop with Christ incarnate, the symbolism of the bishop's role as vicar of Christ would be furthered and his authority strengthened. We might go as far to say that this bishop's cathedra would reach its full ideological potential if it was employed to host Christ incarnate, the sacred Gospel text.' In addition, see Wedoff's remarks about the purpose of the cathedra on pp. 38, 39.

[43] In regard to the present design of the cathedra see Waddy, 'The Cathedra of Maximian and Other Sixth-Century Ivories from Constantinople', p. 1; Lowden, *Early Christian and Byzantine Art*, p. 116; Wedoff, 'Word and Witness: A Reevaluation of the Function, Form, and Imagery of the Cathedra of Maximian', p. 1. It also features a carved monogram of Archbishop Maximianus (located directly above the carving of the Baptist), along with several decorative vertical and horizontal panels of 'grapevines inhabited by animals and birds' that frame the portrait and narrative series.

[44] For a general survey of these particular panels, see Morath, *Die Maximianskathedra*, pp. 36-45. See also Wedoff, 'Word and Witness', p. 44, who makes the important point that the 'front face of the backrest' is in 'a location second only in prominence and visibility to the evangelist figures, providing the infancy scenes a level of high importance as the only frontally visible narratives'.

8. *Portraits in the First Dream of Joseph and the Annunciation to Joseph*   181

that affirms the positive portrayal of Joseph in the Matthean account and continues to expand his significance in the larger Christian story. Therefore, it offers further evidence for understanding the development of the *Wirkungsgeschichte* of the New Testament representations of Joseph the Carpenter in the middle of the sixth century.

Introduction

Scholars also believe Joseph to be present in a conflated portrayal of the *First Dream of Joseph and Annunciation to Joseph and the Marriage of Joseph and Mary*, seen in Figure 6, which is the source of the image of the *First Dream of Joseph and Annunciation to Joseph*, featured in Figure 7.[45]

Figure 6
Sarcophagus, Le Puy, *First Dream of Joseph and Annunciation to Joseph and the Marriage of Joseph and Mary*, Gallic, Fourth Century, Musée Crozatier, Le Puy-en-Velay, France

---

[45] Edmond Frederic Le Blant, *Les Sarcophages Chretiens de la Gaule* (Paris: Imprimerie Nationale, 1886), p. 75, certainly confirmed his conviction that Joseph is the figure juxtaposed to Mary in in the second scene in Figure 9. He offers an extensive discussion of this scene in this text. Seitz, *Die Verehrung des hl. Joseph in ihrer geschichtlichen Entwicklung bis zum Konzil von Trient dargestellt*, pp. 74-75, also believes Joseph is portrayed in these scenes. G. Koch, *Frühchristliche Sarkophage* (Munich: C.H. Beck, 2000), p. 156, concurs and both believes Joseph is a central figure in these two portrayals and that they are the product of 'a local shop'. Wilpert, *I Sarcofagi Cristiani Antichi*, vol. II, text, p. 279, also identifies both works as examples of Gallic sculpture.

Figure 7
Sarcophagus, Le Puy, *First Dream of Joseph and Annunciation to Joseph*, Gallic, Fourth Century, Musée Crozatier, Le Puy-en-Velay, France (detail of fig. 6)

Little is known about this image of the *First Dream of Joseph and Annunciation to Joseph* in Figure 7 and the larger conflated portrayal (Figure 6) of which it is a part, other than that this sarcophagus fragment was created by an anonymous Gallic sculptor and is quite rare.[46] It is presently located in the Musée Crozatier in Le Puy-en-Velay.[47]

---

[46] Figures 6 and 7 are found in Wilpert, *I Sarcofagi Cristiani Antichi*, vol. I, plate XXVI. 1. His commentary on this work is found in *I Sarcofagi Cristiani Antichi*, vol. I, pp. 23-24, 33-34. While there may have been other portrayals that presented these two particular images together, the example in Figure 6 is the only known extant example in which this is the case. Seitz, *Die Verehrung des hl. Joseph in ihrer geschichtlichen Entwicklung bis zum Konzil von Trient dargestellt*, p. 74, thinks the setting of the *First Dream and Annunciation* is 'the gate of Nazareth'. He believes (pp. 74-75) the second scene in this sarcophagus in Figure 4 portrays the angel of God directing Joseph to 'take Mary to be his wife' and Joseph 'obediently' responding to this direction. While Koch (*Frühchristliche Sarkophage*, p. 156) does not deny that the right part of this portrayal, in Figure 6, may represent the marriage of Joseph and Mary, he refers to it as the scene in which 'Joseph takes Mary into his house'.

[47] Although Le Puy-en Velay is a Gallic city like Arles, it is located some distance north of it. While much less is known about the presence and activity of Christians in this community, its proximity to Lyon (the center of much Christian activity in Gaul in

The Characterization of Joseph in Figure 7

Joseph's portrayal is quite distinctive in the first scene, in the image on the left side of the sarcophagus, which recounts the *First Dream of Joseph and the Annunciation to Joseph*, particularly with respect to the physical size of Joseph. Here, the sculptor casts Joseph as a diminutive figure, something neither specified nor suggested in the canonic or non-canonic texts or in prior art portrayals, indicating this artist's independence. However, his/her representation of Joseph as a seated individual, apparently in a state of dreaming, and possibly asleep, is, as, noted in the prior review of Figure 5, based upon in the aforementioned Matthean narrative account.[48] While this is also provided in IGJames and other non-canonic texts, there is nothing in the present composition to suggest that the creator of this piece used information from those narratives in this artistic composition.

Moreover, as in Figures 1-5, the sculptor provides a particular dress for Joseph that additionally informs the viewer about Joseph's character. In the case of Figure 7, Joseph is dressed in an exomis, 'much like a Roman shepherd, comprising a short, girdled tunic which often leaves

---

the early Christian period), some 60 miles southwest of the city, suggests there may be authenticity to the reports that Christians were active as early as the third century and that it was known for its early devotion to Mary. In this regard, see Ean Begg, *The Cult of the Black Virgin* (New York, NY: Penguin, 1989). See also C. Herbermann, "Le Puy', *Catholic Encyclopedia* (New York: Robert Appleton, 1913).

[48] That the dreaming occurred during sleep is clearly conveyed in the words of Mt. 1.20-24. While Heublein, *Der 'verkannte' Joseph*, p. 34, acknowledges this, in part, in her specific remarks about the portrayal of Joseph in this sarcophagus, her general discussion of the topic of the posture of Joseph seems much too informed by classical images and interpretations. While it can be argued that this position or posture of Joseph may represent what Heublein, *Der 'verkannte' Joseph*, pp. 21-22, 26, suggests ('a gesture of sorrowful contemplation and mourning'), this supposition seems largely unreflective of the character and person of Joseph. Although it may be claimed that it might reflect Joseph's feeling or demeanor in the period prior to the annunciation of the angelic messenger, the canonic (as well as most of the non-canonic) literature related to the nativity suggests this physical posture more likely conveys the role of Joseph as a dreamer and receipient of the revelations of God (a role that is especially highlighted in the first two chapters of Matthew). Further, the same early literature (that informed so many other aspects of the portrayal of Joseph) discloses no indication that Joseph's character, demeanor, or spirit were disheartened or shaken following his brief doubt upon initially discovering that Mary was pregnant. In fact, the literary evidence suggests Joseph acted obediently, boldly, courageously, judiciously, and lovingly, once he understood what his responsibilities were to be. Thus, the idea that this posture indicates Joseph remains in doubt or despair following the birth of the child is unwarranted. Even the idea that Joseph is in 'deep immersion' may be made but not the idea that it is 'deep immersion in itself that is filled with worry and suffering', as some scholars suggest. See also, Seitz, *Die Verehrung des hl. Joseph in ihrer geschichtlichen Entwicklung bis zum Konzil von Trient dargestellt*, p. 74. He notes that in the *Annunciation and First Dream* image, Joseph is 'laying his cheek in his left hand and is supporting the elbow with his right hand on his knee ...'

one shoulder uncovered, his head is bare and he carries a shepherd's staff (pedum), which is crooked at the top'.[49] Standing behind Joseph is an angel of God who is dressed in a Roman toga. Further, while the sculptor's representation of the dress of Joseph and the dress of the angel reflect, along with other factors noted, his/her independence from the canonic and non-canonic narratives, they raise the prospect that he/she may have been influenced by the prior characterizations of the dress of Joseph and the angel found in Figure 1, in the sarcophagus fragment from Arles, a community near Le Puy.

Yet, this possibility seems minimal in light of the substantial differences that do exist between the portrait of Joseph found in this representation of the *First Dream* and the three prior representations (in Figs. 1, 3, and 5). This leads to the conclusion that this visual influence is unlikely and that this sculptor has created his/her own non-canonic composition that is both largely distinct from canonic and non-canonic narratives and from prior visual representations.

The Artist's and the Artist's Community's Perceptions and Beliefs about Joseph in Figure 7

Having acknowledged the sculptor's independence in light of the function of the sarcophagus that this fragment represents, it seems likely, as was stated in the discussion of Figure 1 that because of the size of Le Puy's Christian population and the accompanying demand they would have for the creation of sarcophagi that, by this time, this area would have come to have its own independent marble artisans and workshops.[50] This seems to be the case despite the fact that this composition is part of a two-part conflated portrayal that includes a more positive image of Joseph. For the sculptor could certainly have decided to represent the *First Dream of Joseph* in a more positive light, in a way that would have been more complementary to the portrayal of Joseph found on the right side of the larger conflated configuration. Thus, the characterization of Joseph in Figure 7 raises the prospect that a specific tension existed in the sculptor's community in regard to Joseph. Accordingly, although it stands in sharp contrast to the portrayal next to it, the composition of the *Marriage of Joseph and Mary*, in Figure 7, still confirms this tension and documents the presence of a trajectory in early Christian art that negates the positive portrayal of Joseph in the New Testament.

Nonetheless, in summary of this chapter, it can be concluded that the portrayal of Joseph, in this scene of the *First Dream of Joseph and the Annunciation to Joseph*, in four compositions, highlights the significance of

---

[49] Schiller, *Iconography of Christian Art*, I, pp. 59-60.
[50] See the discussion about these matters on pp. 163-164 above.

8. Portraits in the First Dream of Joseph and the Annunciation to Joseph

his dream and annunciation (as the annunciation of Mary was often highlighted in other art). Therefore, examination of these four compositions of the canonic and non-canonic theme of the *First Dream of Joseph and Annunciation to Joseph* indicates that Gallic, Roman, and Ravennian or Byzantine artists/artisans, working from the fourth century to the sixth century, exercised and exhibited considerable freedom both in their representation of this theme and in their portraits of Joseph. Additionally, it reveals substantial evidence of the presence of a trajectory that affirmed the positive portrayal of Joseph in the Matthean narrative account in Figures 1, 3, and 5 as well as an example of some proof of the presence of a trajectory that diminished this positive portrayal in Figure 7.

9

Portraits of Joseph in Compositions of the Water Test

Figure 8
Ivory Plaque, *Water Test*, Cathedra for Archbishop Maximianus of Ravenna, Byzantine, 546–556, Archiepiscopal Museum, Ravenna, Italy

9. Portraits in Compositions of the Water Test

The second theme to be considered is the Water Test, which is not found in canonic narratives but is well-documented in non-canonic narratives. A textual reference to it first appears in IGJames 15–16. Another account is also found in the GPM 12. Likewise, portrayals of it are also present in early Christian and early medieval art. Two portraits of Joseph in compositions of this theme are illustrated in Figures 8 and 9.

The first, created in the medium of ivory, is from the sixth century, and is a panel, as Figure 3, from the cathedra of Maximianus, located in the Archiepiscopal Museum in Ravenna. The second is from the sixth century and presents a carved section of a liturgical ivory book cover presently in the Bibliothèque Nationale in Paris.

Introduction

The second of the portrayals to be examined from the cathedra of Maximianus is seen in Figure 8 above. While it has been suggested that the male character in the left side of this carving is someone other than Joseph, most scholars adhere to the assumption, made in the present analysis, that this figure is Joseph.[1]

The Characterization of Joseph in Figure 8

In this representation Joseph is portrayed as a bearded figure who, dressed in the formal garb of an upper-class Roman citizen, holds a staff (or rod) in his left arm. He stands before Mary and the angel and, with his right hand raised, and his eyes directed toward Mary, addresses her. This occurs as Mary, dressed in much the same garb as Joseph, looks sadly upon a large cup she has raised with her right hand and appears reluctant to drink. At the same time, the angel, standing behind and above Mary looks down toward Joseph and with his/her right hand

---

[1] Wedoff ('Word and Witness', p. 54) believes the 'identity of this figure is in question' and seems inclined, in light of contemporary portrayals of the *Water Test* in the Etchmiadzin Gospel and Saint-Lupicin Gospel cover and the location of this male figure in front or within the context of the temple, as well as other matters, to believe it is most appropriate to identify this figure as Zacharias. However, Joseph's intimate involvement in this event (as recorded in both IGJames and the GPM) and the similarities in construction and composition between this representation of Joseph (including his composition with a staff) and the other 'established' portrayals of Joseph in the *First Dream of Joseph and the Journey to Bethelehem*, the *Nativity*, and the *Adoration of the Magi*, suggest this figure may be identified as Joseph. In addition, there is nothing in the dress of this figure or in other elements associated with his character (this figure carries a staff, not a pyxis) to indicate that this figure is Zacharias. Morath (*Die Maximianskathedra*, pp. 38-39) also believes this figure is Joseph. In addition, Schiller (*Iconography of Christian Art*, vol. I, p. 57) is not hesitant to identify the male figure in this scene as Joseph and to state that Mary's 'face expresses greater distress than does that of Joseph, who comforts her and at the same time listens to the angel's voice'.

raised, addresses him. They all appear in front of a large columned temple-like structure (featured directly behind Joseph and before a stream of water that may be the source for the water of the test as well as symbolize the spiritual differences between Joseph and Mary).

This composition appears to reflect the fact that Joseph has already taken and passed the 'water test'.[2] It also seems to reveal that Joseph's lifting of his right hand may well be at the instruction of the angel, who, standing next to Mary, also has his right hand raised. Thus, Joseph's act may well be one of comfort, aimed at reassuring the younger, pregnant, and troubled Mary that she should do as he did and drink the water and not be afraid.[3] It is also possible that Joseph may be drawing attention to Mary and to this particular event (as his raised hand appears to signify in the last two portrayals in this set of panels) and to the fact that, despite her sadness, she is willing to have her purity tested because she is the pure virgin through whom God will bear the Christ. Thus, by his prior example (having already taken the 'water test'), his actions in this scene and his position in the foreground of the image, directly across from Mary, Joseph appears both to encourage her and to bear witness to her purity and virginity. While the angel stands closest to Mary, above whom he is positioned, the angel's attention and direction seem focused upon Joseph who, in turn, appears to focus his attention upon Mary and provide her the instruction and encouragement she needs to face this particular test.[4]

While it is certainly clear that the carver of this work had somehow become aware of the basic details of the story of the Water Test that was first related in IGJames 15–16 and assimilated them (some centuries later, represented in GPM 12), it is clear that this artist has chosen to add details not found in IGJames in order heighten the illustrative quality of this work. Thus, here, in Figure 8, the carver inserts an angelic figure alongside Joseph and Mary and a stream of flowing water, as well as other details. At the same time, by placing the characters in the positions he/she does and portraying each in the particular ways he/she does, so as to suggest specific roles they have in the portrayal the artist enhances the drama of the theme. Further, it is also clear that he/she has chosen

---

[2] Morath, *Die Maximianskathedra*, p. 38.

[3] Schiller (*Iconography of Christian Art*, I, p. 57) states that there is no 'straightforward explanation' for the presence of an angelic figure in the *Water Test* scenes. In any case, she does think it can be argued that the 'angel stands in the place of the high priest; he is probably intended to underline the fact that the ordeal is a divine one'. Having suggested this, she cautions that it 'is hardly possible to interpret this relief, as has sometimes been done, as combining the trial by water and Joseph's dream, for the dream is depicted on the next plaque of the Throne (of Maximian), above the journey to Bethlehem'. This is contrary to the opinion of the present argument and is explained here and in the forthcoming pages.

[4] Again, see Schiller, *Iconography of Christian Art*, I, p. 57.

to portray Joseph as the pivotal and significant figure that he is in this scene as a result of his/her sense of Joseph's importance in this event and in the life of Mary and that of her child. Thus, the carver has asserted his/her aesthetic independence from non-canonic literary images of Joseph as well as from the earliest gospel narratives of Matthew, Luke, and John that did not relate this account and theme. What is also clear is that in Figure 8 the creator of this ivory panel from the cathedra chair of Archbishop Maximianus of Ravenna has gone to great efforts to create an image of Joseph as a helpmate of Mary and in the process, given the impression that he is responding to her as one who cares and loves her and seeks to make sure that she comes to no harm in the present challenge she faces.

The Artists' and the Artists' Community's Perceptions and Beliefs about Joseph in Figure 8

As was recognized in the discussion of the panel of the *First Dream of Joseph*, in Figure 5, the presence of the Archbishop's carved monogram, in the front center of this cathedra, serves as an imprimatur on the work and indicates his approval of its content, including the portrait of Joseph in the representation of the *Water Test* in Figure 8. Therefore, one cannot talk about the carver and his/her community without acknowledging the role of the Bishop and the hierarchy associated with the church and ecclesiastical community in Ravenna (and in light of the fact that the cathedra did include the representation of a non-canonic theme, the Water Test, found first in the Infancy Gospel of James). Further, as noted with respect to Figure 5, the carved monogram may also suggest that the Bishop acted as the patron for this piece and suggested what should be included within it. While it may be hypothesized that the cathedra was a gift of Justinian I and originated in Constantinople, the evidence of the monogram of the Archbishop on the cathedra lends more support to the idea that the cathedra originated in Ravenna and had the patronage of the Archbishop, himself.[5]

In addition, this analysis of Figure 8 permits one to conclude two things with respect to the perceptions and beliefs of the carver of these images and his/her community. First, the inclusion of Joseph in this scene of the *Water Test* indicates a very high regard for Joseph. Second, the placement of Joseph in close proximity to the angelic messenger (who appears to represent and symbolize the presence of God) and Mary in each of these images, suggests they believed Joseph's role was not only necessary but critical to this theme as well as the larger salvation story.

[5] Williamson, *An Introduction to Medieval Ivory Carvings*, pp. 8-9.

Consequently, this portrayal of Joseph, visible in Figure 8, from the cathedra of Maximianus, a significant Christian artifact, offers evidence of the presence of a trajectory that continues to confirm the earlier positive portrayals of Joseph the Carpenter in Matthean, Lukan, and Johannine narratives even into the period of the middle of the sixth century. This is the case even though the literary inspiration of this theme likely had its source in the non-canonic account of IGJames 15–16 that, as previously acknowledged, presented largely diminished representations of Joseph.

Figure 9
Ivory Book Cover, St. Lupicin Gospels, *Water Test*, Byzantine, Sixth Century, Bibliothèque Nationale, Paris, France

Introduction

Figure 9, illustrated opposite, is part of a five-part ivory book cover that has been reused on the St. Lupicin Gospels, now located in Paris in the Bibliothèque nationale.[6] Created around 550 CE, possibly in Constantinople or some other location in the Byzantine east, the recto of this cover has one composition in the right vertical panel that features an older and bearded Joseph in the scene of the *Water Test*.[7]

The Characterization of Joseph in Figure 9

In this second composition of the *Water Test*, as in the previous carving of Joseph, in Figure 8, his right hand is raised and he appears to direct and encourage Mary to drink the water in the cup. While it is possible that the male character in the left side of this carving is someone other than Joseph, in keeping with the prior discussion of Figure 8, it is here assumed that this figure is Joseph.[8] Thus, from this perspective, in this representation Joseph is portrayed as a bearded figure who, dressed in a Roman toga, holds a staff (or rod) in his left arm. In contrast to the image in Figure 8, Joseph and Mary are the only figures featured, and they both appear to stand in front of the entrance to a large arched stone doorway. Therefore, here, the focus of the scene is upon the interaction between them. With respect to this interaction, it should also be noted that Joseph stands before Mary and, with his right hand raised, and his eyes focused upon Mary, addresses her. This occurs as Mary, dressed in much the same clothing as Joseph, looks reluctantly upon a large cup she has raised with her right hand and appears hesitant to drink.

It also appears that Joseph's lifted right hand, as before, in Figure 8, indicates an effort by him to provide comfort to the younger, pregnant

---

[6] The panels of the the St. Lupicin Gospels are discussed in some detail in F.Steenbock, *Der kirchliche Prachteinband im frühen Mittelalter: Von den Anfängen bis zum Beginn der Gothik* (Berlin: Deutscher Verlag für Kunstwissenschaft, 1965), pp. 76-77 and in Lowden, 'The Word Made Visible: The Exterior of the Early Christian Book as Visual Argument', pp. 40-41.

[7] Steenbock, *Der kirchliche Prachteinband im frühen Mittelalter: Von den Anfängen bis zum Beginn der Gothik* , pp. 76-77; in Lowden, 'The Word Made Visible: The Exterior of the Early Christian Book as Visual Argument', p. 43. This narrative account was previously discussed in the chapters on IGJames and the GPM.

[8] In this regard, again, see Morath, *Die Maximianskathedra*, pp. 38-39; Schiller, *Iconography of Christian Art*, vol. I, p. 57. She is not hesitant to identify the male figure in this scene as Joseph and to state that Mary's 'face expresses greater distress than does that of Joseph, who comforts her and at the same time listens to the angel's voice'. Joseph's intimate involvement in this event (as recorded in both IGJames and the GPM) and the similarities in construction and composition between this representation of Joseph and the other 'established' portrayals of Joseph, noted in this discussion, suggest this figure should be identified as Joseph.

and concerned Mary; to reassure her that she should do as he did and drink the water and not be afraid. Thus, by his actions in this scene and his position in the foreground of the image, Joseph offers support to Mary.

In light of the similarities that exist between the portrait of Joseph in this representation (in Figure 9) and the prior portrayal (in Figure 8) which is a contemporary work, it can be concluded that the carver of this work may well have been influenced by the former design. Nonetheless, as the creators of the prior compositions, the carver of Figure 9 demonstrates his/her independence from the non-canonic narrative of IGJames 15–16 that details this theme. This is evident in light of both the additional details he/she provides and because the carver's portrayal of Joseph suggests he plays a critical role and has a significant position in relationship to Mary and her forthcoming child.

The Artist's and the Artist's Community's Perceptions and Beliefs about Joseph in Figure 9

While it has been noted that some scholars believe this composition and the set of compositions of which it is a part originated in Constantinople, other scholars, focused upon the study of the creation of early Christian books, offer more ideas about both the type of possible communities in which carvers of book covers could be found and their location. Since this ivory represents the first of several ivory works used in book covers that will be examined it is appropriate to broach this issue in this particular discussion.

Although little is known about specific ivory carvers in this period, the research of O.M. Dalton and Chrysi Kotsifou, among others, has established that there were 'centers of book production [which naturally included the creation of ivory book covers] ... in monasteries in the Early Christian and early medieval periods as well as later'.[9] In these monastic communities different members engaged in different aspects of book production – from the creating or copying of books to the illustrating and binding of books. While they sometimes worked on their own in order to create texts for their monastic communities, they also earned income from those outside their communities who sought books

---

[9] Chrysi Kotsifou, 'Books and Book Production in Monastic Communities of Byzantine Egypt', in William E. Klingshirn and Linda Safran (eds.), *The Early Christian Book* (Washington: Catholic University of America Press, 2007), p. 50. See also Dalton, *Catalogue of the Ivory Carvings,* p. xliv, who states that 'in the earlier centuries of the Middle Ages ivories were chiefly made in the great monasteries' and also (p. xli) asserts that this remained the case in the Carolingian period when most of the 'ivories probably came from the great monasteries on the Rhine and its tributaries ...'

for private devotion or for their churches.[10] Additionally, with respect to the function of most of the ivory carvings in this study, it can be concluded that the intent of the carver (whether the carving was to cover a text created for private devotion or for a public ecclesiastical setting) was to detail certain themes of the canonic and/or non-canonic gospels in a positive way.

Thus, in light of this scholarship serious consideration should be given to the hypothesis that this portrayal of Joseph in this particular sixth century composition of the *Water Test* is the creation of a member of a monastic Christian community located in the Byzantine east. At the same time, while the specific identity of the carver and his community remains uncertain, it is clear that this carving discloses the perceptions and beliefs the ivory carver and his/her community held with regard to Joseph. It reveals, as the prior ivory composition of the *Water Test*, that the inclusion of Joseph, in this significant book cover, indicates he was held in high esteem by both the artist and the community of the artist. Second, the position of Joseph in close proximity to Mary in both of these images, suggests belief that Joseph's role was essential in these accounts. Third, Joseph's importance is also highlighted by the fact that Joseph and Mary are also portrayed as having equal size and stature. Finally, it is also revealed in the fact that Joseph and Mary are presented as a conjoined and respectful couple (Joseph standing up for Mary in the *Water Test*).

So, this portrayal of Joseph, created in the middle of the sixth century and present in Figure 9, in a book cover, offers more evidence of the presence of a trajectory that affirms the positive portrayal of Joseph found in the Matthean, Lukan, and Johannine narratives. At the same time, it reveals more insight into the development of the *Wirkungsgeschichte* of these particular narrative representations of Joseph.

Although this scene has its origin in a non-canonic text (and is later represented in other non-canonic narratives), the character of its artistic representation in Figure 9 reflects the positive spirit of the earliest gospels. Thus, it must be acknowledged that both extant compositions provide substantiation of the presence of this positive trajectory. No artistic portrayals of this account exist that suggest Joseph was represented in a diminished way during the early Christian and early medieval periods.

---

[10] Kotsifou, 'Books and Book Production in Monastic Communities of Byzantine Egypt', in Klingshirn and Safran (eds.), *The Early Christian Book* (Washington: Catholic University of America Press, 2007), p. 55. Dalton (*Catalogue of the Ivory Carvings*, p. xliv) adds that 'monks who were distinguished for any particular craft, whether carving (ivory), enameling, or goldsmith's work, might be summoned to distant houses of their order, or their services, might be requisitioned by high ecclesiastics or secular rulers with whom their own superiors entertained friendly relations: in this way the style of the same man might affect the art of places situated at considerable distances from each other.'

10

Portraits of Joseph in Compositions of the Journey to Bethlehem

Figure 10
Ivory Plaque, *First Dream of Joseph and Annunciation to Joseph and the Journey to Bethlehem*, Cathedra for Archbishop Maximianus of Ravenna, Byzantine, 546-556, Archiepiscopal Museum, Ravenna, Italy

10. Portraits in Compositions of the Journey to Bethlehem

The third canonic theme to be considered is the Journey to Bethlehem. It is well documented in canonic and non-canonic narratives that have been reviewed in Parts II and III and can be found in Luke 2, IGJames 17.1-11, HJC 7, and GPM 13. This theme is also found with some frequency in works of art in the early Christian and early medieval periods. Four examples from these periods are illustrated in Figures 11, 12, 13, and 14. They offer four portraits of Joseph in ivory from the sixth to the eighth centuries.

The seventh portrait of Joseph to be examined is found on an ivory plaque, as were Figures 5 and 8, and is part of the same sixth-century cathedra of Archbishop Maximianus of Ravenna.

Figure 11
Ivory Plaque, *Journey to Bethlehem*, Cathedra for Archbishop Maximianus of Ravenna, Byzantine, 546-556, Archiepiscopal Museum, Ravenna, Italy (detail of Fig. 10)

Introduction

The upper part of the conflated plaque in Figure 10, which includes the *First Dream of Joseph and Annunciation to Joseph*, has been previously discussed in the review of Figure 5. The lower part, illustrated in Figure 11 directly above, portrays the *Journey to Bethlehem* and is the subject of the present analysis.[1]

The Characterization of Joseph in Figure 11

In the narrative account of the Journey to Bethlehem, first recorded in Lk. 2.1-6, readers and listeners are presented with a limited number of details: with the key characters of Joseph and Mary and her forthcoming child and with a reason why Joseph is taking the pregnant Mary to Bethlehem with him. Thus, while these narrative details in Luke 2 help carry the narrative forward, they only reveal part of what the creator of the composition in Figure 11 shows. Much the same may be said in regard to the two non-canonic narratives with which the artist may have had some familiarity. In IGJames 17 the readers and listeners are told that Joseph 'saddled his donkey and had her(Mary) get on it', that he was accompanied by two sons from a previous marriage, and that he and Mary engaged in conversation but only two pieces from this narrative are found in Figure 11: that Mary is seated and on a 'donkey'.[2]

Mention of Mary riding a donkey, Joseph and Mary speaking, and the sudden appearance of a 'beautiful child' who accompanies them is also found in GPM 13.[3] But, again, these additional details do not appear to further inform this carver's art. Thus, both the canonic and the non-canonic narratives only disclose a portion of what the carver creates. For the carver, creating his/her own work provides more details and, in the process, provides a more elaborate portrayal of Joseph; one which shows Joseph physically holding and supporting the pregnant Mary. Moreover, he/she also suggests that God is helping them in their difficult and precarious journey by including the character of a winged angel, who, with his eyes focused on Mary (and her eyes focused on the angel) also walks closely with the couple and guides the donkey upon which Mary sits.

As a result, the carver offers a portrayal, as it were, that goes significantly beyond the text of the Lukan narrative and demonstrates his/her independence from both this canonic narrative as well as the two later non-canonic narratives that also relate this event and theme. In the process, the creator of this composition of the *Journey to Bethlehem* choses, artistically, to add the figure of an angel who assists the couple, and

---

[1] Morath, *Die Maximianskathedra in Ravenna*, pp. 40-41, discusses the carving in this panel in some detail.

[2] Citing the translation of Hock, *The Infancy Gospels*, pp. 61-63. Although some scholars believe the HJC was composed some years before GPM, its dissemination was much more limited than that of GPM. Thus, it is unlikely that the artist of this composition would have been familiar with its account of the Journey to Bethlehem.

[3] Citing the translation of Ehrman and Pleše, *The Apocryphal Gospels*, p. 99.

demonstrates both Joseph's obedience to the earlier message of the angel (that he received in the upper panel of this conflated work) and Joseph's dramatic manifestation of this obedience – his complete physical and emotional engagement with a very pregnant Mary.[4]

At the same time, the carver expands his/her portrayal of the theme by making it evident that both Joseph and the angel are seeking to be very careful and thoughtful with regard to Mary and the child she carries. As such, it is not surprising that both Joseph and the angel 'look to Mary' and have their attention focused upon her as they move along the road to Bethlehem. This care, as has been acknowledged, is also indicated by the way Joseph holds Mary, with his left arm wrapped around her back to hold her steady and his right arm positioned on her right knee to brace her. Likewise, it is exemplified by the action of the angel who, tightly holding the reins of the donkey, guides the movement of the animal. Finally, it is also clear that, as Joseph and Mary make their journey, Mary openly acknowledges her dependence upon Joseph and her need of his support as she leans upon him.

Thus, in this image, in Figure 11, the carver reveals a desire to emphasize the importance and significance of Joseph in the *Journey to Bethlehem*.

The Artists' and the Artists' Community's Perceptions and Beliefs about Joseph in Figure 11

In light of this work's relationship to the prior panels in Figures 5 and 8, it can be assumed that the present composition and portrayal of Joseph shares certain similarities with these objects.

Although Figures 5, 8, and 11 offer portrayals of Joseph in different contexts and in different roles, it should be noted that they each portray him as an older bearded figure dressed in the formal garb of a Roman toga. Further, similarities are also seen when the carved configurations of the characters of Mary and the angel in Figure 11 are compared with those in Figure 5 (with respect to the angelic figure) and Figure 8 (with respect to the Mary and angelic figures). And yet this composition, in Figure 11, as the prior compositions related to it in Figures 5 and 8, demonstrates the carver's significant independence from prior canonic

---

[4] Reflecting upon the way the top scene leads to the bottom, Wedoff ('Word and Witness', p. 55) asserts that 'Joseph's obedience to the angel of his visionary dream is realized in the bottom portion of the composition. Not only is Joseph responding to civil law which required that he enroll in a census in the town of his origin, Bethlehem, but Joseph's obedience to his angelic vision is evident in his assistance to Mary.' Morath (*Die Maximianskathedra in Ravenna*, p. 41) notes Joseph's direct and personal engagement with Mary in this second scene and believes its inspiration lies with Lk. 2.1-7 rather than with the account in IGJames.

and non-canonic narratives and previous iconographic works as well as his/her commitment to characterize and portray Joseph in a very positive way, in the same spirit, disclosed in the other portrayals from the cathedra of the Archbishop Maximianus. This is substantiated in three ways. First, by the emphasis the carver gives Joseph in this composition of the *Journey to Bethlehem*.

Second, the placement of Joseph in close proximity to the angelic messenger (who appears to represent and symbolize the presence of God) and Mary in this image, suggests the artist believed Joseph's role was not only necessary but critical to the salvation story. Third, the fact that Joseph and Mary are placed in such close proximity, represented as being of equal size and stature, and portrayed as a loving couple (Joseph helping to carry her and her child in the *Journey to Bethlehem*), may well reflect the belief (as found in the nativity and infancy accounts in the canonic Gospels of Matthew and Luke) that they were indeed conjoined as husband and wife and father and mother in the period of the nativity and the infancy of Jesus and beyond.

Accordingly, this portrayal of Joseph, visible in Figure 11, reveals the presence of an ongoing trajectory that affirms and expands upon the positive narrative portrayal of Joseph in the Journey to Bethlehem found in Luke 2. Consequently, it offers additional information for comprehension of the development of the *Wirkungsgeschichte* of the earliest gospel portrayals of Joseph in the middle of the sixth century.

Introduction

The next composition is found in another five-part ivory book cover that has been reused on the St. Lupicin Gospels, now located in Paris in the Bibliothèque nationale.[5] Created around 550 CE, possibly in Constantinople, the recto of this cover has two scenes in the right vertical panel that feature an older and bearded Joseph. The first, illustrated in Figure 9, and reviewed earlier, details the *Water Test*, while this composition, featured in Figure 12, provides an image of the *Journey to Bethlehem*.[6]

---

[5] The panels of the the St. Lupicin Gospels are discussed in some detail in Steenbock, *Der kirchliche Prachteinband im frühen Mittelalter: Von den Anfängen bis zum Beginn der Gothik*, pp. 76-77; Lowden, 'The Word Made Visible: The Exterior of the Early Christian Book as Visual Argument', pp. 40-41.

[6] Steenbock, *Der kirchliche Prachteinband im frühen Mittelalter: Von den Anfängen bis zum Beginn der Gothik*, pp. 76-77; Lowden, 'The Word Made Visible: The Exterior of the Early Christian Book as Visual Argument', p. 43. This narrative account was previously discussed in the chapters on IGJames and GPM.

10. *Portraits in Compositions of the Journey to Bethlehem* 199

Figure 12
Ivory Book Cover, St. Lupicin Gospels, *Journey to Bethlehem*, Byzantine, Sixth Century, Bibliothèque Nationale, Paris, France

The Characterization of Joseph in Figure 12

Here, Joseph is shown with his left arm around the back of a pregnant Mary and the left side of his body leaning into Mary while his right arm and hand are extended to the bridle of the beast in order to control its movement. In turn, Mary has her right arm wrapped around the shoulder and head of Joseph.[7] Again, as in Figure 11, here, in Figure 12, the artist's focus is upon the closeness and interconnectedness of Joseph and Mary, and upon Mary's dependence on Joseph in her circumstance – which is even more strikingly portrayed, in contrast to the composition in Figure 11, because Joseph and Mary are seemingly alone. There is no

---

[7] Strong similarities clearly exist between this portrayal of Joseph and the one found in the *Journey* in the cathedra of Maximianus in Figure 11. While this may indicate that Figure 12 was based upon Figure 11, the similarity may suggest the different images were based upon the same model (that could have been current or available to different ivory carvers in the period) and is now lost.

angelic figure or other person who appear to assist them on their journey. In addition, in this representation, it is Joseph, who also has to guide the animal. Thus, the viewer is left with little doubt that the couple feel on their own, clearly dependent upon each other, alone in the reality and challenge of their journey. Accordingly, it is evident that this carver (as the creator of Figure 11) has probably only relied upon certain narrative details related to Luke 2 and IGJames 17 and created a largely independent composition. At the same time, he/she has also shown aesthetic independence in his/her specific carvings of the figures of Joseph, Mary, and the donkey and in the architectural setting in which these figures are portrayed. However, the different ways in which the carver has chosen to portray the interaction between these three characters, as detailed above, suggests that he/she was likely dependent upon an earlier or contemporary configuration and possibly that found in the earlier image of Figure 7 although the present work is more primitive.

Thus, in Figure 12, as was the case in Figure 11, Joseph continues to play an important role and is presented as God's obedient and righteous servant, the loving spouse and husband of Mary, and the guardian of the expected child.

The Artist's and the Artist's Community's Perceptions and Beliefs about Joseph in Figure 12

The prospect and likelihood that this carving was created by a member of a monastic Christian community located in the Byzantine east, has already been suggested in the discussion about the community of the artist who composed Figure 9 and there appears no better explanation, at present. Nonetheless, as was also noted in the earlier analysis of Figure 9, the nature and character of the carver's portrayal of Joseph and the other figures in this figure, does reveal at least three perceptions and beliefs of the ivory carver and his/her community with respect to Joseph. First, the inclusion of Joseph, once again, in the *Journey to Bethlehem*, in this significant book cover, indicates he was held in high esteem by both the artist and the community of the artist. Second, this carving shows that both the artist and the community of the artist believed Joseph was conjoined with Mary, familially, and spiritually, and as a result, familially and spiritually connected to Jesus. Third, this representation suggests Joseph's position and role are essential to the Christian story.

Therefore, this portrayal of Joseph, created in the middle of the sixth century and present in Figure 12, in a carving of the *Journey to Bethlehem*, located on a book cover found on the St. Lupicin Gospels, offers more specific evidence of the presence of a trajectory that affirms both the particular positive representation of Joseph in Luke 2 as well as the positive spirit with which he is portrayed in the other early gospels.

10. *Portraits in Compositions of the Journey to Bethlehem* 201

Figure 13
Ivory Pyx, *Journey to Bethlehem*, Syrian-Palestinian, Sixth Century, Staatliche Museen Preußischer Kulturbesitz, Berlin, Germany

Introduction

The next portrayal of the *Journey to Bethlehem*, illustrated in Figure 13, and presently located in the Staatliche Museen Preussischer Kulturbesitz in Berlin, also includes a representation of Joseph. Probably created in the region of Syria-Palestine in the sixth century, this composition of Joseph in this ecclesiastical object parallels similar images of Joseph found in other ivory portrayals of this subject, namely, in Figures 11 and 12.[8] Properly identified as a 'pyx' or 'pyxide', these ivory cylindrical (or rectangular) boxes were 'employed' by Christians 'to contain relics of saints, or, more rarely, perhaps the consecrated bread.'[9]

The Characterization of Joseph in Figure 13

Here again, as in previous images, Joseph is portrayed as an older, bearded figure. With his head and eyes looking toward the sky (perhaps

---

[8] Dalton, *Catalogue of the Ivory Carvings*, p. xxii and Weitzmann (ed.), *Age of Spirituality: Late Antique and Early Christian Art, Third to Seventh Century*, p. 497.

[9] Dalton, *Catalogue of the Ivory Carvings*, pp. xxii-xxiii.

for direction from God), he supports Mary, as she sits side-saddle upon a donkey. While Joseph does these things, Mary, in contrast, with her right arm firmly locked around his neck and her left arm and hand raised, appears dependent upon Joseph and engaged in conversation with him.[10] At the same time, in the right side of the image, an angel, with his head and eyes turned toward the couple, tightly holds the reins of the donkey and guides the movement of the animal.

In light of the tight and close interaction between these three characters, it is quite evident that both Joseph and the angel are seeking to exercise great care and regard for Mary and the child she carries. As such, it is not surprising that Joseph looks to the heavens (or to God) as he does while he attempts to keep Mary secure and steady and that the angel concentrates his attention upon both as they move along the road to Bethlehem. Joseph's care is highlighted by the way he holds Mary, with his left arm wrapped around her back to hold her steady and his right arm seemingly thrust forward to hold her saddle in place to keep her and the child she bears, safe.

While this particular carving would seem to suggest the dependence of it upon the two prior iconographic compositions (especially Figure 11 which also incorporates an angelic figure), there are also signs of distinction in this liturgical work. This is best seen in the actual carvings of the four figures of Joseph, Mary, the angel, and the donkey, which appear significantly different from the earlier carved representations of the same figures. Still further, the character of the event is more dynamic and fluid than those before, particularly in light of the conversation that appears to be occurring between Joseph and Mary. Additionally, as has been noted with respect to the influence of canonic and non-canonic narratives, the carver uses only certain details and adds much of his/her own creativity to the composition.

Most importantly, perhaps, the carver's work in this piece, as that of the artists' work in Figures 11 and 12, indicates his/her desire to provide a clearer and more intimate portrait of the relationship between Joseph and Mary than is related in the canonic and non-canonic narrative accounts of the Journey to Bethlehem.

Thus, in this ivory pyx (Figure 13), once again, Joseph is presented as an important character in the foreground of a scene who, by his actions, discloses his love and care for both Mary and the child she bears.

---

[10] Joseph and Mary are also represented as being of equal size and stature.

The Artist's and the Artist's Community's Perceptions and Beliefs about Joseph in Figure 13

While there is no documentary evidence to establish clearly the identity of the artist and his/her community, the purpose of this liturgical work, the quality of its carving, and its probable region of origin, make it possible to hypothesize that its origin, as those of the carved sections in the book covers that have been examined, in Figures 9 and 12, lie with a monastic or ecclesiastical community. However, in this case, Weitzmann believes the community of its origin is located in the Syrian-Palestinian region that was home to numerous monasteries.[11]

Additionally, the amount of space devoted to this composition of this event that highlighted Joseph and his relationship with Mary and her forthcoming child on this cylindrical pyx (a liturgical piece of significant value to the Christian community in which it was used) indicates that the carver and his/her community perceived Joseph to be a very important figure in the Christian story and held him in very high esteem.

Hence, this portrayal of Joseph, illustrated in Figure 13, in this sixth century ivory pyx, of possible Syrian-Palestinian origin, offers extra documentation of the presence of a trajectory that affirmed the positive portrayal of Joseph in both Luke and the other early gospel accounts.

Figure 14
Ivory Book Cover, Murano Ivories, *Journey to Bethlehem*, Syrian, Sixth-Eighth Century, Louvre, Paris, France

---

[11] Weitzmann (ed.), *Age of Spirituality: Late Antique and Early Christian Art, Third to Seventh Century*, p. 497.

Introduction

The final composition of the *Journey to Bethlehem* under consideration is featured in Figure 14. It is found in another five-part ivory book cover, known as the Murano ivories, possibly created in Syria between the middle of the sixth century and the eighth century and now situated in different locations.[12] With respect to this analysis, only this bottom horizontal panel of the recto, located in a collection in the Louvre in Paris, will be considered for only it features a portrayal of Joseph.[13]

The Characterization of Joseph in Figure 14

Luke 2.1-6 is the first and earliest text to make a reference to the event and theme of the *Journey to Bethlehem*. But, while it presents us with the key characters of Joseph and Mary and the child inside her who is to be born and suggests a reason why Joseph is taking the pregnant Mary to Bethlehem with him, it offers little more. Thus, while it offers sufficient details to move the story forward, it does not reveal either what earlier artists of this theme have conveyed or what the carver of this artistic composition in Figure 14 relates. For, here, an angel of the Lord appears to guide a young pregnant Mary who, with her head turned back toward Joseph, rides an animal, while a seemingly older Joseph (with a bent back), and a raised right hand, follows behind. Joseph and Mary, both apparently dressed in Roman togas, interact with one another and appear engaged in conversation, as they make their way, with the angel, to their destiny.

Thus, while the three characters found in two of the three previous artistic compositions are also present, their portrayal is markedly different in this representation of the *Journey to Bethlehem*. This is particularly evident in the carver's decision to place Joseph some distance from both Mary (and, thus, the child with whom she is pregnant) and the angelic figure; a decision which suggests he/she believes that the prior portrayals of closeness (whether the carver was or was not aware of them) and Mary's physical dependence upon Joseph, previously seen in Figures 11, 12, and 13, would be inappropriate. In so doing, he/she demonstrates his/her independence from prior canonic narrative sources and prior visual iconographies. However, there is a real possibility that, here, there is

---

[12] The Murano ivories are discussed in detail in Steenbock, *Der kirchliche Prachteinband im frühen Mittelalter*, pp. 73-75; Danielle Gaborit- Chopin, *Ivoires medievaux: Ve-XVe siècle* (Paris: Département des Objets d'Art, Musée du Louvre, Editions de la Réunion des musées nationaux, 2003), pp. 60-62, and in Lowden, 'The Word Made Visible: The Exterior of the Early Christian Book as Visual Argument', pp. 41-43.

[13] Steenbock, *Der kirchliche Prachteinband im frühen Mittelalter*, pp. 73-75; Gaborit-Chopin, *Ivoires medievaux: Ve-XVe siècle*, pp. 60-62; Lowden, 'The Word Made Visible: The Exterior of the Early Christian Book as Visual Argument', p. 41.

an allusion to the representation of this subject found in IGJames 17 and GPM 13 for both make mention of a verbal exchange between Joseph and Mary that may well be illustrated in this particular composition where such an exchange appears to be portrayed.[14] Nonetheless, even if this is the case, it must be concluded that the carver of this composition of the *Journey to Bethlehem* has revealed much independence in his/her work.

The Artist's and the Artist's Community's Perceptions and Beliefs about Joseph in Figure 14

Although it is likely, as has been asserted with respect to other images carved for book covers that the author and the origin of this composition can be found in a monastic community, further information is difficult to discern. However, both the general configuration of the event of the *Journey to Bethlehem* in Figure 14 and the characterization and representation of the figure of Joseph and of his interaction with Mary, indicate that the artist's and the artist's community's perceptions and beliefs about Joseph were quite different from those identified in the three prior images in Figures 11, 12, and 13. In sharp contrast to those, here, in Figure 14, the artist has created a clear space of separation between Joseph and Mary, placed Joseph at the end of the line, behind Mary, and implied, by his/her placement of the angel in the front and right side, that Joseph had lost his pivotal role as the guide and main supporter of Mary.

Therefore, it can be concluded that the portrayal of Joseph, visible in Figure 14, from this book cover associated with the Murano ivories and possibly created in Syria, proffers an example of a representation of Joseph that minimizes the earliest portrayal of Joseph in Luke 2 and negates the positive spirit of his representation in other accounts in Matthew, Luke, and John. Thus, it provides substantiation of the presence of an ongoing trajectory that diminishes the significance of Joseph and his place within the salvation story in the period between the middle sixth century and the eighth century.

Consequently, in summary, both the positive representations of Joseph in Figures 11, 12, and 13, and the negative portrayal of Joseph in Figure 14, offer significant evidence for understanding the development of the *Wirkungsgeschichte* of the earliest gospel portrayals of Joseph.

---

[14] In this regard see both the translation of IGJames 17 in Hock, *The Infancy Gospels*, pp. 61-63 and the translation of GPM 13 in Ehrman and Pleše, *The Apocryphal Gospels*, p. 99.

11

Portraits of Joseph in Compositions of the Nativity

The fourth theme to be considered is the Nativity. It is well-documented in canonic and non-canonic narratives that have been reviewed in Parts II and III and can be found in Luke 2, IGJames 18-19, HJC 7, and the GPM 13-14. It was also a subject of interest in the early Christian and early medieval periods as extant works of art from the period indicated. Four examples from these periods are illustrated in Figures 15, 16, 17, and 18. They offer four portraits of Joseph (three in ivory and one on parchment), from the sixth to the ninth centuries.

Figure 15
Ivory Book Cover, *Nativity*, Italian, Fifth Century, Cathedral Treasury of Milan, Italy

Introduction

This eleventh portrait of Joseph is found in the earliest surviving ten-part ivory and jeweled ecclesiastical book covers (with five parts to each cover), now located in the Cathedral Treasury of Milan (Tesoro del Duomo).¹ Created between 450 and 500 CE, the five-part recto of this set has the only scene that features Joseph, notably, as seen in Figure 15, in an account of the *Nativity*, found in the upper panel of this liturgical book cover.²

The Characterization of Joseph in Figure 15

In the account of the Nativity in Luke 2, the readers are only provided the 'bare-bones' with respect to the event. They are told who is present and where the birth occurs and little more. As a result, much is left to the imagination of the reader. Accordingly, it is not surprising that the creator of this illustration seeks to provide more information; to present a picture that his/her viewers can keep in their minds; a visual mnemonic device as it were; something that, as with many other compositions, attempts to provide much more information about this special event for early Christians. In the process, the carver provides a clear and distinct physical context for the birth that includes a raised brick/stone and thatched resting place for the child, under a thatched roof that also provides cover for two animals. Just outside the boundaries of the roof lines, Joseph, sits upright on an apparent stone seat, at the feet of the child in the crib, and directly across from Mary. From his position 'he gazes upon the child' as Seitz recognizes, 'as if in reflection'.³ Here, he is dressed in an exomis, the dress of a shepherd or tradesman.⁴ Likewise, Joseph is represented as a slightly smaller figure than Mary. Additionally, he appears to hold the handle or top of a saw (a framing saw?) in his left hand; thereby confirming his association with carpentry.⁵ Similarly, though Joseph seems to be bearded, the additional details in the faces of Joseph and Mary do not suggest he is necessarily older than her.

Thus, once again, it can be concluded that while key characters and certain details suggest the carver of this ivory was familiar with Luke 2, this portrayal in Figure 15 reveals particular details neither found in this

---

¹ The panels of this ten-part ivory are discussed in detail in Steenbock, *Der kirchliche Prachteinband im frühen Mittelalter*, pp. 69-71; Lowden, 'The Word Made Visible: The Exterior of the Early Christian Book as Visual Argument', p. 36.

² Steenbock, *Der kirchliche Prachteinband in frühen Mittelalter*, pp. 69-71 and in Lowden, 'The Word Made Visible: The Exterior of the Early Christian Book as Visual Argument', p. 37.

³ Seitz, *Die Verehrung des hl. Joseph in ihrer geschichtlichen Entwicklung bis zum Konzil von Trient dargestellt*, p. 78. Seitz discusses this image in some detail.

⁴ Heublein, *Der 'verkannte' Joseph*, pp. 22-23.

⁵ Heublein, *Der 'verkannte' Joseph*, p. 22. She notes that the portrayal of Joseph with his tool is quite rare and occurs only 'occasionally up until the 14th century ...' With regard to this portrayal of the *Nativity*, see also Schiller, *Iconography of Christian Art*, I, p. 60.

early gospel or in the later non-canonic literary referent of IGJames 18-19.[6] He/she also configures the characters as he/she envisions they may have been positioned – all to give the viewer a better sense of what the context of the birth was and what kind of relationship existed between the main characters. In the process, the artist offers the viewer a more elaborate portrait of Joseph that indicates he played an important role and had a significant position in relationship to Mary and to the child.[7] At the same time, the carver demonstrates his/her independence from both canonic and non-canonic narratives and earlier visual sources and the special nature of his/her own interpretation of this event.[8]

The Artist's and Artist's Community's Perceptions and Beliefs about Joseph in Figure 15

The person who created these ivory ecclesiastical book covers (which contain this portrayal of Joseph) likely wanted them to be representative of their beliefs and also suitable for liturgical purposes in their fifth-century Christian community (it would seem most unlikely that they would seek or wish to use such detailed work that was not representative of their beliefs and suitable for their liturgical purposes). Thus, it was likely the carver who executed this specific design and portrayed Joseph as he is portrayed, did what he did for use within his/her monastic or ecclesi-

---

[6] While this image does include the presence of an 'ox and an ass' which are noted for the first time in the non-canonic account of GPM 14, Cartlidge and Elliott (*Art and the Christian Apocrypha*, pp. 18-19) point out that it is quite possible that artists first introduced these figures to scenes of the Nativity and that only later were they incorporated into Christian literature. It is very possible that the initial origin of this reference in this image would have been the reference in the Hebrew scripture of Isaiah 1.3-4 (LXX, AT) where it is stated that 'The ox knows its owner and the donkey its lord's manger ...' Some early Christian artists would be familiar with this prophetic reading. The Hebrew prophetic literature was very popular with some early Christians. It would not be surprising that a Christian artist was familiar with it or had heard it read at one time or another. If this were true it would certainly provide one explaination for how this information came to be found in a much later non-canonic text, such as GPM.

[7] This is the case although Joseph's role and position are not as important and significant as those of Mary. It is indicated in both the specific context of this composition (where Mary's physical dominance is quite notable) and in the larger context of the nine scenes found on the recto (Figure 14) of this set of ivory book covers from Milan. Mary is represented on at least two other occasions – in the smaller scenes of the *Annunciation to Mary* and in her *Introduction to the Temple in Jerusalem* – found just below the carving of the *Nativity*.

[8] This is not to say that this design and its clients and/or the carver might not have been influenced by a prior non-iconic artistic design. A very similar design is present in another image of the nativity in the Werden Casket. It is discussed in some detail in Joseph Natanson, *Early Christian Ivories* (London: Alec Tiranti, 1953), p. 27 and illustrated in Figure 15 of his catalogue.

11. *Portraits in Compositions of the Nativity* 209

astical community or for clients from another particular religious community. In light of the specific placement of the composition of the *Nativity* at the top of the recto of this multi-faceted ivory book cover, it is appropriate at least to conclude, first, that the inclusion of Joseph, here, in Figure 15, indicates the high respect for Joseph's roles in the nativity and infancy accounts within the ecclesiastical community for which this object was created. Second, Joseph's close proximity to Mary and the child as well as his central location within the upper panel in this ivory book cover additionally substantiates their respect for Joseph and the positive nature and character of his relationships with the virgin and the baby.

Subsequently, it can be concluded that this positive representation of Joseph in this fifth-century ivory book cover, likely from Milan, is another example of a work that enhances the canonic portrayal of Joseph. Therefore, there is no question that this work of art in Figure 15 further substantiates the presence of a trajectory that affirms Joseph's significance in the Lukan narrative as well as in the rest of the earliest gospels' representations of the Christmas story.

Figure 16
Illumination, Parchment Folio Sheet of Rabbula Codex, Syrian, Monastery of St. John Zagba, 586 CE, Biblioteca Laurenziana, Florence, Italy

Introduction

Created in 586, in a Syriac Christian community in the Monastery of St. John of Zagba in Mesopotamia by a scribe who identified himself as Rabbula, this illumination in Figure 16 is one of several marginal miniature images found on this folio parchment sheet in which this portrayal was created (identified as Plut. I, 56, Folio 4 v) of 'canon tables'.[9] This particular folio page, which offers a 'canon table' and images of *Solomon* and *David*, the *Baptism of Christ*, the *Nativity of Christ, Herod,* and the *Massacre of the Innocents* (in two separate images – with the portrayal of Herod in the bottom left corner and the portrayal of the massacre in the bottom right corner), is one page of an extant two hundred and ninety-two page codex.[10] One of only four extant illustrated Gospels to have survived from the pre-iconoclastic East, this codex contains the Peshitta version of the Syriac translation of the canonic Gospels and an inserted 'gathering (not formally part of the text) of fourteen folios of full-page illustrations and other decorations at the beginning of the text'.[11] Twenty-eight images are found in these fourteen folios.[12] Nineteen of these images (including the present folio sheet) are 'designs of architectural arcades enclosing canon tables between columns' that feature, along with portrayals from the Hebrew scriptures (especially the Old Testament prophets), compositions from the New Testament (as this one of the *Nativity*) 'in the margins'.[13]

The Characterization of Joseph in Figure 16

Presently located in the Biblioteca Laurenziana in Florence, Italy, the portrayal of this scene of the *Nativity* presents an important representation of Joseph.[14] In this portrayal Mary is presented as a nimbed figure,

---

[9] Heublein, *Der 'verkannte' Joseph*, pp. 21-22.

[10] Robert Deshman, 'The Illustrated Gospels', in Gary Vikan (ed.), *Illuminated Greek Manuscripts from Armenian Collections* (Princeton: The Art Museum and Princeton University Press, 1973), p. 29. K. Weitzmann (ed.), *Late Antique and Early Christian Book Illumination* (New York: George Braziller, 1977), p. 17, is convinced that 'Gospel Books' such as this large codex 'were produced not to be kept on the library shelf, but to be deposited on the altar table, as the focal point of the service'.

[11] Weitzmann (ed.), *Late Antique and Early Christian Book Illumination*, p. 40.

[12] Weitzmann (ed.), *Late Antique and Early Christian Book Illumination*, p. 42, states that these 28 images constitute 'the most extensive cycle in early manuscript decoration'.

[13] Weitzmann (ed.), *Late Antique and Early Christian Book Illumination*, p. 40. In addition to the images mentioned, Weitzmann notes (p. 40) that there are six full-page portrayals of New Testament accounts, a folio with images of Ammonius and Eusebius, 'who had contributed to the organization of the Canons of Concordance', and two decorated text pages 'with Eusebius' letter to Carpianus and the prologue to the canon tables ...'

[14] While Weitzmann (ed.), *Late Antique and Early Christian Book Illumination*, p. 97, acknowledges the presence of Joseph in this folio, Heublein, *Der 'verkannte' Joseph*,

dressed in a purple and bluish gown, sitting on an unknown object, in the foreground of the image; in a position and location often occupied by Joseph in both earlier and later images. In contrast, Joseph is presented right next to the child in the crib, directly behind the crib.[15] While it is unclear if he is sitting or standing, it is clear that he is leaning over the crib and looking at the face of the child and, with his right hand raised, speaking with the child or reflecting upon the presence of the child. Moreover, he is also portrayed as a nimbed figure, and it is this, as well as his very intimate position in relationship to the child (in contrast to Mary's position in the image) that make this image so unusual and possibly unique among the extant images in the period of this study.[16] In addition, it should also be noted that an ox and ass appear directly behind Joseph and are separated from him and the child by a large horizontal object that suggests the animals are in a stable.

As has been noted, the canonic narrative of Luke 2 only provides certain basic pieces of information about what happened, where it happened, and who was present in the event of the Nativity. As a result it is not surprising that the artist incorporates these pieces into his portrayal. While much more can be imagined, in light of these details, the creator of this composition chose to highlight only certain things – the close proximity of Joseph to the child, his engagement with the child, the significance of Joseph's role, and the distance of Mary. However, neither these details nor others are found in a non-canonic literary source in this period. Thus, with so little to go on, the illuminator has a lot of freedom to portray the characters and the context of this theme. So he can nimb Joseph, place him as close as he does to the child, and put him in a very nurturing role while at the same time, setting Mary some distance from Joseph and the child. In so doing, this sixth-century Syrian monastic artist and member of the Monastery of St. John of Zagba, creates one of the most remarkable compositions of the Nativity and of Joseph in the history of Christianity.[17]

---

pp. 21-22, highlights his importance in this portrayal and the rarity of it. Still, many scholars have simply overlooked the significance of this portrayal of Joseph.

[15] Weitzmann (ed.), *Late Antique and Early Christian Book Illumination*, p. 97, believes the 'background' of this composition 'is reminiscent of the cave turned into a sanctuary as it existed in the Nativity Church (in Bethlehem), and thus the representation (in this particular illumination) is a *locus sanctus* picture from Bethlehem'.

[16] Heublein, *Der 'verkannte' Joseph*, pp. 21-22.

[17] In fact, this monastic artist appears to have created a work that is unique among compositions that represent the theme of the Nativity. There is no evidence of his direct dependence upon the work of other artistic compositions in his portrayal of Joseph.

The Artist's and the Artist's Community's Perceptions and Beliefs about Joseph in Figure 16

Much more is known about the illuminator and his relationship with his community with respect to Figure 16. This is the case because the specific ecclesiastical community with which he is affiliated is identified and also because the artist names himself, 'Rabbula', and relates that he is a scribe (and obviously a manuscript illustrator) within his monastic community. Furthermore, the relationship between the illuminator and the 'clients' or community for whom he works or serves is also quite different since he is both associated with this group and a functioning member of this community (in this case, the late sixth century Syriac monastic community of St. John of Zagba). Subsequently, both the information provided by the artist and his intimate relationship within his community make it clear that both he and the other members of his Syrian monastic ecclesiastical body held Joseph in very high regard. This seems verified by the concluding words at the end of this codex where Rabbula suggests that responsibility for both the writing and the illuminations within this codex lies with all the members of the seemingly small community of the Monastery of St. John of Zagba. For in these words, he gives credit to his 'presbyter and abbot' of his convent, 'Sergius', and his fellow monks and several individuals from 'the convent of Larbik' (presumptively a neighboring convent), including one 'noble Monsignor Damian ... of Bet Perotagin', who have devoted themselves to revising and finishing and arranging and collating and sewing and writing these book' within his convent.[18]

Likewise, the perceptions and beliefs of Rabbula's monastic community can be seen in the two ways in which he presents Joseph in the context of this composition of the birth of Jesus. First, the fact that Joseph is portrayed in very close proximity to the child and is clearly engaged with him, suggests that the artist and his community believed Joseph to be essential to the life of the child, absolutely necessary to the child's life and well-being. Second, these facts and the fact that Joseph is nimbed also suggest they held Joseph in high esteem.[19]

---

[18] http://sor.cua.edu/Bible/RabbulaMs.html, p. 6.

[19] Some insight into these illuminations can be found in the calligraphic 'subscription of all the Gospels of the Codex', located at the end of the codex that has been translated by Giuseppe Furlani. A copy of this translation by Guiseppe Furlani can be found in Carlo Cecchelli, Guiseppe Furlani, and Mario Salmi (eds.), *Facsimile Edition of the Miniatures of the Syriac Manuscript in the Medicaean-Laurentian Library* (Olten and Lausanne: Urs Graf-Verlag,1959). This translation can be found at the website for Syriac Orthodox Resources under the heading, 'Miniatures from the Rabbula Gospels.ms.' These online pages can be located at http://sor.cua.edu/Bible/RabbulaMs.html. In these concluding remarks, the scribe Rabbula, asks that 'whoever reads this book ... pray for me so that I may obtain mercy on the terrible Day of Judgment as the robber on the right side found

Thus, it seems appropriate to conclude that Joseph's portrayal in Figure 16 reflects the beliefs of the sixth-century Syriac monastic scribe, Rabbula, and his fellow monks and others within the communities of St. John Zagba and the convent of Larbik. At the same time, it offers another illustration of the composition that both affirms the representation of Joseph in the account of the Nativity in Luke 2 and the spirit of the Joseph traditions in the other early gospels narrative accounts. Subsequently, Figure 16 provides more evidence of the presence of an ongoing trajectory that positively affirms the significance of Joseph and his place within the salvation story.

Figure 17
Ivory Book Cover, Dagulf Plaque, *Nativity*, Court of Charlemagne (?), Eighth-Ninth Century, Bodleian Library, Oxford, England (detail)

Introduction

The thirteenth composition of Joseph is found in the ivory carving identified as the Dagulf plaque that is a cover for the Douce 176 manuscript,

---

mercy through the prayer of our Lady Mary, the Godbearer, the ever-virgin ...' While such references to Mary certainly provide an explanation for why she is nimbed, placed in the foreground of the image, and highlighted as she is, they do not provide an explanation for the very positive portrayal of Joseph. Nonetheless, in this context, they do indicate that Joseph could be highly esteemed and represented accordingly even in contexts where Mary was emphatically identified as 'Lady Mary, the Godbearer, the ever-virgin ...'

presently located in the Bodleian Library in Oxford.[20] Illustrated in Figure 17 above, it is believed to have been created in the late eighth or early ninth century, possibly in the Court School of Charlemagne.[21]

The Characterization of Joseph in Figure 17

Reflective of the freedom of artists of the period and the different ways they could perceive Joseph, this portrayal of Joseph in a small scene of the *Nativity* in the upper right corner of a larger plaque, stands in sharp contrast to the representations of Joseph in Figures 15 and 16. While the general literary referent for this theme is obviously Luke 2, as noted in regard to these earlier images, and this is reflected in the presence of key characters, the creator of this account includes other elements in this portrayal. In light of the late date of this composition and its likely geographical locale, it is possible that these elements reflect evidence of the influence of the GPM in this work which was accessible in this period and area. This can be substantiated by the presence of the 'ox and the ass', which may have been incorporated in this composition in light of their mention in GPM 14. But, more significantly, it seems suggested by the demeaning way in which Joseph is featured in this ivory carving. For his position and characterization in this image reflects the spirit and tone of his characterization in the GPM where his position and characterization serve to severely limit his role as well as to create a substantial spiritual wall between himself and Mary, as noted in the discussion of his characterization in GPM in Part III. This seems likely since, here, Joseph is represented as an older and diminutive figure whose role has been minimized. Situated on the ground, at the bottom of the composition, below the Christ-child in the manger, a large and reclined figure of Mary, and the two beasts of burden, Joseph's position in relationship to the other figures in the image and within the composition, suggests he is the least important of all the characters. At the same time, his limited significance appears to be highlighted in particular, by the way a dominant Mary is juxtaposed with him. Thus, in this representation, in contrast to the two prior portrayals, Joseph's role and importance are substantially diminished.

---

[20] P. Harbison, *Earlier Carolingian Narrative Iconography: Ivories, Manuscripts, Frescoes, and Irish High Crosses* (Mainz: Jahrbuch des Römisch-Germanischen Zentralmuseums, 1984), pp. 458-63.

[21] Schiller, *Iconography of Christian Art*, I, pp. 208-209; Harbison, *Earlier Carolingian Narrative Iconography: Ivories, Manuscripts, Frescoes, and Irish High Crosses*, pp. 455-63.

The Artist's and the Artist's Community's Perceptions and Beliefs about Joseph in Figure 17

Little definitive can be determined about the creator of this image and the tentative hypothesis that this ivory carving was created in the late eighth to early ninth century in the Court School of Charlemagne does not significantly help to clarify the issue of its authorship. Nonetheless, the composition itself, the fact that it is one of several carvings used in a book cover is suggestive, as has been noted in prior discussions of book covers, that the author may have been a member of a monastic Christian community.[22]

Moreover, the manner in which Joseph is portrayed and what that says about his roles and relationships with respect to Mary and the child does offer specific clues as to the perceptions and beliefs the artist and the artist's community held with regard to Joseph. In light of these factors, it seems reasonable to believe that the position and size of Joseph (when compared with the position and size of Mary – who is represented as not only clearly above Joseph but also as a much larger and important figure), and his proximity to Mary and the child (beneath and some distance from both of them – as well as from the animals), all suggest Joseph played a very diminished role in this artistic portrayal. Subsequently, it seems fair to conclude that the artist and his/her community had a limited vision of the significance and role of Joseph.

These conclusions with respect to the perceptions and beliefs of the carver and his/her community, in turn, suggest that they certainly perceived Mary to be the most important adult in the Nativity and associated very positive characteristics with her character and personality; characteristics they did not appear to associate with Joseph.

For this reason, this single portrayal of Joseph, illustrated in Figure 17, in the book cover identified as the Dagulf plaque, and possibly created in the Court School of Charlemagne, provides more specific evidence of the presence of an ongoing trajectory that negates the positive portrayal of Joseph in the account of the Nativity in Luke 2 and diminishes his role and significance in the larger Christian story in the late eighth or early ninth century.

---

[22] Dalton, *Catalogue of the Ivory Carvings*, xli-xlii.

Figure 18
Ivory Plaque, *Nativity*, Syrian-Palestinian, Seventh-Eighth Century, Dumbarton Oaks, Washington, DC

Introduction

Joseph is also featured in the single ivory plaque of the *Nativity*, illustrated above in Figure 18 and believed to have been created in the region of Syria-Palestine in the late seventh-eighth century.[23] Located in the collection of Dumbarton Oaks in Washington, DC, it presents Joseph as an older and bearded figure, dressed in traditional classical garb.

The Characterization of Joseph in Figure 18

The level of freedom in artistic expression in early medieval Christianity and in perceptions and beliefs about Joseph is even more dramatically revealed in this composition of the *Nativity* in Figure 18 where Joseph, seated on the left side of the image, is juxtaposed to a very large and reclined figure of Mary, who is posed in front of the crib of the child (a second adult figure, possibly a midwife, is situated on the right side of the ivory).[24] As the composition reveals, Mary clearly overshadows both Joseph and this other woman, whose poses suggest they are reflecting upon what has taken place. At the same time, both Joseph and this other female seem to have their attention focused upon Mary, as she rests following her delivery. Thus, while Joseph is physically represented, here, as he is sometimes portrayed (in a reflective and contemplative pose), and may be said (as the figure on the right side) to function in this work as a witness, his position, posture, and size suggest his role is limited. For

---

[23] With regard to this image, see Weitzmann (ed.), *Age of Spirituality: Late Antique and Early Christian Art, Third to Seventh Century*, pp. 582-83.
[24] Heublein, *Der 'verkannte' Joseph*, p. 36.

the central focus of this composition, as the carver has made clear, is the very large and dominant figure of Mary. Thus, while it is clear that the artist has been informed by the early gospel referent of Luke 2, with respect to certain characters, it is even clearer that this carver has demonstrated significant independence from this narrative referent of Luke 2 and turned to later non-canonic narrative referents as well as his/her own imagination in order to compose this piece as he/she wishes. Both the late date of the work and its geographic region suggest that the artist would have had access to IGJames which introduced another female figure during the birth and established a basic dichotomy between Mary and Joseph, and marginalized Joseph. And yet this is not to deny the carver's freedom in this work, which is expressed with an unusual boldness.

The Artist's and the Artist's Community's Perceptions and Beliefs about Joseph in Figure 18

Therefore, in light of the way this carver has chosen to portray Joseph, especially in relationship to Mary and the child, it seems fair to conclude that the artist and his/her community did not believe Joseph had a significant role in the *Nativity* as it is represented, here, in Figure 18.

This conclusion with respect to the perceptions and beliefs of the carver and his/her community, in turn, suggests that they certainly perceived Mary to be the most important adult in the nativity account and associated very positive attributes with her character and personality; attributes they did not appear to also associate with Joseph. They also seem to indicate that the artist and his/her community believed tremendous authority could be attributed to certain non-canonic accounts.

Thus, it is evident that this portrayal of Joseph in Figure 18 offers additional proof of the presence of an ongoing trajectory in the late seventh to eighth century that negates the positive portrayal of Joseph found in Luke 2 as well as the positive attitude toward Joseph found in the other earliest gospels.

Furthermore, the significant differences between the four compositions of the *Nativity* and their portraits of Joseph in Figures 15, 16, 17, and 18, provides more documentation for comprehending the evolution of the *Wirkungsgeschichte* of the earliest narrative representations of Joseph and for verifying the presence of two distinct trajectories in the early Christian and early medieval periods.

12

Portraits of Joseph in Compositions of the Adoration of the Magi

The fifth and final theme to be considered is the Adoration of the Magi. As with most themes, it is found in canonic and non-canonic narratives that have been reviewed in Parts II and III and can be found in Matthew 2, IGJames 21, and GPM 16. It was also a very common theme in extant works of art from the early Christian and early medieval periods. Four examples from these periods are illustrated in Figures 19, 20, 21, and 22. They offer portraits of Joseph in marble and mosaic, from the fourth, fifth, and eighth centuries. The first of these, the fifteenth portrait of Joseph (illustrated in Figure 19) is found on a marble frieze, and is part of a fourth century Roman sarcophagus.

But, before engaging in formal analysis of this work, it is appropriate to recall that the Adoration of the Magi was the most common scene in Christian sarcophagi in the early Christian period and, as Panofsky notes, that 'prefigurative or symbolical interpretation' may well inform the understanding of 'historical (or narrative) events'.[1] Thus, the Adoration of the Magi may be seen as one of several 'manifestations and promises of salvation' that represent the 'dominating principle of Early Christian funerary art', that being 'deliverance from death and sin'.[2]

While 'the Christianization of ... mythological themes' may be acknowledged, the influence of key narrative accounts from the Hebrew scriptures and the earliest Christian scriptures, appear to have been pivotal to the creation of much of the content of these sarcophagi.[3] It is not

---

[1] E. Panofsky, *Tomb Sculpture* (New York: Harry N. Abrams, 1992), pp. 41-42. Early on Seitz, *Die Verehrung des hl. Joseph in ihrer geschichtlichen Entwicklung bis zum Konzil von Trient dargestellt*, pp. 71-72, noted that this 'scene was reproduced often in the early years'.

[2] Panofsky, *Tomb Sculpture*, p. 42.

[3] A.Seta, *Religion and Art* (trans. Marion C. Harrison; New York: Charles Scribner's Sons, 1914), pp. 341-42. According to Seta the key narrative accounts from the Hebrew scriptures and the earliest Christian scriptures include 'Adam and Eve near the tree in the terrestrial Paradise, the sacrifice of Abraham, Noah in the ark, Moses striking the rock, Daniel among the lions, Jonah swallowed and thrown up by the monster, the coming of the Magi, the cure of the man sick of the palsy, of the blind man and of the woman with the issue of blood, the miracle of the loaves, the resurrection of Lazarus,

12. Portraits in Compositions of the Adoration of the Magi

surprising to find accounts based upon canonic texts pertaining to the nativity and infancy of Jesus represented in sarcophagi, which, in turn, incorporate and detail portrayals of Joseph. Alessandro della Seta believes some insight into their content as well as their meaning can also be found by recognizing the similarities between early Christian sarcophagi and early Christian cemetery painting. Addressing these similarities, della Seta notes that they 'correspond to the same funerary requirements and the same spirit, and follow a parallel road both in the contents of the scene and the treatment of form' and adds that the presence of other subjects in the sarcophagi 'such as ... the Nativity' only suggests 'they may have been included in cemetery paintings which have since disappeared ...'[4] Thus, he believes the 'symbolic and allegorical nature of the subjects is indicated, as is the case of the cemetery paintings', by first, 'the sobriety of the elements of which they are constituted'; second, 'by the great number if not by the prevalence of Old Testament subjects'; third, by 'the isolation of each subject'; fourth, 'by their grouping without regard for chronological succession'; fifth, by 'the art of the Christian sarcophagi'; and sixth and finally, by the fact that 'there is no subject that is not taken from the past,' and 'no scene which displays the joys or pains of the future life.'[5]

Although della Seta's and Panofsky's comments have certain value as far as they go, they do not really explain the substantial emphasis given to the Adoration of the Magi in early Christian sarcophagi (the scene in which most prospective images of Joseph are found).[6] One explanation may be found in the 'decline in hermeneutic subtlety' that Brilliant believes 'can be traced through the evolution of visual narratives in Roman art during the second and third centuries'.[7] 'It led,' as he asserts, 'to a

---

and S. Peter's denial of Jesus.' E. Dinkler, 'Abbreviated Representations', in K. Weitzmann (ed.), *Age of Spirituality: Late Antique and Early Christian Art, Third to Seventh Century* (New York: The Metropolitan Museum of Art, 1979), p. 402, writing some years later, supports this contention. He states that these Christian 'types ultimately go back to narrative contexts and thus enhance the likelihood that these were the source of the abbreviated composition. Adaptation and integration within a given context, however, do not exclude the possibility that some iconographic scenes are original in conception ...' Nevertheless, Dinkler ('Abbreviated Representations', p. 402) qualifies these remarks somewhat by later adding that 'Although the abbreviated representation is always rooted in a biblical episode, its symbolic allusions transcend that text. It is intended, at least by the person who gave the commission, as a reference to the function of the object or to the patron's life.'

[4] Seta, *Religion and Art*, pp. 341-42.
[5] Seta, *Religion and Art*, p. 342.
[6] Wilpert, *I Sarcofagi Cristiani Antichi*, vol. II, p. 285, notes that scenes of the *Adoration of the Magi* occur most frequently 'among the childhood scenes' of Jesus.
[7] R. Brilliant, *Visual Narratives: Storytelling in Etruscan and Roman Art* (Ithaca and New York: Cornell University Press, 1984), p. 163.

concentration of effects and to a growing reliance on typological formulations because they were readily perceived by the available audience.'[8] Thus, it is not surprising, as Dinkler asserts, that 'the Adoration of the Magi is a favored theme' often portrayed by Christian artists as 'abbreviated representations ... reduced to the most essential figures, yet maintaining the recognizability of the scene ...'[9] Further, as Soper suggests, it was likely the case that scenes like the Adoration of the Magi were 'of the sort that could hardly fail to become fixed in a simple iconographic formula from the start'.[10]

Another explanation for the emphasis given to the Adoration of the Magi may be found in the purposes (or theological goals) of the owner, the artist, and the communities with which they were associated. Again, as Brilliant affirms, 'the narrative program was surely developed for an active audience, the purchaser and his associates, who chose the sarcophagus from the collection in the workshop and who wished to satisfy the urgings of their beliefs in anticipation of death.'[11] For example, with regard to the emphasis given to scenes of the Adoration it is certainly possible that their presence on several sarcophagi constitutes an affirmation that the homage of the person(s) entombed has been and remains focused upon the Christ, the Word incarnate (and to a lesser but still notable extent upon the Christ's earthly parents), just as that of the magi.

Similarly, as Grabar suggests, the emphasis upon the Adoration of the Magi, in both the early Christian catacombs and sarcophagi, may also reflect the worship of the early Christians who, in contrast to modern Christians, 'celebrated his (Jesus') birth either on the day of the Epiphany of Baptism (January 6) or the day of the theophany of the Magi (January

---

[8] Brilliant, *Visual Narratives*, p. 163.

[9] Dinkler, 'Abbreviated Representations', pp. 400, 396. Dinkler, p. 402, later adds that 'in the West abbreviated scenes ... predominated.' He believes, p. 400, that this theme of the *Adoration* was 'fashioned after a composition pertaining to the imperial cult. Such imperial traits as scepter, nimbus, and acceptance of homage by prostration were transferred to Christ in the fourth century. The epitaph of Severa in Rome, from 325-350 (fig. 57), shows this theme in an interesting version, as does the engraved ring stone at Oxford (no. 393).' E.L. Cutts, 'Traditions of Christian Art, Chapter II, The Sarcophagi and Mosaics', *The Art Journal*, 2 (1876), p. 141, noted the 'popularity of the subject' several decades earlier.

[10] A.C.Soper, 'The Latin Style on Christian Sarcophagi of the Fourth Century', *The Art Bulletin*, 19.2 (1937), p. 160.

[11] Brilliant, *Visual Narratives*, p. 126.

5)'.¹² From their perspective, the Adoration, deserved a 'special place' and encompassed all of the events of the nativity and infancy.¹³

Thus, it could be said that in contrast to others before them, whose focus may well have been upon the emperor or members of the emperor's family or another god or goddess – as was the case in other processional portrayals – the attention of Christian believers was quite different. If the focus of the early Christian was different, then it further suggests that the portrayals of the Adoration of the Magi, although abbreviated by the limited space in which they have been sculpted, may well testify to the faith of deceased Christians and, thereby distinguish them from pagans associated with the imperial cult.¹⁴ At the same time, in light of their visual character and position on the sarcophagi, they also offer a witness of the veracity of the Christian faith to others who might later see the sculpted image.

Figure 19
'Sarcophagus of the Two Testaments' or 'The Dogmatic Sarcophagus,' *Adoration of the Magi*, Roman, Fourth Century, Museo Pio Cristiano (Vatican Museum), Rome

---

¹² Grabar, *Christian Iconography: A Study of Its Origins*, p. 12. Kathleen M. Irwin, 'The Liturgical and Theological Correlations in the Associations of Representations of the Three Hebrews and Magi in the Christian Art of Late Antiquity', PhD dissertation (Berkeley, CA: Graduate Theological Union, 1985), pp. 141-46, concurs with Grabar's assumption about why images of the *Adoration* were common and expresses some additional ideas. She writes: 'Although the traditional assumption has been that the adoration scenes represent Matthew's magi story, some art historians and theologians have proposed various meanings for this scene and reasons for its use in the art of Late Antiquity, including (1) it proclaims the announcement of the gospel to the Gentiles and the rejection of Christ by the Jews, (2) it represents the Epiphany and the establishment of feasts commemorating the birth and early childhood of Jesus, and (3) it is a reflection of imperial art and an acknowledgment of Christ as king.'

¹³ Grabar, *Christian Iconography: A Study of Its Origins*, p. 12.

¹⁴ Dinkler, 'Abbreviated Representations', p. 400. See also Dinkler, p. 419. He agrees that sarcophagi can reveal the 'faith of the deceased ...'

The first portrayal to be examined will be that of a representation of the Adoration of the Magi (found in Figure 19) that typically presents a male figure standing behind Mary and the child as the magi approach.

Introduction

The large marble sarcophagus, seen in Figure 19, and identified as either the 'Sarcophagus of the Two Testaments' or 'The Dogmatic Sarcophagus', presents a common pictorial formula found in many portrayals of the Adoration of the Magi.[15] However, its unadorned lid and its central medallion, with the unfinished couple, suggest this sarcophagus was never sold or used. Thus, it is likely that it was part of a remaining stock of an early sarcophagus sculptor.[16] Probably carved in the second quarter of the fourth century CE by a Roman artisan, the face of this two-registry sarcophagus frieze, presently located in the Museo Pio Cristiano (the Vatican Museum) in Rome, also features a variety of scenes from the Hebrew scriptures and the New Testament.[17] Originally discovered in the Basilica of St. Paul beyond-the-walls in Rome in the nineteenth century, it also includes a portrayal of Joseph in a representation of the *Adoration of the Magi* that is very similar to many others.[18]

---

[15] This piece is portrayed in Wilpert, *I Sarcofagi Cristiani Antichi*, vol. I, plate LXXXVI. His discussion of the image is found in *I Sarcofagi Cristiani Antichi*, vol. I, p. 128. Irwin, 'The Liturgical and Theological Correlations in the Associations of Representations of the Three Hebrews and Magi in the Christian Art of Late Antiquity', p. 300, also records Figure 2 in her list of sarcophagi that feature the *Adoration of the Magi*. See also Soper, 'The Latin Style on Christian Sarcophagi of the Fourth Century', pp. 151 (Figure 6), 155; Panofsky, *Tomb Sculpture*, p. 44 and Figure 167; Koch, *Frühchristliche Sarkophage*, plate 46.

[16] Lowden, *Early Christian and Byzantine Art*, p. 49.

[17] Dinkler, 'Abbreviated Representations', pp. 399-401, sees similarities between the figures in this image and those in 'historical reliefs of the Arch of Constantine' (313-315 CE). Thus, he concludes that both were likely 'produced' in the same workshop or in a workshop where the artisans were very familiar with pagan sculpture.

[18] As has been noted, not all scholars even acknowledge the presence of a male figure behind Mary and the child in this image; let alone suggest the figure may be Joseph. Johann Wilhelm Appell, *Monuments of Early Christian Art* (London: George E. Eyre and William Spottiswoode, 1872), p. 17, exemplifies this position. Although he provides extensive commentary on the numerous characters and scenes in this sarcophagus, he does not mention the presence of a male figure in this context. However, other scholars accept the idea that this male figure is Joseph. Cutts, 'Traditions of Christian Art, Chapter II, The Sarcophagi and Mosaics', p. 142 identifies the figure behind Mary as Joseph. While recognizing that all scholars do not agree that this figure is Joseph, Seitz (*Die Verehrung des hl. Joseph in ihrer geschichtlichen Entwicklung bis zum Konzil von Trient dargestellt*, p. 73) concurs with Cutts and notes that this figure and the others put forward in portrayals of the *Adoration*, bear a real similarity to each other. Offering another alternative, Schiller (*The Iconography of Christian Art*, vol. I, pp. 100-101), in speaking about Figure 19, says 'Behind Mary's chair stands Balaam, the prophet, an allusion to the prophecy of the star of Jacob and to the fact that the Child is indeed the Messiah'.

The Characterization of Joseph in Figure 19

Here, with his body turned out slightly to the right, a slightly diminutive, bearded, and fully clothed (in a toga) Joseph, stands directly behind Mary and the child.[19] With his right hand holding onto the side of the back of her wicker cathedra with a suppedaneum, he looks at the three magi as they approach with their gifts.

In the context of this portrayal of the *Adoration of the Magi*, the location of Joseph, behind Mary and the child, within this pictorial formula initially may appear to suggest his role is limited. However, the fact that Joseph stands as closely as he does to Mary and the child and looks directly toward the approaching magi indicates he has an important position in this image. This can be asserted when it is recalled that the compositional pattern presented in this image (that includes Joseph) was not the only pictorial formula offered for the *Adoration of the Magi*. There are portrayals of this scene, found within the period of the fourth and fifth centuries and later that include Mary, the child, and the magi but exclude Joseph.[20] Thus, while the artist has certainly been informed by the account in Matthew 2, where Joseph is not formally mentioned, he/she have felt free to include him in this composition. Although there is mention of the Adoration in the later non-canonic account of IGJames 21, there is no indication that this literary referent informed this artist's work.

Consequently, although he stands behind (or to the side of) the figures of Mary (who is typically seated on a throne or stone seat) and the child, Joseph still plays a significant role by acting as the evangel and guardian who watches over the mother and child and witnesses to them.[21] Therefore, his presence in this extant image is both important and, it seems, indicative of the significance he held for some early Christian communities in the fourth century.

---

[19] Wilpert, *I Sarcofagi Cristiani Antichi*, vol. II, p. 287, certainly concurs with the idea that this image presents a portrayal of Joseph. He notes (p. 287) that the figure behind Mary in this so-called 'Dogmatic' sarcophagus is not only in 'the same clothes' (as in other parallel scenes of the Adoration of the Magi) but also in 'the same place' and location. This image can be seen in Wilpert, *I Sarcofagi Cristiani Antichi*, vol. I, plate CXV 2.

[20] Wilpert, *I Sarcofagi Cristiani Antichi*, vol. I (plates), and vol. II (plates) presents several of these images in his multi-volume set.

[21] As Wedoff, 'Word and Witness', p. 59, notes, 'the enthronement of mother and child, while partly narrative, is also devotional. Mary and the Christ child are presented to us, not only by their enthronement, but by ... Joseph's mannerisms. We are instructed as viewers to join the Magi and venerate the enthroned couple, perhaps in a similar manner that veneration would be shown to an enthroned Gospel text.'

The Artist's and Artist's Community's Perceptions and Beliefs about Joseph in Figure 19

In this composition of the *Adoration of the Magi* and the portrayal of Joseph, it is, once again, evident that early Christian artists or artisans who worked for Christian clients had significant liberty in their work, including the freedom to represent the themes and events of canonic and non-canonic narrative accounts in a way that permitted them to create their own independent non-canonic interpretations. This is certainly clear in this composition with respect to the earliest narrative account of this theme and event in Matthew 2 and can be seen in the fact the sculptor has inserted Joseph into the *Adoration* and associated him with Mary and the child and the other characters as he/she has. It can also be seen in the way he/she has represented Mary and the child and the roles the sculptor has given them in their positions on the cathedra and in the ways they have been dressed. And, yet, it is reasonable to assume that these factors incorporated into this particular portrayal of the *Adoration of the Magi*, in the context of several other images, must have been considered appropriate by this sculptor and those he imagined to be prospective clients. This is probable with respect to this specific sarcophagus since it appears to have never been used and, as was noted in the discussion in the introduction, was probably part of a remaining stock. This is likely because this particular portrayal of the *Adoration* followed a pictorial pattern (that usually moves from left to right, with Joseph standing behind Mary, who is holding the child while seated on a chair or cathedra, as three magi approach) and has its roots in both imperial iconography as well as earlier Christian iconography (a very similar pictorial pattern can even be found in a very early composition – apparently sans Joseph – in early Christian catacomb art).[22] For, as previously recognized in earlier discussions of sarcophagi compositions, the personal character of this type of artistry and the reasons surrounding the need for the creation or purchase of such works, and the fact that most clients of these works were people of means, would suggest that the client would interact directly with the artist or with the supervisor of the atelier or guild of sculptors with respect to their wishes.

Finally, at the same time, the sculptor's insertion of Joseph and placement of him in close proximity to Mary and the child and the approaching magi, makes it clear that he/she sought to highlight him and his role as guardian and witness, in a compositional context where others had left him out. On that account, his presence and role in this sarcophagus portrayal of the *Adoration of the Magi*, in Figure 19, created in fourth-century Rome, is an example of a work that imitates the positive canonic

---

[22] du Bourguet, *Early Christian Art*, p. 46.

portrayals of Joseph in Matthew, Luke, and John, and provides more evidence of the presence of a trajectory that confirms Joseph's significance in the Christian proclamation.

Figure 20
Sarcophagus, *Adoration of the Magi*, Cherchell, Algeria, Fourth Century, Louvre, Paris, France

Introduction

Probably created in the latter half of the fourth century CE, this marble sarcophagus lid, located in the Louvre in Paris, France, was discovered in the seaport of Cherchell, Algeria, according to Metzger.[23] This portrayal of the *Adoration of the Magi*, visible in Figure 20, is found on the left side of this fragment. In contrast to the prior image, in Figure 19, that follows the pictorial pattern mentioned in the discussion of that composition, the portrayal on this lid, particularly that of the magi and the camels, has a more dynamic style.

---

[23] Figure 20 is noted in the list and commentary of Irwin, 'The Liturgical and Theological Correlations in the Associations of Representations of the Three Hebrews and Magi in the Christian Art of Late Antiquity', p. 297. Catherine Metzger, 'Les sarcophagus chretiens d'Afrique du Nord', in Koch (ed.), *Akten des Symposiums 'Frühchristliche Sarkophage'*, Sarkophag-Studien (Deutsches Archäologisches Institut), vol. II (Mainz: Verlag Philipp von Zabern, 2002), pp. 153-55, makes no mention of Joseph in her analysis of this image. Initially named Iol or Jol, Cherchell, a town on the Mediterranean Sea, was later named Caesarea in honor of Augustus Caesar. Despite its relatively small size, it was a significant city in the Roman period. By the time this sarcophagus was created, it is estimated that a considerable portion of its population may have been Christian. Ramsey MacMullen, *The Second Church: Popular Christianity, A.D. 200-400* (Atlanta: Society of Biblical Literature, 2009), p. 127, states that there is mention of a martyr's shrine or chapel (cella) in the 4th century according to an inscription found in Y. Duval, *Loca sanctorum Africae. Le culte des martyrs en Afrique du IVe au VIIe siècle* (Rome: École Française, 1982), n.p. Further information can be found in S. Petrides, 'Caesarea Mauretaniae' and 'Chercell', *Catholic Encyclopedia* (New York: Robert Appleton, 1913), n.p.

The Characterization of Joseph in Figure 20

As can be seen, it features Joseph in a Roman toga, bearded, and slightly smaller than Mary. Thus, in many respects, he is represented in Figure 20 in much the same way as he is found in the prior portrayal in Figure 19. Here, Joseph's (and Mary's and the child's) figure has been carved and turned so that his head, torso, and feet suggest he is observing both the viewer as well as the unfolding event. Thus, in this image, in contrast, Joseph appears to stand both behind and to the side of Mary and child, who sit upon a cathedra. Nonetheless, as in the prior sarcophagus, with his right hand holding onto the side of the back of Mary's cathedra, in Figure 20, Joseph appears to fulfill the same roles of guardian and witness as he looks out at the viewers, while simultaneously, acknowledging the approach of the magi. While no explicit evidence is present of the influence of any non-canonic text that relates this scene, it has its basis in the literary account in Matthew 2.

As was seen in the discussion of Figure 19, so it is the case here that in the context of this portrayal of the *Adoration of the Magi*, the location of Joseph, behind Mary and the child, within this pictorial formula, may initially appear to suggest his role is limited. Even so, the fact that Joseph stands as closely as he does to Mary and the child, looks toward the approaching magi and, simultaneously looks out at the viewers, in contrast to Figure 19, indicates he has an important position in this image.

Therefore, although he stands behind (or to the side of) the figures of Mary (who is typically seated on a throne or stone seat) and the child, Joseph still plays a significant role by acting as the evangel and guardian who watches over the mother and child and witnesses to them.[24] Accordingly, his presence in this extant image is both significant and suggestive of the esteem with which he was held in some early Christian communities, including the fourth century Algerian Christian community of Chercell.

The Artist's and Artist's Community's Perceptions and Beliefs about Joseph in Figure 20

Having examined this sarcophagus fragment and the role and position of Joseph in this composition, it is now appropriate to ask what might be deduced from this portrayal of the *Adoration of the Magi* in Figure 20, with respect to the perceptions and beliefs of its sculptor and his/her

---

[24] As Wedoff notes ('Word and Witness', p. 59), 'the enthronement of mother and child, while partly narrative, is also devotional. Mary and the Christ child are presented to us, not only by their enthronement, but by ... Joseph's mannerisms. We are instructed as viewers to join the Magi and venerate the enthroned couple, perhaps in a similar manner that veneration would be shown to an enthroned Gospel text.'

Christian community in fourth century Cherchell, Algeria. First, the inclusion of Joseph in these representations of the *Adoration of the Magi* indicates a clear regard for Joseph and his position within salvation history. Second, the location of Joseph in close proximity to both Mary and the child in this image, suggests they believed Joseph's role was essential to the revelation of this them and event. Third, Joseph's position, proximity, and actions indicate that he was perceived as the guardian of Mary and the child (with his arm typically extended to the side of the chair or cathedra upon which she sits) and as a witness (Joseph calling the attention of the magi to Mary and the child in the *Adoration of the Magi*) to Mary and the child. Further, these factors may well reflect the belief that Joseph and Mary were indeed conjoined as husband and wife and father and mother in the period of the nativity and the infancy of Jesus and beyond.[25]

Although the inclusion of key characters and elements from Matthew 2 (Mary, and Jesus, and the magi expressing adoration) indicates the influence of this text, it is also important to realize that the sculptor of this sarcophagus portrayal of the *Adoration of the Magi*, as the sculptor of the previous composition in Figure 19, goes significantly beyond the information of this text as well as beyond the details of the non-canonic texts that relate this theme and event. In the process, he/she creates an image that reveals its independence of these texts while, at the same time, showing its aesthetic dependence upon a basic pictorial pattern found in both earlier Christian portrayals of the *Adoration of the Magi* and earlier pagan portrayals that recount themes and events related to the honoring of the emperor and other dignitaries in Graeco-Roman history. Perhaps, most importantly, as is the case with regard to Figure 19 but is not the case with respect to all artistic portrayals of this theme and event, the sculptor of Figure 20 includes Joseph in his/her representation and interpretation and places him in a special position in relationship to Mary, the child, and the three magi.

So it seems appropriate to conclude that the portrayal of Joseph in Figure 20, born in a fourth-century Algerian Christian community in north Africa also offers evidence of the presence of a trajectory that affirms the specific portrayal of Joseph found in Matthew 2 and the broad positive tradition found in the other canonic Gospels.

---

[25] To state this is not to suggest that this belief necessarily negates the early Christian belief that Jesus was born of a virgin.

Figure 21
Mosaic, *Adoration of the Magi*, Roman, Fifth Century, Santa Maria Maggiore, Rome, Italy

Introduction

Figure 21 offers the second of two themes from the fifth-century mosaic narrative cycles found in Santa Maria Maggiore, as noted in the discussion of the prior composition of Figure 3. This representation of the *Adoration of the Magi*, in Figure 21, is a very public liturgical work, explicitly designed through a commission of Pope Sixtus III. Therefore, as previously asserted, it is very probable that the size and complexity of the mosaic work in the immense architectural structure was carried out by a guild of mosaicists rather than a single artisan. Further, this composition is different from most of the other portrayals reviewed in this study because it has more characters and is one of several large mosaic images in a series on the birth and childhood of Jesus. Likewise, in this mosaic, in contrast to the prior compositions of the *Adoration* in Figures 19 and 20, the Christ-child appears in the center of the image as a royal or imperial figure, seated on a large ornate throne, is older, and is portrayed with a nimbus, as are the four angels standing directly behind his throne.[26] Here, surrounded by his mother (who sits to his left), another

---

[26] There is no explicit or implicit reference to an angel or group of angels being present with the holy family in the Matthean account of the *Adoration of the Magi*. However, there is a reference to the magi receiving direction through a dream (which may imply an encounter with an angelic figure) in Mt. 2.12 and a reference to their receiving direction from a star in 2.2, 9, 10. Further, there is a reference in the account of the *Adoration* in IGJames to the magi receiving direction 'by the heavenly messenger'. With respect to this see ch. 21 in IGJames in Hock, *The Infancy Gospels*, pp. 71-73. In addition, there is a reference in the narrative of the *Adoration of the Magi* in the GPM to the ap-

woman (an unknown figure who sits to his right), four angels, and Joseph (who stands in the left corner), the child receives the three magi.

The Characterization of Joseph in Figure 21

In sharp contrast to the portrayal of the Christ child, and even Mary, Joseph, positioned at the very end of the scene, appears marginalized and disengaged. Situated as far as possible from the center of the composition, apart from both the child and Mary, Joseph is the only figure in the scene who looks out toward those whom might view the event.

Although the mosaic reflects what the text states in the emphases it places upon Mary and the child and the magi, it constitutes an obvious expansion and elaboration of this literary account. While part of this expansion, notably, the positioning of Joseph at the very edge of the composition, may well reflect the spirit of the literary trajectory that sought to diminish the role and character of Joseph, there is little indication (aside from the presence of a second woman) of the insertion of specific elements from the early non-canonic text of IGJames that did reflect this trajectory and would have been available in this period. Consequently, the facts of the inclusion of the numerous characters, the representations of their interactions with each other, the staging of the event in an imperial-like setting, the size of the child and the placement of Joseph, all highlight both the uniqueness of this composition of the *Adoration* and its aesthetic independence from other images as well as its distinction from the canonic and even non-canonic narratives.

The Artists' and the Artists' Community's Perceptions and Beliefs about Joseph in Figure 21

There is no evidence within the mosaics or in tradition pertaining to them that provides specific reference to a particular artist or group of artists/artisans.[27] Accordingly, the identity of the mosaicist(s) remains uncertain.

---

pearance of an angel. See ch. 16 in the *GPM* in Ehrman and Pleše, *The Apocryphal Gospels: Texts and Translations*, pp. 103 and 105. But, there is no reference to an angel or group of angels being present with the holy family at the time of the *Adoration* in any of these texts. While some scholars date the *GPM* to a much later period, to one or two or three centuries after the construction of these mosaics, it is possible that earlier versions of this text may well have influenced these matters.

[27] Determination of the artist(s) involved in the creation of these mosaics is complicated, as Spain, 'The Program of the Fifth Century Mosaics of Santa Maria Maggiore', p. 38, states by the fact that significant portions of the iconography of the triumphal mosaics are 'unique', in particular, 'the Annunciation and Adoration of the Magi differ in composition and iconography from other illustrations of the same theme'. This fact and the fact, which Spain later acknowledges (p. 41), that there is a 'paucity of surviving

However, as was previously acknowledged in the discussion of a composition of the *First Dream of Joseph* in Figure 3, the historical patron of this series has been identified as Pope Sixtus III. The dedication to him, believed to be instituted by him in order to indicate his approval of the art and architecture substantiates this. It is found in a mosaic circle, in the center of the triumphal arch, beneath images of Peter and Paul, images of the symbols of the four evangelists, and images of the apocalyptic throne and the Book of the Seven Seals. The unusual artistic organization of this composition, the configuration of the characters, and the inclusion of many additional characters and elements not found in either the canonic or non-canonic accounts of this theme and event, indicate that Sixtus III believed it was appropriate to respond with a certain freedom and creativity with respect to canonic and non-canonic nativity texts and passed this belief on to the mosaicist and his/her associates who completed this composition and the rest. Therefore, in light of his role and involvement in this massive project, it can be assumed, among other things, that Sixtus III thought it was important to expand upon prior literary portrayals of Joseph in this artistic representation of the *Adoration* as well as upon other portrayals within this mosaic series and to do so in ways that acknowledged, to some extent, the existence of both trajectories in regard to Joseph, that were present in this period. This belief is exemplified, in part, by the contrast that can be found in the portrayal of Joseph in this composition, in Figure 21 (which, as has been noted presents Joseph as a marginalized and disengaged figure) with the way he was represented in Figure 3 (where is presented as a very significant and engaged figure).

Of course, in this specific composition of the *Adoration of the Magi*, in Figure 21, what is seen is evidence of the presence of an ongoing trajectory that diminishes the positive portrayal of Joseph found in the New Testament. Its presence, in a series of mosaics that present largely positive portraits of Joseph indicates that Pope Sixtus III was willing to permit the presence of both trajectories even in this large series in such a public liturgical setting.

---

monuments from this 75 to 100 year period' makes, as she states 'any attempt at comparative analysis futile and inconclusive. The stylistic relationship of mosaic monuments in this period and the geographical origins of style remain elusive.'

12. *Portraits in Compositions of the Adoration of the Magi* 231

Figure 22
Mosaic, St. Peter's Basilica, *Adoration of the Magi*, Roman, Eighth Century, Basilica of Santa Maria in Cosmedin, Rome, Italy

Introduction

Commissioned by Pope John VII in the early years of the eighth century for the chapel of John VII in the first St. Peter's Basilica, this fragment of a mosaic features an image of the *Adoration of the Magi* that includes a portrayal of Joseph.[28] Considering the size and quality of this composition and the rest of the work that initially surrounded it, it would have been necessary that the mosaicist who created this fragment was part of a guild and worked with many other mosaicists on this composition.

---

[28] With regard to Pope John VII who was the ecclesiastical leader of Rome from 705 to 707, see Hugh Chisholm (ed.), 'John VII (pope)', *Encyclopædia Britannica* (Cambridge: Cambridge University Press, 1911), n.p.; C. Herbermann, 'Pope John', *Catholic Encyclopedia* (New York: Robert Appleton Company, 1913), n.p.; J.N.D. Kelly, *The Oxford Dictionary of Popes* (Oxford and New York: Oxford University Press, 1986), p. 84. For further information on the additional commissions executed by John VII see Per Jonas Nordhagen, 'The Frescoes of John VII in S. Maria Antiqua in Rome' in *ACTA III* (Rome: Institutum Romanum Norvegiae, 1968), n.p.

The Characterization of Joseph in Figure 22

Illustrated in Figure 22, and presently located in the sacristy of Santa Maria in Cosmedin, it appears to represent Joseph in a formulaic fashion, as he is found in Figures 19 and 20, with his eyes focused on the movement of the magi as he stands positioned behind the cathedra in which Mary and the child sit. However, this portrayal stands in sharp contrast to not only his representations in Figures 19 and 20 but even in contrast to his portrayal in Figure 21. For, in Figure 22, the three other 'adult' characters, Mary, the angel, and the one wise man (disclosed in the extended visible arm in the lower right corner) are each represented as much larger than Joseph. Further, three of the other four characters – Mary, the child, and the angel (and perhaps the magi whose head is not visible) – are also nimbed, which, additionally, distinguishes them from Joseph. Still further, while Joseph's position, on the far left side, permits him to be a witness, the enlarged figures of Mary and the angel appear to act as a symbolic wall that effectively sets him apart from the action of the event in which the other four characters are obviously engaged.

While the basic construction and organization of this composition (with Joseph behind Mary and the child and others placed in front of her or to her side), indicates that it shares specific similarities with certain prior compositions, as noted, especially those in Figures 19 and 20, Figure 22 stands as a largely unique work of art created to represent this important theme and event of the *Adoration of the Magi*. At the same time, it is evident that in the configuration of the size, dress, and positions of the five figures of Joseph, Mary, the child, the angel, and the wise man that the mosaicist has created a portrayal that reflects significant independence from both the Matthean account and prior non-canonic narrative accounts. However, this does not dismiss the idea that the artist's location and configuration of Joseph may have been influenced by the spirit and tradition of the negative trajectory found in the non-canonic narratives of IGJames and GPM that sought to inhibit and diminish the significance of Joseph.

The Artist's and the Artist's Community's Perceptions and Beliefs about Joseph in Figure 22

The mosaicist's approach to the characterization of Joseph discloses much about his/her beliefs about Joseph as well as his/her community's perceptions about Joseph. For although he/she includes Joseph, and positions him behind Mary and the child and the magi, this mosaicist has chosen to let Joseph be overshadowed by the four other characters in the composition whom he/she has made clear are proportionally (and salvifically?) larger than Joseph. Included in this group, opposite Joseph, is a very large portrait of Mary (situated to the right and front of a Joseph), a comparably large portrait of an angelic messenger (also to the right of Joseph), and a similarly large portrait of one of the magi (who kneels in front of Mary and the child), whose size is suggested by the comparable proximity of his extended arm to the arms of Mary and the angel; three of the four characters of which the mosaicist has also chosen to nimb. Thus, although the artist has included Joseph, he/she has gone to considerable effort to delineate a sharp contrast between Joseph and the other figures he/she portrayed. For this reason, this mosaicist has left little question that he/she sees Joseph as a necessary but ancillary figure in this portrayal of the *Adoration of the Magi*.

Since this mosaic was commissioned by Pope John VII for St. Peter's Basilica, it is likely that he was involved in the initial planning and design and gave final approval to the content of the designs that were scheduled to be developed in this holy sanctuary, especially in light of the significance of this artistic and architectural project. While the mosaicist and his/her guild were likely granted significant leeway in how they created this composition and others, it would seem only natural and reasonable, because of their desire for further commissions, that they would want their work to please the pontiff. Subsequently, it can be concluded that although the inclusion of Joseph in this composition of the *Adoration of the Magi* indicates an effort to acknowledge Joseph, that the manner of his representation suggests he is held in much less esteem than the other figures in this piece, especially Mary.

Thus, in this portrayal of Joseph, the mosaicist reveals Pope John VII's limited appreciation of Joseph. In the process, he/she also discloses further evidence, in Figure 22, of the ongoing presence of a theological trajectory that sought to diminish Joseph's significance in the first quarter of the eighth century in the important and influential Christian community of Rome.

Consequently, as was the case with the theme of the Journey to Bethlehem, here, with the theme of the *Adoration of the Magi* in Figure 22, there is evidence of both similarities and differences in the basic designs of the compositions, with the first two compositions in Figures 19 and 20 showing very close similarity and the last two, in Figures 21 and 22, exhibiting not only significant differences from Figures 19 and 20 but even significant differences between themselves. This then, as has been noted with respect to the prior compositions in this study, permits the conclusion that most artists responded to the canonic and non-canonic accounts as well as prior visual iconographies with great freedom and creativity. In the process, as has been seen in this chapter on the portrayals of Joseph in the Adoration of the Magi, some (Figures 19 and 20) provided proof of the presence of an ongoing trajectory that affirmed the positive portrayal of Joseph in the earliest gospels while others (Figures 21 and 22), in contrast, substantiated the presence of an ongoing trajectory that diminished this positive portrayal. At the same time, these four final compositions, created between the fourth and eighth centuries, offer further documentation for comprehending both the evolution of the *Wirkungsgeschichte* of the earliest gospel portrayals of Joseph in Matthew, Luke, and John and the presence of two distinct trajectories in the interpretation of Joseph in the early Christian and early medieval periods.

Conclusion: The Portrayals of Joseph in Early Christian and Early Medieval Art

The general goal of Part IV has been to engage in an analysis of eighteen works of art from the early Christian and early medieval periods in order to determine what they might reveal about the development of the *Wirkungsgeschichte* of the early gospel portraits of Joseph. In order to reach this goal, consideration had to be given to several issues.

First, attention had to be directed to the ways Christian artists received and assimilated canonic as well as non-canonic texts related to narrative portrayals of Joseph. Second, notice had to be given to the different ways Joseph is portrayed in each composition; to the similarities and dissimilarities found in his characterization. Third, consideration had to be focused upon the independence or dependence an artist's work revealed in relationship to possible canonic and non-canonic literary referents as well as prior visual portrayals of Joseph; thus, upon the distinctiveness of the representation of Joseph found in these artistic works. Fourth, attention was next directed to the perceptions and beliefs these specific art works suggested their artists/artisans and their respective ecclesiastical communities, patrons, commissioners or guilds, held with respect to Joseph. Fifth, and finally, consideration had to be given to whether or not these portrayals of Joseph revealed any patterns or evidence of trajectories that affirm or disconfirm the representation of Joseph found in the early gospel accounts.

As attention has been given to these different matters, it has become possible to come to conclusions about what these eighteen representations of Joseph reveal about the development of the *Wirkungsgeschichte* of the Matthean, Lukan, and Johannine portraits of Joseph. Consequently, several have emerged.

The first, while seemingly simple and perhaps obvious to some, has been long ignored by most art historians: Christians in the early Christian and early medieval periods had significant interest in Joseph. This interest is manifest not only in the number of times he is portrayed (of which only 18 of 47 extant representations of Joseph have been selected for this study) but also in the fact that Joseph is represented in different types of art, materials, media, contexts, and geographical locales.

Consequently, evidence of this interest in Joseph appears in marble sculpture, ivory carving, glass work, and painting found in sarcophagi, ecclesiastical book covers and pyxes, mosaics, and an illumination and a cathedra. Further, it can be found in both public and private contexts, in both public ecclesiastical creations (as seen in Figures 3, 5, 8, 9, 11, 12, 13, 14, 15, 16, 17,18, 21, and 22) that were composed in order to be seen and appreciated by many people and, at the same time, in private art (as seen in Figures 1, 7, 19, and 20), that was created for familial and individual use and appreciation. Additionally, this interest in Joseph existed among Christians located throughout Europe, the Middle East, and North Africa. Therefore, it is present in the works of artists from the Gallic communities of Arles and Le Puy-en-Velay and the Italian communities of Rome, Milan, Ravenna to a monastic center and other communities in Syria and Palestine and to the community of Cherchel (Caesarea) on the Mediterranean coast of Algeria in North Africa, among other places.

The second conclusion that has emerged from this analysis is that while the work of many artists was informed, in different ways, by canonic and non-canonic narrative accounts (or summaries of such) that were directly related to the subject or theme they were representing and, on occasion, informed by prior visual portrayals, that most works show a remarkable independence from these referents. This is not to suggest that their portrayals of the themes that have been analyzed (with the exception of the Water Test) did not show clear evidence of reliance upon the earliest gospels. After all, these texts were the earliest sources of these themes and provided basic content (in the way of characters and details) for the artists' compositions. Nonetheless, as was noted in earlier remarks, related as the canonic and non-canonic texts and the early Christian and early medieval works of art are, the art that has been examined is never simply a copy or reproduction of the text, and typically presents the interpretation of these events in more illustrative ways as a result of the addition of more (and, sometimes, new) characters and details. So it is that in the process of creating their work of art, the artist not only creates his/her own interpretation of a prior narrative account but their own account; their own portrayal, that has narrative, historical, and aesthetic integrity in and of itself, and provides an important record of early Christian perception and belief with regard to many matters – including the understanding of Joseph. In fact, it can be said that the artist often tells us 'more' because he/she addresses issues such as the 'characterization' and 'proximity' of the characters in different ways. This is the case because he/she has the ability, in his/her composition, to more completely address the issues of the size and age of characters and their proximity to each other and their relationship to each other and the roles they play. Thus, the artistic works from the period provide complementary and parallel data and evidence that has its own authenticity and importance and goes far beyond being ancillary or supplementary.

Similarly, much the same may be said with respect to the influence of prior visual portrayals of Joseph. Christian artists (and even secular or pagan artists engaged in work for Christians) exercised a considerable amount of interpretive and stylistic independence from each other. With the exception of their obvious dependence upon the figurative art of the Graeco-Roman world and upon certain general compositional patterns found in earlier representations of the Journey to Bethlehem and the Adoration of the Magi (and even here the different creators added their own interpretations), the artists exercised significant independence with respect to their creations. Therefore, they were largely independent not only of the canonic and non-canonic narrative referents that informed the particular themes with which they were engaged but also significantly independent of the work of earlier artists and of prior visual portrayals, even with regard to the portrait of Joseph.

Third, diverse and independent as the characterization of Joseph is in these early Christian and early medieval works, they, nevertheless, reveal a third conclusion, affirmed in the analysis of the non-canonic literature of IGJames, IGThomas, HJC, and GPM: two diverse schools of thought and trajectories(based upon two very different sets of perceptions and beliefs about Joseph), existed in this period of Christianity. While it may not be possible to date precisely the trajectories of these tendencies in artistic works (since the earliest compositions of Joseph cannot be dated before the early fourth century), as was concluded in the discussion on the canonic and non-canonic narratives, they must have emerged early and may well have been present, as was the case with the narratives, by the latter half or last quarter of the second century CE.[29]

One school/trajectory, representing a majority of the art works, believed patrons, additional persons of influence, and artists should see and portray Joseph in the spirit and positive ways in which they thought he was represented in the Matthean, Lukan, and Johannine accounts – as an important and essential figure in the holy family (and in no way a challenge or threat to the virginity and purity of Mary or the divinity of Jesus). The other school/trajectory, in contrast, representing a minority of the art works, placed priority on Mary and Jesus and diminished the

---

[29] This would seem to be the case for both the trajectory inclined to expand the canonic portraits of Joseph in ways that affirmed and enhanced the early gospel portrayals of Joseph and the one inclined to diminish these.

role of Joseph. Thus, it is not surprising that these trajectories presented different artistic characterizations of Joseph that were often differentiated by the ways the two trajectories' respective artists aesthetically addressed the issues of Joseph's size, age, physical proximity to Mary and Jesus, and role. This can be seen in portrayals of both trajectories but is perhaps most noticeable in the one which sought to represent Joseph in the spirit and ways in which it was believed he was presented in the earliest gospel accounts. For in this trajectory the issues of Joseph's size, age, physical proximity to Mary and Jesus, and roles are addressed in ways that enhance the image of Joseph, are more in concord with the portrayals found in these earliest narratives, and reflect the respect and esteem many held for Joseph.

This respect and esteem is certainly evident in a significant majority of the art objects which feature Joseph in similar roles to those he held in the Matthean and Lukan portrayals. Therefore, it is not surprising to find him represented in roles related to his first dream and annunciation as a 'recipient of divine communications' and an 'obedient servant of God'. Representations of Joseph in one or more of these roles can be found in Figures 1, 3, and 5, which feature scenes of his first and second dreams and parallel scenes that feature both the first dream of Joseph and his response to the message of the dream.

At the same time, it is not unexpected to find him in numerous compositions of the scene of the *Nativity* in which he could be portrayed in at least four roles: 'witness' (or 'evangel' to the birth of the child), 'guardian' (or 'protector' or 'shepherd' of Mary and the child), 'earthly father of Jesus', and 'spouse of Mary'. Examples of these can be seen in Figures 15 and 16.

Additionally, other artists portrayed Joseph in the roles of 'witness' (or 'evangel' to the birth of the child) and 'guardian' (or 'protector' or 'shepherd' of Mary and the child) in scenes of the *Adoration of the Magi* in Figures 19 and 20.

Joseph is also represented with regard in works based on events found in non-canonic literature, such as the subject of the *Water Test*, as can be seen in Figures 8 and 9. Here, he is represented as acting in very particular roles with respect to Mary: as 'comforter' and 'witness to the purity and virginity of Mary'. Therefore, respect and esteem for Joseph seem abundantly present in the roles in which he is found in many of the eighteen works of art reviewed and analyzed for this study.

Respect and esteem for Joseph is also suggested in many of the ways Joseph is positioned in relationship to Mary and Jesus. Review of the eighteen compositions in this study indicates that most artists felt it appropriate to place Joseph in close proximity to Mary and Jesus (as the early gospel narratives imply), despite certain beliefs about Joseph's age, size, and roles (probably developed in response to specific beliefs related to the protection of the virtue and virginity of Mary and the divinity of Jesus). This is especially evident in his portrayals in scenes of the *Water Test*, the *Journey to Bethlehem*, the *Nativity* and the *Adoration of the Magi* in Figures 8, 9, 11, 12, 13, 15, 16, 19, and 20, in which artists place Joseph close to Mary alone or to Mary and the child. This is further substantiated by closer examinations of particular positions in which Joseph is placed in relationship to Mary and of specific positions in which he is placed in relationship to the child.[30] In the first case, respect and esteem for Joseph seems quite evident in the several scenes in which he is closely tied to Mary and is shown either standing in spiritual and public support of her (especially in the *Water Test*) in Figures 8 and 9 or is shown spiritually and physically supporting her as well as the expectant child (in the *Journey to Bethlehem*) in Figures 11, 12, and 13. In the second case, it is manifested in the scenes in which Joseph is presented as a central figure in relationship to the child. Thus, evidence of this attitude can be found in scenes of the *Nativity*, especially in Figures 15 and 16.

In contrast, the other school/trajectory, represented in far fewer objects in this study, thought patrons, other persons of influence, and artists should see and portray Joseph quite differently from the positive ways he was represented in the Matthean, Lukan, and Johannine accounts. Subsequently, in this trajectory the characterization of Joseph's size, age, physical proximity to Mary and Jesus, and roles are approached in ways that diminish his image. This is especially evident in Figures 7, 14, 17, 18, 21, and 22. As such, while the figure of Joseph is included in scenes of the *First Dream*, the *Journey to Bethlehem*, the *Nativity*, and the *Adoration of the Magi*, his portrayal is devalued because the creators of these compositions make him smaller and older than Mary, and usually separate Joseph from both her and Jesus. This occurred because followers of this school/trajectory believed this was necessary in order to affirm and protect the virtue and virginity of Mary and the virtue and divinity of Jesus. Thus, they thought it was acceptable to represent Joseph in these ways.

Therefore, in this regard, it must be said that although these works of art provide clear evidence of esteem for Joseph, they also provide proof of the existence and persistence of an ongoing struggle within the

---

[30] To acknowledge that most felt it was appropriate to place Joseph in close proximity to Mary or to the child or to both is not to suggest that they believed it was appropriate to make Joseph *the* central figure in the work of art or to present Joseph as the central adult figure in relationship to the child. Further study of these art objects also reveals, in other examples (which portray the *Adoration of the Magi* as well as a few other scenes), that Joseph may be positioned close to Mary and the child (usually behind them) but still not be directly engaged with one or both of them. This can be seen in Figures 19, 20, 21, and 22. It must be noted that in a couple of cases, namely in Figures 14 and 21, that it is also the case that artists went even further and placed Joseph some distance from Mary or from her and the Jesus.

broader Christian community within the period of this study. They proffer substantiation of an ongoing struggle about the appropriate theological and spiritual ways to portray Joseph; about how to respond to the earliest gospel portraits of Joseph, in light of the theological and apologetical concerns reflected in the two different schools of thought and trajectories that appear to have emerged early in the history of Christianity.[31] Consequently, the examination of examples of both trajectories provides specific and extensive documentation of the development of the *Wirkungsgeschichte* of the Matthean, Lukan, and Johannine representations of Joseph the Carpenter from the early Christian to the early medieval periods.

Fourth, and finally, although it is believed that these two diverse schools of thought and trajectories did exist, analysis of these eighteen portrayals of Joseph has led to the conclusion that the trajectory that offered positive artistic portrayals of Joseph and, in the process, affirmed the earliest gospel portraits of Joseph, was dominant in the first centuries of Christianity. This can be determined by the fact that twelve of the eighteen art works (representing a variety of material, media, subjects, and locales) show Joseph in a positive light, as that has been described in comments in this conclusion.

---

[31] The existence of this ongoing struggle was also documented in the examination of the four non-canonic narratives.

Part V

Conclusions and Implications

This examination has led to several conclusions that make a contribution to scholarship with respect to the development of the *Wirkungsgeschichte* of the earliest gospels' portrayals of Joseph in early Christian and early medieval literature and art.

First, the literary analysis of the representation of Joseph in the canonic narratives is the most intentional in scholarship at this point. Prior analyses have not necessarily sought to treat these narratives as portraits to which later interpreters would have access.

Second, the examination of the development of the reception history of the portrayals of Joseph in these same narratives is the most extensive to date. Although Joseph has been discussed as a subject in certain commentaries and some studies have focused upon him, none of these have centered upon the development of the *Wirkungsgeschichte* of these narrative portrayals.

Third, the analysis of the portrayals of Joseph in IGJames, IGThomas, HJC, and GPM is also the most extensive that these non-canonic narratives have received. While periodic commentary has been offered with respect to the role of Joseph in individual narratives in this list, there has not been an effort to focus formally upon the nature and character of his portrayal in these texts nor an attempt to document the roles of these early Christian non-canonic texts upon the development of the reception history of the Matthean, Lukan, and Johannine portrayals of Joseph.

Fourth, this examination of the portrayals of Joseph in specific sarcophagi, mosaics, ivories, and other works of art is also the most extensive survey that these images have received. While scattered analyses have been proffered with respect to the nature and character of the portrayal of Joseph in certain works of art, there has not been a systematic review of his portrayal in such a variegated and extensive array of early Christian and early medieval art. Nor has there been an effort to document the role of these images in the evolution of the reception history of the Matthean, Lukan, and Johannine portrayals of Joseph.

Fifth, building upon the ideas and methodologies of Gadamer, Jauss, and Luz, this study has proposed a creative methodology for the exploration of the *Wirkungsgeschichte* of these early gospel texts. In this methodology the selected Christian non-canonic literature that is believed to be part of the *Wirkungsgeschichte* has been analyzed by addressing the following issues with respect to each narrative: first, the date, provenance, language, stability of the text, history of translation and dissemination, availability and accessibility, purpose, and content, to the extent to which they can be ascertained; second, to the characterization of Joseph; the particular way(s) he is portrayed within the text; third, the independence the narrator's work reveals between itself and canonic and earlier non-canonic literary referents and prior visual portrayals of Joseph, as appropriate; i.e. to the distinctiveness of the portrayal of Joseph; fourth, the perceptions and beliefs these specific narratives suggest their narrators and their respective ecclesiastical communities appear to have held with regard to Joseph; and fifth, and finally, if the representation of Joseph in each non-canonic narrative reveals evidence of a pattern or trajectory that largely affirms and enhances his portrayal in the canonic accounts or evidence of a pattern or trajectory that largely dismisses and diminishes this portrayal. In turn, the selected Christian art that is believed to be part of the development of the *Wirkungsgeschichte* has been analyzed by addressing the following issues with respect to each artistic work: first, the theme/subject, date, provenance, purpose and content; second, the ways in which Joseph is characterized; third, the independence the artist's work reveals between itself and possible canonic and non-canonic literary referents and prior visual images; i.e the distinctiveness of the representation of Joseph found in these artistic works; fourth, the perceptions and beliefs these specific art works suggest their creators and their respective ecclesiastical communities, patrons, commissioners or guilds, appear to have held with respect to Joseph; and fifth, and finally, whether or not a portrayal of Joseph reveals evidence of a trajectory that largely affirms and enhances the portrayal and role of Joseph found in the canonic accounts or evidence of a trajectory that largely dismisses and diminishes this portrayal and role.

Sixth, this examination has documented and substantiated that there was much more interest in the character and role of Joseph the Carpenter in both literature and art in the early Christian and early medieval periods than has been often acknowledged and recognized. This study has revealed that more scholars than not have ignored the significance of the character of Joseph. It has drawn attention to many scholars of canonic and non-canonic literature who, while acknowledging Joseph's presence, have disregarded Joseph's importance even in particular works of literature where references to him are abundant. At the same time, it has highlighted many scholars of early Christian and early medieval art who, likewise, have overlooked Joseph's role in Christian images of the period, even in works of art where it is significant. In contrast, in the analysis of the canonic and non-canonic literature of this period substantial interest in Joseph has been revealed. Using the tools of literary and narrative analysis as well as other means, it has been shown that both canonic and non-canonic narrators detail significant information about their beliefs about Joseph's person and character as well as their perceptions of the nature of his relationships with Mary and Jesus. Similarly, significant interest in Joseph has been found in artistic compositions. As was noted, this interest has been uncovered not only in the number of times Joseph is portrayed but also in the fact that he is represented in different types of art, materials, media, contexts, and geographical locales.

Seventh, the study has also revealed that Christian narrators and artists (and their theological and financial patrons) believed they had the theological warrant to expand and contract the portrayals of Joseph in the Matthean, Lukan, and Johannine Gospels for their own theological and apologetical reasons (particularly in order to clarify the nature of the relationships between Joseph and Mary and Jesus). Thus, not surprisingly, as has been documented, both groups exercised considerable independence in their work in relationship to prior literary and artistic referents. There is little question that the later Christian non-canonic narrators were generally informed by either what they read or heard of the early different canonic gospel referents but a simple comparison between their texts and the earliest canonic narratives makes it evident that they largely sought to create rather than imitate. This does not mean that some of the narrators did not let themselves be influenced by the spirit and tradition of the canonic literature. It is very clear, as has been demonstrated, that both the narrators of IGThomas and HJC were influenced by the positive portrayals of Joseph in these earlier gospels. And, yet, they also exercised significant independence in their own writings. Much the same may be said with regard to Christian artists. While there is proof (noted in the introduction to Part IV) that some artists were supplied very specific instructions by certain patrons and commissioners about who and what they would include in relating specific biblical subjects and themes, it can be concluded that there is no explicit evidence of this type of instruction in any of the eighteen artistic compositions examined in this study. This is not to say, as has been made clear, that patrons, commissioners, and other influential individuals did not provide specific directions and give guidance about the design and content of compositions that is no longer extant. In all likelihood, they did offer both at some level. But, no formal proof of this has emerged in this study in the analysis of the eighteen works of art. Finally, it is also the case, that there has been little evidence to suggest that these artists received and assimilated a significant amount of material from non-canonic literary accounts (with the obvious exception of portrayals of the Water Test). While there is little question that the spirit of certain non-canonic narratives in this period (notably IGJames and GPM – that were widely disseminated) was influential, particularly those that sought to constrict and inhibit the character and roles of Joseph, few characters and details were taken directly from these narratives and placed in works of art. Thus, although Christian artists were clearly dependent upon their general aesthetic environment (the Graeo-Roman world), as Grabar argued, for 'the presentation of the human figure, its common accessories, and the architecture or furnishings that surround the figure' and could follow certain prior icongraphic patterns with certain themes and subjects (as previously acknowledged) such as the Journey to Bethlehem and the Adoration of the Magi, they also sought to create rather than imitate and this is evident in these eighteen portrayals of Joseph.[1]

Eighth, at the same time, this extensive interest in Joseph and the freedom both narrators and artists exhibited, has also helped confirm the hypothesis that two trajectories are present in the development of the *Wirkungsgeschichte* of the earliest gospels' portrayals of Joseph in early Christian and early medieval literature and art. Although a limited number of Christian narratives and artifacts remain from the early Christian and early medieval periods, it has been shown that most extant works provide proof of the esteem with which Joseph was held (they represent the first trajectory – the one inclined to expand the canonic portraits of Joseph in ways that enhance portrayals of Joseph). However, this review has also disclosed that two non-canonic texts as well as six artistic compositions (a much smaller number) provide proof of a trajectory that significantly constricts the portrayal of Joseph (they represent the second trajectory – the one that minimized the canonic portraits of Joseph in ways that diminish Joseph's representations). Evidence of these two trajectories has been seen by means of the analyses of the narrative portrayals of Joseph in the later Christian non-canonic gospels of IGJames, IGThomas, the HJC, and the GPM. At the same time, interest in Joseph and verification of the existence of these two trajectories is indicated in the presence and manner of his portrayals in the eighteen artistic representations found on graves, on the covers of books, within the walls and decorations of churches, and in elaborate artifacts and documents. Thus, interest in Joseph and the substantiation of the presence of two trajectories in the development of the history of reception of the early gospel portrayals of him has been exemplified in a variety of narratives and artifacts spanning the period of this study.

Ninth, review of the eighteen portrayals of Joseph considered in this study has led to the conclusion, as previously acknowledged, that the

---

[1] Grabar, *Christian Iconography: A Study of Its Origins*, pp. xlv-xlvi.

trajectory that offered positive images of Joseph and, in the process, affirmed the earliest gospel portrayals of Joseph, was dominant in the first centuries of Christianity.

Tenth, and finally, the discovery and acknowledgment of these two trajectories has provided an explanation for the development of and presence of different types of portraits of Joseph in Christian literature and art and documented the presence of certain tensions with the Christian community with respect to the interpretation of the person, character, and role of Joseph the Carpenter.

Having identified some of the more significant contributions of this study, how might they be used or further developed in the future? Perhaps, first, the design of this study and the methodology that has been constructed for it might be used to explore further the topic of the development of the reception history of the earliest gospels' representations of Joseph in both later Christian literature and art, in assessing the presence or absence of these early trajectories in later Christianity. Second, it seems to be self-evident that this methodology could be applied to the study of the development of the reception history of additional biblical characters, notably, the figures of the Joseph or Moses in the Hebrew scriptures or to analyses of the figures of Paul and Peter in the Christian scriptures. Third, and finally, this methodology could be applied to the study of the development of the reception history of further biblical scenes. For example, it could be applied to the analysis of a singular scene such as that of the sacrifice of Issac in the Hebrew scriptures or to analyses of the multiple scenes of the death of Jesus or the resurrection of Jesus found in the Christian scriptures.

Appendix

Artistic Portrayals of Joseph c.300 CE–800 CE According to Theme

Theme	Figure	Medium	Function	Provenance	Date	Location	Trajectory
FIRST DREAM OF JOSEPH AND ANNUNCIATION TO JOSEPH	Fig. 1	marble	sarcophagus	Gallic	4th cent.	Arles, France	Positive portrayal of Joseph
	Fig. 3	marble	Church illiustration for Santa Maria Maggiore	Roman	5th cent.	Rome, Italy	Positive portrayal of Joseph
	Fig. 5	ivory	Plaque in church cathedra for Archbishop	Italian, Byzantine	6th cent.	Ravenna, Italy	Positive portrayal of Joseph
	Fig. 7	marble	sarcophagus	Gallic	4th cent.	Le Puy-en-Velay, France	Negative portrayal of Joseph
WATER TEST	Fig. 8	ivory	Plaque in church cathedra for Archbishop	Italian, Byzantine	6th cent.	Ravenna, Italy	Positive portrayal of Joseph
	Fig. 9	ivory	Ecclesiastical book cover	Byzantine	6th cent.	Paris, France	Positive portrayal of Joseph
JOURNEY TO BETHLEHEM	Fig. 11	ivory	Plaque for catehdra for Archbishop	Italian, Byzantine	6th cent.	Ravenna, Italy	Positive portrayal of Joseph
	Fig. 12	ivory	Ecclesiastical book cover	Byzantine	6th cent.	Paris, France	Positive portrayal of Joseph
	Fig. 13	ivory	Ecclesiastical communion cup	Syrian-Palestinian	6th cent.	Berlin, Germany	Positive portrayal of Joseph
	Fig. 14	ivory	Ecclesiastical book cover	Syrian	6th-5th cent.	Paris, France	Negative portrayal of Joseph
NATIVITY	Fig. 15	ivory	Ecclesiastical book cover	Italian	5th cent.	Milan, Italy	Positive portrayal of Joseph
	Fig. 16	parchment	Ecclesiastical illuminated ms.	Syrian	6th cent.	Florence, Italy	Positive portrayal of Joseph
	Fig. 17	ivory	Ecclesiastical book cover	Court of Charlemagne?	8th-9th cent.	Oxford, England	Negative portrayal of Joseph
	Fig. 18	ivory	Ecclesiastical plaque	Syrian-Palestinian	7th-8th cent.	Washington, DC	Negative portrayal of Joseph
ADORATION OF MAGI	Fig. 19	marble	sarcophagus	Roman	4th cent.	Rome, Italy	Positive portrayal of Joseph
	Fig. 20	marble	sarcophagus	Algerian	4th cent.	Paris, France	Positive portrayal of Joseph

ADORATION OF MAGI (CONT.)	Fig. 21	mosaic	Church illustration for Santa Maggiore Basilica	Roman	5th cent.	Rome, Italy	Negative portrayal of Joseph
	Fig. 22	mosaic	Church illustration	Roman	8th cent.	Rome, Italy	Negative portrayal of Joseph

Bibliography

Aasgaard, R., *The Childhood of Jesus: Decoding the Apocryphal Infancy Gospel of Thomas* (Eugene, OR: Cascade Books, 2009).
Achtemeier, P.J., '*Omne verbum sonat*: The New Testament and the Oral Environment of Late Western Antiquity', *Journal of Biblical Literature* 109 (1990), pp. 3-27.
———, J.B. Green, and M.M. Thompson, *Introducing the New Testament: Its Literature and Theology* (Grand Rapids and Cambridge: William B. Eerdmans, 2001).
Agnello, S.L., *Il Sarcofago di Adelfia*, Societa Amici Delle Catacombe, Volume 25 (Roma: Pontifico Istituto di Archeologia Cristiana, 1956).
Albright, W.F. and C.S. Mann, *Matthew* (Garden City, NY: Doubleday, 1971).
Allen, W.C., *A Critical and Exegetical Commentary on Matthew* (Edinburgh: T. & T. Clark, 1965).
Appell, J.W., *Monuments of Early Christian Art* (London: George E. Eyre and William Spottiswoode, 1872).
Arnason, H.H., 'Early Christian Silver of North Italy and Gaul', *The Art Bulletin* 20.2 (1938), pp. 193-226.
Augustine of Hippo, *Harmony of the Gospels* in *NPNF*, 1st series, Vol. 6 (Peabody, MA: Hendrickson Publishers, 2004).
Bal, M. and N. Bryson, 'Semiotics and Art History', *The Art Bulletin* 73.2 (1991), pp. 174-208.
Balough, J., 'Voces Paginarum: Beiträge zur Geschichte des lauten Lesens und Schreibens', *Philologus* 82 (1927), pp. 84-109.
Balz, H. and G. Schneider (eds.), *Exegetical Dictionary of the New Testament* (3 vols.; Grand Rapids: Eerdmans, 1990-93).
Bardill, J., *Constantine, Divine Emperor of the Christian Golden Age* (Cambridge and New York: Cambridge University Press, 2011).
Barrett, C.K., *The Gospel According to St. John* (London: SPCK, 1955).
Basser, H.W., *The Mind behind the Gospels: A Commentary to Matthew 1-14* (Brighton, MA: Academic Studies Press, 2009).
Bauckham, R. and C. Moser (eds.), *The Gospel of John and Christian Theology* (Grand Rapids: Eerdmans, 2008).
Baxandall, M., *Patterns of Intention* (New Haven and London: Yale University Press, 1985).
Beare, F.W., *The Gospel According to Matthew* (Peabody, MA: Hendrickson, 1987).
Beasley-Murray, G.R., *Word Biblical Commentary: John* (Waco, TX: Word Books, 1987).

Beck, B.E., *Christian Character in the Gospel of Luke* (London: Epworth Press, 1989).
Beckwith, J., *Early Medieval Art: Carolingian, Ottonian, Romanesque* (London: Thames and Hudson, 1969).
Begg, E., *The Cult of the Black Virgin* (New York, NY: Penguin, 1989).
Benoit, F., *Sarcophages Paléochrétiens d'Arles et de Marseille* (Paris: Centre National de la Recherche Scientifique, 1954).
Bernard, J.H., *A Critical and Exegetical Commentary on the Gospel According to St. John* (Edinburgh: T. and T. Clark, 1928).
Bertrand, G., 'Saint Joseph dans les écrits des Peres', *Cahiers de Joséphologie* 14 (1966), pp. 5-201.
Bienert, W. A., 'The Relatives of Jesus', in Wilhelm Schneemelcher (ed.), *The New Testament Apocrypha: Gospels and Related Writings* I (trans. Robert McL. Wilson; Louisville, KY: Westminster/John Knox Press, 1991), pp. 470-85.
Bigham, S., *Early Christian Attitudes toward Images* (Rollinsford, NH: Orthodox Research Institute, 2004).
Blomberg, C.L., *Matthew* (Nashville, TN: Broadman Press, 1992).
Bock, D.L., *Luke, Volume 1, 1:1–9:50* (Grand Rapids: Baker Books, 1994).
Bonanno, A., 'Sculpture', in Martin Henigy (ed.), *A Handbook of Roman Art* (Ithaca, NY: Cornell University Press, 1983), pp. 90-98.
Bonnard, P., *L'Évangile selon Saint Matthieu* (Neuchâtel, Paris: Delachaux et Niestlé, 1963).
du Bourguet, P., *Early Christian Painting* (trans. Simon Watson Taylor; New York: The Viking Press, 1965).
_____ *Early Christian Art* (trans. Thomas Burton; New York: Reynal & Company in association with William Morrow & Company, Inc., 1971).
Bovini, G., *I Sarcofagi Paleocristiani* (Citta del Vaticano: Pontificio Istituto di Archeologia Cristiana, 1949).
Bovon, F., *A Commentary on the Gospel of Luke*, I (trans. James E. Crouch; Minneapolis, MN: Fortress Press, 2002).
Brilliant, R., *Visual Narratives: Storytelling in Etruscan and Roman Art* (Ithaca, NY: Cornell University Press, 1984).
Brown, C., (ed.), *New International Dictionary of New Testament Theology* (3 vols.; Grand Rapids: Zondervan, 1975-78).
Brown, P.R.L., 'Art and Society in Late Antiquity', in K. Weitzmann (ed.), *The Age of Spirituality: A Symposium* (New York: The Metropolitan Museum of Art; Princeton, N.J.: Princeton University Press, 1980).
Brown, R., *The Gospel According to John*, I-XII (Garden City, NY: Doubleday, 1966).
_____, *The Birth of the Messiah* (Garden City, NY: Doubleday, 1977).
_____, *The Birth of the Messiah* (New Haven and London: Yale University Press, 1993).
Bruce, F.F., *The Gospel of John* (Grand Rapids: Eerdmans, 1983).
Bruce, J.A., 'The Flight into Egypt: the Dreams of Fathers', *Saint Luke's Journal of Theology* 27 (1984), pp. 287-96.
Bruner, F.D., *The Christbook: A Historical-Theological Commentary, Matthew 1-12* (Waco, TX: Word Books Publisher, 1987).

Bultmann, R., *The Gospel of John: A Commentary* (Philadelphia: The Westminster Press, 1971).

Burkett, D., *An Introduction to the New Testament and the Origins of Christianity* (Cambridge: Cambridge University Press, 2002).

Callaway, M.C., 'What's the Use of Reception History?', pp. 1-14. Paper presented at the Annual Meeting of the Society of Biblical Literature, 2004.

Carnevale, L., 'The Bible and Early Christian Art', in Martin O'Kane (ed.), *Imagining the Bible: An Introduction to Biblical Art* (London: SPCK, 2008), pp. 21-40.

Carroll, J.T., *Luke: A Commentary* (Louisville: Westminster John Knox Press, 2012).

Carson, D.A., *The Gospel According to John* (Grand Rapids: Eerdmans, 1991).

Carter, W., *Matthew and the Margins: A Socio-Political and Religious Reading*, (JSNTS 204; Sheffield: Sheffield Academic Press, 2001).

Cartlidge, D., 'The Christian Apocrypha: Preserved in Art', *Bible Review* 13 (1997), pp. 24-31.

―――― 'Which Path at the Crossroads? Early Christian Art as Hermeneutical and Theological Challenge', in Julian V. Hills (ed.), *Common Life in the Early Church: Essays Honoring Graydon F. Snyder* (Harrisburg, PA: Trinity Press International, 1998), pp. 357-72.

Cartlidge, D., and J. Elliott, *Art and the Christian Apocrypha* (London and New York: Routledge, 2001).

Cassiday, B., 'Introduction : Iconography, Texts and Audiences', in Brendan Cassiday (ed.), *Iconography at the Crossroads* (Princeton, NJ : Index of Christian Art, Princeton University Press, 1993), pp. 3-15.

Casson, L., *Travel in the Ancient World* (London: Allen and Unwin, 1974).

Cecchelli, C., *La cattedra di Massimiano ed altri avorii romano-orientali* (Rome: La Libreria dello Stato, 1936-44).

Cecchelli, C., Guiseppe Furlani, and Mario Salmi (eds.), *Facsimile Edition of the Miniatures of the Syriac Manuscript in the Medicaean-Laurentian Library* (Olten and Lausanne: Urs Graf-Verlag,1959).

Chartier, R., 'Texts, Printing, and Readings', in L. Hunt (ed.), *The New Cultural History* (Berkeley and Los Angeles: University of California Press, 1989), pp. 154-75.

Chartrand-Burke, T., 'The Infancy Gospel of Thomas: The Text, is Origins, and its Transmission', PhD dissertation (Toronto: University of Toronto, 2001).

―――― 'Completing the Gospel: *The Infancy Gospel of Thomas* as a Supplement to the Gospel of Luke', in Lorenzo di Tomasso and Lucian Turcescu (eds.), *The Reception and Interpretation of the Bible in Late Antiquity: Proceedings of the Montreal Colloquium in Honour of Charles Kannengiesser* (Leiden and Boston: E.J. Brill, 2008), pp. 101-16.

Chisholm, H., (ed.), 'John VII (pope)', *Encyclopædia Britannica* (Cambridge: Cambridge University Press, 1911), n.p.

Clayton, M., *The Apocryphal Gospels of Mary in Anglo-Saxon England* (Cambridge and New York: Cambridge University Press, 1998).

Cohen, G., 'Le personnage de saint Joseph dans les plus anciens nativités françaises', *Cahiers de Joséphologie* 14 (1966), pp. 221-25.

Coleridge, M., *The Birth of the Lukan Narrative: Narrative as Christology in Luke 1–2* (JSNTS 88; Sheffield: Sheffield Academic Press, 1993).
Creed, J.M., *The Gospel According to St. Luke* (London: Macmillan, 1950).
Culpepper, R.A., *The Gospel and the Letters of John* (Nashville, TN: Abingdon, 1998).
―― *Anatomy of the Fourth Gospel* (Philadelphia: Fortress Press, 1983).
Cumont, F., *Oriental Religions in Roman Paganism* (New York: Dover Press, 1956).
Curschmann, M., 'Images of Tristan', in A. Stevens and R. Wisbey (eds.), *Gottfried von Strassburg and the Medieval Tristan Legend Papers from an Anglo-North American Symposium* (London: D.S. Brewer, 1990), pp. 1-17.
Cutts, E.L., 'Traditions of Christian Art, Chapter I: The Catacomb Paintings', *The Art Journal* 2 (1876), pp. 86-90.
―― 'Traditions of Christian Art, Chapter II: The Sarcophagi and Mosaics', *The Art Journal* 2 (1876), pp. 141-44.
D.C.A., 'Le Développement historique du culte de S. Joseph', *Revue Bénédicte* 14 (1897), pp. 104-14, 145-55, 203-209.
Dalton, O.M., *Catalogue of the Ivory Carvings of the Christian Era* (London: Trustees of the British Museum, 1909).
Davies, M., *Matthew: Readings* (Sheffield: Sheffield Academic Press, 1993).
Davies, W.D. and D.C. Allison, *The Gospel According to Saint Matthew* (Edinburgh: T & T Clark, 1988).
Davis-Weyer, C., *Early Medieval Art 300-1150* (Toronto: University of Toronto Press, 1986).
Deasey, C.P., 'St. Joseph in the English Mystery Plays', PhD dissertation (Washington: Catholic University of America, 1937).
Desert Fathers (trans. Helen Waddell; New York: Vintage Books, 1998).
Deshman, R., 'The Illustrated Gospels', in Gary Vikan (ed.), *Illuminated Greek Manuscripts from Armenian Collections* (Princeton: The Art Museum and Princeton University Press, 1973),
Dinkler, E., 'Abbreviated Representations', in K. Weitzmann (ed.), *Age of Spirituality: Late Antique and Early Christian Art, Third to Seventh Century* (New York: The Metropolitan Museum of Art, 1979), pp. 396-419.
Dodd, C.H., *Historical Tradition in the Fourth Gospel* (London: Cambridge University Press, 1963).
Dodson, D., *Reading Dreams* (Library of New Testament Studies 397; London: T. & T. Clark, 2009).
Dresken-Weiland, J., (ed.), *Repertorium der christlich-antiken Sarkophage: Italien mit einem Nachtrag Rom und Ostia, Dalmatien, Museen der Welt* in *Repertorium der christlich-antiken Sarkophage,* vol. II (Mainz am Rhein: Verlag Philipp von Zabern, 1998).
Duval, N., et al. (eds.), *Naissance Chrétiens: Atlas des Monuments Paleochrétiens de la France* (Paris: Imprimerie Nationale, 1991).
Duval, Y., *Loca sanctorum Africae. Le culte des martyrs en Afrique du IVe au VIIe siècle* (Rome: École Française, 1982).
Eagan, Sister M.C., *Prudentius* (Washington: Catholic University of America Press, 1962).

Ehrman, B.D. and Z. Pleše, *The Apocryphal Gospels: Texts and Translations* (Oxford and New York: Oxford University Press, 2011)

Elliott, J.K., *A Synopsis of the Apocryphal Nativity and Infancy Narratives* (Leiden and Boston: Brill, 2006).

_____ *The Apocryphal Jesus: Legends of the Early Church* (Oxford: Oxford University Press, 1996).

_____ *The Apocryphal New Testament* (Oxford and New York: Oxford University Press, 2004).

Ellis, E., *Gospel of Luke* (San Francisco: HarperCollins, 1981).

Elsner, J., *Art and the Roman Viewer: The Transformation of Art from the Pagan World to Christianity* (Cambridge and New York: Cambridge University Press, 1995).

Elsner, J., (ed.), *Art and Text in Roman Culture* (Cambridge and New York: Cambridge University Press, 1996).

_____ *Imperial Rome and Christian Triumph: The Art of the Roman Empire AD 100 – 450* (Oxford and New York: Oxford University Press, 1998).

Evans, C.A., *Luke* (Peabody, MA: Hendrickson, 1990).

Evans, C.F., *Saint Luke* (London and Philadelphia: SCM Press and Trinity Press, 1990).

Falcetta, A., 'The Call of Nazareth: Form and Exegesis of Luke 4:16-30', *Cahiers de la Revue Biblique* 53 (Paris: J. Gabalda, 2003), pp. 1-120.

Farmer, D.H., *The Oxford Dictionary of Saints* (Oxford: Oxford University Press, 1978).

Ferguson, E., *Backgrounds of Early Christianity* (Grand Rapids: Eerdmans, 2003).

Fiedler, P., *Das Matthäusevangelium* (Stuttgart: Kohlhammer, 2006).

Filas, F., *The Man Nearest to Christ: Nature and Historic Development of the Devotion to St. Joseph* (Milwaukee, WI: Bruce, 1944).

_____ *Joseph and Jesus: A Theological Study of Their Relationship* (Milwaukee, WI: Bruce, 1952).

_____ *Joseph Most Just: Theological Questions about St. Joseph* (Milwaukee, WI: Bruce, 1956).

_____ *Joseph, the Man Closest to Jesus: The Complete Life, Theology, and Devotional History of St. Joseph* (Boston: Daughters of St. Paul, 1962).

Finke, L.A. and M.B. Schichtman, *Medieval Texts and Contemporary Readers* (Ithaca, NY: Cornell University Press, 1987).

Finney, M., 'Jesus in Visual Imagination: The Art of Invention', in J. Cheryl Exum and David J.A. Clines (eds.), *Biblical Reception* 1 (Sheffield: Sheffield Phoenix Press, 2012), pp. 21-43.

Finney, P.C., *The Invisible God: The Earliest Christians on Art* (New York and Oxford: Oxford University Press, 1994).

Fitzmyer, J.A., *The Gospel According to Luke* (Garden City, NY: Doubleday, 1981).

_____ *Saint Joseph in Matthew's Gospel* (Philadelphia: Saint Joseph's University Press, 1997).

Fornberg, T., 'The Annunciation: A Study in Reception History', in Mogens Müller and Henrik Tronier (eds.), *The New Testament as Reception* (Library of New Testament Studies 230; London: T.& T. Clark, 2002), pp. 157-80.

Foster, J.D., 'Les origines de la dévotion à Saint Joseph', *Cahiers de Joséphologie* 1 (1953), pp. 23-54 and 2 (1954), pp. 5-30.
Foster, M.B., 'The Iconography of St. Joseph in Netherlandish Art, 1400-1550', PhD dissertation (Lawrence, KS: University of Kansas, 1978).
France, R.T., *The Gospel of Matthew* (Grand Rapids and Cambridge: Eerdmans, 2007).
Frankemölle, H., *Matthäus: Kommentar*, I (Düsseldorf: Patmos Verlag, 1994).
Freed, E.D., *The Stories of Jesus' Birth* (Sheffield: Sheffield Academic Press, 2001).
Frend, W.H.C., *The Rise of Christianity* (Philadelphia: Fortress Press, 1984).
Gaborit-Chopin, D., *Ivoires médiévaux: Ve-XVe siècle* (Paris: Département des Objets d'Art, Musée du Louvre, Éditions de la Réunion des musées nationaux, 2003).
Gadamer, H., *Truth and Method* (trans. J. Weinsheimer and D. Marshall; London: Sheed & Ward, 1975 and 1989).
―――― *Wahrheit und Methode: Grundzüge einer philosophischen Hermeneutik* (Tübingen: J.C.B. Mohr, 1960).
Gambero, L., *Mary and the Fathers of the Church: The Blessed Virgin Mary in Patristic Thought* (San Francisco: Ignatius Press, 1999).
Gamble, H., *Books and Readers in the Early Church: A History of Christian Texts* (New Haven and London: Yale University Press, 1995).
Garland, D.E., *Reading Matthew: A Literary and Theological Commentary* (New York: Crossroad, 1999).
―――― *Luke* (Grand Rapids: Zondervan, 2011).
Geldenhuys, N., *Commentary on the Gospel of Luke* (Grand Rapids: Eerdmans, 1979).
Gennaccari, C., 'Rilevanza dei documenti editi ed inediti nello studio dei sarcophagi del Museo Pio Cristiano in Vaticano', in G. Koch (ed.), *Akten des Symposiums 'Frühchristliche Sarkophage'*, Marburg, vol. 2, pp. 115-16.
Gerke, F., *Die christlichen Sarkophage der vorkonstantinischen Zeit* (Berlin: Walter de Gruyter, 1978).
Gijsel, J., *Libri de Nativitate Mariae: Pseudo-Matthaei Evangelium Textus et Commentarias*, vol. 9 (Corpus Christianorum, Series Apocryphorum; Brepols-Turnhout: Association pour l'étude de la littérature apocryphe chrétienne, 1997).
Godet, F., *Commentary on the Gospel of John*, vol. I (New York: Funk and Wagnalls, 1886).
Gospel of Pseudo-Matthew in *ANF*, 2nd series, vol. 8 (Peabody, MA: Hendrickson, 2004).
Goulder, M.D., *Luke: A New Paradigm* (JSNTS 20; Sheffield: Sheffield Academic Press, 1989).
Grabar, A., *Early Christian Art: From the Rise of Christianity to the Death of Theodosius* (trans. Stuart Gilbert and James Emmons; New York: Odyssey Press, 1968).
―――― *Christian Iconography: A Study of its Origins* (Princeton: Princeton University Press, 1968).
Green, H.B., *The Gospel According to Matthew* (Oxford: Oxford University Press, 1975).

Green, J.B., *The Gospel of Luke* (Grand Rapids: Eerdmans, 1997).
Gundry, R.H., *Matthew* (Grand Rapids: Eerdmans, 1982).
Gurevich, A., *Medieval Popular Culture: Problems of Belief and Perception* (trans. Janos M. Bak and Paul A. Hollingsworth; New York and Cambridge: Cambridge University Press,1988).
Haenchen, E., *John 1: A Commentary on the Gospel of John* (Philadelphia: Fortress Press, 1984).
Hagner, D.A., *Word Biblical Commentary: Matthew 1-13* (Dallas, TX: Word Books, 1993).
Hamann, H.P., *Chi Rho Commentary on the Gospel According to Matthew* (Adelaide: Lutheran Publishing House, 1984).
Harbison, P., *Earlier Carolingian Narrative Iconography: Ivories, Manuscripts, Frescoes, and Irish High Crosses* (Mainz: Jahrbuch des Römisch-Germanischen Zentralmuseums, 1984).
Harnack, A. von, *The Mission and Expansion of Christianity in the First Three Centuries* (trans. J. Moffatt, 2 vols.; New York: Putnam, 1904).
Harrington, D.J., *The Gospel of Matthew* (Collegeville, MN: The Liturgical Press, 1985).
Harris, W., *Ancient Literacy* (Cambridge, MA: Harvard University Press, 1989).
Hauerwas, S., *Matthew* (Grand Rapids: Brazos Press, 2007).
Herlihy, D., *Medieval Households* (Cambridge, MA: Harvard University Press, 1985).
Heimann, A., 'Trinitas Creatrix Mundi', *Journal of the Warburg Institute* II (1938), pp. 42-52.
Hendrickson, G.L., 'Ancient Reading', *Classical Journal* 25 (1929), pp. 182-96.
Hendriksen, W., *The Gospel of Matthew* (Edinburgh: The Banner of Truth Trust, 1974).
―― *The Gospel of Luke* (Edinburgh: The Banner of Truth Trust, 1979).
Herbermann, C., 'Archdiocese of Aix', *Catholic Encyclopedia* (New York: Robert Appleton, 1913), n.p.
―― Le Puy, *Catholic Encyclopedia* (New York: Robert Appleton, 1913), n.p.
―― 'Pope John', *Catholic Encyclopedia* (New York: Robert Appleton, 1913), n.p.
Heublein, B., *Der 'verkannte' Joseph: Ein Beitrag zur mittelalterlichen Ikonographie des Heiligen im deutschen und niederländischen Kulturraum* (Weimar: VDG, 1998).
Hill, D., *The Gospel of Matthew* (London: Marshall, Morgan and Scott, 1972).
Hock, R.F., *The Infancy Gospels of James and Thomas* (Santa Rosa, CA: Polebridge Press, 1995).
Hoffmann, R.J., *Jesus Outside the Gospels* (Amherst, NY: Prometheus Books, 1984).
Hoskyns, E., *The Fourth Gospel* (London: Faber and Faber, 1947).
Irwin, K.M., 'The Liturgical and Theological Correlations in the Associations of Representations of the Three Hebrews and Magi in the Christian Art of Late Antiquity', PhD dissertation (Berkeley, CA: Graduate Theological Union, 1985).
Iser,W., *The Implied Reader* (Baltimore: Johns Hopkins Press, 1974).
―― *The Act of Reading* (Baltimore: Johns Hopkins Press, 1978).

James, M.R., *The Apocryphal New Testament* (Oxford: Clarendon Press, 1953 corrected edition).

Jauss, H.R., *Toward an Aesthetic of Reception* (trans. Timothy Bahti; Minneapolis, MN: University of Minnesota Press, 1982).

Jensen, R.M., 'Giving Texts Vision and Images Voice: The Promise and Problems of Interdisciplinary Scholarship', in Julian V. Hills (ed.), *Common Life in the Early Church: Essays Honoring Graydon F. Snyder* (Harrisburg, PA: Trinity Press International, 1998), pp. 344-56.

—— *Understanding Christian Art* (London and New York: Routledge, 2000).

—— 'Witnessing the Divine: The Magi in Art and Literature', BibbiaBlog, *Bible Press Review* (November 2006).

Johnson, L.T., *The Gospel of Luke* (Collegeville, MN: The Liturgical Press, 1991).

—— *The Writings of the New Testament* (Minneapolis, MN: Fortress Press, 1999).

Jungmann, J.A., *The Early Liturgy to the Time of Gregory the Great* (Notre Dame, IN: University of Notre Dame, 1959).

Just, A.A., *Luke 1.1–9.50* (St. Louis, MO: Concordia Publishing House, 1997).

Kampen, N.B., 'On Writing Histories of Roman Art', *The Art Bulletin* 85.2 (2003), pp. 371-86.

Katz, M.R. and R.A. Orsi, *Divine Mirrors: The Virgin Mary in the Visual Arts* (Oxford and New York: Oxford University Press, 2001).

Katzenellenbogen, A., 'The Sarcophagus in S. Ambrogio and St. Ambrose', *The Art Bulletin* 29.4 (1947), pp. 249-59.

Keener, C.S., *A Commentary on the Gospel of Matthew* (Grand Rapids and Cambridge: Eerdmans, 1999).

Kehrer, H., *Die Heiligen Drei Könige in Literatur und Kunst*, vols. I and II (Leipzig: Seemann, 1908-1909).

Kelber, W., 'Narrative as Interpretation and Interpretation as Narrative: Hermeneutical Reflections on the Gospels', *Semeia* 39 (1987).

Kelly, J.N.D., *The Oxford Dictionary of Popes* (Oxford and New York: Oxford University Press, 1986).

Kent, W.H., 'Eastern Devotion to St. Joseph', *Dublin Review* 116 (1895), pp. 245-56.

Kessler, H.L., 'Pictures as Scripture in Fifth-Century Churches', *Studia Artium Orientalis et Occidentalibus* 2 (1985), pp. 22-31.

Kessler, H.L. and M.S. Simpson (eds.), *Pictorial Narrative in Antiquity and the Middle Ages* (Studies in the History of Art; Washington, DC: National Gallery of Art; Hanover, NH: University Press of New England, 1985).

Kingsbury, J.D., 'The Birth Narrative of Matthew', in David E. Aune (ed.), *The Gospel of Matthew in Current Study* (Grand Rapids and Cambridge: Eerdmans, 2001), pp. 154-65.

Kirschbaum, E., 'Der Prophet Balaam und die Anbetung der Weisen', *Römische Quartalsschrift* 49 (1954), pp. 155-56.

Kitzinger, E., *The Art of Byzantium and the Medieval West: Selected Studies* (Bloomington, IN: Indiana University Press, 1976).

Klein, B., 'Christliche Ikonographie und künstlerische Tradition in der Sarkophagplastik der ersten Hälfte des 4. Jahrhunderts', in G. Koch (ed.),

Akten des Symposiums 'Frühchristliche Sarkophage', Marburg, vol. II (Mainz am Rhein: Verlag Philipp von Zabern, 2002).

Klingshirn, W.E. and L. Safran (eds.), *The Early Christian Book* (Washington: Catholic University of America Press, 2007).

Koch, G., *Frühchristliche Sarkophage* (Munich: C.H. Beck, 2000).

Koch, G., (ed.), *Akten des Symposiums 'Frühchristliche Sarkophage'*, Marburg, vol. II (Mainz am Rhein: Verlag Philipp von Zabern, 2002).

Kostenberger, A.J., *John* (Grand Rapids: Baker Academic, 2004).

Kotsifou, C., 'Books and Book Production in Monastic Communities of Byzantine Egypt', in William E. Klingshirn and Linda Safran (eds.), *The Early Christian Book* (Washington: The Catholic University of America Press, 2007), pp. 48-66.

____ 'Bookbinding and Manuscript Illumination in Late Antique and Early Medieval Monastic Circles in Egypt', in Juan Pedro Monferrer-Sala, Herman Teule, and Sofia Toralles Tovar (eds.), *Eastern Christians and Their Written Heritage: Manuscripts, Scribes, and Context*, Eastern Christian Studies 14 (Leuven, Paris, and Walpole, MA: Peeters, 2012), pp. 213-44.

Kovacs, J. and C. Rowland, *Revelation* (Oxford: Blackwell, 2004).

Krautheimer, R., 'S. Maria Maggiore', *Corpus Basilicarum Christianarum Romae*, vol. III (Vatican City: Pontifico istituto di archeologia Cristiana, 1937-1980), pp. 1-60.

Kreitzer, L.J., *Gospel Images in Fiction and Film* (London: T. & T. Clark, 2002).

Lactantius, *Of the Manner in which the Persecutors Died* in *ANF*, 2nd series, vol. 7 (Peabody, MA: Hendrickson, 2004).

Lasareff, V., 'Studies in the Iconography of the Virgin', *The Art Bulletin* 20.1 (1938), pp. 26-65.

Lawrence, M., 'City-Gate Sarcophagi', *The Art Bulletin* 10.1 (1927), pp. 1-45.

____ 'Columnar Sarcophagi in the Latin West', *The Art Bulletin* 14.2 (1932), pp. 103-85.

Leadbetter, B., *Galerius and the Will of Diocletian* (Oxford and New York: Routledge, 2009).

Leaney, A.R.C., *A Commentary on the Gospel According to St. Luke* (New York: Harper and Brothers, 1958).

Le Blant, Edmond Frederic, *Étude sur les Sarcophages Chrétiens Antiques de la Ville d'Arles* (Paris: Impérial Nationale, 1878).

____*Les Sarcophages Chrétiens de la Gaule* (Paris: Imprimerie Nationale, 1886).

Lee, D., *Luke's Stories of Jesus: Theological Reading of Gospel Narrative and the Legacy of Hans Frei* (JSNTS 185; Sheffield: Sheffield Academic Press, 1999).

Lefkowitz, M.R., 'Mary and the Ancient Goddesses', in Melissa R. Katz (ed.), *Divine Mirrors: The Virgin Mary in the Visual Arts* (Oxford and New York: Oxford University Press, 2001), pp. 133-35.

Lenski, R.C.H., *The Interpretation of St. Luke's Gospel* (Minneapolis, MN: Augsburg Publishing House, 1971).

Lienhard, J., *St. Joseph in Early Christianity* (Philadelphia: St. Joseph's University Press, 1999).

Lieu, J., *The Gospel of Luke* (London: Epworth Press, 1997).

____ 'Anti-Judaism, the Jews, and the Worlds of the Fourth Gospel,' in Richard Bauckham and Carl Moser, eds., *The Gospel of John and Christian Theology* (Grand Rapids: Eerdmans, 2008), p. 176.

Lincoln, A.T., *The Gospel According to Saint John* (London and New York: Continuum, 2005).

Lindars, B., *The Gospel of John* (London: Marshall, Morgan, and Scott, 1972).

Lightfoot, R.H., *St. John's Gospel* (Oxford: Clarendon Press, 1956).

Lowden, J., *Early Christian and Byzantine Art* (London and New York: Phaidon Press, 1997).

____ 'The Word Made Visible: The Exterior of the Early Christian Book as Visual Argument', in William E. Klingshirn and Linda Safran (eds.), *The Early Christian Book* (Washington: The Catholic University of America Press, 2007), pp. 13-47.

Luz, U., *Matthew 1–7* (trans. Wilhelm C. Linss; Minneapolis, MN: Augsburg Press, 1989).

____ *Matthew 1–7* (trans. James E. Crouch; Minneapolis, MN: Fortress Press, 2007).

____ *Matthew 8–20* (trans. James E. Crouch; Minneapolis, MN: Fortress Press, 2001).

____ *Matthew 21–28* (trans. James E. Crouch; Minneapolis, MN: Fortress Press, 2005).

____ *Matthew in History: Interpretation, Influence, and Effects* (Minneapolis, MN: Fortress Press, 1994).

____ *The Theology of the Gospel of Matthew* (trans. J.B. Robinson; Cambridge: Cambridge University Press, 1995).

Macgregor, N. and E. Langmuir, *Seeing Salvation: Images of Christ in Art* (New Haven and London: Yale University Press, 2000).

MacMullen, R., *The Second Church: Popular Christianity AD 200-400* (Atlanta: Society of Biblical Literature, 2009).

Malbon, E.S., *The Iconography of the Sarcophagus of Junius Bassus* (Princeton: Princeton University Press, 1990).

Marsh, J., *Saint John* (London: Penguin Press, 1983).

Marshall, I.H., *Gospel of Luke: A Commentary on the Greek Text* (Grand Rapids: Wm. B. Eerdmans Publishing Company, 1978).

Marucchi, O., *Manuel of Christian Archaeology* (trans. Hubert Vecchierello; Whitefish, MT: Kessinger Publishing, 2003).

____ *I Monumenti del Museo Cristiani Pio-Lateranense* (Rome: Museo Cristiano, 1910).

Mathews, T.F., *The Clash of Gods* (Princeton: Princeton University Press, 1993).

Mathews, T.F. and N. Muller, 'Isis and Mary in Early Icons', in Maria Vassilaki (ed.), *Images of the Mother of God* (Aldershot, UK and Burlington, VT: Ashgate Publishing, 2005), pp. 3-11.

McNeile, A.H., *The Gospel According to St. Matthew* (London: Macmillan, 1915).

Mcquire, M., 'Letters and Letter Carriers in Christian Antiquity', *Classical World* 53 (1960), pp. 148-53, 184-85.

Meeks, W., *First Urban Christians* (New Haven and London: Yale University Press,1983).
Meier, J.P., *Matthew* (Wilmington, DE: Michael Glazier, 1985).
Metzger, B., *A Textual Commentary on the Greek New Testament* (Stuttgart: Deutsche Bibelgesellschaft, 2007).
Metzger, C., 'Les sarcophagues chrétiens d'Afrique du Nord', in G. Koch (ed.), *Akten des Symposiums 'Frühchristliche Sarkophage'*, Marburg, vol. II, (Mainz am Rhein: Verlag Philipp von Zabern, 2002), pp. 153-55.
Michaels, J.R., *John* (Peabody, MA: Hendrickson, 1989).
_____ *The Gospel of John* (Grand Rapids: Eerdmans, 2010).
Miles, M.R., *Image as Insight: Visual Understanding in Western Christianity and Secular Culture* (Boston: Beacon Press, 1985).
_____ 'Santa Maria Maggiore's Fifth-Century Mosaics: Triumphal Christianity and the Jews', *Harvard Theological Review* 86 (1993), pp. 155-76.
Mitchell, M.M., *The Heavenly Trumpet: John Chrysostom and the Art of Pauline Interpretation* (Tübingen: Mohr Siebeck, 2000).
Molinier, E., *Catalogue des Ivoires* (Paris: Librairies-Imprimeries Réunies, 1896).
Morath, G.W., *Die Maximianskathedra in Ravenna: Ein Meisterwerk christlich-antiker Reliefkunst* (Freiburg: Herder, 1940)
Morenz, S., *Die Geschichte von Joseph dem Zimmermann* (Berlin: Akadmie-Verlag, 1951).
Morgan-Guy, J., 'The Bible and Medieval Art', in Martin O'Kane (ed.), *Imagining the Bible: An Introduction to Biblical Art* (London: SPCK, 2008), pp. 41-62.
Morris, L., *The Gospel According to John* (Grand Rapids: Eerdmans, 1971).
_____ *The Gospel According to Matthew* (Grand Rapids:Eerdmans, 1992).
Morson, G.S. and C. Emerson, *Mikhail Bakhtin: Creation of a Prosaics* (Stanford: Stanford University Press, 1990).
Mounce, R.H., *Matthew* (Peabody, MA: Hendrickson, 2002).
Murray, M.C., 'Art and the Early Church', *Journal of Theological Studies* 28 (1977), pp. 304-45.
_____ 'The Image, the Ear, and the Eye in Early Christianity', *Art, Religion, and Theological Studies* 9/1 (1997), pp. 17-24.
Natanson, J., *Early Christian Ivories* (London: Alec Tiranti, 1953).
National Council of Churches of Christ in the United States of America, *New Revised Standard Version Bible*, 1989, *The HarperCollins Study Bible* (New York: HarperOne, 2006).
Needham, P., *Twelve Centuries of Bookbindings: 400-1600* (New York and London: The Pierpont Morgan Library and Oxford University Press, 1979).
Nees, L., *Early Medieval Art*, issue 5970 (New York and London: Oxford University Press, 2002).
Neyrey, J.H., *The Gospel of John* (Cambridge: Cambridge University Press, 2007).
Nicholls, R., *Walking on Water: Reading Mt. 14:22-33 in the Light of Its Wirkungsgeschichte* (Leiden and Boston: Brill, 2008).
Nichols, S., 'Philology in a Manuscript Culture', *Speculum* 65 (1990), pp. 1-9.
Nolland, J., *Luke 1–9:20* (Dallas, TX: Word Books, 1989).
_____ *The Gospel of Matthew* (Grand Rapids and Cambridge: Eerdmans, 2005).

Nordhagen, P.J., 'The Frescoes of John VII in S. Maria Antiqua in Rome', *ACTA* III (1968), n.p.
Oden, T. and M. Simonetti (eds.), *Ancient Christian Commentary on Scripture: Matthew 1–13* (Downers Grove, IL: Intervarsity Press, 2001).
Oden, T. and A.A. Just, Jr. (eds.), *Ancient Christian Commentary on Scripture: Luke* (Downers Grove, IL: Intervarsity Press, 2003).
Oden, T. and J.C. Elowsky (eds.), *Ancient Christian Commentary on Scripture: John 11-21* (Downers Grove, IL: Intervarsity Press, 2007).
O'Kane, M., 'The Bible and the Visual Imagination', in Martin O'Kane (ed.), *Imagining the Bible: An Introduction to Biblical Art* (London: SPCK, 2008), pp. 1-20.
Palmer, W. and J.S. Northcote and W.R. Brownlow, *An Introduction to Early Christian Symbolism: A Series of Compositions from Fresco Paintings, Glasses, and Sculptured Sarcophagi* (London: Kegan Paul, Trench, & Co., 1885).
Panofsky, E., *Tomb Sculpture* (New York: Harry N. Abrams, 1992).
Parrinder, G., *Son of Joseph: The Parentage of Jesus* (Edinburgh: T. & T. Clark, 1992).
Patte, D., *The Gospel According to Matthew* (Philadelphia: Fortress Press, 1987).
Pelikan, J., *The Christian Tradition: A History of the Development of Doctrine*, vol. I (Chicago and London: University of Chicago Press, 1971).
_____ *Mary through the Centuries* (New Haven: Yale University Press, 1996).
Petrides, S., 'Caesarea Mauretaniae', *Catholic Encyclopedia* (New York: Robert Appleton, 1913), n.p.
_____ 'Chercell', *Catholic Encyclopedia* (New York: Robert Appleton, 1913), n.p.
Pitts, T., 'The Origin and Meaning of Some Saint Joseph Figures in Early Christian Art', PhD dissertation (Athens, GA: University of Georgia, 1988).
Plummer, A., *An Exegetical Commentary on the Gospel According to St. Matthew* (London: Robert Scott, 1928).
_____ *A Critical and Exegetical Commentary on the Gospel According to St. Luke* (Edinburgh: T. and T. Clark, 1896).
Ridderbos, H.N., *The Gospel according to John: A Theological Commentary* (trans. John Vriend; Grand Rapids: Eerdmans, 1997).
Robb, D.M., *The Art of the Illuminated Manuscript* (South Brunswick, NJ and New York: A.S. Barnes, 1973).
Di Rossi, G.B., 'Delle immagini di S. Giuseppe nei monumenti dei primi cinque secoli', *Bullettino di Archeologia Cristiana* 3 (1865), pp. 25-32.
Di Rossi, G.B., and J.S. Northcote, and W.R. Brownlow, *Roma Sotterranea* (London: Longmans, Green, Reader, and Dyer, 1869).
Sanders, E.P., *Judaism: Practice and Belief* (Valley Forge, PA.: Trinity Press International, 1992).
Sawyer, J.F.A., 'The Role of Reception Theory, Reader-Response Criticism and/or Impact History in the Study of the Bible: Definition and Evaluation', pp. 1-15. This article is found at http://www.bbibcomm.net.
Schapiro, M., 'The Joseph Scenes on the Maximianus Throne in Ravenna', in Meyer Schapiro (ed.), *Late Antique, Early Christian and Medieval Art: Selected Papers* (New York: George Braziller, 1979), pp. 34-47.

Schiller, G., *The Iconography of Christian Art*, vol. I (trans. Janet Seligman; Greenwich, CT: New York Graphic Society, 1971).

Schmidt, T-M., 'Die verzweifelte Zweiflerin Salome auf dem Sarkophag in Boville Ernica', in G. Koch (ed.), *Akten des Symposiums Frühchristliche Sarkophage*, Marburg, vol. II, p. 223.

Schnackenburg, R., *The Gospel According to St. John*, vol. I (New York: The Seabury Press, 1980).

—— *The Gospel of Matthew* (Grand Rapids and Cambridge: Eerdmans, 2002).

Schneemelcher, W., 'General Introduction', in Wilhelm Schneemelcher (ed.), *The New Testament Apocrypha: Gospels and Related Writings* I (trans. Robert McL. Wilson; Louisville, KY: Westminster/John Knox Press, 1991), pp. 9-75.

Schwartz, S. 'Symbolic Allusions in a Twelfth-Century Ivory', *Marsyas* 16 (1972-73), pp. 35-42.

—— 'The Iconography of the Rest on the Flight into Egypt', PhD dissertation (New York: New York University, 1975).

Schweizer, E., *The Good News According to Matthew* (London: SPCK, 1976).

Seitz, J., *Die Verehrung des hl. Joseph in ihrer geschichtlichen Entwicklung bis zum Konzil von Trient dargestellt* (Freiburg im Breisgau: Herder, 1908).

Senior, D., *The Gospel of Matthew* (Nashville, TN: Abingdon Press, 1997).

Seta, A., *Religion and Art* (trans. Marion C. Harrison; New York: Charles Scribner's Sons, 1914).

Sheeley, S.M., *Narrative Asides in Luke–Acts* (JSNTS 72; Sheffield: Sheffield Academic Press, 1992).

Shorr, D.C., 'The Iconographic Development of the Presentation in the Temple', *The Art Bulletin* 28.1 (1946), pp. 17-32.

Sidebottom, E.M., *The Christ of the Fourth Gospel* (London: SPCK, 1961).

Sieger, J.D., 'Visual Metaphor as Theology: Leo the Great's Sermons on the Incarnation and the Arch Mosaics at S. Maria Maggiore', *Gesta* 26 (1987), pp. 83-91.

Smid, H.R., *Protevangelium Jacobi: A Commentary*. Apocrypha Novi Testamenti, I (Assen: van Gorcum, 1965).

Smith, R.H., *Augsburg Commentary on the New Testament: Matthew* (Minneapolis, MN: Augsburg Publishing House, 1989).

Snyder, G. F., *Ante Pacem: Archaeological Evidence of Church Life before Constantine* (Macon, GA: Mercer University Press, 1985).

Soper, A.C., 'The Latin Style on Christian Sarcophagai of the Fourth Century', *The Art Bulletin* 19.2 (1937), pp. 148-202.

Sottocornola, F., 'Tradition and the Doubt of St. Joseph concerning Mary's Virginity', *Marianum* 19 (1947), pp. 127-41.

Spain, S., 'The Program of the Fifth Century Mosaics of Santa Maria Maggiore', PhD dissertation (New York: New York University, 1968).

—— 'The Promised Blessing: The Iconography of the Mosaics of Santa Maria Maggiore', *The Art Bulletin* 61 (1979), pp. 518-40.

Spier, J. (ed.), *Picturing the Bible: The Earliest Christian Art* (New Haven and New York: Yale University Press in association with Kimball Art Museum, 2009).

Steenbock, F., *Der kirchliche Prachteinband im frühen Mittelalter: Von den Anfängen bis zum Beginn der Gothik* (Berlin: Deutscher Verlag für Kunstwissenschaft, 1965).
Stein, R.H., *Luke* (Nashville, TN: Broadman Press, 1993).
Stramare, T., 'Son of Joseph from Nazareth', *Cahiers de Joséphologie* 24.1 (1978), pp. 1-59.
Strauss, M.L., *The Davidic Messiah in Luke–Acts* (JSNTS 110; Sheffield: Sheffield Academic Press, 1995).
Strycker, E. (ed.), *La Forme la plus ancienne du Protévangile de Jacques*, Studia Hagiographica 33 (Bruxelles: Société des Bollandistes, 1961).
Swindell, A., 'Mapping the Afterlife of Biblical Stories', in J. Cheryl Exum and David J.A. Clines (eds.), *Biblical Reception*, I (Sheffield: Sheffield Phoenix Press, 2012), pp. 281-296.
Szirmai, J.A., *The Archaeology of Medieval Bookbinding* (Aldershot,UK: Ashgate, 1999).
Taggart, A.M., *Roman Sarcophagi in The Metropolitan Museum of Art* (New York: Metropolitan Museum of Art, 1978).
Tannehill, R.C., *The Narrative Unity of Luke-Acts* (Philadelphia: Fortress Press, 1986).
_____ *Luke* (Nashville, TN: Abingdon Press, 1996).
Tasker, R.V.G., *The Gospel According to St. Matthew* (Grand Rapids: Eerdmans, 1976).
Tatian, *The Diatessaron* in *ANF*, 2nd series, vol. 9 (Peabody, MA: Hendrickson, 2004).
Taylor, V., *The Historical Evidence for the Virgin Birth* (Oxford: Clarendon Press, 1920).
Thiselton, A.C., *The First Epistle to the Corinthians: A Commentary on the Greek Text* (Cambridge and New York: Eerdmans, 2000).
Tiede, D.L., *Luke* (Minneapolis, MN: Augsburg Publishing House, 1988).
von Tischendorf, C., *Evangelia Apocrypha* (Hildesheim: Georg Olms, 1966; repr. of 2nd ed., Leipzig, 1876).
Tosato, A., 'Joseph Being a Just Man (Matt 1:19)', *Catholic Biblical Quarterly* 41 (1979), pp. 542-51.
Toynbee, J.M.C., *Death and Burial in the Roman World* (Ithaca, NY: Cornell University Press, 1971).
Trexler, R.C., *The Journey of the Magi* (Princeton: Princeton University Press, 1997).
Via, D.O., 'Narrative World and Ethical Response: The Marvelous and Righteousness in Matthew 1-2', *Semeia* 12 (1978), pp. 123-50.
Volbach, W.F., *Early Christian Art: The Late Roman and Byzantine Empires from the Third to the Seventh Centuries* (trans. Christopher Ligota; New York: Harry N. Abrams, 1961).
Waddy, P.A., 'The Cathedra of Maximian and Other Sixth-Century Ivories from Constantinople', MA thesis (New Orleans, LA: Tulane University, 1965).
Webb, M., *The Churches and Catacombs of Early Christian Rome* (Brighton: Sussex Academic Press, 2002).

Wedoff, B., 'Word and Witness: A Reevaluation of the Function, Form, and Imagery of the Cathedra of Maximian', MA thesis (Dekalb, IL: Northern Illinois University, 2009).

Weitzmann, K. (ed.), *Late Antique and Early Christian Book Illumination* (New York: George Braziller, 1977).

_____ (ed.), *The Age of Spirituality: Late Antique and Early Christian Art, Third to Seventh Century* (New York: The Metropolitan Museum of Art, 1979).

Westcott, B.F., *The Gospel According to St. John* (Grand Rapids: Eerdmans, 1881, repr. 1981)

_____ *The Gospel According to St. John: The Greek Text with Introduction and Notes* (London: John Murray, 1908).

White, L.M., *The Social Origins of Christian Architecture*, 2 vols. (Valley Forge, PA: Trinity Press International, 1996-97).

Williamson, P., *An Introduction to Medieval Ivory Carvings* (London: Her Majesty's Stationery Office, 1982).

Wilpert, G., *I Sarcofagi Cristiani Antichi*, vols. I-V (Rome: Pontificio Istituto di Archeologia Cristiana, 1929-1936).

Wilpert, J., 'Early Christian Sculpture: Its Restoration and Its Modern Manufacture', *The Art Bulletin* 9.2 (1932), pp. 89-141.

Wolter, M., *Handbuch zum Neuen Testament, 5: Das Lukasevangelium* (Tübingen: Mohr Siebeck, 2008).

Yassin, A.M., 'Funerary Monuments and Collective Identity: From Roman Family to Christian Community', *The Art Bulletin* 87.3 (2005), pp. 433-57.

Index of Names

Aasgaard, R. 7, 96, 97, 98, 100, 107
Achtemeier, P.J. 25
Alexandria, C. of 83
Albright, W.F. and Mann, C.S. 31, 36, 37, 43
Allen, W.C. 37, 43
Appell, J.W. 222
Aune, D.E. 36

Bardill, J. 149, 150, 151
Barth, K. 20
Barrett, C.K. 71, 73, 74
Basser, H.W. 32, 36, 40, 43
Beare, F.W. 29, 31, 32, 37, 43
Beasley-Murray, G.R. 72
Begg, E. 183
Bernard, J.H. 71, 73
Bienert, W.A. 7, 111
Bloch, E. 20
Blomberg, C.L. 28, 32, 36, 38, 40, 43
Bock, D.L. 48, 50, 56, 59, 60, 62, 67
Bonnard, P. 25, 28, 30, 31, 35, 36, 38, 40, 42, 43
Bourguet, P. du 150, 224
Bovon, F. 46, 47, 52, 55, 62, 67
Brilliant, R. 219, 220
Brown, R. 2, 3, 25, 28, 32, 36, 38, 40, 41, 43, 46, 47, 58, 61, 62, 63, 66, 71
Bruce, A.J. 41, 70
Bruce, F.F. 72, 73
Bruner, F.D. 26, 28, 30, 32, 36, 43
Bultmann, R. 71, 72, 74

Burkett, D. 25

Callaway, M.C. 17
Calloud 4?
Carroll, D. 54, 57, 59, 64, 65
Carson, D.A. 72, 74
Carter, W. 28, 32, 35, 36, 38, 40, 43
Cartlidge, D. and Elliott, J. 98, 130, 208
Cassidy, B. 153
Charles, R.H. 20
Chartrand-Burke, T. 96, 98, 99, 100, 109
Clarke, G. 150
Clayton, M 129, 130, 132, 133
Coleridge, M. 52, 54, 55, 56, 58, 59, 60, 62, 63, 65
Creed, J.M. 46, 49, 50, 53, 58, 66, 68
Culpepper, R.A. 70, 76
Cutts, E.L. 221, 222

Dalton, O.M. 21, 148, 177, 192, 193, 201, 215
Darby, J.N. 20
Davies, M. 28, 29, 34, 36, 43
Davies, W.D. and Allison, D.C. 26, 28, 29, 32, 37, 38, 40, 42
Davis-Weyer, C. 155, 156, 157, 169
Deasey, J.C.P. 81, 132
Degering, H. and Boekler, A. 157
Deshman, R. 210
Dinkler, E. 219, 220, 221, 222

Dodd, C.H. 72
Dodson, D.S 35
Duval, Y. 225

Eagon, M.C. 168
Ehrman, B.D. and Pleše, Z. 83, 84, 85, 96, 97, 99, 111-129, 131-139, 140, 141, 142, 205, 229
Elliott, J.K. 7, 8, 83, 84, 85, 86, 87, 93, 96, 109, 111, 112, 113, 128, 130, 132, 133, 140
Ellis, E. 52, 58, 59, 60, 66, 67
Eusebius 150
Evans, C.A. 49, 53, 54, 55, 58, 59, 61, 62, 66, 67, 68

Falcetta, A. 68
Farrer, F.W. 18
Filas, F. 9, 10, 11, 86, 128, 132
Fiore, Joachim of, 20
Fitzmyer, J.A. 2, 6, 7, 48, 56, 58, 59, 61, 66
Fornberg, T. 17, 18, 19, 20
Foster, M.B. 81, 87, 100, 128, 130, 132, 133
France, R.T. 26, 30, 32, 36, 37, 40
Freed, E.D. 26, 28, 36, 48

Gaborit-Chopin, D. 204
Gadamer, H.-G. 16, 17, 20
Gamble, H.Y 153, 154
Gambero 86
Garland, D.E. 28, 30, 32, 43, 59
Geldenhuys, N. 53, 58, 59
Gijsel, J. 128, 129, 130, 131, 132, 140
Godet, F. 71
Goldschmidt, R.C. 155, 156
Goulder, M.D. 52, 56, 59, 61, 66, 67
Grabar, A. 150, 160, 221, 244
Green, J.B. 25, 28, 32, 35, 36, 42, 43, 46, 47, 54, 55, 61, 62, 63, 64, 65
Greimas, A.J. 3, 4

Grotius, H. 20
Gundry, R.H. 29, 32, 37, 38, 42, 43

Haenchen, E. 72, 74
Hagner, D.A. 28, 32, 36, 38, 43
Hamann, H.P. 36
Hanna, W. 18
Harbison, P. 214
Harrington, D.J. 26, 28, 30, 32, 36, 43
Harvey, J. 149, 158, 159
Hauerwas, S. 28, 36
Hendriksen, W. 30, 32, 36, 38, 48, 53, 56, 60
Herbermann, C. 164, 183, 231
Heulbein, B. 13, 15, 16, 183, 207, 210, 211, 215
Hill, D. 37, 43
Hock, R.F. 7, 8, 9, 83, 84, 85, 86, 87, 88, 89, 90, 91, 92, 94, 96-109, 132, 205, 229
Hoskyns, E. 72, 73

Irwin, K.M. 221, 222

James, M.R. 111, 112, 113, 128, 130, 131, 140
Jauss, H.R. 16, 17, 20
Jensen, R.M. 150, 153
Johnson, L.T. 25, 47, 52, 53, 58, 61, 64
Just, A.A. 49
Justin Martyr 12

Keener, C.S. 26, 28, 30, 32, 36, 37
Kingsbury, J.D. 36
Koch, G. 222
Kostenberger, A.J. 70, 71, 72
Kotsifou, C. 192, 193
Kovacs, J. 19, 20
Krautheimer, R. 172

Lactantius 149, 150
Le Blant, E.F. 182
Leadbetter, B. 149
Leaney, A.R.C. 60, 64

Index of Names

Lee, D. 51
Lenski, R.C.H. 50, 53, 59, 62, 65, 66, 67
Lienhard, J. 9, 12, 86, 87, 97, 100, 132, 133
Lieu, J. 48, 62, 68, 74
Lightfoot, R.H. 71, 72
Lincoln, A.T. 70, 72
Lindars, B. 72, 73
Lindsey, H. 20
Lowden, J. 150, 151, 168, 172, 174, 176, 179, 180, 191, 198, 204, 205, 222
Luz, U. 2, 5, 6, 16, 17, 20, 28, 32, 35, 36, 37, 38, 39, 40, 41, 43, 49

Macgregor N. and Langmuir, E. 150
MacMullen, R. 225
Marsh, J. 74
Marshall, I.H. 48, 53, 54, 58, 66
Mathews, T.F. 150
Mathews, T.F. and Muller, N. 172
McNeile, A.H. 31, 37, 43
Mede, J. 20
Meeks, W. 154
Meier, J.P. 29, 33, 35, 36, 38
Metzger, B.M. 62, 225
Meyer, H.A.W. 30, 31, 36, 38, 43
Michaels, J.R. 71, 73, 74
Mitchell, M.M. 17
Morath, G.W. 179, 180, 187, 188, 191, 196
Morenz, S. 111, 112, 113, 124, 125
Morris, L. 26, 37, 42. 43, 75, 76
Mounce, R.H. 28, 32, 35, 36, 43
Mozley, J.B. 18
Murray, M.C. 151

Natanson, J. 208
Needham, P. 177
Nees, L. 167, 173
Neyrey, J.H. 75
Nicholls, R. 18, 19

Nolland, J. 26, 30, 32, 36, 40, 46, 48, 49, 53, 56, 58, 65, 66, 67, 68
Nordhagen, P.J. 231

Panofsky, E. 218, 222
Parrinder, G. 9, 11
Patte, D. 28, 29, 33, 34, 35
Paulus, H.E. 18
Petrides, S. 225
Pitts, T.R. 13, 14, 15
Plummer, A. 28, 40, 48, 51, 62, 67, 68
Pope Sixtus III 13

Ridderbos, H.N. 71, 72
Rossi, G.B.de, Northcote, J.S. and Brownlow, W.R. 164
Rowland, C. 19, 20

Sanders, E.P. 63
Sawyer, J.F.A. 17, 19, 93
Schiller, G. 13, 150, 172, 184, 187, 188, 191, 207, 214, 222
Schleiermacher, F. 18
Schnackenburg, R. 28, 32, 38, 42, 43, 70, 71, 72, 73
Schweizer, E. 25, 28, 30, 32, 36, 37, 38
Seitz J. 9, 10, 162, 167, 170, 171, 182, 183, 205, 218, 222
Senior, 32, 35, 37
Seta, A. 218, 219
Sheeley, S.M. 59, 67
Sieger, J.D. 172
Sidebottom, E.M. 71
Smid, H.R. 83, 86, 87, 93
Smith, R.H. 26, 28, 32, 36,
Soper, A.C. 220, 222
Spier, J. 150
Steenbock, F. 191, 198, 204, 205
Stein, R.H. 48, 50, 56, 62, 67
Stramare, T. 25, 30, 32
Strauss, D.F. 18
Strauss, M.L. 49, 50, 52
Szirmai, J.A. 177

Taggert, A.McC. 162, 164
Tannehill, R.C. 46, 59, 63, 68
Tasker, R.V.G. 29, 37, 43
Tatian 169
Thiselton, A.C. 17
Thompson, M.M. 25
Tiede, D.L. 49, 53, 60, 63, 67,
Tischendorf, C. 128
Tosato, A. 32
Trench, R.C. 18
Trexler, R.C. 17

Via, D.O. 2, 3, 4, 5, 29, 31, 32,
    33, 36, 37
Volbach, W.F. 150
Voragine, Jacques of 131

Waddy, P.A. 179, 180
Webb, M. 150, 169
Wedoff, B. 179, 180, 187, 197,
    223, 226
Westcott, B.F. 18, 70
Weyden, Rogier van der 6
Wilbert, G. 13, 162, 164, 165,
    182, 183, 219, 221, 223
Williamson, P. 176, 177, 189

Index of Biblical and Other Source References

Genesis
37–50 35

Exodus
13 59

Leviticus
12 59

1 Samuel
1.1–2.11 59

Isaiah
1.3-4 208
7.14 36
8.8 36

Jeremiah
31.15 41

Hosea
11.1 41

Matthew
1–7 5
1–2 4, 5
1 162, 171, 178
1.1-17 5, 93, 110
1.1–1.21 35
1.1–1.17 27, 140
1.1-16a 28
1.1-16b 29
1.1 34, 39
1.2-16 28

1.2-16a 29
1.2 27
1.3 28
1.5 28
1.6 27, 28
1.16 27, 29, 30, 36, 37
1.16b 28, 30
1.18–2.23 30
1.18-26 116, 165
1.18-25 5, 28, 29, 30, 31, 33, 34, 36, 37, 41, 122, 169
1.18-21 93, 110
1.18-20 1
1.18 31, 36, 37, 122
1.19-21 36, 123
1.19-20 33
1.19 31, 32, 33, 122
1.20-26 174
1.20-25 33, 42
1.20-24 123, 169, 183
1.20 29, 30, 33, 34, 35, 170
1.21-23 33, 39
1.21 35, 37, 39, 57
1.23-25 34
1.23 37, 39
1.24-25 29, 93, 110, 139
1.24 36, 170

1.25 5, 34, 36, 37
2 218, 223, 224, 226, 227, 228
2.1-12 6, 37, 39, 40, 139
2.2 229
2.3-4 40
2.3 40
2.9 229
2.10 229
2.11 36, 39
2.12 40, 42, 228
2.13-23 5, 6, 36, 37, 39
2.13-15 34, 35, 38, 39, 40, 41, 42, 93, 122, 123, 139, 168
2.13-14 40, 41
2.13 36, 39, 40, 41
2.14-15 34
2.14 36, 40
2.15 39, 41
2.16-18 38, 41
2.16-17 47
2.18 41
2.19-23 34, 35, 42, 93, 122, 123, 140
2.19-22 38
2.19-21 34, 168
2.19 42
2.20 36
2.21-22 34, 41
2.21 36, 42

2.22 34, 168
2.23 34, 43, 44
3.15 33
9.8 8
13.1-5 8
13.6-10 8
13.54-58 27, 44
13.54 44
13.55 27, 44, 83, 109
19.1-13 8

Mark
6.3 85, 109
15.40 85

Luke
1 171
1.4 58
1.5-26 51
1.5 50, 51, 58
1.16 58
1.19 58
1.21 58
1.24 3
1.26-38 18, 26, 47, 48, 50, 66, 169
1.26-28 49,
1.26-27 93, 110, 140
1.26 48, 50
1.27 47, 48, 49, 50, 51, 66
1.27a 49,
1.27b 49, 50
1.31 51, 57, 58
1.32 51
1.33 51
1.34 49
1.35 170
1.36 50
1.39-45 26, 50, 51
1.43 50, 51
1.46-56 26, 50
1.57-1.80 51
1.57-63 57
1.69 51

2 54, 195, 196, 198, 200, 205, 206, 207, 211, 213, 215, 216
2.1-21 49, 58
2.1-7 26, 50, 52, 56, 91, 123, 139, 197
2.1-6 196, 204
2.1-2 52
2.1 54, 93, 110
2.3-5 52, 53
2.3 91, 93, 110
2.4-7 47, 49, 54
2.4 3, 47, 51, 52, 66
2.5-7 52
2.5-6 52
2.5 52, 91, 93, 110
2.6-7 91, 93, 110
2.8-20 55, 93, 110
2.10-12 56
2.11 51, 55, 64
2.12 55
2.16-19 26
2.16-17 55
2.16 47, 54, 55, 56
2.17-18 56
2.17 56
2.19 56
2.20 55
2.21-40 50, 56, 57
2.21-38 93, 110, 139
2.21-24 59
2.21 57, 58
2.22-38 49
2.22-32 60
2.22-28 57, 58
2.22-24 3
2.22 47, 54, 58, 59
2.24 47, 54
2.27 47, 54, 59, 60
2.33-34 47, 60
2.33 47, 54, 60
2.34-35 26
2.34 54, 58

2.39-40 61, 93, 110, 140
2.39 3, 47, 54
2.41-52 50, 61, 62, 93, 98, 107, 109, 110, 140
2.41-46 47
2.41-42 62
2.41 3, 54, 62
2.42 54, 62, 63
2.43 54, 63, 64
2.44 54, 63
2.45 54, 63
2.46 54, 63, 64
2.47 64, 107
2.48-52 108
2.48-51 26, 47
2.48-2.50 64
2.48 3, 47, 54, 63, 65
2.49 54, 63, 64, 65
2.50 54, 63
2.51 54, 63, 65, 108
3.6 64
3.23-38 46, 66, 93, 110, 140
3.23 46, 47, 66
4.16-30 46, 67
4.21 67
4.22 46, 47, 50, 67

John
1.1 69, 71
1.2 69
1.3 69
1.5 78
1.14 69, 71
1.16 77
1.18-20 78
1.18-19 77
1.18 69, 71
1.20-21 77
1.24-25 77, 78
1.27 78
1.29 69
1.32 78

Index of Biblical and Other Source References

1,35-51 73
1.36 69
1.38 69
1.41 69
1.43-51 70
1.43-45 70
1.45 26, 69, 70, 75, 76, 77, 80
1.46 70, 72
1.47-48 73
1.49 73
1.69 78
2 79
2.1-20 79
2.1-5 79
2.1 75, 76
2.3 75, 76
2.4-7 78, 79
2.5 75, 76
2.6-7 79
2.12 75, 76
2.13-15 77
2.13 78
2.14-15 77, 78
2.16-18 79
2.19-21 77
2.19-20 78
2.21-24 79
2.21 77, 78, 79
2.22-38 79
2.22-23 78
2.22 78
2.27-34 79
2.27 79
2.33 79
2.39-40 79
2.41-43 79
2.41 79
2.43 79
2.44-50 79
2.48 79
2.51-52 79
2.51 79
3-5 75
4.16-30 79
4.22 79
6.24 70, 73, 80
6.29 73, 80
6.41-51 73, 80
6.42 26, 69, 73, 74, 75, 76, 77, 80
6.59 70
13.54-58 78
13.54 78
13.55 78
18.5 70, 72
18.7 70, 72
19.19 70, 72
19.25-27 76, 77
19.25 75, 76
19.26b-27 77
19.27 76

Gospel of Pseudo-Matthew
1-24 129
1-17 140
1-8 131
6 141
8 133, 134, 140, 141, 142
9 134
10 134, 139, 140
11 134, 139, 140, 162
12 135, 140, 187, 188
13-14 206
13 136, 139, 140, 195, 196, 205
14 136, 139, 208, 214
15 136, 139
16 137, 139, 140, 218
17 137, 139, 140
18-24 128, 137
18-22 130
18-20 138
18 137
19 137, 138
20 138
21 138, 139
22 139
23 139
24 139
25-42 129

History of Joseph the Carpenter
1 115, 116, 117, 122, 124
2-31 125
2-11 114
2 115, 116, 117, 118, 119, 122, 123, 124, 125
3 116, 117, 119, 124, 125
4 116, 117, 119, 124, 125
5-9 117
5 116, 117, 118, 122, 123, 124
6 116, 117, 118, 123, 124, 162
7 116, 117, 123, 124, 195, 206
8 117, 118, 123, 125
9 116, 117, 118, 123, 125
10 114, 118
11 114, 117, 119, 124, 125
12-29 114
12 117, 119, 125
13 117, 118
14 116, 119, 124, 125
15 117, 119, 125
16 118, 124
17-19 119
17 116, 119, 123, 124, 125
18-29 120
18-20 120
18-19 120
18 117, 119, 120, 124, 125
19 120, 125
20 120, 125

21–23 120
21–22 119
21 117, 119, 120, 121, 125
22 117, 119, 120, 121, 125
23 121
24 117, 119, 120, 121, 125
25 119, 120, 121, 125
26 119, 121, 122, 125, 127
27 116, 119, 120, 121, 123, 125
28 119, 125
29 116, 117, 119, 125
30–32 114
30 114, 115, 116, 117, 119, 125, 127
31 119, 125

Infancy Gospel of James
1–17 128
1–5 85
1.1-3 86
2.1 86
4.2 86
6–7 85
6.4-5 86
6.6-7 86
6.9 86
7.1 86
7.4 123
7.7-8 86
7.8 87
8–10 85
8 87, 88
8.1-9 123
8.2 86
8.3-9 87
8.3-4 124
8.6–9.12 87
8.7-9 124

8.7-8 86
8.7 87
8.8 87
8.9 87
8.12 87
9 87, 88, 140
9.1-8 123
9.7 86, 87, 88, 94, 124
9.8 87, 88, 124
9.11-12 86, 123, 124
9.11 86, 87, 88, 94
9.12 88
10.2-4 86, 88
11–12 85
11 88
11.1-7 86
11.2-3 88
11.2 86
11.5 86
11.7-9 88
11.7-8 86, 87
11.8 86
12.2 86, 88
12.5-6 88
12.5 86
12.6 88
13 85, 88, 91, 93, 140
13.1–14.8 87, 94
13.1-10 88
13.1-3 88
13.1 87
13.2-3 88
13.5-7 88
13.6-7 86
13.7 86
13.9 88
14–15 85
14 88, 89, 91, 93, 140, 165
14.1-8 88
14.2-4 89, 105
14.5-6 86
14.5 89
14.6-7 89
14.6 86, 87

15–16 187, 188, 190, 192
15 89, 140
15.1–16.8 87, 94,
15.8 90
15.10 89
15.11-12 86
15.13 89
15.15 90
15.16-17 90
16–17 85
16 89, 140
16.3 90
16.4-6 90
16.4 90
16.6-8 90
16.7-8 90
17 93, 110, 140, 196, 200, 205
17.1–19.17 87, 90
17.1–18.2 94,
17.1-11 195
17.1-4 90
17.1-3 90
17.2-11 91
17.2-3 91
17.5–18.2 91
17.5 91
17.6-11 91
17.7 91
17.9 91
17.10–18.2 91
17.10-11 86
17.10 91
17.11 87, 91
18–20 85
18–19 206, 208
18 93,
18.1-2 86
18.1 91, 123
18.2-11 91
18.2 91
18.3-11 94
19 140
19.1-16 86
19.1-15 94
19.1-9 92
19.6-9 92

Index of Biblical and Other Source References

19.6 92
19.8-9 108
19.9-11 92
19.11 92
19.12-13 92
19.15-16 87
19,15 92
19.16 92
20 140
21 140, 118, 223, 229
21.1-12 87, 92
21.1-2 92
21.10-11 87
22 85, 140
22.1 87
23 85

Infancy Gospel of Thomas
1.1 98, 99, 11
2.1–10.4 99
2.1-7 101
2.4 100, 101, 102
2.5 100, 101
3.1-4 101
3.1 101, 108
3.3 100, 102
3.4 100, 101, 102
4–5 101
4.1-5.6 101
4.1 101
4.3 101
4.4 100, 102, 103
5.1 100, 102
5.2 102
5.3 103
5.4 100, 102
5.5 102
5.6 102
6.1–10.4 99
6.1–8.4 99, 103
6.1–8.3 108
6 103
6.1 100, 103
6.2 100, 103
6.3 100, 101
6.4 100

6.6-7 103
6.9 101
6.11 101
6.13 100
6.14 100, 103
6.15 101
6.16 101
7.1 101
7.3 101
7.4 100, 101
7.9 101
7.11 100, 103
8.1 101
8.3 101
9.1–10.4 99
10.4 101
11–13 103
11 105
11.1–13.4 99, 101
11.1-4 105, 107
11.1 101, 103
11.3 101
11.4 101, 104
12–13 103
12.1-4 104
12.1 101, 104
12.3 100, 104
13 104, 109
13.1-4 108
13.2 100, 101
13.3 100, 101
13.4 100, 101
14–15 104
14.1–15.7 99
14.1-5 104
14.1 100, 101
14.2 100, 101
14.4 104
14.5 100, 101, 104, 106, 107
15.1-7 100, 104
15.1 100, 101, 105
15.2 100, 101, 105
15.5 100
15.6 100, 101, 105
15.7 100, 101, 105
16–17 105
16 109

16.1-2 100
16.1 105
17 105,
17.1 105
17.1-4 100
17.2 101
17.4 101
18.1-3 100
18.3 101
19 98, 105, 108, 109
19.1-13 100, 107
19.1-12 101
19.1-9 109
19.1 101, 106
19.2 101 106
19.5 107
19.6-13 108
19.6-11 105
19.6-10 108
19.6-9 109
19.6 101, 108
19.8-10 108
19.8 101
19.11 101, 106, 108, 109
19.12-13 109
19.15 109
19.16 109

www.ingramcontent.com/pod-product-compliance
Lightning Source LLC
Chambersburg PA
CBHW071811300426
44116CB00009B/1278